The
Second
Comforter

Conversing *with*
The Lord
Through *the* Veil

DENVER C. SNUFFER, JR.

MILL CREEK PRESS
Salt Lake City, Utah

Published in the United States by Mill Creek Press.

MILL CREEK PRESS is a registered trademark of Mill Creek Press, LLC

Library of Congress Control Number 2006925193

ISBN-10: 0-9740158-7-3
ISBN-13: 978-0-9740158-7-3

Printed in the United States of America on acid-free paper
Mill Creek Press website address: www.millcreekpress.com
pfb32975

Second Edition

Cover design by George Foster www.fostercovers.com.

Dedicated to the
"few who are the humble followers of Christ."
(2 Ne. 28:14)

Table of Contents

SUMMARY OF ABBREVIATIONS USED:

The following abbreviations will be used for the authorities frequently cited in this work:

History of the Church of Jesus Christ of Latter-day Saints, 7 Volumes, published by the Church of Jesus Christ of Latter-day Saints; will be cited as *"DHC"* followed by volume number and page (i.e., *DHC* 6: 23).

Teachings of the Prophet Joseph Smith, arranged by Joseph Fielding Smith, published by Deseret Book Company; will be cited as *"TPJS"* followed by the page number (i.e., *TPJS,* p. 23).

The Words of Joseph Smith, compiled by Andrew F. Ehat and Lyndon W. Cook, published by the Religious Studies Center, Brigham Young University; will be cited as *"WJS"* followed by the page number (i.e., *WJS* p. 23).

The Journal of Discourses, 26 volumes, will be cited as *"JD"* followed by the volume and page number (i.e., *JD* 6: 23).

Lectures on Faith, compiled by N.B. Lundwall, published by Bookcraft; will be cited as *"Lectures"* followed by Lecture Number, paragraph and page number (i.e., *Lectures, Fourth Lecture,* paragraphs 50-54, pp. 90-91)

References to the Bible are to the King James Version.

All other authorities are cited at length.

PREFACE TO THE SECOND EDITION:

The printed text of *The Second Comforter: Conversing With the Lord Through the Veil* has always had a number of minor, technical errors. Eighteen of those errors were corrected early in the printing. However, many have remained. Because of the success of this book, we have gone back and corrected almost all of the minor errors. We say "almost" because we have learned by sad experience it takes the next life to attain perfection and publishing a book is a humbling technical experience.

Because of the importance of this book's contents, we feel it necessary to explain the differences between the first and second editions. In this edition the original text has been unaltered except for minor errors which needed correcting. In addition to line spacing, margins, punctuation and minor spelling changes, there have been some minor changes to the text. Two changes will illustrate the kinds of minor changes made: Early in the book Sam was referred to as the "younger brother" in the first edition and in this edition is referred to as the "brother" of Nephi. There has always been an omission in one sentence due to an "auto-correction" function which has now been corrected. That sentence reads in the first edition: "I will doubt itself." It should have read and now reads in the second edition: "I will doubt doubt itself." The other minor changes involve rewordings to clarify meanings.

In the first edition the two spellings of "fullness/fulness" were used. When the quotes used the spelling of "fulness" they were unaltered; however the text used the spelling of "fullness." In this second edition all instances of the word have been conformed to "fullness" both in the quoted material and in the text.

The Richard L. Bushman paper from the Library of Congress Symposium on Joseph Smith was not in print at the time of the first edition but is now in print. Therefore it is now cited and included in the bibliography. A talk by Paul Toscano was provided by the J. Reuben Clark Law Library at Brigham Young University and it now is also quoted and cited in the bibliography.

The single greatest change to the second edition is the addition of a greatly enlarged word index. We have received enough feedback to know this book will be of more use to readers if an enlarged word index allowed for quick return to passages for use in study or lessons.

The first edition has now sold in excess of 2,500 copies. Since this book is not advertised, sales only come through word of mouth. We appreciate all those who have recommended this book to others. The importance of this book cannot be measured in sales but in the effect it has upon the readers, however few or many the total.

One final note to this second edition. Since this book was released, Denver C. Snuffer, Jr. has written two follow up books. *Nephi's Isaiah* was released late in 2006 and *Eighteen Verses* was released in 2007, just before this second edition. Although these three are not a trilogy in the traditional sense, the second two follow up on questions raised in this book but which are beyond the scope of the main text. Those who read all three will see they address common themes and issues.

We are grateful to readers for comments which have improved this second edition. One of these readers spent two days with the author and his wife reviewing and improving the text. As a result of her efforts a number of sentences have been clarified or reworded.

Mill Creek Press
April, 2008

PREFACE TO THE FIRST EDITION

How vain and trifling have been our spirits, our conferences, our councils,
our meetings, our private as well as public conversations — too low, too
mean, too vulgar, too condescending for the dignified characters of the called
and chosen of God, according to the purposes of His will, from before the
foundation of the world!
> — *Joseph Smith writing from Liberty Jail, found in DHC 3:*
> *295, also found in TPJS, p. 137.*

With Joseph's complaint in mind, this book will attempt to proceed with an appropriate sobriety in the discussion of Christ's Gospel. The attempt grows out of over thirty years of effort to obey and understand the Gospel of Jesus Christ, as taught through the Church of Jesus Christ of Latter-day Saints. To the extent this work proves helpful to that process for others, it is offered as one lay member's contribution. I alone am responsible for the effort, errors and mistakes contained in this book, though in truth, I have not been alone in this effort. Any credit, therefore, for its positive contributions should be given to the Lord, who has been the inspiration for this writing.

Over three decades ago I joined the Church of Jesus Christ of Latter-day Saints. What followed was a long struggle to realize promised blessings from following the restored Gospel. The process has not always been upward, nor has it been consistent. There have been challenges, set-backs, failures and successes. There have been moments of profound insight and clarity. There have been seasons of darkness and confusion. Overall, the struggle has always been upward, although that would not have been true at some moments in these thirty-some years. This text grows out of that struggle.

There is a hunger among the Saints which this book attempts to fill. Perhaps there will be others inspired by this effort to carry the dialogue yet further toward appropriate discussion of these significant teachings. The 'light-mindedness' of the 1830s which attended the general discussion of Gospel principles troubled Joseph in Liberty Jail. The one-hundred-sixty-five years since then have not produced significantly less 'low, mean, vulgar or condescending' discussions among us. What now passes as attempts at serious discussion is among Latter-day Saint scholars, whose writings are more often than not flawed by their excessive academic orientation, in which 'light' is not the objective. I fear we may be entering a period of 'Rabbinical Mormonism' in which discussions of the 'deep things of the Gospel' are nothing like what they should be. Instead, they are typified by esoteric discussions which fail to address the simple Gospel truths which save. Although I regularly read a wide sampling of these serious modern publications, I find them less edifying than I had hoped. There is a great deal of pride about the whole academic approach which, in the end, serves more to alienate us from God than draw us toward Him. There seems to be a preoccupation with academic credentials and with padding one's bibliography among some of those who claim serious interest in Christ's restored Gospel. Nor is the academic approach devoted to actually finding answers. Their effort is to bring advances, incrementally, and then invite further study. They are ever learning but not able to settle on a final truth, rather like Paul described in his letter to Timothy,[1] even when the process involves a Latter-day Saint scholar. This is because the techniques of the scholar are by necessity tentative and governed by a process which dictates only tentative results.

The academic process is well described by Noel B. Reynolds in the "Acknowledgment" found in his recent publication *Early Christians in Disarray: Contemporary LDS Perspectives on the Christian Apostasy,* edited by Noel B. Reynolds. Provo: FARMS, 2005 (a very interesting book, by the way). There he describes the process of informal discussion, leading to

---

[1] 2 Tim. 3: 1-2, 7: "[I]n the last days perilous times shall come. For men shall be... Ever learning, and never able to come to the knowledge of the truth."

preparation of papers and a conference, followed by peer reviews and criticisms, culminating in the final publication of the book, which represents the outcome. He states, "Good critics are essential to progress in academic research and thinking, and the present volume has been significantly improved as it has been filtered and re-filtered through a series of critical reviews." (*Id.*, p. viii.) He goes on to write about the book: "the explanations and extrapolations it contains are not intended to be official or final in any way. Some of the chapters included in this volume present snapshots of ongoing research. Others identify and recommend questions that will require further examination. The contents have generally been improved by dialogue among the various authors and other colleagues, and it is my hope that this volume will stimulate and support a new beginning to a much broader conversation." (*Id.*, p. 26.)

It is certain Latter-day Saint scholars are necessary and their process is both valid and useful. Without the scholar's contribution, the progress of the Church would be impaired. However, academic discussions have never been the primary tool the Lord has commended to His Saints for following Him or discovering His truths. If such tools were capable of determining saving truths, the great councils of Christianity would have succeeded in avoiding the apostasy. They did not, as is so ably discussed in Noel B. Reynolds' recent book. This book, therefore, makes no effort to employ those tools. Rather, it attempts to follow an alternate, and more certain path for determining truth based upon the tools outlined in scripture. It was those tools which brought to the author a testimony of the Restoration of the Gospel. And it has been those tools which have continued to bring light and truth.

The Church's Sunday curriculum is primarily influenced by the relentless gathering of new converts into the Church whose need for basic instruction must be addressed. That material cannot go beyond the things which are suitable for establishing a foundation of basic Gospel knowledge. It would be unwise of the Church to do otherwise.

FARMS publications seem to have replaced the prophetic voice among some Saints as the rallying point for serious orthodox students of the Gospel. While FARMS continues to make significant contributions, it does not address the subject of this book nor does it adopt the approach taken here. This book does not take issue with FARMS' efforts, but neither does it attempt to duplicate the scholar's approach nor employ the scholar's tools.

This is a topic that needs to be written, and I write based upon my own struggles and experiences. I am an obscure Latter-day Saint who has no claim on the reader's attention because of Church office or position. This book would probably be less meaningful if it were written by someone with position or rank. It is written for the least Latter-day Saint. As one of them, I claim the right to speak about difficulties and struggles among the rank and file who will always constitute the backbone of the Church.

The title is not misleading. This book is about receiving an audience with Christ, as He promised. He is the promised Second Comforter and this book is about the process of having a personal visit from Him.

An effort to expound on truth requires two witnesses of the truths taught. The Divine standard for establishing truths always requires two witnesses. One is the author. The other must be the Holy Spirit. If, as you read this work, you receive a witness from the Spirit that its teachings are true, you have the required two witnesses. If you do not, then you should feel free to dismiss it. Above all, do not take the author's word on this subject without a second confirming witness, for the author does not ask you to do so.

The contents of this book have been shaped in large measure by Cyndi Fowler Clark, a convert to the Church whose relentless questions have produced the clarity to set out in one place a continuous explanation of the material covered. It has been aided by the inquiries of students who have met at my home to study the Book of Mormon for the last several years, including Nathan Snuffer, Lara Skousen Snuffer,

Benjamin Snuffer, Cassidy Rona, Moshe Rona, Kalisa Carli, Cyndi Clark, Richard Snowball, Brandon Blair and various visitors who have attended occasionally, as well. My wife, Stephanie Snuffer, has aided in editing the second draft and provided the opportunity to write. Without her contribution, the final draft would not have been improved, and the time to write it would not have been available. Jerine Watson provided the final editing and Mike Eldredge provided layout. The galley proofs were checked by Rita Bennett, Stephanie Snuffer, and others. The index was prepared by Mill Creek Press.

Denver C. Snuffer, Jr.
Salt Lake City, Utah
April 6, 2006

The
Second
Comforter

Conversing *with*
The Lord
Through *the* Veil

Chapter One

OVERVIEW

In 1973, I was in the Air Force, stationed at Pease AFB in Portsmouth, New Hampshire. Although I came from Idaho, I was at that moment a New Englander.

While attending a University of New Hampshire night class taught on base, visiting Professor Cal Colby from Brandeis University, began an unrelated discussion about Mormonism and the corruptions of all organizations, including that one. "Odd," I thought, "that a college professor would trouble to mention Mormonism all the way out here in New Hampshire." Mormons were a small cult in Utah, who spilled over into Idaho, where I had run across them frequently in my youth. I hadn't given them any serious thought though, other than to accept at face value the criticisms my Baptist mother supplied to me. I was certain there wasn't a Mormon infestation in New Hampshire.

To my surprise, a student raised his hand and confronted the professor about his criticism of Mormonism. He mounted a defense against the professor that displayed either courage or bad judgment or both. It was a noble enough effort to attack the professor, evoking my admiration of the fellow-student in spite of myself.

After class, I made the mistake of complimenting the fellow on his courage. This he confused with interest in "The Church," as I later learned it is called by the Mormons. He then proceeded over the following months to pamphleteer, film-strip and testify to me with such vigor I was at a loss to know how to disabuse him from the notion I was a candidate for his faith.

Even when I showed up drunk for missionary discussions, my inebriation seemed to have little effect on the enthusiasm he and his missionary friends had about explaining their religion to me. When they finally got to the lesson on the "Word of Wisdom," I was surprised to learn they wanted me not to drink any more and realized why they hadn't allowed cigars to be lit during discussions.

For six months I tolerated this process with no genuine interest in what was being said. I was a polite skeptic. They confused politeness for interest and regarded me as a "golden contact." Their persistence probably had much more to do with the slim interest in Mormonism in New England than it did with any of my outward signs of interest.

After a while I was asked to read a few passages in the Book of Mormon and tell the missionaries what I thought. I agreed and finished the assignment before the next "lesson." When they later asked what I thought of the passages, I responded: "It must be scripture. It's every bit as boring as the Bible." The response did nothing to curb their enthusiasm.

Eventually, I was invited to a campout at the birth place of Joseph Smith in Sharon, Vermont. I stayed overnight there with Mormons from all over New England. During the evening I happened across a book in the Visitor's Center containing what were supposed to be revelations given to Joseph Smith. I asked if I could buy a copy, and the elderly lady offered me one free of charge.

While glancing through the volume I chanced across Section 76. As I read it for the first time I was taken by the depth of the material. Here in majestic simplicity was a vision of things which had never been revealed about the afterlife and the definition of "many mansions" which was both clear and soul stirring. It startled me. "If Joseph Smith wrote this, then perhaps there is more to him," I thought to myself.

My real investigation of Mormonism finally began that moment, at the birthplace of the Mormon prophet, whose birth was 200 years prior to the date of this writing.

There are two Comforters. The first is the Holy Ghost. Christ promised His followers He would send a "Comforter" to them. He said, "I will pray the Father, and he shall give you another Comforter, that he may abide with you forever; Even the Spirit of truth; whom the world cannot receive, because it seeth him not, neither knoweth him; but ye know him; for he dwelleth with you, and shall be in you." (John 14: 16-17.)

The promise of this first Comforter is followed by this verse: "I will not leave you comfortless: **I will come to you**." (*Id.* verse 18, emphasis added.) Joseph Smith elaborated on this by explaining Christ was promising to come to comfort you Himself. Joseph explained, "When any man obtains this last Comforter, he will have the personage of Jesus Christ to attend him, or appear unto him from time to time, and even He will manifest the Father unto him." (*DHC* 3: 381 also found in *TPJS,* p. 151.)

Referring to these same verses Joseph elaborated:

After a person has faith in Christ, repents of his sins, and is baptized for the remission of his sins and receives the Holy Ghost (by the laying on of hands), which is the first Comforter, then let him continue to humble himself before God, hungering and thirsting after righteousness, and living by every word of God, and the Lord will soon say unto him, Son, thou shalt be exalted. When the Lord has thoroughly proved him, and finds that the man is determined to serve Him at all hazards, then the man will find his calling and election made sure, then it will be his privilege to receive the other Comforter, which the Lord hath promised the Saints [at which point Joseph refers to these verses in John's Gospel]. (*DHC* 3: 380, also *TPJS,* p. 150.)

Joseph's explanation is clear and its import unmistakable. He is saying this promise is to be taken literally. Joseph claimed to have been visited by "the personage of Jesus Christ" who "appeared unto him from time to time." Therefore, he had personal knowledge about the Second Comforter. Joseph wanted the Saints to understand the visitations he received from Christ were actual, literal and physical. Similarly, his explanation that Christ will "not leave you comfortless: [He] will come to you" means just that. Christ will be comforting you by coming to visit with you. This involves having the heavens open to you, just as they have opened to others before you. It is the culminating part of Christ's Gospel, in which Christ ministers to you as He has ministered to others before.

The promise about the Comforter is preceded and followed by two important conditions. It is preceded with the statement: "If ye love me, keep my commandments." (*Id.*, verse 15.) There is a direct and unavoidable connection between the Comforter and the scriptural requirements to both love the Lord and keep His commandments. You cannot love Him and reject His commandments. More importantly, He cannot send this Comforter to you if you disregard, disobey or neglect His commandments. It is through obedience to the commandments the Comforter (Holy Ghost) is obtained. The connection of these two principles to the two Comforters (both the Holy Ghost and Christ) will be explained in this book. If you are not prepared to obey His commandments, it is not possible to receive these two Comforters.

In the D&C there is also a confirmation the Second Comforter is Christ appearing to us. Section 130, verse 3 discusses these same verses from John. It states: "John 14:23— The appearing of the Father and the Son, in that verse, is a personal appearance; and the idea that the Father and the Son dwell in a man's heart is an old sectarian notion, and is false." Therefore, it is a personal appearance of these Divine Personages which Christ promises to us in John's fourteenth chapter.

These promised Comforters are the inheritance of the Saints. Today it remains a promise from Christ set out in scripture and reaffirmed by

His Prophet Joseph Smith. Whether Joseph, as prophet, or Christ made this promise to the Saints, it is the same: "What I the Lord have spoken, I have spoken, and I excuse not myself" is the Lord's assurance in Section 1 of the D&C (v. 38). The Lord takes His promises seriously, even if we do not. The Lord remains committed to follow through whether men have faith to follow Him and receive these things or not. When men do as He asks, the Lord will "excuse not" Himself. If you come to Him in obedience, He has no intention of leading you along only to disclose an exception. He intends for us to rely upon His promises. When we do, He will react just as He promised and invited.

To press the point further, the Lord went on to say in this last verse: "though the heavens and the earth pass away, my word shall not pass away, but shall all be fulfilled, **whether by mine own voice or by the voice of my servants, it is the same.**" (*Id.*, emphasis added.) The Lord's promises made directly or through His servants, are promises He intends to keep.

In a comment on the Second Comforter, Elder Bruce R. McConkie wrote:

> The Millennial day is the day of the Second Comforter, and whereas but few have been blessed with this divine association in times past, great hosts will be so blessed in times to come.
>
> What, then, will be the nature of worship during the Millennium? It will be pure and perfect, and through it men will become inheritors of eternal life. And in this connection, be it known that **it is the privilege of the saints today** to separate themselves from the world and to receive millennial blessings in their lives. And **any person who today abides the laws that will be kept during the Millennium will receive, here and now, the spirit and blessings of the Millennium in his life**, even though he is surrounded by a world of sin and evil. (McConkie, Bruce R. *Millennial Messiah*, p. 682. Salt Lake City: Deseret Book Company, 1982.)

Though this principle may be ignored or even denied as possible, the promise is a part of the Gospel of Jesus Christ. It is the fullness of the Gospel. And in this regard, just as with the fundamentals of the Gospel, many are "only kept from the truth because they know not where to find it." (D&C 123: 12.) Neglect cannot remove it from the Gospel. Doubt cannot remove it, either. Though neglect and doubt may disqualify the doubter, it cannot disqualify you if you obey the Gospel and have faith.

Some teachings of the Gospel of Jesus Christ are not for the novice. They require maturity, time and patience. The Church of Jesus Christ of Latter-day Saints has such great numbers of new members added yearly, the curriculum of the Church cannot accommodate both the large numbers of new members who require milk on the one hand, and those who are ready for meat on the other hand (to use the Apostle Paul's analogy).

The Church of Jesus Christ has weighed the varying interests and has properly determined to address in classes and conferences the primacy of the interests of the newly converted. It is to these Saints the Church must give its first concerns. As to those who seek for more, they are properly left in large measure to their own study. However, oftentimes people looking for "more" look beyond the mark and develop strange, arrogant or hobbyhorse views of the Gospel. This happens so often the notion someone is seeking to know "mysteries" has come to be regarded as a bad thing. Done in the right way, with the right understanding, approached in humility and as it was intended to be pursued, it is altogether right. Done in the wrong way, it can lead to weird results, even apostasy. Throughout this book, you will be reminded the Second Comforter comes only to those who follow the fullness of Christ's Gospel. You can never outgrow the programs of the Church of Jesus Christ of Latter-day Saints. You can never outgrow the need for the Church of Jesus Christ's saving ordinances. It is His medium for delivering the Gospel. Therefore, it will not be something you leave behind.

Many Church members want a deeper understanding of the Gospel. This has resulted in increased numbers of publications and organizations trying to append themselves to the Church, attempting to satisfy the desire for higher knowledge.

Dialogue is an independent periodical started in the 1960s addressed to Mormon intellectuals.[2] The Sunstone organization followed and also publishes a periodical for the same audience.[3] Both of these efforts occasionally drifted from friendly commentary into more critical views. Sunstone has become outright hostile to the Church's views in many of its papers and conferences and provoked indirect criticisms from Apostles Boyd K. Packer and Dallin Oaks.[4] One of Sunstone's recent

---

[2]*Dialogue: A Journal of Mormon Thought* is a magazine published by the Dialogue Foundation. Its first journal was published in the spring of 1966 with Eugene England and G. Wesley Johnson as editors. Dialogue describes itself in these terms: "*Dialogue* Journal is an independent quarterly established to express Mormon culture and to examine the relevance of religion to secular life. It is edited by Latter-day Saints who wish to bring their faith into dialogue with the larger stream of world religious thought and with human experience as a whole and to foster artistic and scholarly achievement based on their cultural heritage. The journal encourages a variety of viewpoints; although every effort is made to ensure accurate scholarship and responsible judgment, the views expressed are those of the individual authors and are not necessarily those of the Church of Jesus Christ of Latter-day Saints or of the editors." (Taken from the *Dialogue* website www.dialoguejournal.com.)

[3]Sunstone Foundation was established in 1974 by a group of graduate students. The organization's backbone is the *Sunstone* magazine. For an interesting recount of the Foundation's history, see *The Origin and Evolution of the Sunstone Species: Twenty-five Years of Creative Adaptation*, by Elbert Eugene Peck, available at the Sunstone Foundation's website. Their self-defined mission is "to sponsor open forums of Mormon thought and experience. Under the motto, 'Faith Seeking Understanding,' we examine and express the rich spiritual, intellectual, social and artistic qualities of Mormon history and contemporary life. We encourage humanitarian service, honest inquiry, and responsible interchange of ideas that is respectful of all people and what they hold sacred."

[4]See, e.g., Dallin Oaks' General Conference address *Alternative Voices* from the 1989 April Conference, *Ensign*, May 1989 beginning at p. 27. There

conferences invited excommunicated former members to come and present papers on their experiences and complaints. FARMS[5] grew out of the need to respond to the critics who employ scholarship or pseudo-scholarship to accuse the Church of alleged failings. Recently a more direct and combative approach to our critics has been undertaken by FAIR.[6] These non-affiliated groups[7] carry on a dialogue of pro and con in which matters are discussed which are not included in the Church's internal teaching materials. More often than not they provoke debate, and contentious debate among the Saints has never been unifying.

BYU's Religion Department also regularly publishes articles and books dealing with Mormon studies.[8] These and other sources attempt

---

he states, among other things: "There have always been alternative voices whose purpose or effect is to deceive. Their existence is part of the plan. The prophet Lehi taught that there 'must needs be ... an opposition in all things.' (2 Ne. 2: 11; italics added.) And there have always been other alternative voices whose purpose or effect is unselfish and wholesome. ... Alternative voices are heard in magazines, journals, and newspapers and at lectures, symposia and conferences."

[5] FARMS is the acronym for the Foundation for Ancient Religious and Mormon Studies. Currently it is a defender of the faith, and affiliated with Brigham Young University. Originally a private research organization founded in 1979, it was taken into Brigham Young University in 1997 and remains a part of BYU. Overwhelmingly their publications are from faculty members and students or former students of BYU.

[6] The Foundation for Apologetic Information and Research (FAIR) was formed in 1997 to defend the Church of Jesus Christ of Latter-day Saints. It was inspired by a desire to respond to on-line criticism of the Church. Their explanation of their purpose and history can be found at their website www.fairlds.org.

[7] FARMS is now part of Brigham Young University, and therefore affiliated with the Church.

[8] See, e.g., *BYU Studies*, a magazine forum dedicated to publishing scholarly religious literature. It was founded in 1959. Their mission statement is: "*BYU Studies* is dedicated to publishing qualified, significant, and inspiring scholarly religious literature in the form of books, journals, and dissertations.

to advance Mormon intellectual inquiries; and all of these sources provide some interesting reading. Sometimes the polemics are entertaining, even when they are not enlightening. While they can be useful in defining issues or providing a source for further study,[9] these sources stop short of addressing the subject of this book and when they have brushed up against it, their treatment makes no attempt to instruct in the process of receiving the Second Comforter.

This book is about receiving the Second Comforter. It is an attempt to show the reader a roadmap for going from where he or she is now to the position where Lord can be received. This is not about the afterlife or some future millennial day when all mankind will see the Lord. Rather it is about receiving the Second Comforter during your present lifetime.

No book devoted solely to this subject exists. In an effort to prevent these matters from being misunderstood or neglected, we will explain what it means to receive the Second Comforter, and outline a course of conduct to apply these teachings in your life.

We will focus on doctrine and scripture, but also intend to present a practical guide. The value of reading will come only as a result of actually **doing** the things set out in the scriptures. We are going to examine what you must do in order to receive the Second Comforter. This isn't a book for a merely academic inquiry. If that is what you are looking for you might want to read something else. This is not a scholarly work but rather, it is a simple book about how the scriptures teach us to grow in light and truth until we reach a perfect day. This is

We want to share these publications to help promote faith, continued learning, and further interest in our Latter-day Saint heritage with those in the world who have a positive interest in this work."

[9]Without relentless inquiries into faith and the reasons for faith, souls stagnate. These publications supply many useful subjects worthy of further individual study and reflection. Therefore it is not the purpose of this work to condemn or censure these sources. They are important. But this work is independent from such discussions and does not attempt to contribute to the world of Mormon intellectual studies, as will become apparent as you read it.

about the fullness of Christ's Gospel. Many of the things discussed will be "foolish" to the academic. Scholars are some of our harshest critics, and it is good that scholars are among our defenders and apologists, too. But this work does not participate in the scholars' debates.

Knowledge of theological subtleties alone will not produce light and truth. The greatest theologians in history have failed to crack open the heavens in the slightest. St. Augustine was a formidable intellect, whose reasoning and theology changed Western culture. But he was wrong in many conclusions, and never pretended to have received an angel, much less to have been visited by the Lord. Similarly, the other great theological minds of Catholicism, as well as the Reformers, contributed wonderfully to mankind's thinking about religious issues. But reason alone does not produce light and truth. There are some irrational -- or more correctly extra-rational -- sources of truth as well. Angels do not come to us because we have an interesting paper to present to them.

The well-schooled are not the ones who have received the greatest truths revealed to mankind. It was fishermen and plow boys who were called both anciently and in modern times to be the Lord's greatest prophets and revelators. Angels visited them, and Christ ministered to them. The greatest prophets of history came with less education than most modern-day high school graduates. They had access to truth from another source. That source provided them the revealed light and truth from heaven itself.

Theologians rely on the records and written words of the prophets who actually saw angels and the Lord to reach their reasoned conclusions. There is a significant distinction between the process followed by the revelators and the reasoning of theologians and scholars. More often than not the theological arguments, which are purportedly based upon the words of the simple inspired messengers, mangle the original message to the point it brings more darkness than light to the reader.

Divine revelation will never come through the scholar's tools. Instead, it comes as people follow the Gospel principles. People who rely upon their reasoning may become great rabbis, doctors of law and great theologians. These, however, must ultimately base their reasoning on the basic truths revealed to simple but faithful people of revelation. Here we are going to look at the truths themselves. We must do so if we hope to have an audience with the Second Comforter. Therefore, this subject is approached through the scriptures and the teachings of latter-day prophets and apostles who have commented on the subject.

Scholars attempt to teach others to use analytical tools to reach reasoned conclusions. They use logic, reason and supporting studies to establish their "truths." Prophets attempt to duplicate their experiences by teaching others to obey God and to ask Him to reveal hidden knowledge. Prophetic knowledge is not obtained merely by study, reason or logic. It is obtained by obedience to God's will and from revelation. We will examine that here and approach it as a practical matter. We want to know what is required to get revelation, and then we want to get revelation. We want the truth through revelation. We will look at how to recognize it as it begins, and the process by which it grows in light. Standing in the "perfect day" does not come about spontaneously. It comes at the end of a process. We want to look at the process.

The scriptures tell us how to get the "mysteries of God."[10] Learning these "mysteries" is the fullness of Christ's Gospel. We are going to examine how these things come together in a planned pattern Christ has offered to us all. Scholars do not pretend to uncover new mysteries or revelations from God. They may attempt to uncover what has been lost from the prophets from long ago, or to expound on what the prophets meant in a cultural or historic setting. They do not attempt to open the heavens for us. On the other hand, the scriptures do attempt to open the heavens to all, under specific conditions.

---

[10]This term has a specific meaning and refers to that knowledge which is hidden from the world and only made available through revelation to the faithful. Such knowledge may be learned but is not to be taught. This work will set out the way in which it is learned, but does not intend to set out any particular mystery for the reader. You will have to apply the materials in your life, if you intend to learn the mysteries themselves.

In Sunday School and Sacrament meetings, the primary focus is always going to be the fundamental principles of the Gospel. That is as it should be. As Elder Henry Eyring reminded us in April 2005's General Conference, the majority of the Church of Jesus Christ today is comprised of converts.[11] The primary education in the Church must therefore be addressed to teaching the foundational doctrines of the Gospel to this convert majority. Discussing the "mysteries" before the foundations have been adequately established is more destructive than edifying. The Apostle Paul put it in these words: "I have fed you with milk, and not with meat: for hitherto ye were not able to bear it, neither yet now are ye able." (1 Cor. 3: 2.) Immaturity leads some curious but unprepared folks to seek these things prematurely. Encouraging them in this before they are ready may result in deep frustration or even losing their testimony altogether. In most lives it will take many years of development before this process is appropriate for them. Those many years of development can best, perhaps only, be acquired by faithful service within the Church. Church service is the best means for preparation because that is why the Church has been restored. There is an inspired genius behind the programs of the Church. From Home Teaching to Relief Society service programs, the Church reflects a higher intelligence. The Church is literally preparing its members for citizenship in heaven. Even the least Saint, who has no curiosity about higher learning, is preparing herself for something much greater by following the programs of the Church. Nothing in this text will contradict those programs. And if you are a critic of the Church you will find no comfort or support for your views in this work. The Church is the work of God. Through its institutions the ordinances which must precede and accompany the acquisition of mysteries are given to the members. Seeking further light and knowledge is not independent of the Church, but utterly reliant upon it.

---

[11] "My message is to those who are converts to the Church. More than half the members of the Church today chose to be baptized after the age of eight. So you are not the exception in the Church." (*Ensign*, May 2005, Vol. 35, no. 5, *Hearts Bound Together.*)

As to the institutional reluctance to address deeper mysteries publicly, Joseph Smith cautioned about revealing things to those unprepared to receive them. Throughout his ministry Joseph was always torn between the desire or requirement to teach on the one hand, and the preparedness and willingness of the Saints to receive instruction on the other. In Nauvoo, Joseph lamented: "I could explain a hundredfold more than I ever have of the glories of the kingdoms manifested to me in the vision, were I permitted, and were the people prepared to receive them." (*DHC* 5: 402; also *TPJS,* p. 305.) Permission to reveal and preparation to receive go together. No one is "permitted" to reveal something unless "the people are prepared to receive them." That limit applies not just to men but also to angels. God waits for each person's preparation before giving them light and truth. After all is said and done *we* determine how much God is able to give to us. This work will focus on that, and your ability to accept further light and truth. It is not only in a collective sense people qualify to receive hidden mysteries, but rather it is primarily individually.

Brigham Young commented on this in these words: "Twenty-two years ago, Joseph said, 'Brother Brigham, if I were to tell this people all the revelations I have, every man would leave me.' **I do not want to know things faster than I can obey. Everything that is received must be lived up to** by the people, and when this people are ready to receive further light, I promise you in the name of Israel's God it will be given every son and daughter." (McConkie, Mark L. *Remembering Joseph; Personal Recollections of Those Who Knew the Prophet Joseph Smith.* Salt Lake City: Deseret Book Company, 2003, page 217.) Here again Joseph and his successor President of the Church teach the same principle. We decide what we are willing to receive. If you decide you are willing to receive more, then you must follow the path to do so. There are rules which govern these things. We want to find and follow these rules. You cannot avoid the rules and then hope to get what they offer.

There is a direct connection between what is permitted to be revealed to others, and the preparation of the **audience** to receive them. This precaution is merciful. It keeps those who are unprepared from receiving things they will be unable to incorporate into their lives. It prevents those who cannot live a higher standard from being judged against that standard before they have first had a merciful season to prepare. Almost anyone will accept truth if they are prepared to identify it as truth. But many people are unprepared, and cannot recognize it as true. So, for them, the Lord withholds information to allow them to prepare first. You have no right to impose upon unprepared souls higher information than they are able to bear.[12]

This book may not be appropriate for a number of readers and you might well ask yourself if this book is a good fit for you. It is intended only for a specific audience: active, faithful members of The Church of Jesus Christ of Latter-day Saints with many years of faithful living. It is for those faithful members who have felt there is something more to the Gospel, but who do not have a secure sense of how to proceed to receive it. It is for those who would like to grow in their understanding, but who feel at a loss to understand how. It is for people whose lives have been filled with years of active service in the Church supporting its programs and providing service to others. It is for those who have attended the Temple, and consistently returned to worship there. It is for the few, humble followers of Christ as described by Nephi.[13]

This book is not for critics or the curious whose devotion to the Lord is lacking in some material respect. If your life has serious sins you have not resolved through repentance, this book will provide you with very little. It is not for the faithless, or the skeptical.

---

[12]Anti-Mormon crusaders have learned long ago that the most effective way to interfere with Church success is not to lie about us, but instead to reveal some truth about us outside of a context in which it can be understood. They try to choke people with meat when their capacity is limited to milk.

[13]In 2 Ne. 28: 14 he mentions about our day that "they have all gone astray save it be a few, who are the humble followers of Christ; nevertheless, they are led, that in many instances they do err because they are taught by the precepts of men." We are going to look at this.

To receive the Second Comforter we must allow others who have been so blessed to serve as our guides. Their instructions and testimony need to be accepted and followed: You can't ignore the recipe and expect a perfect cake.

The steps in this book are not innovative. They are based entirely upon the scriptures and the information and instruction given there, together with inspired teachings of authorities in the Church leadership. But these sources are arranged in a single place, rather than scattered throughout the Standard Works and conference talks. We are going to put the mosaic into a comprehensible picture.

This book will show the propriety of these things from scripture, and then show the reader how to approach the task. If this subject makes you uncomfortable, this book may not be suitable for you. Certainly if this subject amuses you and strikes you as a fairy tale, then it is not for you. Anyone can read this book, but it will only help those who apply the teachings in their lives. Heaven will not open to the skeptic (except on those occasions when they have reached the point of being judged and condemned[14] for their inordinate wickedness).

On the other hand, if you believe there is a deeper level available through faith which you long to experience but is just beyond your reach because you are unsure how to proceed, this book can help you. You may already have the faith required, but you may lack the knowledge or the confidence to realize these things are in fact available to you. Rest assured they are part of Christ's Gospel. And they are as much a part of the Gospel today as they have been at any time in the past. It is not just ancients who have seen God. Nor is it only the founding Prophets of this Dispensation. There are people alive today who have received the Second Comforter. It can be done by any Saint who is

---

[14]For example, angels visited Sodom in judgment. They rebuked Laman and Lemuel as well. Christ promises to return and make a public appearance also which the wicked and righteous alike will see. But these experiences are not what this work intends to provoke. Here we are looking at the process of passing through the veil into God's presence in compliance with His Gospel.

willing to abide the conditions set to receive this kind of comfort. It can be done by you.

Joseph admonished the Saints: "I advise **all** to go on to perfection, and search deeper and deeper into the mysteries of Godliness." (*DHC* 6: 363; also *TPJS*, p. 364, emphasis added.) The notion you should "leave the mysteries alone" has become a mantra for some Saints. Perhaps that is an appropriate mantra for most Saints and in most settings and for all those whose maturity in the Gospel has not prepared them for receiving the deeper things of Christ's Gospel. As Paul put it in his letter to the Corinthians quoted above, novices in the faith should be fed with milk, and not meat. But there are some Saints who have a legitimate right to these things. This is not meant to appeal to your pride. Gospel understanding is not meant to make you popular or garner acclaim. It is meant to remake you into a humble servant, to change your heart so you, like the Good Samaritan, will minister to others in need. There was no audience applauding (or even noticing) the Good Samaritan. Nor did he later stand on a street corner calling attention to himself. He merely served. You will not get recognition for pursuing this effort. It must be a private struggle, about which the world will never know. If you hope for status from the experience, you will be disappointed. But if you wish to know God, you will not.

Receiving these things does not mean you are authorized to get in front of the Brethren who preside as authorized agents, and begin teaching doctrines either in addition to or different from their authorized message. No one, at any time, is authorized to teach beyond what the Lord's chosen authorities have taught. Hiram Page was receiving revelations in 1830 through a stone. Oliver Cowdrey was misled by this. In a revelation given to Oliver Cowdrey which remains applicable to us today, the Lord commanded: "But, behold, verily, verily, I say unto thee, no one shall be appointed to receive commandments and revelations in this church excepting my servant Joseph Smith, Jun.[or his successor as President of the Church], for he receiveth them even as Moses." (D&C 28: 2.) Joseph added additional counsel on this requirement by explaining:

> I will inform you that it is contrary to the economy of God for any member of the Church, or any one, to receive instruction for those in authority, higher than themselves; therefore you will see the impropriety of giving heed to them; but if any person have a vision or a visitation from a heavenly messenger, it must be for his own benefit and instruction; for the fundamental principles, government, and doctrine of the Church are vested in the keys of the kingdom. (*DHC* 1: 338; also *TPJS,* p. 21.)

The mysteries can be received by any person who will follow the process to receive them, but they cannot be taught. This book will teach existing doctrine, and not new or hitherto unrevealed principles or doctrine. Anyone who would attempt to do so is out of harmony with the scriptures and teachings of the Church.[15]

You should note that implicit within this last quote from Joseph is the expectation there will be those who will receive "a vision or visitation from a heavenly messenger." That is the right of the Saints. It is one of the characteristics of true faith that the heavens communicate to men and women on the earth.

This principle involving limited disclosure of things received in personal revelation is explained by Alma. He taught:

> It is given unto many to know the mysteries of God; neverthe-less they are laid under a strict command that they shall not

---

[15]Joseph F. Smith gave a discourse on Sunday, June 21, 1883, found beginning in *JD* 24: 187, where he said at p. 188: "so long as the Lord has any communication to make to the children of men, or any instructions to impart to His Church, **He will make such communication through the legally appointed channel of the Priesthood; He will never go outside of it,** as long, at least, as the Church of Jesus Christ of Latter-day Saints exists in its present form on the earth." (Emphasis added.)

impart only according to the portion of his word which he doth grant unto the children of men, according to the heed and diligence which they give unto him. And, therefore, he that will harden his heart, the same receiveth the lesser portion of the word; and he that will not harden his heart, to him is given the greater portion of the word, until it is given unto him to know the mysteries of God until he know them in full. And they that will harden their hearts, to them is given the lesser portion of the word until they know nothing concerning his mysteries... (Alma 12: 9-11.)

If you are incapable of obeying these requirements, then you cannot receive any new mystery by revelation. Heaven will not permit any soul to receive mysteries if they cannot resist revealing them unwisely to others. The constraint that they may be learned but cannot be taught is enforced by withholding them from those who will not abide by this constraint. If you are one of those who cannot respect this limitation, then the process will not work for you.

Joseph said: "The reason we do not have the secrets of the Lord revealed unto us, is because we do not keep them but reveal them; we do not keep our own secrets, but reveal our difficulties to the world, even to our enemies, then how would we keep the secrets of the Lord?" (*DHC* 4: 479; also *TPJS*, p. 195.) Elsewhere Joseph admonished: "If God gives you a manifestation; keep it to yourselves." (*DHC* 2: 309; also *TPJS*, p. 91.) The Second Comforter is for your individual comfort and instruction. Not for public display or to gratify your pride or serve your vain ambition.[16]

Sacred things tend to lose their luster as they are profaned by being made common. Just as the white snow tends to stain the longer it is

_____

[16]In this it is no different than the limitations on authority found in Section 121 of the D&C: "when we undertake to cover our sins, or to gratify our pride, our vain ambition, or to exercise control or dominion or compulsion upon the souls of the children of men, in any degree of unrighteousness, behold, the heavens withdraw themselves." (Verse 37.)

trodden underfoot by men, so also does the purity of revelation become denigrated by being revealed without regard to the audience's preparation and worthiness to learn of sacred things. This is a binding limitation and an essential part of the process. To be qualified you must be someone who can be trusted to keep sacred things sacred.[17]

The Second Comforter is not provided in order to produce faith. Rather, He comes in response to faith. If you are seeking a sign, it will not be given. He comes to you at the end of a path, and not merely to begin or move you along. If you hope to receive a sign as a result of the message in this book, you will be disappointed. "Faith cometh not by signs, but signs follow them that believe." (D&C 63: 9.) And again: "dispute not because ye see not, for ye receive no witness until after the trial of your faith." (Ether 12: 6.) We often pay attention to the beginning of these verses, but the real meaning for us in this book is the promise contained in the end of them. Both promise signs which follow faith, and a witness after the trial of faith. So we will turn our attention to the verses' end and seek for faith to bring us there.

These things are given in follow-up to a lengthy process. They are not given before then. "Those that are the most anxious to see these things, are the least prepared to meet them, and were the Lord to manifest His power(s) as He did to the children of Israel, such characters would be the first to say, 'Let not the Lord speak any more, lest we His people die.'" (*DHC* 5: 31; also *TPJS*, p. 247.)

There is a process, and it must be followed. The revelation comes after a maturation process, not before. How long you take to grow

---

[17]Of course, when required to testify of something by the Lord, the Lord's insistence upon that testimony always takes precedence. The general rule is you keep them to yourself. The exception is when the Lord constrains you to do otherwise.

depends entirely upon you.[18] It needn't take long, but almost always does.

The expression "practice makes perfect" is really incorrect. If you practice imperfectly you cannot hope to become perfect. The expression should be "perfect practice makes perfect." Two thoughts may help understand this process:

Having the veil open to you is like seeking to open something kept shut by a combination lock. To an uninformed observer watching the lock being opened, they may conclude what is needed is spinning the dial back and forth a few times and the lock disengages. However, no amount of turning the dials on the combination lock will open it until you have the right sequence and the right numbers. So it is here. Unless you have the right sequence and the right information, it is not possible to have the veil open. We are going to attempt to put those things into

---

[18]Joseph Smith taught: "We consider that God has created man with a mind capable of instruction, and a faculty which may be enlarged in proportion to the heed and diligence given to the light communicated from heaven to the intellect; and that the nearer man approaches perfection, the clearer are his views, and the greater his enjoyments, till he has overcome the evils of his life and lost every desire for sin; and like the ancients, arrives at that point of faith where he is wrapped in the power and glory of his Maker, and is caught up to dwell with Him. But we consider **that this is a station to which no man ever arrived in a moment**: he must have been instructed in the government and laws of that kingdom by proper degrees, until his mind is capable in some measure of comprehending the propriety, justice, equality, and consistency of the same." (*TPJS*, p. 51, emphasis added.) Elsewhere he taught: "**A man is saved no faster than he gets knowledge**, for if he does not get knowledge, he will be brought into captivity by some evil power in the other world, as evil spirits will have more knowledge, and consequently more power than many men who are on the earth. Hence it needs revelation to assist us, and give us knowledge of the things of God." (*Id.*, p. 217.) He also taught: "**if you do right, there is no danger of your going too fast**. He said he did not care how fast we run in the path of virtue: resist evil, and there is no danger; God, men, and angels will not condemn those that resist everything that is evil, and devils cannot; as well might the devil seek to dethrone Jehovah, as overthrow an innocent soul that resists everything which is evil." (*Id.*, p. 226, emphasis added.)

an overall pattern you can understand, then feel, then do, and finally become so you can receive what is being offered.

These things cannot, however, be rushed. When you train a young baseball player to hit baseballs, you do not start correcting at once his hands, shoulders, wrists, elbows, foot position, stride, upper body loading, torque at the mid-body, counter-rotation, release, contact, and follow through in one lesson. If you do, you are neither a good instructor nor will the batter develop any skill. There is too much going on for anything to actually improve. You teach complicated or intricate skills one step at a time. There should be in the mind of the student only *one* thing to do. There is always only *one* thing to do. There is never more than the single thing to be addressed. It is the thing most wrong at the moment. Once that is addressed and corrected, then you can move on to the next thing, where again there is only *one* thing to do—and it is the next thing in the sequence. When the next skill is acquired, then there is still only *one* thing to do.

So it is here. There is only one thing for you to do. You will know what you need to do within the context of your own life. We will discuss that further. But whatever it is that most hinders you is the one and only thing you have to do. When it is resolved, then you move on to the next thing. Sometimes we all have blind spots about our own shortcomings. If you cannot figure out what the thing you most need to resolve is, then ask the Lord. He has always been willing to answer the sincere inquiry of "what lack I yet?" The answer to that question is the one thing you should work on. But never work on three, or thirty, or fifty things at once. We will be further discussing this issue later in the work.

Finding the balance point in baseball is always a good starting point. If you can stay centered, in balance, then you are not fighting against gravity to accomplish a skill. Any athletic activity is best accomplished by keeping the body's center of gravity in balance. This makes the body nimble and mobile. So it is with these things, as well. There is harmony and balance to this process when it is being done correctly. You can feel it more than think it.

Good batting in baseball is reactive and instinctive. It does not involve a batter reciting to himself a dozen different batting techniques or rules as he awaits a 90-mile per hour pitch. If he does, the ball is going to pass him by every time. The Gospel is no different. You need to seek for balance in your life. It is the object of this work to get you to become balanced, nimble, and more attuned to feeling than to thought.

Finally, you should understand that the writer of this book holds no high Church office. There is no reason to rely upon me as an authority on anything. I am not someone who should command your attention or respect because of position. The content of this work alone stands as the authority for these things. If you accept anything from this book, you must do so on the strength of what it says and not who is saying it.

Just as no power or influence can or ought to be maintained by virtue of the priesthood or reason of standing or office, but should only be acquired through persuasion and that by gentleness and meekness, and by love unfeigned;[19] so this work should not be accepted for any reason other than it persuades you it is true. If it does not persuade you, then you should reject it. If this work seems to have the wrong 'spirit' about it, then feel free to discard it. You are not rejecting any Church authority if you discard this book as meaningless.

---

[19] See D&C 121: 41-42: "No power or influence can or ought to be maintained by virtue of the priesthood, only by persuasion, by long-suffering, by gentleness and meekness, and by love unfeigned; By kindness, and pure knowledge, which shall greatly enlarge the soul without hypocrisy, and without guile-"

On the other hand, if you find this work does "greatly enlarge the soul without hypocrisy, and without guile" then you should be willing to use it as a basis for an experiment. Test its teachings. See if they do or do not provide you with growth in your walk with Christ. Take from this book such things as you find to be good and true, and then discard the rest.

We are going to walk through the process from beginning to end. Although this work is inspired by deeply personal experiences, this work is about you. The only personal materials discussed are to illustrate points the text is trying to communicate. Some experiences are of course too sacred to discuss in full in a work like this and therefore may receive only the briefest of notices, if any.

Chapter Two

FOUNDATION BEDROCK

I**t had been over thirty-two years, but I can still recall the scenes as if they happened earlier this morning. After concluding to investigate Mormonism sincerely, I heard in the lessons taught by the missionaries an echo of what I had been searching for. Something familiar was here, even though it was coming from an odd place. "How," I thought, "could Mormonism have the answers? After all, my Baptist mother had taught me that it was a false cult. How, then, could they be offering anything of enduring value?"**

The things I had been taught before during months of insincere investigation needed to be re-taught. This time I had questions. I began to check the references in the New Testament, and to ponder these things. I finally concluded to do as they asked me to, and to ask God, with real intent, if this cult of Mormonism was not true:

"Oh God, the Eternal Father, I believe in you, and have tried to follow you in my life. These missionaries have taught me that you have spoken again. And that you have done so to a young boy named Joseph Smith. If this is true, can you make it known to me? I do not know how to be certain that you are answering me, so I will need help in recognizing that it is you speaking, and you who are answering. But if you answer, and if these things are true, then I will be willing to change."

To go where the Second Comforter is you have to do it the way the scriptures teach. There is a specific way to get there. It makes no sense to think the promised results are not linked to the requirements to get them. These foundational things need to be done or accepted. This chapter will begin to describe a context. It is introductory and foundational, and will be expanded in the later chapters. But here we will begin with an overall 'big-picture' context.

First, of course, is faith in Jesus Christ. Why would you expect to be able to see Him if you don't have faith in Him? It would be an odd sort of expectation, to say the least. Somewhat akin to expecting to see Harvey, the invisible six foot rabbit, when you are sure he doesn't exist.

Everyone will see Christ at some point whether they have faith in Him or not.[20] To meet Him here in mortality however, you must have

---

[20] Alma 40: 11: "Behold, it has been made known unto me by an angel, that the spirits of all men, as soon as they are departed from this mortal body, yea, the spirits of all men, whether they be good or evil, are taken home to that God who gave them life." Alma 11: 44: "Now, this restoration shall come to all, both old and young, both bond and free, both male and female, both the wicked and the righteous; and even there shall not so much as a hair of their heads be lost; but every thing shall be restored to its perfect frame, as it is now, or in the body, and shall be brought and be arraigned before the bar of Christ the Son, and God the Father, and the Holy Spirit, which is one Eternal God, to be judged according to their works, whether they be good or whether they be evil."

faith in Him. If you want to see the Lord you must believe in, trust, and act in reliance upon Him so you can develop[21] faith in Him.

You must receive the ordinances of baptism, laying on of hands for the Gift of the Holy Ghost, and thereafter take the sacrament regularly as a means of 'always remembering Him and having His Spirit to be with you.' You need to have been washed and anointed, and received your endowments. These rites are essential tools that will be discussed further in this book. They have been restored to help you in the path toward godliness. If you don't have these tools, you can't build the required faith.

These ordinances are not ends in themselves. They are provided to take you to another level of preparation and of cleanliness. It would be good, therefore, to have more than just a passing familiarity with their meaning and potential power. We will look at them closely as we move along. Hopefully, you have already formed some views about these rites and their deep meaning.

All these ordinances are required to follow God. He has provided them so you can begin to become dissociated from the world and associated with Heaven. Through the ordinances of the Gospel you become an heir[22] and a member of God's family. He comes to visit with

---

[21] All those things are necessary to have faith. "Confessing with the lips" as some evangelicals contend brings salvation, without some obedience to Him, does not constitute faith. We'll take a brief look at that later, but you need to have FAITH and not mere belief in Him. If you don't know the difference, then you ought to read the *Lectures on Faith*. Some of that work will be quoted here, but pay careful attention to that whole little book if you don't understand the difference between belief and faith.

[22] 1 Jn. 3: 1-2: "Behold, what manner of love the Father hath bestowed upon us, that we should be called the sons of God: therefore the world knoweth us not, because it knew him not. Beloved, now are we the sons of God, and it doth not yet appear what we shall be: but we know that, when he shall appear, we shall be like him; for we shall see him as he is."

members of His family, but not with strangers and foreigners.[23] The rites collectively are adoption rites, through which you are restored to God's family.

God could have required anything of us as a demonstration of our faith in Him. He has chosen the ordinances of the Gospel for that purpose. Christ worked out the Atonement and holds all the keys to forgive sins. He can choose any means for conditioning how He forgives us. He has chosen to require baptism, laying on of hands, washings, anointings, endowment, sealing, etc. as the rites He wants us to receive. That is His prerogative. Rather than trying to debate their necessity, we are going to accept they are necessary. We accept they should be done to show you have faith in Him. It makes little sense to think He provided these rites and then decided to make them superfluous to the Second Comforter. If that were so, why would He waste the effort and ask us to waste the time? Why ask us to do the irrelevant?

It also seems self evident that you must accept and believe in the latter-day scriptures including the four standard works. They are authoritative texts from which you derive hope to receive[24] Gospel blessings. Without them there is no map to follow.

The scriptures are accounts written about and by people who have received the Second Comforter. They did something to qualify. They tell us what to do. If, therefore, we want to get there, we should be eager to look carefully at what they tell us about how they got there. It is futile to travel other paths and hope to obtain the same things the authors of scriptures obtained while going in another direction -- especially when the authors repeatedly tell us there is only one way. We

---

[23]Paul contrasted the two statuses in Eph. 2: 19: "Now therefore ye are no more strangers and foreigners, but fellowcitizens with the saints, and of the household of God." In the verse before this Paul promised: "For through him we both have access by one Spirit unto the Father." (*Id.*, v. 18.)

[24]All things, including an eternal reward, come from having a firm hope anchored in God's promises. As Ether 12: 32 mentions in passing, "…man must hope, or he cannot receive…" This is good doctrine. And if you cannot have a firm hope of these things you cannot receive them.

are going to allow those who wrote the scriptures, who passed through the veil before us, who have seen the face of God, and who have been ministered to by angels, to teach us. Accepting His scriptures is necessary because without them we can't determine what He is asking us to do. So we get familiar with what He wants us to do first. Then we must do it.

God ordained the conditions. He had the right to do that. Rather than argue theological propositions, we would be better served to accept that God is trustworthy and isn't fooling with us. So we are going to proceed with that commonsensical notion in mind.

God sent His Son to fulfill the conditions as the great example to mankind. His Son tells us He is "the way, the truth and the life."(John 14: 6.) Let's look at His example and His teachings as the path back to see God.

In contrast with those who have seen God through their obedience to Him, there is no example of anyone who has used their reasoning to bring them face to face with God. Since no one has returned from the library and reported they met God there, we won't attempt that course. He has been seen in rather specific settings, and those settings have witnesses who tell us how they got to see Him there. We are going to look carefully at enough of these accounts in this book to learn how it happens.

Philosophical arguments do not get Him to visit. Philosophy has been used to tell us everything about His nature and being (or lack thereof) and has even presumed to tell us what He must conform to in order to really be God. But philosophy hasn't gotten a single great mind an audience with Him. We will abandon philosophical arguments in this work, as they don't provide any light on the subject. Instead, we are going to look exclusively to the prophets for guidance.

The prophets who have seen Him tell us to set aside self will and become both acquainted with and obedient to His will. For a proud and 'self-reliant' person this is a difficult thing to do. But there is no getting around it. Christ is the most intelligent being who lived on this earth.[25] Yet He had to gain what He gained through obedience.[26] When He cited His credentials to the Nephites, it is His utter submission to the Father that defines who He is and what He had accomplished.[27] In this He is our great example. So if we want to arrive where He arrived, we should expect to travel on the same path He traveled. Fortunately, the path has been cleared before us by His trailblazing. His guidance, example, and teachings are designed to bring us back to the Father. So we needn't experiment along the way by supplementing steps or changing directions. The Son tells us He is the "way, truth and life" and that "no man cometh unto the father, except by me." (John 14, *supra.*) There is no need for trial and error. He worked out all the problems, and now it is only necessary to accept His leadership and follow Him.

He assures us He knows how to lead us there. His experiences in mortality along with the profound difficulties of the Atonement, equip Him to know everything there is to know about human frailties and pains. His suffering informed Him about how to minister to all of us in our suffering.[28] He is the perfect comforter because He has suffered in

---

[25] Abraham 3: 19: "I am the Lord thy God, I am more intelligent than they all."

[26] Heb. 5: 8: "Though he were a Son, yet learned he obedience by the things which he suffered."

[27] 3 Ne. 11: 10-11: "Behold, I am Jesus Christ, whom the prophets testified shall come into the world. And behold, I am the light and the life of the world; and I have drunk out of that bitter cup which the Father hath given me, and have glorified the Father in taking upon me the sins of the world, in the which I have suffered the will of the Father in all things from the beginning."

[28] Alma 7: 11-13: "And he shall go forth, suffering pains and afflictions and temptations of every kind; and this that the word might be fulfilled which saith he will take upon him the pains and the sicknesses of his people. And he will take upon him death, that he may loose the bands of death which bind his people; and **he will take upon him their infirmities, that his bowels may be filled with mercy, according to the flesh, that he may know accord-**

full degree all that mankind has or can suffer. Through this He has qualified to be our Savior. But we must allow Him to save us from our sins. He is not going to compel us to follow Him. Instead, He invites us to do so. Much of the work of getting past our sins remains our own work. He will forgive us on condition of repentance. But we must work to replace the forgiven sin with virtue.

We have all made mistakes. Even serious ones have been commonly made by His Saints. Our culture is the culture of big mistakes. We are entertained by violence and infidelity, two of the more serious kinds of sin. Hollywood caters to our hedonistic impulses and if you look at what passes for entertainment, we are rather addicted to serious sins as our common fare. The last few seasons of the touring theatrical performances in Salt Lake's Capitol Theater have offered us musicals set in a whore house in Chicago,[29] a whore house set in Southeast Asia,[30] and a whore house set in Paris,[31] not to mention *The Best Little Whorehouse in Texas*. Singing, dancing whores are the stuff our theaters are filled with. While entertaining, they reveal something more of our culture than we may first suspect. Primetime television mixes sex with violence instead of song, but it is the same fare. So it is little wonder we have commonly committed serious sins.

The past is forgivable. Even serious sins are forgivable. That's the

---

ing to the flesh how to succor his people according to their infirmities**. Now the Spirit knoweth all things; nevertheless the Son of God suffereth according to the flesh that he might take upon him the sins of his people, that he might blot out their transgressions according to the power of his deliverance; and now behold, this is the testimony which is in me." (Emphasis added.)

[29]Maurine Dallas Watkins, *Chicago.* New York: American Play Company, 1996.

[30]Claude-Michel Schönberg and Alan Baubil, *Miss Saigon,* New York: Hal Leonard Corporation, 1992.

[31]Victor Hugo, trans. by Charles E. Wilbur, *Les Miserables,* New York: Modern Library (Reprint Edition), 1992.

point of what Christ did. He wants us to recover from our errors. He associated with sinners, and held company with harlots and publicans. Your own past sins, even serious sins, are no impediment to His power to forgive. With His guidance and succor, He wants us to build a new nature under His tutelage. There is no magic to this process. He will heal, guide, succor and forgive us. He will suffer the punishments of sins for us. He will bestow mercy upon us. But we have to follow Him. We must leave our sins in the past. Given what He will do for us in exchange for following Him, it is rather the fool's bargain to refuse.

If we follow Him, He will lead us to the Father. If we refuse His leadership, then we cannot get there.

Though it may sound odd, it is nonetheless true: You must be willing not to judge God. He knows more than we do. He intends to elevate us to be better than we are now. He knows better than any of us how to make that happen. Fearing Him,[32] distrusting Him, judging Him and questioning whether or not He is asking us something which He ought not to be asking erodes faith and confidence in Him. We can't be skeptical and believing at the same moment. So we need to quiet our fears and find our trust in Him.

He has sent a latter-day prophet and restored His Church and Kingdom on earth. Joseph Smith was a flawed mortal. He received the Lord's censure and condemnation for his shortcomings.[33] He is not

---

[32]The term "fear" here is not used in the older sense of 'respecting Him' as the scriptures use the term "fear of the Lord;" e.g., Ps. 19: 9, "The fear of the Lord is clean, enduring for ever." Rather it is used in the modern sense of being reluctant or fearful to accept Him because of some reticence or disgust of Him. The notion of a father-figure offends some feminists whose belief about a male deity have been eroded as a result of cultural norms, thus interfering with acceptance of Him. It is this kind of fear that is used here.

[33]Section 3 of the D&C contains this rebuke: "And behold, how oft you have transgressed the commandments and the laws of God, and have gone on in the persuasions of men. For, behold, you should not have feared man more than God. Although men set at naught the counsels of God, and despise his words -- Yet you should have been faithful; and he would have

worthy of worship, and if anyone worships him they get damned for that.[34] Worshiping the messenger rather than the One who sent him completely misses the mark.

Similarly, worship of the Church that Joseph was an instrument in restoring, or of the presiding authorities within that Church, will damn us. This is not an inconsequential distinction. Christ has never asked anyone to worship men or institutions. He has, however, commanded us to worship the Father and to obey His commandments. A golden calf, or golden angel, or golden-aged leaders are *not* God. No true messenger has ever asked that adoration of God be diverted to them. So we shouldn't spontaneously do what none of them have ever asked us to do.

---

extended his arm and supported you against all the fiery darts of the adversary; and he would have been with you in every time of trouble. Behold, thou art Joseph, and thou wast chosen to do the work of the Lord, but because of transgression, if thou art not aware thou wilt fall." (V. 6-9.) He lamented: "I often felt condemned for my weakness and imperfections." (JSH, 1: 29.)

[34]Claiming to be Joseph's disciple will serve you no better than claiming to be Moses' or John's or even Christ's, if you are unwilling to accept the Gospel with all its teachings and requirements. See, e.g., D&C 76: 98-101: "And the glory of the telestial is one, even as the glory of the stars is one; for as one star differs from another star in glory, even so differs one from another in glory in the telestial world; For these are they who are of Paul, and of Apollos, and of Cephas. These are they who say they are some of one and some of another — some of Christ and some of John, and some of Moses, and some of Elias, and some of Esaias, and some of Isaiah, and some of Enoch; But received not the gospel, neither the testimony of Jesus, neither the prophets, neither the everlasting covenant." God's ministers are sent by God. They are accountable to Him, just as you are. They are unworthy of worship, just as the angels are unworthy of worship. See, e.g., when John fell to worship the angel messenger he was told: "And I fell at his feet to worship him. And he said unto me, See thou do it not: I am thy fellow servant, and of thy brethren that have the testimony of Jesus: worship God: for the testimony of Jesus is the spirit of prophecy." (Rev. 19:10.) This reaffirms the deference of worship is reserved for God alone, and not His messengers, even if the messenger is a prophet or angel.

God alone is worthy of worship. Yet, despite Joseph's limitations and flaws, he was a prophet and restorer used by God for our salvation. The Lord has stated to us, through Joseph Smith: "But this generation shall have my word through you. ... And behold, whosoever believeth on my words, them will I visit with the manifestation of my Spirit." (D&C 5: 10, 16.) Did you notice that? God is saying those words Joseph gave to us were HIS words. And if we believe on "my words" – meaning God owns and accepts complete responsibility for them – then we get manifestations from His Spirit. Accepting the word of God delivered to you through the Prophet Joseph Smith is also bedrock in the process. God did not send a Prophet and establish a binding testimony through him by having his blood shed as a witness of the truthfulness[35] of the message he delivered, only to have us doubt, question, reject or entertain reservations about that message. If you have these doubts, you should resolve them before attempting to do what is set out in this book. If you hold these doubts, the explanation of the process in this text will provide you with nothing more than you already have.

Joseph's mortal flaws should give you hope. If a man whose flaws are on display in his own writings and magnified through the writings of his critics[36] can receive the Second Comforter, it should give hope to all of us. When we measure ourselves against Christ we tend to be discouraged by the gap. It can look like trying to jump across the Grand

---

[35] As D&C 135: 1 states: "To seal the testimony of this book and the Book of Mormon, we announce the martyrdom of Joseph Smith the Prophet, and Hyrum Smith the Patriarch." And D&C 136: 39 states: "Many have marveled because of his death; but it was needful that he should seal his testimony with his blood, that he might be honored and the wicked might be condemned."

[36] Many of his critics have taken more than liberty in proclaiming weaknesses for Joseph. His flaws do not need magnifying by his enemies, and an overstatement of his shortcomings may well interfere with a proper assessment of the man God called as the head of a dispensation. Choose your historians carefully on this subject. There will be no recommended reading list given here.

Canyon at the North Rim where the sides are ten miles apart. But when you consider Joseph Smith's limited education, his primitive cultural setting, his limited opportunity for knowledge of history and culture, and his lack of scholarly attainment, this looks more hopeful. That distance is more like crossing the Colorado River upstream at Marble Canyon, where there is a bridge. People do that every day. So Joseph's example is hopeful and far less discouraging.

Still in all, some of what is regarded as "weaknesses" in Joseph turn out to be strengths. So we have to be careful about how harshly we assess him. We will look carefully at some of that, too, as we pass along.

The next notion is we should be doing what we know is expected from us if we want to receive more from God. It doesn't make sense to expect Him to shower down more truth and light when we aren't paying heed to what He has given to us already. In the economy of heaven, we generally should not expect miracles when our own effort will do the trick. Christ didn't use miraculous means to open Lazarus' tomb. He had people do that. Nor did He use a miracle to unwrap the burial cloth. The miracle was confined to what men *couldn't* do; which in that case was resurrecting a dead man to life. If we have scriptures that tell us some great truths, it is contrary to the economy of heaven to expect those same great truths will be given to us by independent revelation. You can read them. We don't need angels to read the scriptures to us. We just need a little initiative. Rather than being ungrateful for His revelations already contained in scriptures, we should study them before expecting more. So if you are not familiar with the scriptures, you need to become so. They answer more questions, as well as more prayers, than any other source. They are a great repository of past revelations, and therefore need to be studied.

When we are wearing sunglasses, we need to take them off before complaining about the dark. If there is some serious transgression, we should resolve it first. If we are neglecting the duties we have been given, leaving our responsibilities owed to family -- particularly to minor children -- not paying our tithing, or not attending Church meetings regularly, it is unlikely reading this book will make any meaningful difference for you. We can't omit the weightier matters and expect performing the lesser matters will suffice.[37] All things move forward together. If our balance is off, we are more likely to fall aside than to move in the right path. So we need to get back into balance.

Holding high Church office does not matter one way or the other for this subject. Lehi was just a family man whose extended family was not particularly large. Though he was a great prophet, his ministry was among a small group of family members. Nephi not only didn't hold high office, as a younger brother he couldn't get his "flock" to accept him. Ultimately he had to flee from them for his life. Abraham presided over a family and following smaller than most ward Relief Societies. We lose sight of that because their stories are now read by millions; but in their time and setting, they were obscure, as was the Lord Himself obscure in His day. His largest single audience may have been the Nephites, which came after His resurrection. So you mustn't think great spiritual experiences are related to lives led before great audiences. Many of the greatest experiences in scripture involved obscure or private lives.

It is not required that you have the priesthood to receive the Second Comforter. Everyone is invited to come to Him. The promises He made are clearly directed to both men and women. If you are a man, however, you will, of course, need to receive the priesthood to enter the Temple and receive the rites there. But that is incidental to receiving the Second Comforter and not required for it. The ordinances of the Melchizedek Priesthood are required; but those are available to all, men and women. God is no respecter of persons and is universally willing to accept **all** who come unto Him. The first person to receive a visit from the resurrected Second Comforter was a woman. It was some time later

---

[37]Matt. 23: 23 "Woe unto you, scribes and Pharisees, hypocrites! For ye pay tithe of mint and anise and cumin, and have omitted the weightier matters of the law, judgment, mercy, and faith: these ought ye to have done, and not to leave the other undone." That is, you should be paying your tithing, but without the virtues of mercy, faith and fair judgment you cannot qualify.

before the Church leaders caught up with her and got a witness of their own. Culturally we get sensitive, jealous, protective, and somewhat insecure about this. We ought to relax and accept that God is no respecter of persons. He loves us all. He set a precedent with Mary at the tomb the morning of the resurrection which tells us women are entitled to see, witness, and touch Him. We'll need to return to this subject again later and develop it more fully.

There is a profound difference between the mind we have as 'Western rational thinkers' and what we need to take the step through the veil. This change of mind is no small accomplishment. We are going to look at the impediments in our thinking. You may find it distressing as we look at this subject, but nonetheless it is also part of the foundation required to move from where you are to where God is.

There is a centuries-old compulsion in the West to use the rational and scientific method in approaching all subjects. This subject does not get approached that way. It gets approached on its own terms or not at all. If we want an audience with the Second Comforter, and to behold His face and know that He is, then we must do so in the way He established.

The scriptures tell us we need to "experiment," as Alma put it.[38] The experiment alone is not enough, though, because thereafter we must be willing to accept the results of the experiment on its terms and take the next step. The process is not without its proofs and promises along the way, but they come on the Lord's terms, and not as a result of other kinds of study, experimentation, or testing. If you do as asked, you will receive the proof promised. But you will **only** receive that proof, and nothing different. This proof begins in small ways, and requires you exercise faith along the way. It is personal. It must be personal, and every person must receive these things for herself and not for others. As

---

[38]See, e.g., Alma 32: 27: "But behold, if ye will awake and arouse your faculties, even to an experiment upon my words, and exercise a particle of faith, yea, even if ye can no more than desire to believe, let this desire work in you, even until ye believe in a manner that ye can give place for a portion of my words." See also the verses which follow in Chapter 32.

you develop faith and accept the small proofs, then you become ready to receive greater proofs. But we can't jump from small proofs to greater proofs without accepting and trusting the small proofs first. This process requires anyone hoping to move along to persist and grow in the process until fit to receive the next step.

The nature of the "proof" given will require faith. It does not begin with certitude. It starts with the still, small voice. We need to listen to it and act in conformity with its answers before there are more dramatic proofs. If we ignore or reject the small proofs, we won't get more. If you do accept them, and act in reliance upon them, they will form the foundation for more. Through these steps of asking, receiving, trusting and acting, we develop stronger faith. Everyone must follow this same process. Anyone willing to move along with this will grow in light and truth. The scriptures talk about things getting "brighter" until at last we have "the perfect day."[39] This is a remarkably apt description of how it progresses from a lesser to a greater kind of light, until the Being who is light itself comes to comfort you.

The Gospel is not anti-intellectual, but it requires learning through a different method than that used by academics. There is a passage in the D&C which gets quoted in support of the proposition that academic learning is the preferred way to gain understanding. However, the quote is misused. It reads: "And as all have not faith, seek ye diligently and teach one another words of wisdom; yea, seek ye out of the best books words of wisdom; seek learning, even by study and also by faith." (D&C 88: 118.) What gets neglected are the first six words. This statement does not endorse academic methods as the first, or preferred manner, of getting light and truth. Faith is preferred.[40] But since not everyone

---

[39]D&C 50: 24: "That which is of God is light; and he that receiveth light, and continueth in God, receiveth more light; and that light groweth brighter and brighter until the perfect day."

[40]A revelation given more than a year earlier, Section 46, linked "knowledge" to faith and gifts from the Spirit. (See, D&C 46: 10, 13.) Here, in Section 88, the Lord is lamenting that "as all have not faith" then study becomes necessary.

has faith to do so, academic efforts can be used as a lesser alternative. In this book we will try to focus on the preferred way of getting light and truth. Getting light and truth from God is obtained through experiences. It is experiential rather than academic. Feeling comes before seeing, hearing, and touching. But these experiences are the hallmarks of the process. To some significant extent the traditions of Western thought have developed into impediments to the process. Western skepticism has put up cynical barriers to the proofs. Proofs we get from the process are disputed as being subjective and unreliable. But with every person it always begins with subjective experience.

Anecdotal proof may not be acceptable for most scientific conclusions. But anecdotal proof is what you must be willing to accept throughout this process. Your own experiences are going to be your guide. Children were held up as an example by the Lord for a reason. The Lord's command to us to become as little children was not just a passing comment about innocence of character and conduct. He was instructing us to put our intellect into the overall context as well. We will be looking into this further.

Sterling McMurrin, in his introductory essay[41] in *Studies of the Book of Mormon*, writes this about Brother Roberts: "His special responsibility as an official of the Church was to provide leadership in missionary activities, and he firmly believed missionaries should be adequately armed with knowledge for their task. He was not always supported in this conviction by his colleagues, who often preferred dependence on faith with a minimal concern for relevant learning." (Roberts, B. H. *Studies of the Book of Mormon*, Second Edition. Edited by Brigham D. Madsen. Salt Lake City: Signature Books, 1992, p. XXV.) This comment betrays an intellectual's preference for scholarship over "dependence [upon] faith."

With respect to missionary work, there are advantages to 'relevant learning.' Perhaps Paul put it best when he said, with respect to missionary work: "And unto the Jews I became as a Jew, that I might

---

[41]The essay is entitled: *Brigham H. Roberts: A Biographical Essay.*

gain the Jews; to them that are under the law, as under the law, that I might gain them that are under the law; To them that are without law, as without law, (being not without law to God, but under the law to Christ,) that I might gain them that are without law. To the weak became I as weak, that I might gain the weak: I am made all things to all men, that I might by all means save some. And this I do for the gospel's sake, that I might be partaker thereof with you." (1 Cor. 9: 20-23). Paul had a trained and nimble intellect he used in missionary work. But Paul's conversion and mission came as a result of an experience, NOT from his study. He was a "witness" of the Lord. It was that witness, and not his informed and nimble mind, which qualified him as an Apostle of Christ. Paul was 'dependent upon faith' for this powerful experience. He might argue with the philosophers on Mars Hill, and did quote the pagan poet Aratos from his work *Phaenomena* as a missionary,[42] but Paul is still studied for what he experienced and not for his other learning.

In the context of missionary work, 'relevant learning' and reasoning are crucial to converting some, but within the household of faith, there are limits to the value of mere scholarly learning. When we seek a visit from the Second Comforter, it is faith and experience in feeling God's presence which matter; not your scholarly credentials.

Scholarly accomplishment and intellectual sophistication may actually interfere with this process if it gets overemphasized. As Nephi cautions: "O that cunning plan of the evil one! O the vainness, and the frailties, and the foolishness of men! **When they are learned they think they are wise, and they hearken not unto the counsel of God, for they set it aside, supposing they know of themselves, where-fore, their wisdom is foolishness and it profiteth them not**. And they shall perish. But to be learned is good if they hearken unto the counsels of God." (2 Ne. 9: 28-29, emphasis added.) The intellect can

---

[42]Acts 17: 27-28: "That they should seek the Lord, if haply they might feel after him, and find him, though he be not far from every one of us: For in him we live, and move, and have our being; as certain also of your own poets have said, *For we are also his offspring*." Aratos' words are in italics.

deceive. Pride in our intellect can keep us from accepting the small proofs initially given to us. If learning does that to you, you have been ill-served by your education. A bad education is worse than no education. But, the last verse in this quote adds learning can be a good thing *if* you hearken to the counsel of God. It can be a great benefit to have both this world's learning and still keep the sensitivity to feel what lies behind the veil. There is no veil to our feelings. The veil is to our other senses. But we have learned to trust *everything but* our feelings in modern Western thought. For some readers it will be necessary to go back to trusting their feelings from a time long ago in childhood.

Depending on faith is humbling. Some might think it is humiliating. Perhaps it is both. But it is necessary to this process and you must be humble to receive God. You can take pride in great learning. You can be arrogant and judgmental of others whose learning is inferior to your own. That is one of the flaws inherent in "learning" as Alma pointed out above. But you cannot be proud of being faithful, and of complying with God's commandments for receiving the Second Comforter. Paul commented on this with these words: "Let no man deceive himself. If any man among you seemeth to be wise in this world, let him become a fool, that he may be wise." (1 Cor. 3: 18.) The world regards this process as foolish. The Lord requires it of His faithful. When it happens you cannot take any pride in it. As you seek after God, at first it will begin as feelings and subjective experiences. By the time it reaches the point of seeing, hearing and touching, you will have become different than you were before. That new person will have little reason for pride, and no need for recognition. You will see there are greater things than earthly recognition and status. Similarly, criticism and rejection are less meaningful as well.

There has been tension between faith and scholarship in Western culture since the Renaissance, history has put a skew into modern thought about trusting religious impulses. So we need to take a moment and look back briefly to review how we got here.

Aristotle's dogma on the nature of God was incorporated into Catholic thinking by St. Augustine. The historic fight between faith and reason was between Catholic theologians who were disciples of Augustine/Aristotle and the Copernican disciple Galileo. Neither side in this fight was following the path to receiving revelation. The side of "religion" was held by Aristotelian philosophers/theologians. They no more expected revelation than the other side did. There wasn't a dog in that fight belonging to anyone who believed in an ongoing personal revelation from God.

Many years after Copernicus theorized a different framework for heaven than had Aristotle, the uninspired clerics dismissed it as false and ultimately heretical because of their false religious notions. They mis-read the Bible to conclude the earth was the center of the universe. Galileo turned his telescope upward and found proof for the Copernican model. Galileo even went to the trouble of writing an explanation of why the Bible did not require an earth-centered universe. He explained how the verses could be read as a description from the earth's view, and nothing more. Clerics reacted by banning as heresy any teaching other than an earth-centered universe and dismissing Galileo's better reasoned scriptural exegesis.[43] This disastrous conflict between the scholar and the clergy has resulted in a modern presumption that history has vindicated the scholar as truth detector and condemned the clergy as superstitious. But neither side made any pretense to continuing revelation. The clerics relied on a philosopher's views, mingling them with scripture. Oddly, this historic fight between intellectual traditions handed down from philosophy on the one side, and empirical observation on the other side is used to support a stereotypic view that religion is unreliable and science reliable in finding truth.

When, however, this historic debate occurred there were no prophets. No one spoke *with* God, though one side presumed to speak *for* God. The "precedent" therefore is inapplicable. So relying on it as

---

[43]Ironically, Galileo was a better scriptorian than the Catholic clerics of his day.

a reason to limit your confidence in revealed truth is misplaced.

From political and cultural dominance to full scale retreat, religion has receded as science has advanced. In the ebb and flow of argument, the cultural dominance of science and secularism today has all but evicted God from popular Western thinking. To receive the Second Comforter you must go back to accepting revelation as not only possible, but you must notice and accept it as it happens to you.

Our cultural biases today are the result of struggles which date back centuries. There are good historic reasons why we look at things as we do, and why academics think as they do. From the perspective of history, the academics have been right all along in their criticism of religion. In the past, clergy has been wrong more often than not in the great discussions about truth and learning. Even from the view of science, however, none of their great lights from Galileo to Hawking has seen God through mechanical means. Nor is science seeking the means of finding Him now. Seeing Him is left entirely to those who are willing to do what He asks them to do.

History deserves study and can enlarge views. History affects how the issues are perceived today. We will deal with that legacy in this work, however we are not going to deal with the history itself. This is about the promise of the Second Comforter, and the requirements for receiving an audience with Christ, and not merely about history. The Lord's ground is outside of science and in stark contrast to the historic religious and political powers that fought the intellectual battles of the Renaissance. From the close of the New Testament until a beautiful spring day in the Spring of 1820, there was no system on earth for receiving the Second Comforter. So, while our culture may presume the fight between revealed truth and science has been decided, the issue really wasn't even present when the historic arguments took place.

There are competing approaches for finding truth. We are going to trust one of them and follow its guidance and try to accept its proofs.

This estate is to see if we will obey God.[44] A significant component of obeying Him is accepting His system for acquiring light and truth. We are here to acquire light and truth, or intelligence. "Whatever principle of intelligence we attain unto in this life, it will rise with us in the resurrection. And if a person gains more knowledge and intelligence in this life through his diligence and obedience than another, he will have so much the advantage in the world to come." (D&C 130: 18-19.) Acquiring light and truth in their highest forms comes from God and is gained through His processes.

There is not a significant overlay between what is a valuable education for this life and a valuable education for eternities. A Venn-Diagram of the two would show precious little overlap. That disparity is not often recognized. Getting light and truth from God is not an irrational process, but it is extra-rational. For many people this involves such an adjustment to their thinking that it is offensive.[45] These notions are being introduced here, and will be developed later.

Getting back to bedrock issues, there is also the necessity that we get tested. We all get proven along the way. Before you are ready to receive the Second Comforter you will encounter substantial tests of your faith. Of course, you should expect that. Hearts must be broken.

---

[44]Abr 3:25: "And we will prove them herewith, to see if they will do all things whatsoever the Lord their God shall command them."

[45]The path here is so humbling/humiliating to people of strong intellect that we see the same scene Paul found himself in: "Festus said with a loud voice, Paul, thou art beside thyself; much learning doth make thee mad. But he said, I am not mad, most noble Festus; but speak forth the words of truth and soberness. For the king knoweth of these things, before whom also I speak freely: for I am persuaded that none of these things are hidden from him; for this thing was not done in a corner. King Agrippa, believest thou the prophets? I know that thou believest. Then Agrippa said unto Paul, Almost thou persuadest me to be a Christian." (Acts 26: 24-28.) It would be a shame for you to come so close to the truth that you find yourself only "almost" persuaded of its fullness. If, therefore, you can set aside your pride and be willing to accept the charge of "madness" being leveled at you, this undertaking can bear fruit for you.

That is the only way to get the required "broken heart and a contrite spirit"[46] the Lord demands. Just as the Lord passed through Gethsemane, and Joseph Smith through Liberty Jail, and the ancient Saints through persecutions, and Moses through the wilderness for forty years, so we all must pass through sorrows. It is an essential requirement and you will be tested or more accurately, you will be blessed with these opportunities.

How, when, where, and to what extent you will be tested is an individual matter. But a test which will break your heart will certainly come. You must pass through the very valley of the shadow of death, while relying upon the Lord to guide you and provide you the comfort to endure. The Psalmist was not just composing beautiful prose,[47] but describing a part of the Lord's plan.

On the other side of the test there is "the rest of the Lord." But that kind of "rest" needs defining, too. It is not what you might suppose. None of the insecurities of mortality are removed. Only one thing changes: You will know God. But you will still need to go to work and pay the bills.

The reason Christ calls Himself the "Comforter" is because when He comes, you will need comfort. You will pass through distresses, sorrows and difficulties first, and then He will provide comfort.

We often refuse to accept His comfort because of our pride. When our hearts are broken, however, comfort from any source is welcome. It is in our extremities that we are willing to accept feelings from Him. Even the small "proofs" He asks us to rely upon are welcome relief in our extremities. Below is a description of the suffering and resulting faith produced from the Martin Handcart Company experiences as told by one of its survivors:

---

[46]D&C 59: 8: "Thou shalt offer a sacrifice unto the Lord thy God in righteousness, even that of a broken heart and a contrite spirit."

[47]Psalm 23: 4: "Yea, though I walk through the valley of the shadow of death, I will fear no evil: for thou art with me; thy rod and thy staff they comfort me."

'Cold historic facts mean nothing here, for they give no proper interpretation of the questions involved. A mistake to send the Handcart Company out so late in the season? Yes. But I was in that company and my wife was in it and Sister Nellie Unthank whom you have cited was there, too. We suffered beyond anything you can imagine and many died of exposure and starvation, but did you ever hear a survivor of that company utter a word of criticism? Not one of that company ever apostatized or left the Church, because **everyone of us came through with the absolute knowledge that God lives, for we became acquainted with him in our extremities.**

'I have pulled my handcart when I was so weak and weary from illness and lack of food that I could hardly put one foot ahead of the other. I have looked ahead and seen a patch of sand or a hill slope and I have said, I can go only that far and there I must give up, for I cannot pull the load through it.'
He continues: 'I have gone on to that sand and when I reached it, the cart began pushing me. I have looked back many times to see who was pushing my cart, but my eyes saw no one. I knew then that the angels of God were there.

'Was I sorry that I chose to come by handcart? No. Neither then nor any minute of my life since. **The price we paid to become acquainted with God was a privilege to pay,** and I am thankful that I was privileged to come in the Martin Handcart Company.' *(Hope,* Copyright 1988 Deseret Book Company p. 24; also found in *Relief Society Magazine,* January 1948, p. 8.) (Emphasis added.)

This testimony fits into a pattern. If you expect an audience with the Second Comforter, you should expect that He will come because you *need* comfort. You should expect you will have to fit into the pattern. And so you must not be surprised as He arranges experiences for you, in answer to your search for Him, which will break your heart. That is as it must be.

Chapter Three

KEEPING THE COMMANDMENTS

I *sat alone in the barracks at Pease Air Force Base, in Portsmouth, New Hampshire, reading the journal given to me by Steve Klaproth, himself a recent Mormon convert. Steve had been the one who defended the Church in the UNH night class. He had gained his testimony of the Mormon Church while on guard duty in Southeast Asia, where the Vietnam War was still raging. As I read his journal, I began a debate with myself: "Joseph Smith could not be a prophet because there are no prophets anymore."*

How do you know that?

"Because there haven't been prophets for nearly two thousand years."

Just because it has not occurred for a time, does that make it impossible to happen again?

"Well, no. But the scriptures do not say further prophets should be expected."

What about Christ's test: 'By their fruits ye shall know them.' If there is a test, does it not imply a test is needed? And if a test is needed, then doesn't that suggest more prophets will come?

"I suppose so. But Joseph Smith couldn't be a prophet. After all, he was a fraud, wasn't he? He had multiple wives, and started a religion that is more 'corporate' than religious."

Shouldn't you apply Christ's test? Wasn't that what it was given for?

"Well, what then were Joseph's 'fruits?' I suppose the way to answer that would be to look at these Mormons I am dealing with here. They seem happy enough. They seem to avoid alcohol and drugs, have happy marriages, and live clean lives. They seem to actually enjoy Church as opposed to treating it as an unwelcome obligation. They have large families, and seem to love their children. If these people are the measure of the 'fruits' then I suppose Joseph might be a prophet. But, even assuming Joseph had good fruits, what about the problems of new scripture? There wasn't supposed to be any more scripture. Revelation says you shouldn't add to the scriptures."

Does God not have the right to add or take away? The commandment to not add or detract is addressed to man. Why would that limit God?

"Hadn't thought of it like that...."

Keeping Christ's commandments is not just incidental to the path back to Him. It is the path back. There is nothing optional about it.

"There is a law, irrevocably decreed in heaven before the foundations of this world, upon which all blessings are predicated – And when we obtain any blessing from God, it is by obedience to that law upon which it is predicated." (D&C 130: 20-21.) Commandments have associated blessings.

The commandments were given to shape us. When we are doing something the Lord has asked us to do, we are moving in a direction toward Him. Sometimes commandments may seem odd, irrelevant or counter-intuitive. They are necessary even when we don't see the "why" about them.

When you learn to draw faces, you don't start by sketching faces. You start with basic shapes like circles and triangles. Then you progress to three dimensional simple shapes like cubes and cones. There is a progression which art teachers implement to help develop the needed skills in the student, and these progressions are incorporated into the teaching process. So it is with the Lord. He teaches us more important material than art, but He uses basics to move us along in our development.

The Gift of the Holy Ghost is conferred after baptism. It is intended to be a guide, and to lead you into greater light and truth. It is the still, small voice which helps by whispering or giving impressions. It is a subtle and quiet tool, intended to help us develop sensitivity and reverence. It is the Comforter first promised to us.

This Comforter can help enlighten us as we use the other basic tools we are given. Reading the scriptures while listening to this Comforter allows us to see the meaning of the passages more clearly. When the scriptures were written, the authors were in tune with the Comforter. Inspired passages were put into these words as the Spirit whispered to the writers. That same Spirit can aid you when reading them. Joseph describes the relationship in these words: "Our minds being now enlightened, we began to have the scriptures laid open to our understandings, and the true meaning and intention of their more mysterious passages revealed unto us in a manner which we never could attain to previously, nor ever before had thought of." (JSH 1: 74.)

In traditional Christianity, Theological Seminaries use logic, deductive reasoning, historic precedent and rhetoric among other things to develop the scriptures' meaning. These tools have resulted in opposing interpretations and opposing denominations. Brilliant minds have reached contrary interpretations using these tools. They have their limits.

The original authors were fishermen and farmers who did not write as theologians. They wrote in the common language of their day, speaking about their experiences with God. Animated by the Spirit, they tried to preserve or testify about encounters with God

Rather than using the theologian's tools, the Comforter can guide us to a clearer view of what the inspired writer was saying. It is as if the writer was attuned to and writing about music but using only words to describe the harmony. Without that tune in the mind of the reader, the music cannot be heard and the harmony is lost. The Holy Ghost allows you to resonate with the same frequency as the writer and to "hear" what he is writing about. The process is far more abstract than logic, reason, rhetoric and historic precedent will uncover. Capturing the thought of the inspired fisherman requires an inspired reader. The Holy Ghost is a guide to speak to you as you study the scriptures. It will lead you to understanding, harmony, clarity and truth. If you have not experienced this kind of awareness while studying the scriptures, then you need to attempt it. The scriptures are a great source of inspiration and revelation. Through them you can gain experience in listening to the Spirit. They tutor us, not just in doctrine, but they tutor us in hearing the voice of inspiration as well. Through scripture study you can develop a greater spiritual sensitivity. If you have not begun to do that, you will need to start.

Find time to be alone. Take the time to study, not just read, the scriptures. Pray before you begin. Think about the phrases used, and don't try to digest whole chapters at once. Be silent, so that you can hear the still, small voice. If there is some serious sin in your life, repent of it. Let the Lord know you are doing so because you want the Spirit as a guide in your life. He will respond. You will find He is no respecter of persons. He will send His Spirit to any sincere seeker for truth. And when He does, it will be as a result of you seeking the light and obeying the commandments. The Comforter's purpose is to guide you into greater truths. There is a library of truth waiting to be discovered inside the scriptures. Use this library and experience the inspiration it offers.

There is a point at which this Comforter is no longer adequate to bring the faithful disciple along. At that point, the disciple is tutored and comforted by the Lord Himself. These things build one upon the other. The Holy Ghost, as Comforter, leads one to Christ. Christ, as Comforter, leads the disciple to the Father. Returning to the presence of God is the Redemption from the Fall, which Christ provides to mankind through His Atonement. "Because thou knowest these things, ye are redeemed from the fall," is how Christ described it to the Brother of Jared, as He brought him through the veil for an audience. Ether 3:13. By seeking the Second Comforter you are seeking nothing less than Redemption from the Fall.

There are steps along the way which are set out in scripture. They are clear and concrete. Applying them is left to each disciple.

The interesting thing about the process is that actual light – or enlightenment – is acquired through obedience. It is not acquired in any other way. It is specifically not acquired by study or scholarship alone. Scholars can have some of the greatest difficulties in overcoming the world and acquiring faith. God does not ask whether the believer has been to college and received theological training. Semi-literate but believing youth are more suited for acquiring the Spirit than educated and sophisticated adults. It was to an uneducated boy[48] the Lord came

---

[48]President Wilford Woodruff, at Cache Stake Conference, held at Logan, Sunday Afternoon, November 1st, 1891 stated the following about Joseph: "Now, in our day and generation, we have arrived at a point in the history of the world when this Priesthood is restored. The Lord raised up Joseph Smith. He came forth in the proper time. He organized a Church. Who was Joseph Smith? Was he a lawyer? Was he a doctor of divinity? Was he what is called a great man, a learned man? No, he was but a youth; the world would say an illiterate, ignorant youth. He was an unlearned youth in the things of the world. But he was a pure man." (*Messages of the First Presidency of The Church of Jesus Christ of Latter-day Saints*, 6 vols. James R. Clark, comp., (Salt Lake City: Bookcraft, 1965-75), vol. 3, p.222.)

to open this last Dispensation. None of the Lord's twelve original Apostles were well educated. A significant number were fishermen. The faith of Saints in less sophisticated societies has been greater than among the most sophisticated. Yet it pleased the Lord to establish His Latter-day restoration in the heart of a Western society which prizes self-reliance and individual achievement. A faith based upon cooperation and selflessness has been planted in the heart of a selfish and competitive society. This is not just ironic. It is a hopeful sign that we are just as entitled as less sophisticated and more believing peoples from other cultures, in spite of the handicaps of our own[49]

The scriptures tell us the connection between acquiring light and truth and obedience to the commandments is direct, immediate and

------

[49]We arrogantly assume that our own culture is superior and beneficial. The one thing that the American society in which the Church has been restored *is* superior in is its economy. That economy has fueled and funded the wide ranging programs of the Church. But the American secular, agnostic, hedonistic and selfish culture surrounding the Church is resented around the world. 'Freedom' has become a license for excess and perversion in the eyes of many third-world countries. Islamic nations respect our successes, but fear our secularism. One of the first commercial commodities available in Baghdad after the American led invasion's success was pornography. That confirmed in the minds of many that we are "Satanic" and not that great shining city on a hill as we contend we are. We do not teach people to govern themselves as well as we once did, and have a hard time balancing between freedom and excessively destructive behavior. Societal disagreements over personal conduct have resulted in our Supreme Court resolving questions of this nature in favor of the broadest definitions of freedom. Government has increasingly become less involved in limiting conduct solely on the basis of its "morality" or "immorality" alone. Self-government presumes a moral people. But the secularism of America, along with the "wall of separation" between Church and state, has resulted in less and less agreement on the meaning of morality, and greater and greater tolerance of what was once regarded as clearly immoral. Both sides have dubbed this the "culture war" and have politicized the matter. Tying the Church of Jesus Christ of Latter-day Saints to American society and its changing values is, therefore, a hazardous thing to do, and may in the long run ill-serve the Church as it becomes global. Perceiving the Church as an 'American Institution' may have some unexpected and unpleasant results as these things unfold further.

inescapable. It can be acquired in no other way. "That which is of God is light; and he that receiveth light, and continueth in God, receiveth more light; and that light groweth brighter and brighter until the perfect day." (D&C 50: 24.) A "perfect day" seems clear enough. Cloudless and clear, at the apex of the summer solstice, a "perfect day" would be filled with light and warmth. That kind of symbol powerfully captures an image. The image is suggesting to us what standing in God's presence would be like. The Millennium would be a "perfect day" in which the "light of the earth" will dwell among mankind. So that is what we seek. But how does one "receive light" and "continue in God" so as to receive more light?

Section 93 speaks directly to this. It teaches "And no man receiveth a fullness unless he keepeth his commandments. He that keepeth his commandments receiveth truth and light, until he is glorified in truth and knoweth all things." (V. 27-28.) If we want the fullness, we have to keep His commandments. To make it more clear for us, in that same section it teaches, "I give unto you these sayings that you may under-stand and know how to worship, and know what you worship, that you may come unto the Father in my name, and in due time receive of his fullness. For if you keep my commandments you shall receive of his fulness." (*Id.*, v. 19-20.)

This is how light and truth are received. The commandments are not obligations, but opportunities. They are not burdens to weigh us down. Rather they are the means of lifting us up. Ecc. 12: 13: "Let us hear the conclusion of the whole matter: Fear God, and keep his commandments: for this is the whole duty of man." Elsewhere it is written: "And in nothing doth man offend God, or against none is his wrath kindled, save those who confess not his hand in all things, and obey not his commandments." (D&C 59: 21.) God reveals Himself through His commandments.

The commandments are intended to move our lives into harmony with a higher intelligence. We cannot be in tune with that higher intelligence without bringing our own lives into conformity with something higher. Commandments are the guide, and the scriptures are where we learn the commandments.

All learning should inform our reading of the scriptures. We read the scriptures to learn the commandments. We learn the commandments to be able to obey them. We obey the commandments to receive light and truth.

Culturally, we have been conditioned to question authority and to resent any attempt to curtail our freedom. The great East-West cold war era tensions grew out of the 'freedom v. oppression' dichotomy. Freedom won that war, we presume, and therefore history is on the side of the forces of freedom. Attempts to limit freedom are viewed as politically reactionary and potentially threatening. There are reasons for this attitude. The beliefs people hold on these matters are deep and strong.

Against that cultural background the idea of being required to obey commandments seems 'oppressive' and politically 'reactionary' or on the wrong side of history. If you view this as an exclusively cultural matter, you may find it troubling.

This is not a cultural matter. Keeping the commandments as a personal matter does not involve you oppressing anyone else. If you are trying to impose a standard of conduct upon others you are not only going to fail, you are going to be violating the scriptures' teachings as well. The Gospel is intended to be lived "without compulsory means."[50]

Political history and cultural biases are a poor basis for interpreting the Gospel. We tend to do that. We breathe in the smog of our culture. Although this problem exists, it mustn't influence your thinking on the matter. Realizing it probably does and recognizing that to be so is the first step in stopping it. We will discuss this problem further later in this book.

There is a difference between mere hoping something is true and

[50]D&C 121: 46: "The Holy Ghost shall be thy constant companion, and thy scepter an unchanging scepter of righteousness and truth; and thy dominion shall be an everlasting dominion, and without compulsory means it shall flow unto thee forever and ever."

believing it is true. You can hope something is true without believing it to be. Belief comes after mere hope, and is based upon conviction a proposition is true. There is a difference between belief and faith, and between faith and knowledge. It is a spectrum. At one end there is hope, and it is then followed by belief. By degrees this grows into faith and faith can progress by degrees into knowledge. Knowledge is at the other end of the spectrum.

When we first begin to follow Christ to any degree, the process begins with some hope Christ is who He purports to be. We have a desire or a hope Christ can actually save us. (Alma 32: 28.) That desire needs to change from a hope Christ is the promised Savior into a belief that He is. Belief is a step toward faith. Belief can come from study and trusting others. No matter how your faith in Christ has come to you, it is that faith which is the bedrock requirement for seeking the Second Comforter. Faith is more than belief. It requires action consistent with belief. But let us begin with belief:

Belief can be very weak, or it can be a strongly held conviction. Most of the "Christian"[51] world ends their practice of religion with either hope or belief. But there is much more offered by Christ than this. He offers to us faith, and ultimately knowledge as well.

You can spend a lifetime as a "believer" without ever developing faith. Before belief can turn into faith, action is required. "What blessing would be obtained by believing the words which Christ has spoken, unless we enact them? It is not the person who merely believes in the sayings of Christ who is justified, but it is he who shows his faith by obeying them. When Jesus speaks of believers, He has reference, most

---

[51] I put "Christian" in quotes to make clear that I use the term to mean Historic Christianity. Mormonism is not part of Historic Christianity. Rather it claims to be a restoration of Primitive Christianity. The difference between the two is beyond this work, but has been treated by others, including Hugh Nibley in "*Mormonism and Ancient Christianity*," Volume 4 of the Collected Works of Hugh Nibley, and Barry Robert Bickmore in "*Restoring the Ancient Church, Joseph Smith and Early Christianity*." For someone interested in this subject, these sources are referred.

generally, to those whose faith has been sufficiently strong to lead them to obedience." (*Lectures, True Faith,* p. 75.)

Without some action consistent with belief, a disciple cannot move along from mere belief to developing faith. For faith follows laws irrevocably decreed and can be purchased in no other way. This is why obedience to the commandments is necessary. Without obedience to the commandments, it is not possible to develop beyond belief. Our culture is hostile to faith. That is no accident. There are forces at work which are opposed to faith. The adversary is interested in preventing progress from hope to belief, and from belief to faith, and from faith to knowledge. Progression in this course comes from obedience to the commandments. The forces, arguments, cultural baggage, and social arguments opposing obedience to the commandments are arraigned against faith in Christ. You should not be misled by them. They can cost you something far more valuable than anything they can offer in return.

The Third Lecture, of the *Lectures on Faith*, teaches faith comes only to those who have "an actual knowledge that the course of life which he is pursuing is according to [God's] will." (*Lectures, Third Lecture,* p. 33.) In the Sixth Lecture it is explained, "An actual knowledge to any person, that the course of life which he pursues is according to the will of God, is essentially necessary to enable him to have that confidence in God without which no man can attain eternal life. ... unless [the Saints] have an actual knowledge that the course they are pursuing is according to the will of God they will grow weary in their minds, and faint;" (*Lectures, Sixth Lecture,* p. 57.) This means we must actually do something in order to follow the "will of God" in our lives.

The only way to possess this required "actual knowledge" that one's life is in harmony with God's will is to keep His commandments. It is not possible to disobey and refuse to submit to His commandments, and then develop faith in Him. Disobedience is contrary to the laws ordained before the foundation of the world upon which the blessing of faith is predicated. Therefore, if you want faith, you must obey and if you choose to disobey, you cannot acquire faith.

Christ lamented the difference between merely believing or saying you believe in Him on the one hand, and those that obey His commandments on the other. He said: "Not every one who saith unto me, Lord, Lord, shall enter into the kingdom of heaven; but *he that doeth the will* of my Father which is in heaven." (Matt. 7: 21, emphasis added.) It is action, obedience and living in conformity to God's will which yields faith.

The commandments give us a chance to develop faith. Even when the commandments seem trivial, they are not. Doing His will, even in small ways, brings us closer to Him. Even small reminders can help us "that [we] do always remember him, that [we] may have his Spirit to be with [us]." (D&C 20: 79.)

So if you want to have faith, obedience is the key to acquiring it. Whatever reason you have for disobedience, it is the enemy of faith. You should consider whether it is worth the loss of faith it is costing you.

Faith covers a broad spectrum. It begins embryonic and weak, but can develop into an unshakable faith in the truthfulness of a principle. Jacob describes that kind of faith, which results in actual power, in these words: "Wherefore, we search the prophets, and we have many revelations and the spirit of prophecy; and having all these witnesses we obtain a hope, and our faith becometh unshaken, insomuch that we truly can command in the name of Jesus and the very trees obey us, or the mountains, or the waves of the sea." Jacob 4: 6. He is speaking about mature faith that comes after trusting the many proofs of faith that come from obedience.

Alma tried to describe the proofs that come from obedience. He used a seed in this analogy to help illustrate what they are:

Now, we will compare the word unto a seed. Now, if ye give place, that a seed may be planted in your heart, behold, if it be a true seed, or a good seed, if ye do not cast it out by your unbelief, that ye will resist the Spirit of the Lord, behold, it will begin to swell within your breasts; and when you feel these swelling motions, ye will begin to say within yourselves – It must needs be that this is a good seed, or that the word is good, for it beginneth to enlarge my soul; yea, it beginneth to enlighten my understanding, yea, it beginneth to be delicious to me. Now behold, would not this increase your faith? I say unto you, Yea; nevertheless it hath not grown up to a perfect knowledge. But behold, as the seed swelleth, and sprouteth, and beginneth to grow, then you must needs say that the seed is good; for behold it swelleth, and sprouteth, and beginneth to grow. And now, behold, will not this strengthen your faith? Yea, it will strengthen your faith: for ye will say I know that this is a good seed; for behold it sprouteth and beginneth to grow. (Alma 32: 28-30.)

The first proof comes after you have decided not to reject the commandments, but to try and obey them. When you do that and begin to obey, then he says, "it will begin to swell within your breast." This expression suggests within your heart, where you feel, you will notice that you feel swelling or some emotional feeling in sympathy with the things you are trying to accept. This feeling in sympathy grows to the point that "it beginneth to enlighten" your understanding. That is, you begin to see reasons for faith. You begin to accept the belief system which you are obeying. Your "understanding" of it is increased because you are living in conformity with it. You begin to "see" there is something to the belief system. This is also called "enlarging the soul" of the person who obeys.

This isn't much, but it is proof. The scriptures are telling us how to get the proofs. It begins small. But it does begin. And when it begins it requires action. That action will provoke these feelings, which will then grow into an understanding of the belief system. Action leads to feeling. In turn, action and feeling will lead to understanding. The mind is led through this process by the action and the feeling. The process is not scientific. It is instead an experience.

Alma is trying to get you to take this step and have this experience. He is teaching that if you will take the step and follow the commandments, they will lead you to feelings, and then to "seeing" things the way the belief system is trying to teach you. This is the beginning of faith.

It is subtle and does not come as a result of reasoning. The mind or reason will follow from the experience. Things here are apparently backward. We normally expect the proof will be provided first. Here we are being told the proof comes after the obedience. If you want faith, then you must obey. Then when you obey, you get this subtle form of proof.

Faith begins in very small ways. Emotional, sympathetic feelings are the beginnings of this seed sprouting. Then after that, the mind begins to "get" or to "see" the truthfulness of the system.

Alma says when you have done these things and let this process work inside you, it will begin to be preferable to what you had before. You will conclude "it beginneth to be delicious to" you. This means you are going to come to the point where you rather like this new way of seeing things better than the old way of seeing them. You begin to get a new view of life, its meaning, and God's existence. You begin to feel closer to Him than you did before. It will be familiar to your spirit, even if it is not familiar to your mind. And you begin to resonate with God's frequency, which brings light or enlightenment to you. Though this may sound vague, it is not. It is an actual experience and anyone who decides to go through the experience will witness it. Keep the commandments, hope this commitment will lead you to enlightenment, and you will find your heart or feelings become inclined toward God.

Then Alma asks, "Now behold, would not this increase your faith?" Meaning if you take the steps and get these feelings and begin to see the belief system as more reasonable as a result, will this not cause you to believe in it? Alma answers his own question: "I say unto you, Yea; nevertheless it hath not grown up to a perfect knowledge." If you act on this invitation, you are going to receive the proofs that are promised. When you receive these proofs, they will help you find faith itself. But that is not knowledge. It is only faith. It is a beginning. Much more lies ahead, if you will let it develop in you.

Faith can grow, just like a seed, if you will continue to obey the commandments. As you persist in obedience, your faith will inevitably grow as feelings grow stronger, your mind grows in light, and you begin to "see" more clearly the wisdom of the entire belief system. Christ's mission and Atonement begin to take on a new meaning. His teachings begin to grow in wisdom right before you. In turn, your ability to see their profound depth with greater clarity will follow. You are getting light and truth. It is an actual enlightenment of your mind and it comes through this process. Without engaging in research, you begin to experience added light and truth in your mind as you follow the commandments.

Obedience to the commandments is what God has ordained as the means to gain light and truth. Anyone can do it and receive the same result. No class of people is excluded. No intellectual background is required. No research need be done. Follow this path, accept these feelings, and your mind will begin to see the truthfulness as light and truth flow into it.

Alma describes the continuation of this enlightenment process in these words: "But behold, as the seed swelleth, and sprouteth, and beginneth to grow, then you must needs say that the seed is good; for behold it swelleth, and sprouteth, and beginneth to grow. And now, behold, will not this strengthen your faith? Yea, it will strengthen your faith: for ye will say I know that this is a good seed." Swelling and sprouting is an attempt to tell you about the unfolding inside you of the light and truth that comes from obedience. This is a palpable experience universally available on the same terms to anyone. You just have to keep the commandments to witness these things beginning to happen inside you.

But faith is not the end. Though developing faith will save you, much more is offered if you are willing to receive it. There is another level above in the process of this progression. The end of this process will have your faith transfer into knowledge. Knowledge is what one gets when they are "redeemed from the fall" as Christ explained to the Brother of Jared.

We are going to look carefully at this path; follow it from hope, to belief, to faith, to knowledge, and along the way study the lives of those who have walked it. As we go we will become acquainted with the meaning of the phrase the "fullness of the Gospel of Jesus Christ." (See D&C 20: 8-9.) To receive these things is to receive that Gospel message in its fullness.

Alma said it was a "delicious" process. It might be put differently: It is fun! You will find greater joy in doing as this than in anything else available to mortals. Nothing is quite as satisfying as growing in harmony with God. It fills that void all mortals feel. All the other outlets (addiction, hero-worship, alcohol, politics, becoming a "fan" of an actor/leader, excessive educational attainments, activism, etc.) are attempts to fill the void with a substitute for the real thing. That void inside mankind is because we seek God. Doing as He instructs us is the only way to really find what we lack. He alone is the real thing we are missing. He intends for us to experience Him through obedience to His commandments.

Chapter Four

NEPHI'S WALK:
THE PATH EXEMPLIFIED
Part 1: The Prelude

The journal in front of me spoke of the writer's testimony. It spoke about how this convert had faith in the Gospel as taught by the Mormons. He had been converted while serving in the war zone in Southeast Asia. He had received a spiritual witness that the Gospel was true. The words of the journal seemed so sincere, but remained too good to be true. He could have just been worried about survival in a war zone and may have confused his intense personal longing for safety as an answer from God. Like the cliché my father used to repeat: '"there are no atheists in fox-holes." My father had survived D-Day on Omaha Beach. He believed in God but he wasn't particularly religious. In fact, the trauma of that single day of fighting left him confused about God's will throughout his life. The Vietnam War was nothing if not ambiguous and confusing.*

And, I thought, how was I ever to come to some certainty about these matters? The "truth" had been a raging and elusive subject since the dawn of man. If Pilate got nothing else right, he certainly asked the right question: "What is truth?"

Came the thought: Truth is the knowledge of things as they are, and as they were, and as they are to become.

"How can a religion claim to be the only truth?"

I thought: Christ made similar claims. If He made such claims in His day, shouldn't His Church (if it is His Church) be making similar claims, today?

"Well, I suppose so. But couldn't any Church just assert that? How can this Church be authentic?"

From the New Testament until now there has not been a single Church calling itself The Church of Jesus Christ. There has not been a single Church which claims to have divinely restored authority. There has not been a single Church with the offices found in the New Testament, including Apostles, Prophets, Seventies, Elders, Bishops, Deacons, Priests and Teachers. If you look to the New Testament as a model, only one Church fits that model.

* * * * *

After two hours of raising questions and considering answers alone in the barracks, I reached this final question:

"But how do I know there even is a God? After all, there may not even be a God, and life may not have any real meaning." In response to which came this final thought:

Who do you think you have been talking with these last two hours?

It was that last thought which alarmed me. Had I really been in a conversation with God? The thoughts had come more quickly and easily than I'd experienced before, and came with a quiet feeling of certitude and calm. Perhaps this was what it meant to talk with God. Perhaps I had an answer. Perhaps this was the stuff from which faith flows. If so, then I must then have a testimony, for I had an answer from God. The answer was so subtle, however, that it was nothing more than a still, small feeling. Was that really how God answered prayer?

Nephi's life is a wonderful revelation of how this process unfolds. The D&C testifies the Book of Mormon "contains a record of a fallen people, and the fullness of the gospel of Jesus Christ." (Section 20: 9.) Although some have questioned whether or not the "fullness of the Gospel of Jesus Christ" is in the Book of Mormon. Had we nothing more than First Nephi, we would have the fullness of the Gospel of Jesus Christ set out in plainness there. The Book of Mormon contains much more, of course. Yet the "fullness" is in Nephi's example. So we are going to carefully look at Nephi.

The Book of Mormon begins as Nephi's father, Lehi, hears "many prophets, prophesying unto the people that they must repent, or the great city Jerusalem must be destroyed."[52] (1 Ne. 1:4.) Lehi responds charitably to the message and prays as an intercessor for Jerusalem. (v. 5.) Because of this intercession by Lehi, he receives a theophany set out in verses 6 through 15 of Chapter 1. Lehi then begins to prophesy of

---

[52]Although many LDS authors and commentators assume Lehi was a prophet at the beginning of the Book of Mormon text, the text itself makes no such assertion. In the beginning Lehi reacts to the message of others in verse 5 of 1 Ne. 1. There is no suggestion Lehi was among those warning the people at the beginning of the Book of Mormon. He later joins in the call to repentance as a result of the theophany he receives in verses 6-15. When Lehi begins his ministry as a prophet the text clearly states Lehi "**began** to prophesy" in verse 18, emphasis added. Nothing in the text suggests this "beginning" in verse 18 had any antecedent in an earlier call to Lehi.

the things he now knows, starting in verse 18.[53] Lehi is threatened with death and he flees Jerusalem for the desert, taking his family with him.

In the desert, Lehi instructs his family of the things he witnessed and this spiritual experience he had. His family is understandably skeptical. It is apparent his children, including Nephi, are not able to accept or believe their father's tale about visions from God. (See, 1 Ne. 2: 11-12.[54]) Nephi's own skepticism is apparent from verse 16.[55] This is where the journey begins for Nephi on the path to redemption from the Fall, for in verse 16 Nephi confronts his inability to believe his father's prophetic encounter with God by asking God to help him believe. Nephi writes: "having great desires to know of the mysteries of God, wherefore, I did cry unto the Lord; and behold he did visit me, and did

---

[53]"Therefore, I would that ye should know, that after the Lord had shown so many marvelous things unto my father, Lehi, yea, concerning the destruction of Jerusalem, behold he went forth among the people, and **began to prophesy** and to declare unto them concerning the things which he had both seen and heard." (Emphasis added.)

[54]"Now this he spake because of the stiffneckedness of Laman and Lemuel; for behold they did murmur in many things against their father, because he was a visionary man, and had led them out of the land of Jerusalem, to leave the land of their inheritance, and their gold, and their silver, and their precious things, to perish in the wilderness. And this they said he had done because of the foolish imaginations of his heart. And thus Laman and Lemuel, being the eldest, did murmur against their father. And they did murmur because they knew not the dealings of that God who had created them."

[55]"And it came to pass that I, Nephi, being exceedingly young, nevertheless being large in stature, and also having great desires to know of the mysteries of God, wherefore, I did cry unto the Lord; and behold he did visit me, and did soften my heart that I did believe all the words which had been spoken by my father; wherefore, I did not rebel against him like unto my brothers." If Nephi wasn't skeptical, he would not have needed to "cry unto the Lord" to try and believe. Nor would he report his heart got "softened" so he could "believe" what his father had been teaching. So Nephi, too, was skeptical at first. Perhaps not so rebellious as his older brothers, but skeptical nonetheless.

soften my heart[56] that I did believe all the words which had been spoken by my father; wherefore I did not rebel against him like unto my brothers."

This short verse contains a succinct statement of how the path to a fullness of the Gospel begins. Nephi first had a "great desire" to know. He acted on that desire. He "cried unto the Lord" to get the ability to believe on the things Lehi taught. In response to that "cry" to God, Nephi says "behold he did visit me."

Although that sounds significant, the "visit" is then described. It is the same modest proof Alma says the process begins with, as discussed earlier. God's visit was merely to "soften" Nephi's heart. No rushing wind, no parting veil, nor thunder from on-high accompanies this "visit" from God. In fact nothing material happens at all. It consists merely of Nephi being able to set aside his skepticism about his father's teachings. He was able to believe his father's message. Just "believe." Nothing further happens. That is where all of us must begin. The initial proof offered by God is a still, small encounter that speaks more with feeling than words.

That is where it begins with each of us if we want to follow the path. It must start somewhere, and this is it. By nature Nephi starts out with skepticism, but with a desire in his heart to believe. He couldn't quite muster the faith to accept the principles being taught to him, but he wanted to overcome this skepticism and accept the things taught.

What you need is a true message from God. That is what the restored Gospel says it is. If you would like to know if those claims are true, you must want to believe it and be willing to ask God to find out. You must have a "desire" to believe. Then you must "cry unto the Lord" so the Lord can aid you to overcome unbelief.

Although the end of the process may be great and glorious, it begins very humbly. It began so with Nephi. It begins similarly with everyone

---

[56]Since Nephi needed to have his "heart softened," it is apparent Nephi did not welcome his father's message uncritically or with full acceptance when he first heard of it. But Nephi did not leave the matter there. Rather, he persisted through prayer to try and believe. And God "visited" him as a result.

who will walk that path. Interestingly, wherever you are in the path, the next step is always the first step all over again. Whenever you encounter the doubts and skepticism, the route through them is the same route taken to find faith in the first place.

Nephi's desire has now progressed to belief. He has grown into belief, and he correctly attributes it to God's grace. But the account does not clearly show Nephi to have faith at this point. For faith requires action, as discussed before. So Nephi, like all of us, must act on this belief to develop faith. That is exactly what Nephi does next.

First, Nephi records he "did not rebel against [Lehi] like unto [his] brothers." (Id., v. 16.) Second, he "spake unto Sam, making known unto him the things the Lord had manifested unto me by his Holy Spirit. And it came to pass that he believed in my words." (v. 17.) So Nephi not only believed, he also bore testimony to his brother Sam, and thereby convinced Sam of the same belief. It was necessary for Nephi to do this. Without bearing testimony and taking some action as a result of his belief in his father's words, Nephi's faith would have remained dormant. Action activates faith.

The relationship between Nephi and Sam illustrates two of the gifts to the Church, as well. "To some it is given by the Holy Ghost to know.... To others it is given to believe on their words." (D&C 46: 13-14.) This is also a part of the path. We are all interdependent. In that interdependence we develop our gifts and receive grace. Your gifts were given you to benefit others. Nephi is showing an example of the right pattern.

After the success with Sam, Nephi takes his message of belief to his older brothers. Nephi writes: "But, behold, Laman and Lemuel would not hearken to my words." (1 Ne. 2: 17.) Nephi's testimony to his older brothers did not produce belief in them.

There are mixed results here. One is encouraging, because Nephi's brother Sam believes. But the other effort has failed. Once again Nephi demonstrates how the path is followed. Christ taught we are to "bless them that curse you, do good to them that hate you, and pray for them which despitefully use you, and persecute you," (Matt. 5: 44.) Nephi, faced with critical and unbelieving brothers, does not either turn his back or return their criticism. Instead he says, "being grieved because of the hardness of their hearts I cried unto the Lord for them." (1 Ne. 2: 17.) Nephi returned grace for rejection. He showed charity and he made intercession for them by praying to the Father in their behalf. Just like his father Lehi before, Nephi also shows charity (or love) to the hard-hearted and seeks God's grace for them.

There is something profound in this example. It illustrates exactly what Christ asked us to do in the Sermon on the Mount.[57] The Savior taught His code of conduct in that sermon. If you want to understand Christ's life, that single sermon defines Him. If any person lives these teachings, they become a "type" of Christ or an example that mirrors Him. Of course, He lived the pattern fully, and others live it imperfectly. Even so, when anyone is following His lead they typify His teachings and thereby become "types" of Christ. It is for this reason the scriptures speak of "saviours on mount Zion."[58] Those referred to as "saviors" in this context are types of the One who really saved us all.

Here Nephi's conduct makes him a 'type' of Christ. Just as Christ made intercession for all of mankind through the Atonement, so Nephi also makes intercession on behalf of his unbelieving brothers and "cried unto the Lord" for those who had rejected him. Nephi shows himself to be faithful in the face of adversity. He has been charitable to the critical. As a result of this he is ready to receive more. Everything given him to this point has resulted in his being true and faithful. He has passed the test, secured faith, and now can be trusted with more.

---

[57]It makes no difference that Nephi lived before the Sermon on the Mount was preached. He lived the precepts of that sermon, and therefore merited the results. The laws irrevocably decreed before the foundation of the earth apply throughout history. Therefore Nephi is a suitable example of these teachings even though his life was lived some 600 years before that sermon was preached.

[58]Obadiah 1: 21: "And saviours shall come up on mount Zion to judge the mount of Esau; and the kingdom shall be the Lord's."

Nephi is showing us through his personal history how this process works. He isn't just telling a story. He is living doctrine. When we read the account of his life, we are reading how the Gospel works.

Nephi then receives more. While the first "visit" from the Lord merely resulted in his heart being "softened" so he could believe, now the 'visit' becomes something more. Nephi is ready because he has developed faith. When there is faith already present and a person seeks to grow, they are allowed to grow.

The Lord grants a return of more grace for the grace already shown in Nephi. Nephi writes in response to his charitable intercessory prayer (that is, while he is in the very act of being a "type" of Christ), "it came to pass that **the Lord spake unto me, saying**: Blessed art thou Nephi, because of thy faith." (*Id.*, v. 19, emphasis added.) Now instead of feelings which soften his heart, Nephi is receiving actual words from the Lord in answer to his prayer. Instead of the words coming from Nephi's father, this answer comes in the form of a dialogue with God and God entrusting Nephi with His words. The process has grown. The nature of the "visit" has increased and improved.

Most importantly there is a difference between Nephi's first recorded answer to prayer and his second. In the first, he receives grace to believe. In the second, he receives actual "words" from God. Why the improvement?

Between the first and the second, Nephi has acted consistently with what he was given in the first prayer. In addition to his faithfulness to the promptings first given to him, he shows charity to his rebellious fellow man. God does that. He shows charity to His rebellious children. Christ observed God treated the good and the evil with grace and kindness.[59] As Nephi goes through the account here, this is not just

---

[59] As Christ put it: "But I say unto you, Love your enemies, bless them that curse you, do good to them that hate you, and pray for them which despitefully use you, and persecute you; That ye may be the children of your Father which is in heaven: **for he maketh his sun to rise on the evil and on the good, and sendeth rain on the just and on the unjust.** For if ye love them which love you, what reward have ye? Do not even the publicans the

personal events in a private life. They are words from a Prophet to us about his own prophetic development. Nephi is trying to share with us the path he has walked. He is trying to tell us how he grew into communion with God, so we can do the same thing.

Anyone who is willing to obey God and to accept the answers which come in the form in which they are given can receive them. However, the answers will begin only in these forms. For them to grow into something more, you must be willing to accept in faith the answers in this form first.

This is how it works. There is a gathering momentum to this process. Though it begins small, it becomes a great mountain. We are seeing here a movement in Nephi's life changing from emotion, sympathy, or feeling, to words, dialogue and conversation. "The word of the Lord" is coming to him.[60] This does not mean the Lord's voice was audible to others. The "word" comes more in the mind of the person 'hearing' Him rather than as an audible voice detectible by the

---

same?" (Matt. 5: 44-46, emphasis added.)

[60]This is what prophets have experienced throughout the events in the Old and New Testaments, and Book of Mormon. See, e.g., Jacob 2: 11: "Wherefore, I must tell you the truth according to the plainness of the word of God. For behold, as I inquired of the Lord, thus came **the word unto me, saying**: Jacob, get thou up into the temple on the morrow, and declare the word which I shall give thee unto this people." Moro 8: 7: "For immediately after I had learned these things of you I inquired of the Lord concerning the matter. **And the word of the Lord came to me by the power of the Holy Ghost, saying:**" 1 Chr 22: 8: "**But the word of the Lord came to me, saying,** Thou hast shed blood abundantly, and hast made great wars: thou shalt not build an house unto my name, because thou hast shed much blood upon the earth in my sight." Jer. 2: 1:"Moreover **the word of the Lord came to me, saying,**" Ezek 3: 16: "And it came to pass at the end of seven days, that **the word of the Lord came unto me, saying,**" Ezek 12: 17: "Moreover **the word of the Lord came to me, saying,**" Zech 8: 1: "Again **the word of the Lord of hosts came to me, saying,**" (emphasis added). These are only a few illustrative examples. They show, however, this form of communication has been typical of those whom we regard as prophets and has been the basis for much of the scriptural record of God's dealings with mankind.

vibration of the air.[61] Yet God can and does speak, and His words are heard in the mind, when you are willing to hear Him.

The ability to hear, just like the ability to accept what is heard, is directly related to keeping the commandments. The more faithful you are in keeping the commandments, the more prepared you are to receive His voice. This whole process is how you gather light and truth. These proofs are seemingly small things. Yet it is the way God has elected to speak to mankind. He requires we develop our faith in mortality.

These things move forward together. The cleaner your personal life is the better you can 'hear' His voice. The less clean your life is, the less you are able to 'hear' or trust Him.

Nephi was praying for his unbelieving elder brothers, and in response to this intercession for them the Lord speaks words into the mind of Nephi. Those words cover much more than the subject Nephi raised in his prayer. (That, too, is a part of the path.[62]) His prayer gets

---

[61] Boyd K. Packer has commented on this as follows: "Enos, who was 'struggling in the spirit,' said, 'Behold, the voice of the Lord *came into my mind*' (Enos 1: 10; emphasis added). While this spiritual communication comes into the mind, it comes more as a feeling, an impression, than simply as a thought. Unless you have experienced it, it is very difficult to describe that delicate process." (Packer, Boyd K. *Things of the Soul*. Salt Lake City: Bookcraft, 1996, p. 90.) On this subject Neal A. Maxwell wrote in *If Thou Endure It Well*, at p. 107: "Thus communication from the Lord is most often a voice in which 'I will tell you in your mind and in your heart, by the Holy Ghost' (D&C 8: 2). Such is 'the spirit of revelation' (D&C 8: 3). This particular process is the more secure and sure way of revelation."

[62] It is more often than not the case that the Lord presents us a dilemma or difficulty in order to bring us to prayer to Him. We pray to receive help or an answer. Then the prayer is answered by the Lord with a response which covers much more than the original problem that brought you to Him. You can see this illustrated in the Brother of Jared's experience. He thought the issue was light for his vessels. The Lord used it as an opportunity to get him to pray, as a result of which one of the great theophanies of scripture happens. Ether Chapter 3. We are going to look at this later, in some detail.

answered, but he also receives the prophetic history of many generations.

After the prayer and the ensuing answer from the Lord, Nephi returns to his father's tent. There he learns of another dream his father has had in which Nephi and his brothers are commanded to return to Jerusalem to obtain a record from a relative named Laban. Lehi has already discussed this new dream/revelation with Nephi's brothers. Lehi tells Nephi his brothers "murmur, saying it is a hard thing which I have required of them." (1 Ne. 3: 5.)

As Puck closes *A Midsummer Night's Dream*, he puts the play into this perspective: "And this weak and idle theme, No more yielding but a dream." (Act V, Scene I, l. 416-17, Shakespeare, William. *A Midsummer Night's Dream, The Complete works of William Shakespeare.* New York: Barnes & Noble Press, 1994.) Dreams are the will 'o 'wisp so insubstantial our sophisticated society dismisses them without thought. Yet they are the stuff from which great messages have come from God throughout the scriptures. For example, when God was securing the marriage of Joseph to Mary, Joseph's objections to Mary's pregnant and unmarried condition were removed by a dream.[63] The wise men were warned not to tell Herod about the location of the young child Jesus because God sent His message to them in a dream.[64] To protect Jesus's life and get Him away from the king who was determined to kill Him, God sent His message in a dream.[65] When Herod died, again it was a

---

[63]Matt. 1: 20: "But while he thought on these things, behold, the angel of the Lord appeared unto him in a dream, saying, Joseph, thou son of David, fear not to take unto thee Mary thy wife: for that which is conceived in her is of the Holy Ghost."

[64]Matt. 2: 12: "And being warned of God in a dream that they should not return to Herod, they departed into their own country another way."

[65]Matt. 2: 13: "And when they were departed, behold, the angel of the Lord appeareth to Joseph in a dream, saying, Arise, and take the young child and his mother, and flee into Egypt, and be thou there until I bring thee word: for Herod will seek the young child to destroy him."

dream which brought Christ back from the refuge of Egypt.[66] As a further precaution, it was a dream warning Joseph and his family to flee from Judea to Galilee, away from the son of the King who sought to take away Christ's life.[67] If dreams were a sufficient and reliable way for God the Father to protect the very life of His Only Begotten Son, then dreams should be sufficient for God to speak to you. When they come from God you should revere and respect them as you would any Divine communication found in scripture.

Dreams have been the stuff of prophetic inspiration and the voice of God in scriptures.[68] The scriptures define God's dealings with men in these terms: "And he said, Hear now my words: If there be a prophet among you, I the Lord will make myself known unto him in a vision, and will speak unto him in a dream." (Num. 12:6.) In Job we read this about God speaking with man: "Behold, in this thou art not just: I will answer thee, that God is greater than man. Why dost thou strive against him? for he giveth not account of any of his matters. For God speaketh once, yea twice, yet man perceiveth it not. In a dream, in a vision of the night, when deep sleep falleth upon men, in slumberings upon the bed;"

---

[66]Matt. 2: 19: "But when Herod was dead, behold, an angel of the Lord appeareth in a dream to Joseph in Egypt,"

[67]Matt 2: 22: "But when he heard that Archelaus did reign in Judaea in the room of his father Herod, he was afraid to go thither: notwithstanding, being warned of God in a dream, he turned aside into the parts of Galilee:"

[68]See, e.g., Joseph's (son of Jacob) account of God's great dealings with him in Genesis, chapters 37 to 41 where every great turn of events in his life comes as a result of dreams he received, or his fellow prisoners received, or the Pharaoh received; Solomon received a visit from God in 1 Kings 3: 5 and 15 in a dream; in Jer. 33: 28 Jeremiah is told that when God speaks in a dream, the Prophet is to report the matter faithfully or accurately; Daniel Chapter 2 remains one of the most discussed, studied and read dreams in history as the image of the world's history is foretold in an image with a head of gold and feet of clay and iron; and of course Joel 2: 28 (which Moroni quoted to Joseph Smith) promises of latter-day visions and dreams. These and many other places record as the word of God in scripture the dreams of prophets and kings.

(Job 33: 12-15.) If, therefore, this is one of God's historic and well established ways of speaking to mankind, then you should expect it will be one of the means He will speak with you. If He elects to make Himself known to you in this manner, you have the high privilege and honor of having spoken with God. Do not expect Him to physically appear to anyone who has insufficient faith to accept His messages in dreams. If you will not accept the whisperings of His Spirit, through the feelings He sends to you, then why should He send more? If you are given a dream from Him but cannot accept it in faith, then why should He give more? If you are not willing to accept His proofs in faith, which come exactly as He promises they will come, then why should He send more? He has told us what to expect. When we do not expect them, or refuse to have faith in them, or refuse to accept them as proofs, then we are not following His path. But, if we accept them in faith as His voice, His mind, His will and His voice, then our faith is sufficient. Signs follow faith. They do not produce it.

This new communication comes from the Lord, to Lehi, directing Nephi to do something specific. Nephi does not question, reject, murmur or even hesitate to respond to this new assignment. Rather, he responds, "I will go and do the things which the Lord hath com-manded, for I know that the Lord giveth no commandments unto the children of men, save he shall prepare a way for them that they may accomplish the thing which he hath commanded them." (1 Ne. 3: 7) This is one of the great verses in the Book of Mormon. We do not see this kind of faithfulness very often. It is hard to trust God with no hesitation. Yet that is exactly what Nephi does.

This remarkable response shows Nephi a willingly obedient follower of God who accepts God's word when it comes in a form "no more substantial than a dream." He isn't complaining or skeptical. He is eager to do the things the Lord asks him to do. He accepts his father's revelation/dream as a commandment from God. He has faith God will not require anything of him He will not help him accomplish. These are important things. Nephi's faith is being tested. His brothers do not pass the test. They murmur and complain. They think it hard. Nephi sees the difficulty as a requirement from God, and Nephi trusts God to help him accomplish it.

When David confronted Goliath, he did not see the conflict as between him, a mere boy, and Goliath, an experienced warrior and giant of a man. David saw this as a conflict between mere Goliath and God. David puts the conflict in these terms: "Thou comest to me with a sword, and with a spear, and with a shield: but I come to thee in the name of the Lord of hosts, the God of the armies of Israel, who thou hast defied. This day will the Lord deliver thee into mine hand; and I will smite thee, and take thine head from thee." (1 Sam. 17: 45-46.) To David it is God who is about to fight with Goliath. In those terms, you can almost be amused at Goliath picking this fight. But without faith, this is a boy without armor and experience, getting into a fight with a trained, experienced warrior.

How we perceive our challenges determines how we meet them. If we see God as the overriding influence in life's challenges, then we can trust God to help us through them. Whether the dilemma is a giant of a warrior, or retrieving a brass plate book, or dealing with stresses of everyday life, or paying tithing when it will make payment of other necessary expenses seem unaffordable, the dilemma is never merely physical. It is always a battle between faith and skepticism. Do you see it as a fight between your own willingness to trust God to deliver you, or in merely physical terms? Does God care about your life's dilemmas? Will He help deliver you from your 'Goliaths?' Do you trust Him? Do you believe in Him? Do you believe He is interested and involved in your life? Will you accept the proof of His involvement as His word to you? Do you feel His proofs are not sufficient or substantial enough to have faith in them?

Faith in a distant and unconcerned God may satisfy some Latter-day Saints. But that is not the God Nephi (or David) believed in. In Nephi's example we find a personal God involved in everyday life. We find a God who will give a challenge to us, and then walk beside us to see we succeed. Nephi is trying to teach us this is the way God operates in all of our lives. He is not distant. He is a part of each of our daily lives. We can ignore Him, or acknowledge Him. But whether we accept or reject His involvement, Nephi's view is that He is present and concerned.

If you want to have an audience with God, you must first be willing to see God as someone who does have personal, direct and ongoing involvement with each of our lives. You must accept Him as someone who cares enough about you that He will help you accomplish His commandments. You must be willing to accept the forms of communication He uses to facilitate this.

This example of Nephi's is not limited to retrieving a book from a hostile cousin. It should apply to any of life's challenges. Whatever the difficulties you have with God's commandments, He is not going to ask you to do something you cannot do. Whether the challenge is tithing, fasting, Word of Wisdom, faithfulness in marriage, honesty in dealings with your fellow-man, or any of the other commandments, Nephi's faith is that you can, with God's help, do it. That is how you need to see the challenges you have. No Goliath in your life will destroy you. Rather, God will destroy the Goliaths for you.

In the end, Goliaths are merely opportunities for you to demonstrate your faith. They will be swept away when they no longer serve any purpose. They are there only temporarily to provide you with an opportunity to demonstrate faith.

This life is a time to "prove [you] herewith, to see if [you] will do all things whatsoever the Lord their God shall command [you]." (Abraham 3: 25.) Take an inventory of your life. Look again at your challenges. Those Goliaths you face are opportunities to see if you will proceed in faith to confront them. They are opportunities and blessings, not difficulties. They are mere illusions; here to test your faith. Face them with faith and with the confidence 'the Lord gives you no commandments save he shall prepare a way for you to accomplish the thing which he hath commanded,' as Nephi would put it. Until you are willing to do this, and actually begin to see life's challenges in this light, you are not ready to proceed further.

You have to take the proofs, the feelings, the dreams and the insubstantial communications from God and bring them into the physical and material world in which you live. If you are not willing to bring these things from the spiritual into the physical realities by your faith, then the veil will remain in place. It draws aside only as your faith permits it to be drawn aside. It will be you who brings the Second Comforter into your life by this process. He cannot appear to those who have not broken through the veil by obeying the spiritual commandments in the physical world.

These things are not optional. They lie at the heart of this process. Faith and trust in God must precede development into the fully prepared man or woman of faith. "Faith cometh not by signs, but signs follow those that believe." (D&C 63: 9.) That is, to put it another way: You will need to develop the faith to see first, before you see. Until your faith allows you to see things in this light, you are not prepared to see beyond the veil.

Nephi now has an errand to perform. He accepts that errand faithfully and with confidence the Lord is going to help accomplish it. And he acts in this physical world consistent with faith in the unseen world. That is how we all need to act.

We all have faith in something. And we act consistent with that faith. Whether faith is in God or in science or in philosophy, we all act consistent with our beliefs. Since that is invariably true, you may as well accept Nephi's view and promise of how things really are and try trusting God in that manner. The alternative is to stay as you are now, and not progress in spiritual matters.

Nephi's struggles to fulfill the errand are not going to be discussed at length here, but are found in Chapters 3 and 4 of 1 Nephi. The important highlights are as follows: Nephi and his brothers returned to Jerusalem, a journey of three days. (See 1 Ne. 2: 6 and 3: 9.) When they returned, they cast lots to decide who would make the effort to retrieve the plates. (*Id.*, v. 11.) The result was the oldest brother, and not Nephi, was determined by lot to make the attempt. (*Id.*, v. 11.) This may have been discouraging to some in Nephi's position. After all, Nephi returned willingly to accomplish the assignment. The older brothers did not. They "murmured" and didn't accept the assignment willingly. And now, when the moment arrives to actually seek the plates, the lot falls on Laman. Using lots was a custom at the time for deciding God's will. This suggests that God had chosen Laman, and rejected Nephi, for the honor of getting the plates. Nothing in the text suggests Nephi complained about this, however.

Laman fails in his attempt. He is even accused of "robbery" in his attempt. (*Id.*, v. 13.) Laman flees for his life, and the brothers become "exceedingly sorrowful" the attempt failed. (*Id.*, v. 14.) As the brothers discuss abandoning the attempt, however, Nephi rallies them for another attempt. He vows the effort will not stop "as the Lord liveth" until they have accomplished the responsibility. (*Id.*, v. 15.) Nephi's tenacity in approaching his assignment shows that even in dark and discouraging moments he remains committed to the Lord. Nephi's experience demonstrates that trials, setbacks or temporary failure do not mean the Lord has abandoned you. Nor does it mean the Lord has forgotten His promises to you, anymore than this setback meant that to Nephi. The upside of God's statement, "What I the Lord have spoken, I have spoken, and I excuse not myself, and though the heavens and the earth pass away, my word shall not pass away, but shall all be fulfilled, whether by mine own voice or by the voice of my servants, it is the same" (D&C 1: 38), is that He will not excuse Himself from commitments made you. Your internal reaction (like the older brothers') has no effect on Him. Your faithlessness does not change things He promised (again like the older brothers). It only limits you. If you remain faithful (like Nephi) no difficulty will prevent ultimate success.

A temporary setback in any Godly undertaking is for your benefit. If you were not given these chances to show faith, then you would fail to develop into the person God wants you to become. Growth for any person comes in the same way. It requires persistence in the face of almost certain failure. It requires you to look Goliath in the face and say he is God's problem, not yours. Your problem is to persist in faith. The results will occur, however unlikely they may seem at the moment, in the way God has promised. This is why it is so important to keep His commandments. He has ordained an outcome as a result of following His commandments. If you follow them, you will get the outcome. Keep in mind there are laws ordained before the foundation of the world, upon which all blessings are predicated. When you follow His commandments, you will receive, as a natural and inevitable result, the blessings which flow from keeping the commandments.

Though these things may seem vague and ill-defined or perhaps even chaotic, they are not. As you persist in keeping God's commandments you get an increasingly clear perception. There are concrete and tangible relationships. They are real. Following them will result in anyone, anywhere, from any culture or background, receiving the resulting blessings. Joseph Smith was explaining these things as he taught:

> God has created man with a mind capable of instruction, and a faculty which may be enlarged in proportion to the heed and diligence given to the light communicated from heaven to the intellect; and that the nearer man approaches perfection, the clearer are his views, and the greater his enjoyments, till he has overcome the evils of his life and lost every desire for sin; and like the ancients, arrives at that point of faith where he is wrapped in the power and glory of his Maker and is caught up to dwell with Him. But we consider that this is a station to which no man ever arrived at in a moment: he must have been instructed in the government and laws of that kingdom by proper degrees, until his mind is capable in some measure of comprehending the propriety, justice, equality and consistency of the same. (*DHC* 2: 8; also *TPJS*, p. 51.)

One of the necessary experiences through which you *must* pass is the experience of apparent imminent failure. This experience is as necessary to your development as was Christ's experience on the Cross when the Father withdrew His presence from Christ. When Christ cried out, "My God, my God, why hast thou forsaken me?" (Matt. 27: 46) He was again pointing out the way. He was providing another example in suffering. Paul would explain Christ "was in all points tempted like as we are, yet without sin." (Heb. 4: 15.) Christ therefore necessarily endured the temptation of apparent failure before His ultimate triumph. Paul continued: "Though he were a Son, yet learned he obedience by the things which he suffered;" (*Id.*, 5: 8.) If you are feeling discouraged, and believe the Lord has abandoned you, or your calling, assignment, duty or obligation to the Lord is failing, you are going through no valley which the Lord Himself has not passed. "Yea, though I walk through the valley of the shadow of death, I will fear no evil: for thou are with me; thy rod and thy staff they comfort me." (Ps. 23: 4.) Even facing death, this is only a necessary experience to prepare you for what comes next.

What is the "rod" and "staff" which comfort you? They are the promises made: "What I the Lord have spoken, I have spoken, and I excuse not myself; and though the heavens and the earth pass away, my word shall not pass away, but shall all be fulfilled, whether by mine own voice or by the voice of my servants, it is the same" (D&C 1: 38) These promises remain, as a nail in a sure place, an anchor securing you to Him. He will "comfort" you. He intends to develop you to the point you can receive Him. You will not be ready before you have persisted through discouragement. This is an essential part of the process. Everyone must pass through it.

Nephi is an example of this process, of facing the downside before receiving the upside. The path to heaven passes through hell. Joseph didn't see the Father and the Son until after first being attacked by Satan. (JSH 1: 15.) Moses didn't receive an audience with God without also being subjected to Satan's temptations and efforts to mislead him. (Moses 1: 12-22.) Christ didn't receive angels to minister to Him before His ministry began until after "the tempter came to him." (Matt. 4: 3-

11.) And Joseph and Sidney were not shown the vision of the Celestial Glory (D&C 76: 50-70) until after they beheld the sons of perdition and their punishment (*Id.*, v. 43-49). It is not just that you reach upward. There is a bracket to these things, and it requires what is below, in addition to what is above. This is the necessary balance. Lehi taught: "For it must needs be that there is an opposition in all things." (2 Ne. 2: 11.) You can't get to heaven without passing through hell. You can't develop the required faith without the necessary opposition. You must choose between the apparent failure of faith, and the desire to persist. Facing the end, you must retain hope. This is good for your soul, even though it may be painful to endure. You must face the physical dilemmas and difficulties of life while viewing them in their true spiritual setting. You must rend the veil.

Joseph, who is the greatest commentator on these things, explained this law of opposition in these words: "The things of God are of deep import; and time, and experience, and careful and ponderous and solemn thoughts can only find them out. Thy mind, O man! If thou wilt lead a soul unto salvation, **must stretch as high as the utmost heavens, and search into and contemplate the darkest abyss**, and the broad expanse of eternity—thou must commune with God." *(DHC 3: 295; also TPJS, p. 137, emphasis added.)* It is not heaven alone which will open to you. Hell will also give you an audience. So be prepared for these things to come in balanced pairs. If you would learn to fly, be prepared to fight against and overcome gravity.

Nephi vows, 'As the Lord liveth, and as we live' he will remain true to the undertaking, though every one of his brothers may be prepared to abandon the assignment. (1 Ne. 3: 15.) He sees all of this as an extension of God's will. He continues, "Let us be faithful in keeping the commandments of the Lord" (*Id.*, v. 16), and views this setback in this context: God wants this thing done. He has commanded us to do it. We should spare no thought, no creative alternative, and no effort to find a way to finish the assignment. That is how you should approach this seeking for the Second Comforter, as well. That is the only way in which it will happen.

Nephi suggests they retrieve their family's wealth, and try to buy the plates. They act on this helpful suggestion, and together the brothers return to their previously abandoned home, gather their wealth, and collectively return to Laban to buy the plates. This creative plan backfires, and Laban throws the brothers out without the plates. Then Laban sends his servants to rob the brothers of their wealth, as a result of which Nephi and his brothers flee and abandon their property. (*Id.,* 23-26.)

Now the brothers have lost their property, and narrowly escape with their lives. They are reduced to hiding in a cave. (*Id.,* v. 27.) In these desperate circumstances the older brothers become angry and begin to beat Nephi and his younger brother. As after every other discouragement, Nephi must now endure a physical beating. (*Id.,* v. 28-29.) It is only at this bleak and life-threatening extremity, the Lord's clear hand in the matter returns. God has been with them throughout, of course, but it has not been apparent to any of the participants, though Nephi was faithful, even faithful in the face of adversity. Now in the extremity of being beaten and his life threatened, he is delivered by the Lord. An angel appears to renew the commission to get the plates. "Behold ye shall go up to Jerusalem again, and the Lord will deliver Laban into your hands." (*Id.,* v. 29.) At last Nephi's hope seems more reasonable and less an act of profound faith.

Nephi's brothers are willing to go along with this only because of the angel's admonition. Interestingly, this appearance produces **no** faith in them. They haven't been prepared to accept it through their obedience and the sign produces no faith. These older brothers are not converted to the mission or the Lord. They continue to "murmur, saying: How is it possible that the Lord will deliver Laban into our hands?" (*Id.,* v. 31.)

Here we see the difference between seeing the problem as a purely physical one and as a spiritual one. Laman and Lemuel see only Goliath.

They do not see the offense Goliath has given God. And they certainly do not conceive of themselves as God's assigned servants. They haven't prepared themselves to receive this faith because they have not been obedient. Without obedience and accepting the proofs that come through obedience, they are blind to it all. Nephi sees it all contrariwise. He sees this as a reaffirmation of his earlier beliefs. To him this whole undertaking will succeed because God's hand is in it. He has sight and is not blind because he has done what is necessary to be able to see. He can feel the coming success before it happens. His heart is righteous before God.

When the final attempt is made, it is Nephi alone who enters Jerusalem at night to reclaim the plates. He has his brothers hide outside the walls and goes into the city in the dark. As he approaches Laban's house, he finds Laban intoxicated and on the ground. With Laban in this helpless condition, Nephi takes from him his sword, and while examining it, receives the impression that he should kill Laban. (1 Ne. 4: 5-10.) If he does this, the plates will be his.

Nephi struggles with this impression and strongly objects because he has never killed a man before. While refusing to kill, Nephi again receives words from God. The words direct him: "Behold the Lord hath delivered him into thy hands." (*Id.*, v. 11.) On this thought from God, Nephi reflects on several things: Laban had sought to kill him and his brothers; Laban would not listen to God's command that the plates be given to them; and Laban had robbed them of their property.[69] Unlike

---

[69]Some Saints are troubled by this commandment to kill Laban. It is consistent with Christ's later teachings in the Sermon on the Mount, and consistent with God's dealings with mankind elsewhere. Laban's accusation against Nephi's brother that he was a "robber" (1 Ne. 3: 13) was a ruse to justify Laban in killing Laman. A person was justified in killing a robber. (Exo. 22: 2.) Laban was using this as an excuse to justify his intention to kill Laman. Later, Laban commits the very act which he had earlier accused Laman of committing. In this case, as in the case of David (2 Sam. 12: 1-7), Laban has made his own judgment upon his own head. Just as David condemned the thief in Nathan's allegory, Laban condemned the robbery which he was about to commit. As certain as Nathan's proclamation to David, "Thou art the

the false accusation against Laman, Laban had actually committed a robbery and attempted to commit murder, as well. Laban merited death under the laws of Moses and, further, had pronounced the death penalty against Nephi's brother unjustly. Here, therefore, would be a just killing under the law then in effect.

Nephi's repulsion at the thought of killing is yet another example of the testing and trying process which precedes Nephi's proving himself before God.[70] This difficulty is an essential part of the sacrifices needed for Nephi, or any person, to develop the faith which saves. This is further explained in the discussion on sacrifice.

Nephi again complies with the direction of the Spirit, and gives to Laban that judgment which he first had pronounced on himself. Thereafter Nephi succeeds in obtaining the plates.

Though the route to gaining possession of the plates was circuitous, it was essential. Had his oldest brother succeeded, it would have been Laman and not Nephi who would have had claim of ownership. Had the family property succeeded in purchasing the plates, they would have been the joint property of all of them. It was necessary these other attempts be made first, and fail. After all the efforts had failed, it was Nephi alone who obtained possession, and who would later have the legal right to take the plates when the brothers separated from each other. This testing and trying was for a host of reasons. The most important of which was to prove, or try, Nephi. He performed consistently as one who seeks to please God.

Importantly, Nephi took the insubstantial and spiritual thoughts spoken in his mind, dreams of his father, and impressions given him

---

man," is Laban's condemnation of the robber, "I will slay thee." Christ's instruction "with what judgment ye judge, ye shall be judged: and with what measure ye mete, it shall be measured to you again," is consistent with the commandment the Lord gives here to kill Laban.

[70]This whole mortal experience is to "prove" us to determine whether we will "do all things whatsoever the Lord God shall command them." (Abr. 3: 25.) We are taking an 'open book test' here in mortality. Unfortunately, many people do not appreciate an exam is underway.

while in the act of retrieving the plates, and moved them into the physical world. He acted on these things. He is moving aside the veil by bringing the spiritual into the physical. He is keeping the commandments. He is obedient to the word of God.

That is our challenge, as well. To consistently perform in a way we know will please God. Knowing what will please God is not difficult. Mustering the will to do so is where the difficulty arises. Just because the task becomes difficult or awkward, it does not change whether God has commanded the task. Nor does personal embarrassment excuse us from delivering on our commitments to God. If you know God's will, you must do it. For the necessary faith to seize hold upon God's blessings can be obtained in no other way.

This was the subject of many of the *Lectures on Faith*. In the *Lectures on Faith: True Faith*, by Orson Pratt, he teaches: "The only way to receive additional faith and light is to practise according to the light which we have: and if we do this, we have the promise of God that the same shall grow brighter and brighter until the perfect day." (*Lectures, True Faith,* paragraph 30, p. 84.) You cannot walk in a crooked path. It is essential you walk in a straight path. Moving from knowing God wants you to do something, to then doing something else, cannot produce the needed faith to seize hold upon the blessings. You must practice according to the light you already have if you want the light to grow brighter.

Nephi and his brothers return with the plates containing the scriptures. They return under Nephi's successful leadership. After sacrifices and thanksgiving to God for the success, Lehi receives another revelation saying the brothers are to return, yet again, to Jerusalem. This time, however, Nephi is put in charge of the new mission from the outset. The revelation to Lehi is worded: "that the Lord commanded him that I, Nephi, and my brethren, should again return unto the land of Jerusalem." (1 Ne. 7: 2.) Nephi describes the new mission: "I, Nephi, did again, with my brethren, go forth into the wilderness to go up to Jerusalem." (*Id.*, v. 3.) When the return journey resulted in the older brothers revolting, the revolt is described as, "behold Laman and Lemuel, and two of the daughters of Ishmael, and the two sons of Ishmael and their families, did rebel against us; yea, against me, Nephi, and Sam, and their father, Ishmael." (*Id.*, v. 6.) So as a result of the earlier mission's success, Nephi is the leader of this return second journey. He is placed in that position from the beginning of the assignment, through its completion. From this it is apparent, in addition to the increase of Nephi's faith, the family dynamics changed, too. Nephi is supplanting his older brothers in the family hierarchy. This will lead to later struggles in the family's unfolding history. But for now, it is enough to note Lehi, the prophet-father of the family, recognizes Nephi has earned a position of greater trust for his obedience in the assignment and the ensuing ordeal.

The physical world is altering because of Nephi's faith. This is how mountains are moved at the command of faith. This is how seas part and how the dead are raised. It is through faith. It is through taking the power of the spirit and moving it from behind the veil into the physical world by obedience to God. Anyone can do this. But it must be done in the way God has established.

The family prepares to journey to a new promised land. They have records, provisions, wives and are busily setting about preparing for the journey. But they need another form of preparation as well. It will involve a dispensation of the Gospel. Lehi receives a vision or dream in which he learns of the prophetic future history of the earth. Lehi's dream or vision is described in cryptic and symbolic terms. Nephi also seeks for and obtains a vision of the same material. Nephi's account is much more complete, and describes the future of his descendants and the future of the world. In Nephi's account we see him acting the part of the fully matured prophet.

This vision makes Nephi's journey complete. It began with the hope he could believe his father. You will recall how Nephi's heart was softened as he prayed to believe. He accepted that softening as a "visit" from God. It progressed next to receiving revelation in the form of words in his mind, from God. Then he received commandments as he

was led by the Spirit. In all these things Nephi was faithful. He was
tested, tried, discouraged and thwarted at times. But he persisted and
trusted God.

This is no random history. It is a description of the things which
everyone who seeks to know from God about His great mysteries must
pass through. It is a formula for how this process works. It is the
fullness of the Gospel of Jesus Christ. It is what He would have you do,
as well.

Chapter Five

NEPHI'S WALK:
THE PATH EXEMPLIFIED
Part 2: Final Preparation for the
Audience with Christ

As the missionaries interviewed me for baptism, I acknowledged having a testimony. However I told them I didn't think I would make a very good Mormon. The lifestyle they expected me to lead seemed beyond my capability. It was only because I had received what I believed was an answer to prayer that I felt the need to be baptized. But I had no confidence in my ability to live the Gospel.

As I was interviewed for baptism, I told the missionaries there was perhaps no sin I had not either committed or contemplated committing. I had not been what I regarded as a very good person, and there was no precedent in my life which would lead me to believe I could live a "Mormon" life. They told me that was exactly what Christ was looking for, and I would be forgiven and cleansed through the baptismal ordinance as long as I was willing to repent and follow

Him. I was, of course, willing to attempt that, but believed I would ultimately fail.

On September 10, 1973, I was baptized in the Atlantic Ocean at Kittery Point, on the southern coast of Maine. It was a cool, sunny day. I was confirmed a member while kneeling on the beach, with a small gathering of local Saints who had come to the service.

Kneeling on the beach, as I was given the Gift of the Holy Ghost, I felt a presence from head to toe unlike anything before. I was electrified by this presence and felt a joy unlike anything before. It was palpable. Cold from the water of the North Atlantic, wet and kneeling in the cool Atlantic sand, I felt warmth which transformed me.

Life began anew that day on the beach in the south of Maine as I was 'born again.'

Having been true and faithful in all things, Nephi is prepared to receive further light and knowledge by conversing with the Lord through the veil. Because of this preparation, the Lord will come to Nephi and converse with him. First, however, we are going to look at Nephi's description of his final steps for that audience.

Nephi's vision of Christ and his tutorial from an angel begins with Nephi taking a series of specific steps. Nephi wants us to know these steps. They are described by him in these terms:

> For it came to pass after I had **desired** to know these things that my father had seen, and **believing** that the Lord was able to make them known unto me, as I sat **pondering** in mine heart I was caught away in the Spirit of the Lord, yea, into an exceedingly high mountain, which I never had before seen, and upon which I never had before set my foot. And the Spirit said unto me: Behold, what desireth thou? And I said: I desire to behold the things which my father saw. (1 Ne. 11: 1-3, emphasis added.)

Here is Nephi's list of several concrete steps which must occur for anyone to receive the things of God in vision or revelation:

1. **Desiring** to know.
2. **Believing** the Lord can make them known to you.
3. **Pondering** or thinking deeply and prayerfully.

Nephi isn't just randomly telling a story. This is how these things are accomplished. Read again what preceded the Vision of the Redemption of the Dead (Section 138 of the Doctrine and Covenants), President Joseph F. Smith uses some of the same words while pursuing the same activity as Nephi. He writes he was "pondering over the scriptures." (V. 1.) He desired to know what happened between the time of Christ's death and resurrection. He believed God could make it known. We see President Smith desiring, believing and pondering.

Then read again Joseph's struggles to know the truth preceding the First Vision. He asked, "Who of all these parties is right?" He read and pondered James 1: 5, a passage which "came with more power to the heart of" Joseph than any passage before. "At length [Joseph] came to the conclusion that [he] must either remain in darkness and confusion, or else [he] must do as James directs, that is, ask of God." He did so "concluding that if [God] gave wisdom to them that lacked wisdom, and would give liberally, and not upbraid," then he could ask and get an answer. (JSH 1: 10-13.) Here again we see desire, pondering and believing.

Moses on the Mount, the Brother of Jared at Mount Shelem, Joseph and Oliver after reading about baptism, Peter wondering about Gentile converts, Isaiah in the Temple, Gideon when Israel was under attack, and still others in diverse places and times, have inquired of the Lord after: 1.) Having desire. 2.) Believing the Lord can make them known. 3.) Pondering. Nephi is telling us about a universal pattern.[71]

---

[71]Christ will use an almost identical formulation when instructing the Nephites in how to prepare to be taught deeper truths. After first telling them He was unable to teach them all He was commanded to teach, He admonishes them to prepare their minds to be taught with these words: "Therefore, go ye unto your homes, and ponder upon the things which I have said, and ask of

If all these people have followed a pattern and received answers to their prayers, then why should you not follow the pattern? If you do, what is there to prevent you from a similar experience? We will try to understand these three steps. They deserve careful attention.

Before baptism, although I had an answer to prayer, I was not confident I would make a very good Mormon. There was no power within me which could overcome the temptations to which I had always succumbed in the past.

But everything changed at baptism. The apparent 'heavy lifting' I thought I would be in for turned out to be a light yoke, just as Christ had promised. And I found within me a new power of goodness which came as the Elders laid hands on my head and gave me the Gift of the Holy Ghost. I hadn't reckoned on that.

Despite those pre-baptismal doubts over my own weaknesses, I have found the Lord has provided a constant companion, a Comforter, ever since baptism. He supplies what I have lacked, and living as a Mormon has become comfortable and preferable. I could never go back.

Through the decades that followed I have remained an active member in good standing, through seasons of triumph and success as well as seasons of failure and difficulty. There have been times when I thought I would prefer death to continued life, the despair of some trials has been so great to bear. And there have been times when the joy and happiness has also been overwhelming. Through it all the Holy Ghost, given as a gift at my rebirth, has been a guide and companion.

And now, over thirty-two years later, I have found 'rest' with the Lord, and know the peace of an untroubled conscious. Miraculously I have avoided serious, though certainly not all, sin. Though troubled

the Father, in my name, that ye may understand, and prepare your minds for the morrow, and I come unto you again." (3 Ne. 17: 3.)

by seasons of doubt born from disobedience, I have found persistent faith.

1. "Desiring:"

It seems self evident desire should precede an answer from God. After all, without a desire to know, why would God interrupt your life to speak with you about anything? But desire in the context here has a deeper meaning. Moroni 10: 4 promises this: "And when ye shall receive these things, I would exhort you that ye would ask God, the Eternal Father, in the name of Christ, if these things are not true; and if ye shall ask with a sincere heart, with real intent, having faith in Christ, he will manifest the truth of it unto you, by the power of the Holy Ghost." This is a description of the kind of desire required for an answer.

Desire encompasses "a sincere heart," and also encompasses having "real intent." It requires you have some degree of "faith in Jesus Christ."

Christ touched upon the subject of getting answers to inquiries. He taught us to "ask, and it shall be given you; seek, and ye shall find; knock, and it shall be opened. For every one that asketh receiveth; and he that seeketh findeth; and to him that knocketh it shall be opened." (Matt. 7: 7-8.) Just before these promises about getting answers, He taught in the same sermon: "Blessed are they which do hunger and thirst after righteousness: for they shall be filled." (*Id.,* 5: 6.) There is a direct relationship between "hunger and thirsting" for an answer, and the required "desire" to receive an answer.

Once again, the Book of Mormon's plain superiority in explaining these connections comes through. Alma the High Priest taught: "Behold, I say unto you they are made known unto me by the Holy Spirit of God. Behold, I have fasted and prayed many days that I might know these things of myself. And now I do know of myself that they are true; for the Lord God hath made them manifest unto me by his Holy Spirit; and this is the spirit of revelation which is in me." (Alma 5:

46.) Here "fasting and praying for many days" is related to "the spirit of revelation which is in me." The concept of "hungering and thirsting"[72] and receiving answers to prayers are tied together here in a plain explanation of the path.

When Alma the Younger met the Sons of Mosiah after years of separation, he observed: "They had waxed strong in the knowledge of the truth; for they were men of sound understanding and they had searched the scriptures diligently, that they might know the word of God. But this is not all; they had given themselves to much prayer, and fasting; therefore they had the spirit of prophecy, and the spirit of revelation, and when they taught they taught with power and authority of God." (*Id.*, 17: 2-3.) This principle of asking and receiving on the one hand, and the spirit of prophecy and revelation on the other are directly related. Without an inquiry, you are not able to receive.

The most interesting and sustained illustration of the requirement we must inquire before we learn is found in the Book of Mormon. Since it involves the Lord Himself, we are going to take an extended look at that example. There are, of course, many others. But this is the longest and clearest single example:

Christ's visit with the Nephites resulted in His teaching about His "other sheep." First, Christ explains about the principle of "other sheep" in the context of the Nephites being "other" to the "sheep" in Palestine. He explains the Nephites' status of being "other sheep" was revealed to His disciples in the land of His mortal ministry. But it was

---

[72]One brief comment on fasting: You may not be able to hunger and fast for many consecutive days. Not all of us are Gandhi. But if you reduce your caloric intake, live with "fasting" while still eating enough to subsist, you can subordinate the flesh to the spirit while still eating and maintaining health. And, most of all, you can do so without calling attention to yourself since fasting should always be a private matter. Sometimes it does take days to receive an answer. Do not abandon the powerful tool fasting can provide to you because you cannot fast for many consecutive days. Instead, "fast" while eating enough for subsistence, and you will find you can accomplish the same things without jeopardy to health. Many of us eat too much anyway, and reducing food may be a boon to physical as well as spiritual health.

revealed to them without either explanation or elaboration[73] when Christ said there were other sheep.

Christ explains His disciples in Palestine were not taught about the Nephites and would not be taught about them, **unless they asked.**[74] Without an inquiry, the disciples at Jerusalem would be left with only the Lord's unexplained reference to the "other sheep."

Christ explains why this limited and obscure information was given to His disciples at Jerusalem: "And now, because of stiffneckedness and disbelief they understood not my word; therefore I was commanded to say no more of the Father concerning this thing unto them." (3 Ne 15:18.) If you want to learn from Christ, He explains, you must have belief, make an inquiry and have a soft heart. Since His disciples at Jerusalem lacked some or all of these, He was not going to force the information on them. They simply lacked any desire to know anything further. He would wait for them to follow the required pattern.

---

[73] 3 Ne 15: 13-17: "And behold, this is the land of your inheritance; and the Father hath given it unto you. And not at any time hath the Father given me commandment that I should tell it unto your brethren at Jerusalem. Neither at any time hath the Father given me commandment that I should tell unto them concerning the other tribes of the house of Israel, whom the Father hath led away out of the land. This much did the Father command me, that I should tell unto them: That other sheep I have which are not of this fold; them also I must bring, and they shall hear my voice; and there shall be one fold, and one shepherd."

[74] 3 Ne 16: 4: "And I command you that ye shall write these sayings after I am gone, that if it so be that my people at Jerusalem, they who have seen me and been with me in my ministry, **do not ask the Father in my name, that they may receive a knowledge of you** by the Holy Ghost, and also of the other tribes whom they know not of, that these sayings which ye shall write shall be kept and shall be manifested unto the Gentiles, that through the fullness of the Gentiles, the remnant of their seed, who shall be scattered forth upon the face of the earth because of their unbelief, may be brought in, or may be brought to a knowledge of me, their Redeemer." That is, the disciples at Jerusalem will never be told about the Nephites (or still other sheep) if they do not ask.

At this point, Christ has informed the Nephites of the reference He made in Jerusalem to these "other sheep" and its meaning. In Jerusalem He meant the term to apply to the Nephites. But the disciples at Jerusalem would not have that meaning given to them unless they "asked the father" to know about the Nephites. (Remember He tells us it was "unbelief" which set this limitation on the information given to the disciples at Jerusalem.)

Christ then tells the Nephites He had still "other sheep" which were neither part of Jerusalem nor part of the Nephites. He explains, "And verily, I say unto you again that the other tribes hath the Father separated from them; and it is because of their iniquity that they know not of them." (3 Ne 15: 20.) Here is the first reference to the still "other sheep" (Tribes of Israel) who also existed and who were separated from the people at Jerusalem. He elaborates on this point by adding:

And verily, verily, I say unto you that I have other sheep, which are not of this land, neither of the land of Jerusalem, neither in any parts of that land round about whither I have been to minister. For they of whom I speak are they who have not as yet heard my voice; neither have I at any time manifested myself unto them. But I have received a commandment of the Father that I shall go unto them, and that they shall hear my voice, and shall be numbered among my sheep, that there may be one fold and one shepherd; therefore I go to show myself unto them. (3 Ne 16: 1-3.)

Christ is telling the Nephites they were not alone in the status of "other sheep" belonging to Him. He had still "other sheep" which were not Nephite, and not at Jerusalem. There is another at least third[75] group of His "sheep." He intended to visit with them also.

Christ would like us to have this information. He wants us to know He is the God of Israel and, indeed, the God of the whole earth. He not only ministered in Palestine and visited the Nephites, but He visited all of His sheep wherever located throughout the world. This is what the Book of Mormon was to prove. Although it is only a record of a single group of the "other sheep," it establishes there are "sheep" throughout

---

[75]All of the references made stop short of identifying the "other sheep" who are not part of the Nephites and not part of Jerusalem as a single group. Therefore, it is not correct to conclude this is a reference to a single body of "sheep" and could not be in multiple groups. In the other passages relating to separated peoples who were in bodies of believers and who were to keep records which would be restored at some point which is still yet future, Nephi writes the Lord has said: "For I command all men, both in the east and in the west, and in the north, and in the south, and in the islands of the sea, that they shall write the words which I speak unto them; for out of the books which shall be written I will judge the world, every man according to their works, according to that which is written. For behold, I shall speak unto the Jews and they shall write it; and I shall also speak unto the Nephites and they shall write it; and I shall also speak unto **the other tribes of the house of Israel, which I have led away**, and they shall write it; and I shall also speak unto all nations of the earth and they shall write it. And it shall come to pass that the Jews shall have the words of the Nephites, and the Nephites shall have the words of the Jews; and the Nephites and the Jews shall have the words of **the lost tribes of Israel**; and the lost tribes of Israel shall have the words of the Nephites and the Jews. And it shall come to pass that my people, which are of the house of Israel, shall be gathered home unto the lands of their possessions; and my word also shall be gathered in one. And I will show unto them that fight against my word and against my people, who are of the house of Israel, that I am God, and that I covenanted with Abraham that I would remember his seed forever." (2 Ne. 29: 11-14, emphasis added.) These words also do not limit it to a single record. The "lost tribes" is a plural reference. Therefore, we are left not knowing if there are one or more records to be produced kept by one or more groups of disciples. However, the reference to "all men, both in the east and in the west, and in the north, and in the south, and in the islands of the sea" suggests strongly that the reference here is plural. Finally, the promised return in D&C 133: 21-35 does not clarify if there are multiple bodies bearing multiple records, or a single body of many believers bearing a single record of their dealings with the Lord.

the world to whom He paid a visit after His resurrection. In the title page of the Book of Mormon, it says it was written "to show unto the remnant of the House of Israel what great things the Lord hath done for their fathers; and that they may know the covenants of the Lord, that they are not cast off forever – And also to the convincing of the Jew and Gentile that JESUS is the CHRIST, the ETERNAL GOD, manifesting himself unto all nations – And now, if there are faults they are the mistakes of men; wherefore, condemn not the things of God, that ye may be found spotless at the judgment-seat of Christ." (Emphasis added.) This reference to "all nations" confirms the meaning of the term "other sheep" as Christ elaborated to the Nephites. The term was intended to cover multiple groups of believers who had been separated from Palestine, and not just a single third group of believers. Christ's ministry after His resurrection therefore may have involved many groups who both saw Him and heard His voice, and thereby became part of His sheepfold.[76]

Christ finishes His explanation to the Nephite audience and then pauses. He spends some time looking at the group of Nephites whom He had been teaching. And, after they stare back without question or inquiry, He laments they are just not getting it. They are too spiritually weak to receive what He would like to teach them.[77] He suggests they go home and pray and ponder, and see if they can't be ready to be taught tomorrow.

---

[76]The 5th Chapter of Jacob, although an allegory, may be the most detailed account of these "other sheep." But that is beyond the scope of this work.

[77]3 Ne 17: 1-3: "Behold, now it came to pass that when Jesus had spoken these words he looked round about again on the multitude, and he said unto them: Behold, my time is at hand. I perceive that ye are weak, that ye cannot understand all my words which I am commanded of the Father to speak unto you at this time. Therefore, go ye unto your homes, and ponder upon the things which I have said, and ask of the Father, in my name, that ye may understand, and prepare your minds for the morrow, and I come unto you again."

They are unprepared to receive what He is coming to teach them because they are missing the very point which He just taught! He had told them the disciples at Jerusalem are not going to receive any knowledge of them unless these other disciples ask. If they do not ask, then the disciples at Jerusalem will not know about the Nephites. After making this clear, Christ tells the Nephites there are still other sheep. And in response to this clearest of declarations, there is no inquiry! The Nephites simply do not ask. They listen to what the Lord is willing to tell them, but they are unwilling to ask to learn more! It could not be a clearer example of the **necessity** of asking. Nor a clearer example of how the Lord is disappointed when we fail to ask Him.

It is learning which is the most difficult. It is far easier to perform a miracle. These people are prepared to receive miracles.[78] But they are not prepared to be taught.[79] Today people continue to mistake the

---

[78] 3 Ne 17: 6-10: "And he said unto them: Behold, my bowels are filled with compassion towards you. Have ye any that are sick among you? Bring them hither. Have ye any that are lame, or blind, or halt, or maimed, or leprous, or that are withered, or that are deaf, or that are afflicted in any manner? Bring them hither and I will heal them, for I have compassion upon you; my bowels are filled with mercy. For I perceive that ye desire that I should show unto you what I have done unto your brethren at Jerusalem, for I see that your faith is sufficient that I should heal you. And it came to pass that when he had thus spoken, all the multitude, with one accord, did go forth with their sick and their afflicted, and with their lame, and with their blind, and with their dumb, and with all them that were afflicted in any manner; and he did heal them every one as they were brought forth unto him. And they did all, both they who had been healed and they who were whole, bow down at his feet, and did worship him; and as many as could come for the multitude did kiss his feet, insomuch that they did bathe his feet with their tears." They had faith to be healed.

[79] 3 Ne 17: 2-3: "I perceive that **ye are weak, that ye cannot understand** all my words which I am commanded of the Father to speak unto you at this time. Therefore, go ye unto your homes, and ponder upon the things which I have said, and ask of the Father, in my name, that ye may understand, and prepare your minds for the morrow, and I come unto you again." (Emphasis added.)

things which matter most and are the most difficult to achieve on the one hand, with what is less difficult on the other hand. It is learning, being taught, and receiving further light and knowledge which always challenges the human mind the most. Here we are talking about learning through revelation, not merely by study.

Some Saints assert learning the mysteries of God ought to be avoided, which of course runs directly contrary to the Lord's own teachings.[80] It is little wonder such things remain a formidable obstacle to receiving the Second Comforter. If you want to receive, you must first ask. If you do not seek you will not find.

We have no record of the Lord's extended ministry to the lost tribes of Israel. Other than the single record of the Lord's visit to the Nephites, nothing has been revealed as yet. The Nephite record testifies these visits happened. The Title Page of the Book of Mormon, 2 Ne. Chapter 29, and the Lord's words here from Third Nephi all confirm there was such a ministry and a record was kept. We are also told by the 2 Nephi passages the record of these other visits will be restored. But the Nephites never inquired to know, and therefore their record does not provide any further insight into this subject.

The Lord wants us to know about these things. If He did not want us to know, He would not have taught these things to the Nephites. But the Nephites failed to inquire, and therefore they could not shed any further light on the subject for us.

Importantly, **neither** the disciples at Jerusalem asked, nor the Nephites. It actually came as a surprise to everyone the "other sheep" were not the Gentiles. Until the translation of 3 Nephi, the common understanding of the Christian world was the "other sheep" were the

---

[80]Christ's ministry was punctuated with admonitions to His followers to "seek" and "ask" and "knock" as pointed out throughout this work. Today that has been turned into a 'don't ask, don't tell' approach in which inquiries are discouraged or condemned. That is, of course, the same thing that provoked Christ's earlier rebuke to religious teachers: "But woe unto you, scribes and Pharisees, hypocrites! for ye shut up the kingdom of heaven against men; for ye neither go in yourselves, neither suffer ye them that are entering to go in." (Matt. 23: 13.)

Gentiles. Once Third Nephi was translated, however, that misunderstanding was forever corrected by the Lord's own words.

Here, however, we are concerned with the necessity of asking in order to receive light and knowledge. The Lord made a graphic demonstration of how important this principle is here in 3 Nephi. He is there to teach. He spells out to them the way in which they can learn more. But they refuse to ask; even when it is plain an inquiry is needed to get further information.

In response to this failing on the part of the Nephites, (which was a consistent failing of His followers in both sets of the "sheep") He is distressed. The record says: "And it came to pass that when they had knelt upon the ground, Jesus groaned within himself, and said: Father, I am troubled because of the wickedness of the people of the house of Israel." (3 Ne 17: 14.) This lament by our Lord is reason enough never to be among those who are unwilling to be taught by Him. You are unwilling to be taught if you are unwilling to ask. How awful it is to think our failure to be instructed by the Perfect Teacher causes Him to groan within Himself and be "troubled by the wickedness" of those of us whose lack of faith prevents asking.

The bounds are set. The answers will not be forced upon you. If you are unwilling to ask then the Heavens cannot give what you are unwilling to receive. It would do no good anyway. For those who are willing to receive always ask. Asking is the way those who are ready identify themselves for Heaven.

Another great principle is illustrated in what the Lord does in light of the dilemma He faces. The body of Nephite believers before Him lacks the faith to be taught. They aren't ready to receive what He has to offer. But there is a sub-group of children among them who are ready. Their purity and faith allows Him to minister to them, even though the adults present are unprepared. The Lord then ministers to the worthy and receptive children, and permits the adults to eavesdrop.[81] The Lord

---

[81] 3 Ne 17: 11-17: "And it came to pass that he commanded that their little children should be brought. So they brought their little children and set

gathers the worthy children around Him in a prayer circle. The multitude of adults is put outside the sacred circle. The multitude of adults are permitted to listen in and witness these sacred things, but they do not (in fact cannot) participate in the rites being administered. The children are directly involved in the circle and Christ leads them in prayer and then takes them through the veil.

The first time I spoke in a Fast and Testimony meeting I was inexperienced and inarticulate. But I was filled with desire and wept as I spoke. I had found the truth. I loved the people who had sacrificed to bring me to the truth. The missionaries had given two years of their young lives to be my teachers. I wanted them to know my joy and my gratitude.

Although I testified "I know this Church is true," at the time it would have been much more correct to say that I believed it to be true. I was a long way from knowledge. But I was fervent in my belief.

I did not have any idea the difficulties and sacrifices involved in trading faith for knowledge. If I had known then, I would perhaps have stayed content with belief.

---

them down upon the ground round about him, and Jesus stood in the midst; and the multitude gave way till they had all been brought unto him. And it came to pass that when they had all been brought, and Jesus stood in the midst, he commanded the multitude that they should kneel down upon the ground. And it came to pass that when they had knelt upon the ground, Jesus groaned within himself, and said: Father, I am troubled because of the wickedness of the people of the house of Israel. And when he had said these words, he himself also knelt upon the earth; and behold he prayed unto the Father, and the things which he prayed cannot be written, and the multitude did bear record who heard him. And after this manner do they bear record: The eye hath never seen, neither hath the ear heard, before, so great and marvelous things as we saw and heard Jesus speak unto the Father; And no tongue can speak, neither can there be written by any man, neither can the hearts of men conceive so great and marvelous things as we both saw and heard Jesus speak; and no one can conceive of the joy which filled our souls at the time we heard him pray for us unto the Father."

2. "Believing The Lord Can Make Them Known To You."

This kind of believing requires more than just passive hoping. It requires us to have an active conviction or certitude God will answer our prayers. Most people, even traditional Christians, believe God does answer prayers. Latter-day Saints overwhelmingly believe strongly in Joseph Smith's First Vision. The revelations in the Doctrine and Covenants are also the subject of strong belief. The problem is not with the concept God answers prayer or has revealed Himself to prophets. The problem is the lack the confidence God will do the same thing for you.

In discussing this issue, the *Lectures on Faith* provide this insight:

> But it is also necessary that men should have an idea that he is no respecter of persons, for with the idea of all the other excellencies of his character, and this one wanting, men could not exercise faith in him; because if he were a respecter of persons, they could not tell what their privileges were, nor how far they were authorized to exercise faith in him, or whether they were authorized to do it at all, but all must be confusion; but no sooner are the minds of men made acquainted with the truth on this point, that he is no respecter of persons, then they see that they have authority by faith to lay hold on eternal life, the richest boon of heaven, because God is no respecter of persons, and that every man in every nation has an equal privilege. (*Lectures, Third Lecture,* paragraph 23, p. 36.)

You see, God will make it known to you, just as He has made it known to the prophets. As Joseph Smith taught: "God hath not revealed anything to Joseph, but what He will make known unto the Twelve, and even the least Saint may know all things as fast as he is able to bear them" (*TPJS*, p. 149).[82]

---

[82]In commenting on this passage, Elder Bruce R. McConkie wrote in *A New Witness for the Articles of Faith*, p. 490: "If all things operate by law, and they do; if God is no respecter of persons, and certainly he is perfectly

If you believe these things are possible for others, you should be willing to believe in them for you, as well. Otherwise, you do not really believe at all. For if they are not possible in your life, why do you think them possible in other's lives? Again, from the *Lectures on Faith*:

> He who has no faith to obtain Gospel signs, has no faith to obtain Gospel pardon. He who would thus pervert the Gospel is most woefully deceived, if he supposes himself in possession of any Gospel blessing. Jesus has made no Gospel promises to be trifled with, or to be rejected with impunity by professed believers.
>
> Faith in all ages, and under all dispensations, has always prevailed with God. By faith, signs, miracles, and manifestations of the power of God, were abundantly shown forth under the Patriarchal, Mosaic, and Christian dispensations. Jesus said, 'All things are possible to him that believeth.' – (Mark ix, 23.) Again he said, 'Have faith in God, For verily I say unto you, That whosoever shall say unto this mountain, Be thou removed, and be thou cast into the sea; and shall not doubt in his heart, but shall believe those things which he saith shall come to pass; he shall have whatsoever he saith. Therefore, I say unto you, what things soever ye desire, when ye pray, believe that ye receive them, and ye shall have them.' – (Mark xi, 22, 23, 24.) In another passage He said, 'Verily, verily, I say unto you, He that believeth on me, the works that I do shall he do also; and

---

impartial; if his course is one eternal round, never varying from age to age, and such truly is the case, then all of the gifts and graces and revelations ever given to any prophet, seer, or revelator in any age will be given again to any soul who obeys the law entitling him so to receive. While discoursing about the Second Comforter and in setting forth that those whose callings and elections have been made sure have the privilege of seeing the face of the Lord while they yet dwell in the flesh, the Prophet Joseph Smith said: 'God hath not revealed anything to Joseph, but what He will make known unto the Twelve, and even the least Saint may know all things as fast as he is able to bear them.' (Teachings of the Prophet Joseph Smith, p. 149.)" (McConkie, Bruce R. *A New Witness for the Articles of Faith*. Salt Lake City: Deseret Book Company, 1985.)

greater works than these shall he do; because I go unto my Father.' – John xiv, 12.)

None of these passages limit the miraculous effects of Faith to the Apostles, or to any particular class of true believers, or to any particular age of the world. But on the contrary; each of these promises was made on the broadest terms, general and unlimited as to time or place. The terms, '*He that believeth*,' '*Whosoever shall say*.' & etc, are applicable to all believers, in all ages, and in all the world, unto the latest generations, or to the end of time. ...

Indeed, the miraculous gifts were to be the effects – the results – the signs of faith, by which the true believers could, by the most infallible evidence distinguish himself from an unbeliever. By these gifts he is confirmed; and he obtains the most satisfactory knowledge and absolute certainty of the divinity of the doctrine which he has embraced. By these tokens, he knows that he is in reality a true genuine Gospel believer, that his sins are surely forgiven; and that he has received the gift of the Holy Spirit, and is, indeed, an heir of Salvation.

While on the other hand, without these gifts, he knows that he is not a believer –that he has no genuine gospel faith – that he has no claim to any of the other Gospel blessings – that he is classified with the unbelievers, and with them he must be damned. (*Lectures*, Paragraphs 50-54, pp. 90-91, *True Faith*, by Orson Pratt.)

You may at first think Brother Pratt is being harsh in this analysis. But we find the same thing in the Book of Mormon. It is apparent Elder Pratt took his teaching in this lecture from the Book of Mormon.

We are taught by Moroni quoting Mormon:

If they are true, has the day of miracles ceased? Or have angels ceased to appear unto the children of men? Or has he withheld the power of the Holy Ghost from them? Or will he, so long as time shall last, or the earth shall stand, or there shall be one man upon the face thereof to be saved? Behold I say unto you, Nay; for it is by faith that miracles are wrought; and it is by faith that angels appear and minister unto men; wherefore, **if these**

things have ceased wo be unto the children of men, for it is because of unbelief, and all is vain. For no man can be saved, according to the words of Christ, save they shall have faith in his name; wherefore, **if these things have ceased, then has faith ceased also**; and awful is the state of man, for they are as though there had been no redemption made. (Moroni 7: 35-38, emphasis added.)

You must believe these things are possible for you. You must seek them in the way the scriptures teach. They are not distant gifts given only occasionally to presiding authorities. They are not just historic gifts whose days have passed. They are available to you and they are available now. In all probability, this book is of interest to you because you have this conviction already, but you need help in developing the faith to act on that conviction.

It was a few months after baptism. I was being faithful to everything I had been taught, to the best of my limited understanding and ability. An answer to prayer came in words which I can still quote, though it has been over thirty years: "On the first day of the third month in nine years, your ministry will begin. And so you must prepare."

It was not until some time after the answer it occurred to me I had not been told what I was to prepare for. Nor was I told how I should prepare. These were basic questions which remained unanswered, and to which I could not get an answer.

I proceeded to prepare without knowing just what I was preparing for. But nine years is a long time in the life of a new convert. With the passage of time other responsibilities overwhelmed me and I forgot about this guidance. In the intervening years, I was married, finished military service and went to law school. It is hard to remember revelations when preparing for life and a vocation.

3. "Pondering."

Meditation is needed for answers to prayer. Though we are in a hurry, there is no imposing upon God to answer to our time line. Some answers take decades to receive. But they will always come.

When Elijah was commanded to go forth and stand upon the mount, the Lord showed him a series of signs: "And, behold, the Lord passed by, and a great and strong wind rent the mountains, and brake in pieces the rocks before the Lord; but the Lord was not in the wind and after the wind an earthquake; but the Lord was not in the earthquake; And after the earthquake a fire; but the Lord was not in the fire; and after the fire a still small voice." (1 Kings 19: 11-12.) It was not the dramatic, nor the forceful which revealed God. It was the quiet, almost inaudible voice, which revealed Him.

You might ask yourself, "Why would God choose such an obtuse way of revealing Himself? Wouldn't it make more sense for Him to show Himself in the dramatic and compelling events of the fire, or wind or earthquake?" Certainly God has and does show Himself in the dramatic outcomes of history, and in the epic struggles of mankind. But in the everyday lives of man, it makes more sense to require us to develop a spiritual sensitivity than for us to be compelled by Him overawing us. Fireworks are for Hollywood where the message has so little to recommend, it needs the dramatic. If Hollywood didn't put the "stars" above us on a silver screen, larger than life and shining like a heavenly vision while we sit in the dark, we would not be fooled into respecting these hollow things. They offer us form without substance.

The real thing requires only a whisper. It is so compelling in its own right it does not require a shout. God is clearly more interested in the substance and not at all interested in the form. Substance should be compelling to the sensitive soul whether its delivery is dramatic or mundane.

When the Lord came to visit the Nephites, the Father introduced Christ three times before the audience gathered in Bountiful could recognize the words He spoke. This voice was described in these terms:

"It was not a harsh voice, neither was it a loud voice; nevertheless, and notwithstanding it being a small voice it did pierce them that did hear it to the center, insomuch that there was no part of their frame that it did not cause to quake; yea, it did pierce them to the very soul, and did cause their hearts to burn." (3 Ne. 11: 3.) This is the Father's voice. They had heard it before. It reminds anyone who hears it of their primordial existence, when as a spirit being you dwelt with Him. He is familiar to your spirit, because your spirit came from Him. Yet here in mortality, you have not yet seen Him. And so you are both familiar with Him and will recognize Him the instant you hear His voice again, and you are a stranger to Him because in the flesh you have not yet seen Him. That underlying spiritual familiarity with the Speaker is what caused the Nephites to "quake" to their "very soul."

There is a veil to the flesh. This veil causes the spirit within us to forget what went before. But our spirits retain awareness of this Being. It is the longing for Him which makes mankind search for what is missing in their souls. It is why men resort to hero worship, and want celebrities and people who are 'larger-than-life.' We long for this Being whose seeming lack of presence has left us all incomplete here in mortality.

You may not be able to see Him here without first developing the faith to rend the veil, but you can still feel Him here anytime you are willing to do so. There is no veil to your feelings. Fasting helps in the process because it weakens the flesh, and thereby strengthens the spirit within. Similarly, as we grow old and infirm, the veil of this flesh draws thinner and our spirits are freed, in a measure, to greater promptings of the spirit.[83]

---

[83] It is this thinning of the flesh's grip on the spirit which accounts for the tradition, beginning with Adam, of conferring the patriarch's blessing on his posterity as his death approaches. See, e.g., D&C 107: 56, where Adam blesses his posterity "notwithstanding he was bowed down with age, being full of the Holy Ghost." The power of the Holy Spirit was related to this infirmity of the flesh. See also, Jacob (Israel's) blessing in Genesis, Chapter 49, which ends with: "And when Jacob had made an end of commanding his sons, he gathered up his feet into the bed, and yielded up the ghost, and was gathered

This perfectly mild voice is generally not heard when it is in competition with the distractions, noises and offenses of daily life. You need time apart where you can listen. You will recollect Christ was often found apart, praying and meditating during His ministry.[84] If Christ needed time for contemplation, prayer, and pondering, then how much greater need do we have to do the same?

If you are going to grow into the power of revelation, then you need to begin to develop sensitivity to feel the voice of God. It requires effort to learn to do this. Pondering is a necessary part of the process. Joseph Smith said this about recognizing revelation:

> The Spirit of Revelation is in connection with these blessings. A person may profit by noticing the first intimation of the spirit of revelation; for instance, when you feel pure intelligence flowing into you, it may give you sudden strokes of ideas, so that by noticing it, you may find it fulfilled the same day or soon; (i.e.) those things that were presented unto your minds by the Spirit of God, will come to pass; and thus by learning the Spirit of God and understanding it, you may grow into the principle of revelation, until you become perfect in Christ Jesus. (*DHC* 3: 381; also *TPJS*, p. 151.)

It does not come in a great wave. It begins as a small ripple. Only through heeding the small voice first, will you allow it to grow into something much greater. But along the way, pondering and meditating will be the only way you can develop recognition for the still small voice.

You must lessen the distractions of this life. We move too much, are too noisy, too preoccupied and too distracted. We measure all of this,

---

unto his people." And see Lehi's blessing in the beginning chapters of 2 Nephi, which concludes with: "And it came to pass, after my father, Lehi, had spoken unto all his household, according to the feelings of his heart and the Spirit of the Lord which was in him, he waxed old. And it came to pass that he died, and was buried." (2 Ne. 4: 12.)

[84]See, e.g., Matt. 14: 23; 19: 13; 26: 39; Mark 6: 46; Luke 9: 29.

and call it 'productivity.' Capitalist nations pride themselves on being the most productive people on earth. National "productivity" reports are made and compared with prior years, and with each other, as if this was the most noteworthy measurement of a nation's vitality. There is, of course, no one measuring (at least on this side of the veil) our collective capacity to ponder. Our pondering index goes unnoticed by our fellow man, but is one of the main criteria catching the attention of the angels.

If you want to progress in the power of revelation in your life, it will require you to find time to meditate, and to ponder. Unless you become still, you will not resonate with that still small voice.

And so Nephi has finished his final preparation by these things:

1. Desiring.
2. Believing the Lord could make them known to him.
3. Pondering.
4. Asking

These are the important final parts of the foundation in Nephi's preparation which result in the veil parting for him. We now turn to Nephi receiving an audience with the Second Comforter, which is the fullness of the Gospel of Jesus Christ.

Chapter Six

NEPHI'S WALK:
THE PATH EXEMPLIFIED
Part 3: The Audience with Christ

During law school I became quite critical of the Church authorities. My developing analytical abilities were applied indiscriminately to everything, including the Church. I recall launching into a litany of complaints with the fellow who had loaned me his journal when I was originally investigating the Church. He was also a student at BYU at the time. He responded by asking me, "Are you reading your scriptures?"

I replied, "What has that got to do with it?"

To which he responded, "I would be more convinced by your complaints if you were reading your scriptures."

I was unwilling to abandon my criticisms, and thought he was being obtuse. But to prove him wrong, I began to read the scriptures, and tried all the while to keep up my complaints against the Church. What I found, however, was I could not both study the scriptures and reflect on their meaning, and retain a critical and judgmental attitude. The scriptures held a higher form of knowledge and had an air of transcendence to them. They suggested to me that intellectual, analytical approaches to spiritual things may result in missing the mark. I could see the scriptures warned about having excessive concerns about some virtues, while neglecting others. As I read the Lord's counsel not to worry about specks in other people's eyes when there are beams in our own, I was struck by how I was not really following Him. I was off the mark. Criticism is easy. Anyone can do it. Obedience is hard. Few people ever accomplish that.

At length I went back to my friend and thanked him: First, for helping convert me originally by sharing his testimony and his journal; secondly, for reconverting me when I was struggling with a spirit of criticism and alienation. I was indebted to him for his guidance in both.

So we have Nephi telling us he "desired" to know things.[85] He "believed" God could make them known. And he was "pondering" the things he was seeking. Then, in response to this process, the Lord sent an angel who inquired of Nephi: "For it came to pass after I had desired to know these things that my father had seen, and believing that the Lord was able to make them known unto me, as I sat pondering in mine heart I was caught away in the Spirit of the Lord, yea, into an exceedingly high mountain, which I never had before seen, and upon which I never had before set my foot. And the Spirit said unto me: Behold, what

---

[85]We are now returning to the discussion of the verses: 1 Ne. 11: 1-3; which began NEPHI'S WALK: THE PATH EXEMPLIFIED; PART 2: PREPARATION FOR THE AUDIENCE WITH CHRIST in the preceding chapter.

desireth thou? And I said: I desire to behold the things which my father saw." (1 Ne. 11: 1-3.)

What ought to stick out most in this passage is that Nephi is now granted an audience with an angel, and the angel is inquiring of him: "What desireth thou?" He is in the presence of an angel but before he can learn anything, the angel first asks him: What do you want? That should tell you something of great significance. Heaven responds to inquiries! This is one of those eternal principles. Heaven is controlled by ordained limits or governing principles. Just as we must abide the conditions for obtaining blessings,[86] Heaven's help comes in response to ordained limitations, principles, laws and ordinances. This is why the angel does not launch into a lecture right away. Instead, the angel asks Nephi what he wants to know so the balance and limits are maintained. If you aren't asking you are sealing the heavens. You disqualify yourself from further knowledge.

God did not come in response to Joseph Smith's silent desire to know more. The First Vision came as a result of a specific vocal and private prayer in which he **asked** to know more. When the Father and Son appeared, the first words spoken were: "Joseph: This is my beloved Son. Hear Him!" Then **nothing further happens** until Joseph "asked the Personages who stood above [him] in the light, which of all the sects was right."[87] God did not force an answer upon Joseph, nor comment further until Joseph had first asked a question. **It is not Heaven's responsibility to force upon us answers to questions which we do not ask.** Unless we are willing to ask, we will not (in fact cannot) receive. This is why teaching we should not ask to know more of God's mysteries is so pernicious. It is not only false, it limits Heaven's ability to provide light and truth to us. We seal the heavens when we comply with such instruction.

---

[86]D&C 130: 20-21.

[87]JS-H: 1: 17-18.

Nephi asks, "I desire to behold the things which my father saw." (1 Ne. 11: 3.) Then the angel asks Nephi whether he believed the things his father had been teaching him. Nephi says he did believe. Indeed, Nephi said he believed "all the words of my father." Having now secured from Nephi both a question to answer and a confession of faith in the Lord's spokesman (Nephi's prophet-father), the angel reacts with overwhelming joy: "And when I had spoken these words, the Spirit cried with a loud voice, saying: Hosanna to the Lord, the most high God; for he is God over all the earth, yea, even above all. And blessed art thou, Nephi, because thou believest in the Son of the most high God; wherefore thou shalt behold the things which thou has desired." (*Id.*, v. 6.) An angel shouting for joy! Here we have a clear indication of just how much it pleases God and His holy angels when a person finally shows their willingness to receive further light and truth by conversing with the Lord through the veil. It is a rare thing. Heaven rejoices over someone who comes with a question, and with faith, and with a desire to know these things, believing the Lord can make them known. This particular alignment of things is so rare an event Heaven cannot contain the joy, exultation and wonder when it occurs. The Hosanna Shout comes naturally to the angels in such circumstances.

The Heavens long for communion with mankind. The silence which prevails is due to our wickedness, and not Heaven's unwillingness to open to us.[88] If silence prevails, it is mankind who stopped the dialogue.

Having asked, Nephi is now qualified to receive an answer; for unto him who asks, it is given. Nephi is then instructed he is about to see the Son of God. He is told to bear record of Him after he sees the

---

[88]The scripture says it is we who cause this: "For all flesh is corrupted before me; and the powers of darkness prevail upon the earth, among the children of men, in the presence of all the hosts of heaven -- Which causeth silence to reign, and all eternity is pained, and the angels are waiting the great command to reap down the earth, to gather the tares that they may be burned; and, behold, the enemy is combined." (D&C 38: 11-12.) It is not their choice to be "silent." It is our choice to require them to be so. Our choice causes both 'silence to reign' and pain to the heavens.

Son of God.[89] This explanation given beforehand is designed to prepare Nephi's mind to understand the things he is about to receive. Heaven knows how to instruct. In this instance, Nephi is given an orientation to the coming vision as an aid to comprehension. This kind of care and patience demonstrates Heaven wants us to understand. The word "mystery" is an accurate description of how the world is left without understanding. But "knowledge of the mysteries of God" is accompanied by comprehension. They are no longer "mysteries" to the initiated. They are replaced with knowledge.

Remember, this process began as Nephi wanted to understand the dream of his father, Lehi. Lehi's dream is contained in only one chapter, 1 Ne. 8. It is a dream about a tree, a path, an iron rod, delicious fruit, a river of water, his family members, mists of darkness, a spacious building, people who mocked those who ate the fruit of the tree from inside the building, and multitudes who divided up either to choose to eat the fruit or to join the people in the spacious building who mocked them. The whole presentation of Lehi's dream is symbolic. Although some of the symbols seem readily understandable, the whole of the matter consists of symbols and is a single chapter.

Nephi asks he be able to "behold the things which [his] father saw." (1 Ne. 11: 3.) When Nephi is shown this, the account covers chapters 11, 12, 13 and 14. Moreover the account given by Nephi of the "things which Lehi saw" are covered in distinctly different and much more detailed language. Instead of the symbolic form of the information, history is unfolded, and specific future events are foretold, and promises are made both to Nephi and his posterity, as well as promises to his brothers' descendants. The future ministry of Christ is covered in sufficient detail that Nephi, if he had wanted to and had been permitted to do so, could have written his own Gospel of Christ. He sees Christ's mortal ministry, His death and resurrection, and the unfolding history of the Church which Christ was to establish. He sees the apostasy and restoration of the Gospel. He sees the discovery of America and the

---

[89] 1 Ne. 11: 7.

subsequent effects on his descendants and those of his brothers. Covenant promises are made to the future Gentile Americans in this vision. He even sees events which are entrusted to Christ's Apostle John to write, which he only alludes to in his account.

This vision of Nephi's covers the same material as Lehi previously received. But Lehi's account covers a single, symbol-laden chapter, while Nephi's covers four chapters with extended detailed accounts. As the details in Nephi's account are explained, the symbols of Lehi's dream are seamlessly incorporated. It is clear this is the same vision given to both of them. Yet Nephi's account is qualitatively and quantitatively different. He gives details which make Lehi's dream fully understandable. Lehi's dream is only partly understood until you read Nephi's account.

This tells us something about the nature of symbolic language of scripture. It tells us something about symbolic knowledge itself. The symbol stands for much more than a single point and a single, cryptic message or meaning. The symbols of Gospel teaching have a depth and coverage which take in far more than what we may generally ascribe to them. Nephi is giving us a remarkable key to understanding the use of symbols in his account of this vision.

If we take that lesson to heart, we will find the symbols of the Gospel we have been given have greater richness and depth than perhaps we had assumed at first. The treatment Nephi gives to this same vision by Lehi, and again by himself, stands as one of the most remarkable keys to understanding symbolic language.

It also affirms we can have a prophet's message in symbols and still not know the full picture. If you want the full picture, ask God and seek the same vision. Do what Nephi is teaching. The fullness of the Gospel consists of asking God, receiving answers, revelations, knowledge and, finally, in the Second Comforter. Do not settle for the symbols. Search them and find the underlying truths for yourself.

The place we find the most symbolic Gospel instruction is the Temple. It is literally filled with symbolic teachings. Everything about it is instruction and symbol mixed in a wonderful display of Divine teaching. About this kind of instruction, Elder John Widtsoe of the Quorum of the Twelve wrote in *Temple Worship*, page 63: "Revelation . . . is not imposed upon a person; it must be drawn to us by faith, seeking and working. . . . To the man or woman who goes through the temple, with open eyes, heeding the symbols and the covenants, and making a steady, continuous effort to understand the full meaning, God speaks his word, and revelations come. . . . The endowment which was given by revelation can best be understood by revelation; and to those who seek most vigorously, with pure hearts, will the revelation be greatest." (*Temple Worship*, John A. Widtsoe; address given in Salt Lake City, 12 October 1920.)

In Nephi's great vision we have symbols of the tree, fruit, path, iron rod and the rest set out in a panoramic sweep covering millennia of human affairs. We have Christ's mortal ministry and atonement. In short, we have an example of how symbols can stand for vast meaning and complex detail. Take the Temple symbols and think of them in similar complexity and detail, rather than in cryptic terms or in simplistic meanings. There is a wealth of information there. It is a great Urim and Thummin to you, if you will allow it to be.

In the vision Nephi gets symbolic knowledge from the same set of symbols shown Lehi, followed by the angel asking again: "What desirest thou?"[90] Nephi responds, "To know the interpretation thereof."[91] Again, there is the requirement that Nephi free the angel to respond by asking him a question. You must ask if you want to receive. You cannot receive what you do not ask to receive. Nephi is struggling to convey this message to us in his account. He makes his point over and over. Oftentimes we read these things and remain determined to either ignore the message or to suppress it. Both of these are bad choices.. Heed this message. It will take you somewhere wonderful if you will allow it to.

---

[90] *Id.*, v. 10.

[91] *Id.*, v. 11.

Speaking of how the great revelations of this dispensation had been received, B.H. Roberts made this commentary in *History of the Church of Jesus Christ of Latter-day Saints*, 7 vols. comments by B.H. Roberts, Vol. 5:, p. xxxv – xxxvi:

> I may say that all the great revelations of the Church, as well as those which might be regarded as merely personal, were received in response to earnest inquiries of the Lord. Thus the revelation which in 1831 was regarded as making known the moral law of the Gospel was received after earnest inquiry. (History of the Church, Vol. I, p. 148; Doc. and Cov., Sec. 42, par. 3.) So also the great revelation on priesthood. (History of the Church, Vol. I, p. 287; Doc. and Cov., Sec. 84.) The great revelation on the order of the priesthood and the relations of the quorums to each other was given in response to a formal and very earnest petition on the part of the quorum of the Twelve Apostles. (History of the Church, Vol. II, pp. 219, 220; Doc. and Cov., Sec. 107.) So also as to the revelation on tithing and the disposition of it. (Doc. and Cov., Sec. 119, 120; History of the Church, Vol. III, p. 44.) So the great revelation setting in order the affairs of the Church at Nauvoo, given January 19, 1841. 'Your prayers are acceptable before me,' said the Lord to the Prophet, 'and in answer to them I say unto you,' then continues that great revelation. (Doc. and Cov., Sec. 124: 2.) In fact, to particularize no further, **it may be said that by far the greater number of the revelations received by the Prophet were in response to his petitions and inquiries of the Lord**; and therefore the fact that this revelation on marriage was given in response to inquiries by the Prophet, to know why the Lord justified the worthy patriarchs named, and some of the prophets, in their plural marriage relations, is characteristic of practically all the revelations received by him. (Emphasis added.)

If asking must precede receiving, and if Joseph Smith was also required to ask before the great revelations of this dispensation unfolded to him, then you must ask also. If you do not ask, you hedge up the way and prevent Heaven from answering.

A study of the entire vision given to Nephi would take us away from our subject here. So we are going to pass the many details of Nehi's vision without a full explanation. We will only mention some limited few of them because they relate to the subject of receiving a witness from God through the Second Comforter and what is to be expected from such an experience.

Nephi asks and in turn sees the coming vision of Christ's birth and His mother, Mary.[92] He beholds Christ's baptism, mortal ministry, healing of the sick and afflicted, and His death.[93] This kind of information is the very heart and definition of an Apostolic witness. It gives Nephi the kind of standing which the ancient original Quorum of the Twelve had. You will recall when Judas was replaced, the remaining eleven members met and discussed the kind of person who was to be added to their Quorum. They said, "Wherefore of these men which have companied with us all the time that the Lord Jesus went in and out among us, Beginning from the baptism of John, unto that same day that he was taken up from us, must one be ordained **to be a witness with us of his resurrection.**" (Acts 1: 21-22, emphasis added.) Apostles were to be those who were familiar with Christ's mortal ministry, and a witness of His resurrection.

This requirement for Apostles is the same now as then. When the first Quorum of the Twelve was organized in this dispensation, Oliver Cowdery gave a charge to them which included these words:

> You have been indebted to other men, in the first instance, for evidence; on that you have acted; but **it is necessary that you receive a testimony from heaven for yourselves**; so that you

---

[92]This vision of the future events of history are not only possible, but are commonplace before God. D&C 130: 7: Angels reside "in the presence of God, on a globe like a sea of glass and fire, where all things for their glory are manifest, past, present, and future, and are continually before the Lord." Therefore the vision of these future events may seem to us miraculous, but to the angels they are the usual view of things.

[93]2 Ne. 11: 13-33.

can bear testimony to the truth of the Book of Mormon, and **that you have seen the face of God**. That is more than the testimony of an angel. When the proper time arrives, you shall be able to bear this testimony to the world. **When you bear testimony that you have seen God, this testimony God will never suffer to fall, but will bear you out; although many will not give heed, yet others will. You will therefore see the necessity of getting this testimony from heaven.**

Never cease striving until you have seen God face to face. Strengthen your faith; cast off your doubts, your sins, and all your unbelief; and nothing can prevent you from coming to God. **Your ordination is not full and complete till God has laid His hand upon you. We require as much to qualify us as did those who have gone before us**; God is the same. If the Savior in former days laid His hands upon His disciples, why not in latter days?" (*DHC* 2: 195-196, emphasis added.)

Here, then, we see Nephi was an Apostolic witness of the Lord. Whether he was ordained a member of the Twelve or not (and he was not because there was no Quorum in existence during his day), he nonetheless was Apostolic in stature and witness.

He saw the persecution of the Lamb's Twelve Apostles by the "world" and "the house of Israel."[94] He was shown the unfolding history of the world, the apostasy and ultimately the restoration of the Gospel.[95] He saw and received a promise his descendants would also receive blessings through the final restoration in the latter-days.[96] In short, he was shown the very definition of the truth.[97]

---

[94]*Id.*, v. 35.

[95]1 Ne. chapters 12-14.

[96]*Id.*, chapter 15.

[97]D&C 93: 24: "And truth is knowledge of things as they are, and as they were, and as they are to come." Here Nephi is shown a vision of these unfolding events of history so that he may become acquainted with the truth. One of the great blessings of knowing the mysteries is to gain knowledge of how God's plans apply through all generations. God is in charge. There are no

Now, while Nephi saw the future events in fullness, he was not permitted to disclose or record them[98] in full. This is often the case. God ordains those who are called to know, and from among them there is a limited number who are permitted to reveal. All others who know, but who are not permitted to reveal, must keep these things to themselves. Some who are permitted to reveal things are also commanded to keep a part back, just as Nephi was.[99]

If you think seeing these things will authorize you to either teach or reveal them, you are mistaken. God calls those who are permitted to reveal things to the world. He puts them in a position to preside over His Church. Those alone are permitted to speak **for** Him.[100] But many people are permitted to speak **with** Him.[101] And anyone is permitted to

---

mistakes, nor coincidences. Things are unfolding in exactly the way in which He anticipated, notwithstanding man's freedom to choose for himself.

[98]Nephi is told: "But the things which thou shalt see hereafter thou shalt not write; for the Lord God hath ordained the apostle of the Lamb of God that he should write them." (1 Ne. 14: 25.)

[99]See, e.g., D&C 76: 113-119 where Joseph saw things which were not lawful for him to reveal. "But great and marvelous are the works of the Lord, and the mysteries of his kingdom which he showed unto us, which surpass all understanding in glory, and in might, and in dominion; **Which he commanded us we should not write while we were yet in the Spirit, and are not lawful for man to utter.**" (*Id.*, vs. 114-115, emphasis added.) Similarly the First Vision is not a complete recount (see, JSH, v. 20).

[100]"But, behold, verily, verily, I say unto thee, no one shall be appointed to receive commandments and revelations in this church excepting my servant Joseph Smith, Jun.[or his successor as President of the Church], for he receiveth them even as Moses." (D&C 28: 2.)

[101]"It is given unto **many** to know the mysteries of God; nevertheless they are laid under a strict command that they shall not impart only according to the portion of his word which he doth grant unto the children of men, according to the heed and diligence which they give unto him. And, therefore, he that will harden his heart, the same receiveth the lesser portion of the word; and he that will not harden his heart, to him is given the greater portion of the word, until it is given unto him to know the mysteries of God until he know

learn directly **from** Him. He has never abdicated His right to come to any of His disciples as a Second Comforter. Nor will He abdicate that right so long as men remain on the earth. He is the final authority and the One who remains in ultimate control. Never think any man or men, institution or educational requirements stand between you and the Lord. That mistake has ill-served other religions. It has no place in the restored Gospel. You must not trust responsibility for these things to others.

In his vision Nephi learns these things concerning Christ: "And after he had said these words, he said unto me: Look! And I looked, and I beheld the Son of God going forth among the children of men; and I saw many fall down at his feet and worship him. And it came to pass that I beheld that the rod of iron, which my father had seen, was the word of God, which led to the fountain of living waters, or to the tree of life; which waters are a representation of the love of God; and I also beheld that the tree of life was a representation of the love of God." (1 Ne. 11: 24-25.) Here, Nephi is getting an orientation of the actual events of the Savior's life and how that relates to the symbols of his father's dream. The "iron rod" seen in the vision is the "word of God." Meaning the way to find the path back to the tree of life is found in the revelations from God. They are contained in large measure in the scriptures. Scriptures are of vital importance to us. We have an angel instructing Nephi, and we have Christ being shown to him, and the message includes this specific teaching about the importance of revelations and the scriptures.

It seems obvious, but should be asked anyway: if you are not willing to receive the contents of the revelations already recorded in the scriptures by studying them (and learning such mysteries as they contain), then what makes you think you can qualify to receive revelation of yet greater things? Why would heaven violate the rules of

---

them in full. And they that will harden their hearts, to them is given the lesser portion of the word until they know nothing concerning his mysteries;…" (Alma 12: 9-11, emphasis added.)

its own economy and do for you what you can do for yourself? No miracle is required to teach you many of the mysteries of heaven. They are already here in the scriptures and in the ordinances. But if you ignore them and refuse to receive what is in them, there is little reason to part the veil and teach you more.

We prove our need to be taught by heaven when we have done our part to study what heaven has already revealed. When we have exhausted the available information here, we are permitted to receive more because we ask and we are ready to receive. You can know a person is ready to receive because they have paid heed to what has been delivered to mankind already. Nephi has done this. This is why we find ourselves gaining a new flood of light from him.

As we will see, however, not all scripture is of equal value. When it comes to the scriptures, the Book of Mormon is plainly the best source for learning the mysteries of God. Within its pages is the fullness of the Gospel set out in plainness like no other volume. Joseph Smith was perhaps understating the matter when he proclaimed "the Book of Mormon was the most correct of any book on earth, and the keystone to our religion, and a man could get nearer to God by abiding by its precepts, than by any other book." (*DHC* 4: 461; also *TPJS*, p. 194.) In addition to other important matters, as Nephi's visionary encounter with the Second Comforter will teach us, the scriptures from all other sources have been corrupted.

But first, we learn the doctrine of premortality and foreordination of man from Nephi. Earlier, you will recall he has recorded his father's vision of the tree of life. In his father's vision which Nephi recorded we read this: "And it came to pass that he saw One descending out of the midst of heaven, and he beheld that his luster was above that of the sun at noon-day. And he also saw twelve others following him, and their brightness did exceed that of the stars in the firmament." (1 Ne. 1: 9-10.) This "One" and the "twelve others" are shown as spirits to Lehi. To Nephi they are also shown, but in their future, mortal ministries. Nephi's vision includes this: "And I beheld that he went forth minister-

ing unto the people, in power and great glory; and the multitudes were
gathered together to hear him; and I beheld that they cast him out from
among them. And I also beheld twelve others following him. And it
came to pass that they were carried away in the Spirit from before my
face, and I saw them not." (1 Ne. 11: 28-29.) Lehi's vision recorded by
Nephi records the pre-earth spirits of the future Twelve Apostles.
Nephi's own vision includes the vision of their earthly ministry.
Therefore, we have in his full account a clear reference to the
premortality of spirits.[102] Not only the pre-existence of souls, but of
their foreordination to earthly ministries as well. Of a truth, the Book
of Mormon is a marvelous work and a wonder for what it reveals to us!

Nephi's vision also includes a remarkable description of the
weaknesses of other scriptures. Unlike the Book of Mormon, which
went from prophet-writer to prophet-translator to publication to you,
the scriptures from the Jews (Old and New Testaments) have been
altered. The vision leaves no doubt the reasons for the alterations. They
were done intentionally. Nephi records:

> And the angel of the Lord said unto me: Thou hast beheld that
> the book proceeded forth from the mouth of a Jew; and when
> it proceeded forth from the mouth of a Jew it contained the
> fulness of the gospel of the Lord, of whom the twelve apostles
> bear record; and they bear record according to the truth which
> is in the Lamb of God. Wherefore, these things go forth from
> the Jews in purity unto the Gentiles, according to the truth
> which is in God. And after they go forth by the hand of the
> twelve apostles of the Lamb, from the Jews unto the Gentiles,
> thou seest the formation of that great and abominable church,

---

[102]Although it is beyond the scope of this work, every doctrine of the
restoration, from pre-existence, to foreordination, to the Temple rites are set
out in the Book of Mormon. To the extent they are relevant to this work, we
will set them out. But these doctrines are all in the Book of Mormon. Joseph's
later revelations all had their foundations and foreshadowing in the Book of
Mormon. That is one of the reasons why the Book of Mormon is so
important for the Saints to study. Within its pages is the fullness of the Gospel
of Jesus Christ, provided, of course, you have the eyes with which to see it.

which is most abominable above all other churches; for behold, they have taken away from the gospel of the Lamb many parts which are plain and most precious; and also many covenants of the Lord have they taken away. And all this have they done that they might pervert the right ways of the Lord, that they might blind the eyes and harden the hearts of the children of men. (1 Ne. 13: 24-27.)

With respect to the New Testament, there is little doubt the text underwent alteration. In Erhman's study of the matter[103] he recounts the proof for the alterations and the reasons for them having been made. He writes on p. 3-4: "that theological disputes, specifically disputes over Christology, prompted Christian scribes to alter the words of Scripture in order to make them more serviceable for the polemical task." That is, the changes helped the arguments get resolved. As he goes on to explain, on p. 15: "the ways scribes modified their texts of Scripture in light of the polemical contexts within which they worked, altering the manuscripts they reproduced to make them more orthodox on the one hand and less susceptible to heretical misuse on the other." He admits, however, the definitions of what was "orthodox" on the one hand, and what was "heretical" on the other were determined later by who won the arguments. He makes no allowance for the possibility the wrong side won the argument, and what became orthodoxy was a faction whose beliefs were corrupt. We, of course, know that happened through revelation in the Restoration.

He continues on p. 29:

The vast majority of all textual variants originated during the period of our concern, the second and third centuries. This was also a period in which various Christian groups were actively engaged in internecine conflicts, particularly over Christology. A number of variant readings reflect these conflicts, and appear to have been generated 'intentionally.' Scribes sometimes

---

[103]Ehrman, Bart D. *The Orthodox Corruption of Scripture: The Effects of Early Christological Controversies on the Text of the New Testament.* Oxford: Oxford University Press, 1993.

changed their manuscripts to render them more patently orthodox, either by importing their Christology into a text that otherwise lacked it or by modifying a text that could be taken to support contrary views.

In his conclusions at p. 275 Ehrman writes: "proto-orthodox[104] scribes of the second and third centuries occasionally modified their texts of Scripture in order to make them coincide more closely with the Christological views embraced by the party that would seal its victory at Nicea and Chalcedon." Therefore, today the prevailing creeds of Historic Christianity are all based upon the alterations made in the scriptures to support their creeds. But the original texts may have contradicted or undermined those "orthodox" beliefs. He continues, "The texts of these books were by no means inviolable; to the contrary, they were altered with relative ease and alarming frequency. Most of the changes were accidental, the result of scribal ineptitude, carelessness, or fatigue. Others were intentional, and reflect the controversial mileux [sic] within which they were produced." (*Id.*) The scriptures, including the New Testament, have not escaped corruption.

With respect to Christ's ministry, Nephi confirms Christ did perform miraculous healings and wonders. These were not textual insertions or alterations. Nephi continues his visionary account:

> And he spake unto me again, saying: Look! And I looked, and I beheld the Lamb of God going forth among the children of men. And I beheld multitudes of people who were sick, and who were afflicted with all manner of diseases, and with devils and unclean spirits; and the angel spake and showed all these things unto me. And they were healed by the power of the Lamb of God; and the devils and the unclean spirits were cast out. And it came to pass that the angel spake unto me again,

[104]This is his term which he defines to mean those people who believed what would later become "orthodox" teachings and interpretations. These people were of these views before they became the majority, and later the enforced "orthodox" views. Hence his reference to them as "proto-orthodox."

saying: Look! And I looked and beheld the Lamb of God, that
he was taken by the people; yea, the Son of the everlasting God
was judged of the world; and I saw and bear record. And I,
Nephi, saw that he was lifted up upon the cross and slain for
the sins of the world. (1 Ne. 11: 31-33.)

These two things are juxtaposed by the angel-tutor for a reason. Christ
did wonderful good works, and bestowed blessings and benefits upon
those to whom He ministered. He healed. He cured. He relieved
suffering from demonic sources. And He was killed by people who
judged Him worthy of death.

Nephi needed this lesson. Nephi would later lament his own
inability to succeed in his ministry to convert and teach his brothers. He
suffered similar, though less intense, rejection for his own good
works.[105] Following Christ would require Nephi to endure the same type

---

[105]Nephi's lament in 2 Ne. 4: 17-34: "Nevertheless, notwithstanding
the great goodness of the Lord, in showing me his great and marvelous works,
my heart exclaimeth: O wretched man that I am! Yea, my heart sorroweth
because of my flesh; my soul grieveth because of mine iniquities. I am
encompassed about, because of the temptations and the sins which do so
easily beset me. And when I desire to rejoice, my heart groaneth because of
my sins; nevertheless, I know in whom I have trusted. My God hath been my
support; he hath led me through mine afflictions in the wilderness; and he
hath preserved me upon the waters of the great deep. He hath filled me with
his love, even unto the consuming of my flesh. He hath confounded mine
enemies, unto the causing of them to quake before me. Behold, he hath heard
my cry by day, and he hath given me knowledge by visions in the night-time.
And by day have I waxed bold in mighty prayer before him; yea, my voice
have I sent up on high; and angels came down and ministered unto me. And
upon the wings of his Spirit hath my body been carried away upon exceedingly
high mountains. And mine eyes have beheld great things, yea, even too great
for man; therefore I was bidden that I should not write them. O then, if I have
seen so great things, if the Lord in his condescension unto the children of men
hath visited men in so much mercy, why should my heart weep and my soul
linger in the valley of sorrow, and my flesh waste away, and my strength
slacken, because of mine afflictions? And why should I yield to sin, because
of my flesh? Yea, why should I give way to temptations, that the evil one have
place in my heart to destroy my peace and afflict my soul? Why am I angry
because of mine enemy? Awake, my soul! No longer droop in sin. Rejoice, O

of treatment. Following Christ always requires the sincere disciple to suffer similar rejection by those who should be listening to them.[106] The more closely you follow Him, the more you will experience the same form of treatment. Without the rejection and criticism by the world (i.e., having yourself mocked by the occupants in the "great and spacious building"), you are not really following Him. Good public relations are not a part of Christ's Gospel. Elder Bruce R. McConkie observed, "As with the Master, so with the servant: persecution is always the heritage of the faithful. The Lord's ministers in all dispensations have suffered for his name's sake." (McConkie, Bruce R. *Doctrinal New Testament Commentary*. Salt Lake City: Bookcraft, 1965, 1:751.) There is a remarkable loss of spiritual power associated with worldly popularity. Follow-

---

my heart, and give place no more for the enemy of my soul. Do not anger again because of mine enemies. Do not slacken my strength because of mine afflictions. Rejoice, O my heart, and cry unto the Lord, and say: O Lord, I will praise thee forever; yea, my soul will rejoice in thee, my God, and the rock of my salvation. O Lord, wilt thou redeem my soul? Wilt thou deliver me out of the hands of mine enemies? Wilt thou make me that I may shake at the appearance of sin? May the gates of hell be shut continually before me, because that my heart is broken and my spirit is contrite! O Lord, wilt thou not shut the gates of thy righteousness before me, that I may walk in the path of the low valley, that I may be strict in the plain road! O Lord, wilt thou encircle me around in the robe of thy righteousness! O Lord, wilt thou make a way for mine escape before mine enemies! Wilt thou make my path straight before me! Wilt thou not place a stumbling block in my way – but that thou wouldst clear my way before me, and hedge not up my way, but the ways of mine enemy. O Lord, I have trusted in thee, and I will trust in thee forever. I will not put my trust in the arm of flesh; for I know that cursed is he that putteth his trust in the arm of flesh. Yea, cursed is he that putteth his trust in man or maketh flesh his arm."

[106]In this respect, the treatment of Christ and the treatment of His disciples, generally fit Isaiah's Messianic description in Chapter 53: 3: "He is despised and rejected of men; a man of sorrows, and acquainted with grief: and we hid as it were our faces from him; he was despised, and we esteemed him not." Just as Nephi was despised and rejected by his older brothers to whom he was sent as their prophet-king, so also Joseph Smith was despised and rejected by the religionists of his day. Christian clergy were among those who led the attack on the Carthage Jail.

ers of Christ are always "strangers and foreigners" here. The "royal priesthood" Peter refers to is clarified in terms which make the designation anything but popular. They are further described as "a peculiar people."[107] The oddness or "peculiarity" of such people makes it clear they ill-fit this world.

Nephi was shown the coming ministry of the resurrected Lord to his descendants in the Americas. "And it came to pass after I saw these things, I saw the vapor of darkness, that it passed from off the face of the earth; and behold, I saw multitudes who had not fallen because of the great and terrible judgments of the Lord. And I saw the heavens open, and the Lamb of God descending out of heaven; and he came down and showed himself unto them." (1 Ne. 12: 5-6.) Therefore, had his descendants studied his prophecies, they would have anticipated the Lord's coming to visit them. It is possible Samuel the Lamanite was not teaching a new revelation, but returning to the old prophecies of Nephi as the source of his later prophetic message.

The entire theophany of Nephi is worth careful study. We have covered only as much as is needed here. Nephi has demonstrated through his life history what the "fullness of the Gospel" contains. And he has similarly demonstrated for us how it is obtained. As he ends his record Nephi admonishes us with these words: "Wherefore, now after I have spoken these words, if ye cannot understand them it will be because ye ask not, neither do ye knock; wherefore, ye are not brought into the light, but must perish in the dark." (2 Ne. 32: 4.) Nephi wrote so we might be led to both understand, and then obtain for ourselves the fullness of the Gospel of Jesus Christ. We have the record before us. If we refuse to be informed by its contents, then we are not going to receive what it offers. We will remain as the Israelites who refused the offer made by the Lord to them.

---

[107] 1 Peter 2: 9: "But ye are a chosen generation, a royal priesthood, an holy nation, a peculiar people; that ye should shew forth the praises of him who hath called you out of darkness into his marvelous light."

It should not matter whether you have ever had these things taught to you in plainness by a teacher. The scriptures themselves are given to us as God's intended curriculum. Whether you are fortunate enough to be in a ward with good instruction, or you are not, you are still in a position to receive the fullness for yourself. The scriptures have been given to you for that purpose. The scriptures, and in particular the Book of Mormon, is God's message delivered right over the heads of the inadequate teachers you may have had in your life. The fullness is contained in its pages. Open them, study them seriously, and you will find the fullness there for yourself.

Chapter Seven

TO WHOM THESE THINGS ARE
MADE AVAILABLE

I n a startling passage from my Patriarchal Blessing, it promises I will be blessed with: "an understanding of life and its purposes and its meaning and the great blessing that will come to those who are thus faithful in magnifying this estate to be again in the presence of their Father in Heaven in their second estate." It was a passage which haunted me as I contemplated its meaning. It had the same effect upon my thoughts as the passage from James had on Joseph.[108] I reflected on it again and again.

---

[108] Inspired reflections are one of the ways God communicates with us. This is not limited to prophets, dispensation heads, or even Church leaders. It applies to us all. As one example, in *Hugh Nibley: A Consecrated Life*, p. 60: "Hugh's discovery of his life's work came as a spiritual experience in his mid-teens. ... As he skimmed through the Pearl of Great Price, he read Moses 1: 41 which promised that ancient writings 'shall be had again among the children of men.' 'Oh boy, that hit me,' remembers Hugh. 'That verse wasn't just purely a mental process.' 'Absolutely stunned' by the promise, he lifted his head and 'stared out the window[;] I was looking out across the sky.' Great

I saw in these words a promise to me, given by authority delegated from God to a Patriarch in the Church, which promised if I am faithful I will again be in the presence of my Father in Heaven in this life, this second estate. No passage of the Blessing or even from scripture came with more power to my heart than this did to me. I determined I would be faithful and I would do what needed to be done in my life to obtain this audience with the Father.

If He were willing to receive me, I did not want to do anything to prevent it from happening. It became my study, my focus, my mission, my hunger and thirst.

When the angel Moroni appeared to Joseph Smith, he quoted this scripture:

> And it shall come to pass afterward, that I will pour out my spirit upon all flesh; and your sons and your daughters shall prophesy, your old men shall dream dreams, your young men shall see visions: And also upon the servants and upon the handmaids in those days will I pour out my spirit. And I will shew wonders in the heavens and in the earth, blood, and fire, and pillars of smoke. The sun shall be turned into darkness, and the moon into blood, before the great and the terrible day of the Lord come. And it shall come to pass, that whosoever shall call on the name of the Lord shall be delivered: for in mount Zion and in Jerusalem shall be deliverance, as the Lord hath said, and in the remnant whom the Lord shall call. (Joel 2: 28-32.)

After that statement, Moroni said to Joseph: "this was not yet fulfilled, but was soon to be." (JSH 1: 41.) This prophecy and promise about powerful spiritual experiences is not limited to Church authorities. It is not limited to one sex. But, rather, promises both "sons and daughters" are to receive these things. Nor does age limit the promise,

---

possibilities dawned in that instant. So 'I got into this old stuff,' – ancient literature and history – 'and stayed with the old stuff ever after that."

for "your young men" as well as "your old men" will similarly receive these visions and revelations.

This kind of equal entitlement of all the Saints to "prophesy…, dream dreams…, and see visions" is consistent with the equal treatment promised by Nephi. Nephi wrote: "For none of these iniquities come of the Lord; for he doeth that which is good among the children of men; and he doeth nothing save it be plain unto the children of men; and he inviteth them all to come unto him and partake of his goodness; and he denieth none that come unto him, black and white, bond and free, male and female; and he remembereth the heathen; and all are alike unto God, both Jew and Gentile." (2 Ne. 26: 33.)

All are invited. Male, female, young, old, bond, free, black white, and even the "heathen." Elder Bruce R. McConkie wrote in *A New Witness for the Articles of Faith*, p. 490:

> If all things operate by law, and they do; if God is no respecter of persons, and certainly he is perfectly impartial; if his course is one eternal round, never varying from age to age, and such truly is the case-then all of the gifts and graces and revelations ever given to any prophet, seer, or revelator in any age will be given again to any soul who obeys the law entitling him so to receive. While discoursing about the Second Comforter and in setting forth that those whose callings and elections have been made sure have the privilege of seeing the face of the Lord while they yet dwell in the flesh, the Prophet Joseph Smith said: 'God hath not revealed anything to Joseph, but what He will make known unto the Twelve, and even the least Saint may know all things as fast as he is able to bear them.' (Teachings of the Prophet Joseph Smith, p. 149.)" (McConkie, Bruce R. *A New Witness for the Articles of Faith*. Salt Lake City: Deseret Book Company, 1985.)

This promise is therefore available to all. The Book of Mormon assures us of it. Moroni prophesied it would come in our day. Joseph declared it and Elder McConkie reiterated it. Accordingly, it is available to you. Alma's teaching that "it is given **unto many** to know the mysteries of God" (emphasis added) means what it says.[109] This is God's promise in every age. Even if only few men or women are willing to receive it, that does not cancel the promise.

This process is perfectly natural. We are all incomplete, with a universal void inside us which we all long to fill. The void within us was meant to lead us to search for a substantive way of filling it. People attempt to fill this void with any number of unsatisfying and unfulfilling movements, causes, and things. But it is only through finding God that this void can be filled.

In a revelation through Joseph in 1832, the Lord lamented about the past rejection of this offering during the time of Moses. It says in D&C 84: 23-25: "Now this Moses plainly taught to the children of Israel in the wilderness, and sought diligently to sanctify his people that they might behold the face of God; But they hardened their hearts and could not endure his presence; therefore, the Lord in his wrath, for his anger was kindled against them, swore that they should not enter into his rest while in the wilderness, which rest is the fulness of his glory. Therefore, he took Moses out of their midst, and the Holy Priesthood also." We know from this Moses sought diligently to bring Israel to the point where they "might behold the face of God." But Israel failed, and they could not receive the Second Comforter. The lesser priesthood was instituted, and the possibility of seeing God was closed to them. But in our time, the possibility has been renewed.

Understand, Moses did see the face of God.[110] This passage is not speaking of him. It is speaking of the common residents of Israel. It was to them the offer to see God "face to face" was extended, and in turn declined. Moses individually accepted the offer. The rank and file did not. This unfortunate historic failing of Israel should not be repeated by us. The reason the ordinances are universally available now, and the Temple rites are open to all, and the dialogue at the veil is open to all,

---

[109] Alma 12: 9-11, cited and set out *supra*.

[110] See, e.g., Moses 1: 2; Num. 12: 8; Exo. 24: 9-10.

and the priesthood is so generally spread among all the Church members is to avoid this prior failing by our ancestors. We are supposed to be doing better than they did. We, unlike them, are supposed to behold the face of God.

The universal nature of this opportunity is unmistakably set out in D&C 93: 1, where it is written: "Verily, thus saith the Lord: It shall come to pass that **every soul** who forsaketh his sins and cometh unto me, and calleth on my name, and obeyeth my voice, and keepeth my commandments, shall see my face and know that I am." (Emphasis added.) The promise is to "every soul," not only to leaders, not just to dispensation heads such as Moses or Joseph Smith, and not only to someone who holds office, priesthood, position or heritage. When it comes to heritage, sometimes the presumption there is an "entitlement" because of what one's ancestors did, works to quell the earnest search to obtain a promise in your own right.[111] While having great ancestors is laudable, it is no substitute for individual attention to these things. Your ancestors cannot ask for you, nor can they receive for you. You alone must qualify for these things.

And so you, along with every soul, are invited to take these specific steps and thereby "see [God's] face, and know that [He is.]" The steps are universal. And the invitation is similarly universal. Anyone who will 1) forsake his sins; 2) come unto Him; 3) call on His name; 4) obey His voice; and 5) keep His commandments, can qualify. We will discuss this list later in some detail. We have already considered the need to "call on

---

[111] In addition to the other matters of his ministry, this was one of the messages of Abinadi as well. He came bearing the name of Abinadi as the sole person of that name in the entire record. There is not another person holding that name in the entire thousand-year history. He comes without genealogy, and without so much as a clear indication of whether he is Nephite or Lamanite (or Jaredite for that matter). He comes from an unknown place, and returns temporarily to that unknown place. That suggests he was *not* a Nephite. Yet his message changes the entire unfolding history of the record. This man's message is not limited to what he said. It includes the additional confirmation that God is no respecter of persons. See Mosiah chapters 11-17.

His name" in the discussion about "asking" previously. But it should be noted this requirement appears here again.

When Moses was told there were men prophesying in the camp of Israel he did not react with jealousy. Rather, he expressed his wish that all men were prophets.[112] Today is the day in which all Christ's followers, young and old, male and female, are entitled by ordinance and by prophetic promise to receive dreams, visions and visitations. Today is the day of the prophet and prophetess. When you were confirmed a member of the Church of Jesus Christ of Latter-day Saints you were promised and admonished to "receive the Holy Ghost." This confirmation, blessing and admonishment is given to every baptized member of Christ's Church. The ordinances point to and confer upon every member of Christ's Church the right to receive what Joel and Moroni promised would occur in our day. Yet these blessings and promises suggest a reluctance you must overcome to actually receive the "power of godliness."

The only limit on what you can receive is the limit we have already discussed. Only the President of the Church is entitled to receive revelation **for** the Church. But if the President is to receive all revelation **in** the Church, he is going to have to do so contrary to the scriptures, prophecies and ordinances. For that to happen the Church of this dispensation would fare no better than Israel in Moses' dispensation. If we refuse to behold the face of God, then the restoration of higher rites, higher priesthood, and the prophetic promises about our times will all

---

[112]The incident is found in Numbers, Chapter 11: "But there remained two of the men in the camp, the name of the one was Eldad, and the name of the other Medad: and the spirit rested upon them; and they were of them that were written, but went not out unto the tabernacle: and they prophesied in the camp. And there ran a young man, and told Moses, and said, Eldad and Medad do prophesy in the camp. And Joshua the son of Nun, the servant of Moses, one of his young men, answered and said, My lord Moses, forbid them. And Moses said unto him, Enviest thou for my sake? **would God that all the Lord's people were prophets, and that the Lord would put his spirit upon them!**" (Vs. 26-29, emphasis added.)

have been worth next to nothing. For if the President of the Church alone receives revelation, then he alone will be saved.[113]

Remember, the Church is spread through revelation. New converts are not asked to join the Church because they have been argued into accepting a belief. They are not asked to listen to skilled orators and theologians present the best case for the Church. They are taught by young men and women, whom the Lord calls "the weak things of this world."[114] He does not call the wise, the experienced or the learned. He calls the "weak" to His ministry.

The weak ministers of the Gospel are then told to go forth bearing their testimonies. They are to convert new members by asking them to take the challenge found in Moroni 10: 4. The challenge is to pray and ask God if the Church is true or not. The Gospel promises if you do this in sincerity, then God will tell you the Book of Mormon is true, and in turn, through the Holy Ghost you can know the truth of all things. It is, therefore, a revelatory experience that brings new converts into the Church, not some persuasive, academic presentation. The Spirit, bearing testimony to the truth, is the basis for all conversion.

The Lord does not invite people to join His Church because they have been persuaded by a personality to join. He wants people to convert because they have begun to have a relationship directly with Him, through the Holy Spirit. He wants people to receive a direct witness, through spiritual means. The process disconnects the convert from the way in which things are usually learned, and connects them with a new form of learning. He wants us to experience hearing from Him, and because of that experience with Him, for us to convert and follow Him. This process is involved in every convert's decision to join the Church. We see here the universal nature of revelation in our time.

---

[113]"No man can receive the Holy Ghost without receiving revelations. The Holy Ghost is a Revelator." *(DHC* 6: 58; also *TPJS*, p. 328.)

[114]D&C 35: 13 "Wherefore, I call upon the weak things of the world, those who are unlearned and despised, to thrash the nations by the power of my Spirit."

Though converts may later rebel, fall away or rationalize their experience, they all come to the Church as a result of a personal revelation experience. These things are sensitive, however, and losing that Spirit is easy without consistent effort to follow Him. So there are many who fall away. But when they converted, they had had an experience, a witness, a connection to God which persuaded them God was speaking to them.

As was mentioned earlier, Elder Eyring's April 2005 General Conference talk began with mention that most of the Church is comprised of converts. Therefore, most of the members of the Church entered into its ranks through revelation. This is as it should be. Universal experience with the Holy Ghost in the lives of Church members is the expected norm.

In this respect, it is perhaps the Church's greatest asset that there is this predominate population of converts whose basis for membership stems from a witness of the Holy Ghost. There is a minority population in the Church, however, whose membership was not originally derived from a spiritual witness of the truth of the restoration. For them it is family ties, family tradition and early teaching which originally brought them into membership. There is a vast difference between conversion through the Spirit (which the Book of Mormon not only approves but demands of us) and the traditions of the fathers (which the Book of Mormon more often than not condemns). Church membership grounded upon a Spiritual witness means the convert has had an experience tying them to God, and in turn to Christ's Church. It stems from the heart.

Tradition can be a very unspiritual thing. Feeling obligation or commitment is a poor substitute for feeling a burning belief in the heart that God has spoken to you and made it known to you He lives and His Church has been restored to the earth.

There are Catholics whose ties to Catholicism stem from their family's long connection to Rome. They would feel a deep sense of betrayal to their ancestors and their family heritage if they converted to the Church of Jesus Christ of Latter-day Saints. They are not interested in, nor willing to seek, any form of spiritual witness which would contradict their feeling of obligation or commitment to Catholicism. We look on that type of commitment as a handicap. Latter-day Saints lament anytime someone would forfeit the ability to receive a greater reward in the afterlife and a greater connection to God in this life, exclusively because of the traditions of their fathers.

There is no difference between this form of religious commitment and one that keeps a Latter-day Saint a member of the LDS Church whose ties are familial and traditional rather than spiritual and revelatory. Without a witness from God that the Church of Jesus Christ of Latter-day Saints is the work of God, then you might as well be Catholic, or Presbyterian, or Lutheran or another Historic Christian disciple. In all cases there is a lack of the "power of godliness" which Christ condemned in His opening remarks to Joseph Smith in this dispensation. Holding onto the false "traditions of your fathers" is consistently condemned in the Book of Mormon. (See, e.g., Mosiah 10: 12; Alma 18: 5; 23: 3; 24: 7; 31: 16; 31: 22; 37: 9; 47: 36; 60: 32; Helaman 5: 51; 15: 7, among others.)

Any form of godliness lacking power is of equal value. It is to restore godliness "with power" that the Father and Christ came to open this dispensation. Christ complained all the existing churches had only a form of godliness but lacked spiritual power. He promised to restore the real, spiritual, living, true and powerful faith not then on the earth. But that restoration does no good if the adherents have not received the spirit, nor possess the power of godliness.

Being raised Latter-day Saint, of course, does not prevent anyone from becoming converted to Christ through a spiritual witness. Anyone can receive such an experience. Having the Gospel from birth can be an enormous advantage for the faithful, seeking disciple. It does not need to be a handicap. This book is addressing a single subject, however, and for that subject, if you are a lifelong member your obligation is no different than the obligation of the convert. There are no exceptions based upon parentage.

> In living our lives let us never forget that the deeds of our fathers and mothers are theirs, not ours; that their works cannot be counted to our glory; that we can claim no excellence and no place, because of what they did, that we must rise by our own labor, and that labor failing we shall fail. We may claim no honor, no reward, no respect, nor special position or recognition, no credit because of what our fathers were or what they wrought. We stand upon our own feet in our own shoes. There is no aristocracy of birth in this Church; it belongs equally to the highest and the lowliest; for as Peter said to Cornelius, the Roman centurion, seeking him: ". . . Of a truth I perceive that God is no respecter of persons: But in every nation he that feareth him, and worketh righteousness, is accepted with him. (Acts 10: 34, 35.)" (*They of the Last Wagon*, President J. Reuben Clark, Jr., Conference Report, October 1947, Afternoon Meeting, p.160.)

If your familial experience has prevented you from seeking such a witness, you should do something about that. You should realize God is no respecter of persons. And you should do exactly as converts have done since the restoration began. Your own family came into the Church because someone in your family prayed, sought and received an experience which convinced them Christ had restored His Church to the earth. If He did that for your ancestor, and He does that for converts daily as they pray and ask to know the truth, He will do that for you. You do not need, and should not accept, merely the traditions of your family as your basis for belief. Seek and you will find Christ will testify to you that the Church of Jesus Christ does exist on the earth. When that happens, you will begin the path which this book is discussing.

The difference between relying upon tradition and relying upon a Spirit-led belief is the difference between moving in the dark and living with the light. Through the Spirit you become reconnected with God. You are alive again. You can receive an experience which will form an anchor to your belief and prevent you from ever being blown off course by winds of false doctrine again.

Many things can be faked, but you cannot fake spiritual power. People pretend to espouse beliefs and/or traits all the time which do not belong to them. But power in the Spirit cannot be a mere pretense. Gifts of the Spirit cannot be feigned. New and inventive ways to describe what is passed off as gifts of the Spirit cannot substitute for the absence of the traditional gifts named in scripture. Some talents are commonly possessed by mankind whether they have ever been converted or not. Calling such common talents a "gift of the spirit" may be a humble acknowledgment of the fact all things come from God, but such things are not the "gifts of the Spirit" which are identified in scripture. The scriptures are unequivocal in telling us healing, prophecy, ministering angels, speaking in tongues, etc. are the hallmark gifts of the Spirit.[115] If you have had such a witness and such an experience, you do not need to pretend something is a proof of the power of godliness when it is not. You will experience the real thing.[116] And when you do,

---

[115]Moroni wrote: "And again I speak unto you who deny the revelations of God, and say that they are done away, **that there are no revelations, nor prophecies, nor gifts, nor healing, nor speaking with tongues, and the interpretation of tongues**; Behold I say unto you, **he that denieth these things knoweth not the gospel of Christ**; yea, he has not read the scriptures; if so, he does not understand them. For do we not read that God is the same yesterday, today, and forever, and in him there is no variableness neither shadow of changing? And now, if ye have imagined up unto yourselves a god who doth vary, and in whom there is shadow of changing, **then have ye imagined up unto yourselves a god who is not God of miracles.**" (Mormon 9: 7-10, emphasis added.) A very recent book from Matthew B. Brown, *Receiving the Gifts of the Spirit*, Covenant Communications, Inc., American Fork, Utah, 2005, invites all to receive the Spirit's gifts.

[116]The Book of Mormon presumes the necessity and regularity of revelation. From the references in Helaman alone, we get these descriptions: Hel 4:12: "And it was because of the pride of their hearts, because of their exceeding riches, yea, it was because of their oppression to the poor,

there will be no need for pretending something else is the power of godliness which Christ promised He was returning to the earth.

The Seventh Article of Faith says: "We believe in the gift of tongues, prophecy, revelation, visions, healing, interpretation of tongues, and so forth." This specific statement of belief, composed by the founding Prophet of the Dispensation, does not say we believe in administration, patience, love, listening, tolerating, or other merely human virtues possessed in common with all mankind, are going to be called the gifts of the Spirit. The gifts of the Spirit have something unusual about them and are based upon power from God. There is no need, if you have received a witness from the Spirit, to pretend any longer a mere human virtue is evidence of God's power in your life. You can and will actually find God bestowing upon you the power of prophecy, revelation, visions, healing, tongues and interpretation of tongues, etc. If these things are brushed aside, then faith itself has failed. As Mormon explained about Christ's Gospel:

---

withholding their food from the hungry, withholding their clothing from the naked, and smiting their humble brethren upon the cheek, making a mock of that which was sacred, denying the spirit of prophecy and of revelation, murdering, plundering, lying, stealing, committing adultery, rising up in great contentions, and deserting away into the land of Nephi, among the Lamanites" — (from which we see moral degeneration being connected to the loss of the spirit of revelation.) Hel. 4: 23-24: "And because of their iniquity the church had begun to dwindle; and they began to disbelieve in the spirit of prophecy and in the spirit of revelation; and the judgments of God did stare them in the face. And they saw that they had become weak, like unto their brethren, the Lamanites, and that the Spirit of the Lord did no more preserve them; yea, it had withdrawn from them because the Spirit of the Lord doth not dwell in unholy temples" — (from which we see the connection between dwindling faith and loss of revelation.) Hel 11: 23: "And in the seventy and ninth year there began to be much strife. But it came to pass that Nephi and Lehi, and many of their brethren who knew concerning the true points of doctrine, having many revelations daily, therefore they did preach unto the people, insomuch that they did put an end to their strife in that same year"– (which show daily revelation can be the normal experience.)

Or have angels ceased to appear unto the children of men? Or has he withheld the power of the Holy Ghost from them? Or will he, so long as time shall last, or the earth shall stand, or there shall be one man upon the face thereof to be saved? Behold I say unto you, Nay; for it is by faith that miracles are wrought; and it is by faith that angels appear and minister unto men; wherefore, if these things have ceased wo be unto the children of men, for it is because of unbelief, and all is vain. **For no man can be saved, according to the words of Christ, save they shall have faith in his name; wherefore, if these things have ceased, then has faith ceased also**; and awful is the state of man, for they are as though there had been no redemption made. (Moroni 7: 36-38, emphasis added.)

In an attempt to identify further the things we should expect to find as evidence within the Church of the power of God and the confirming gifts of the Spirit, Section 46 teaches us as follows:

And again, verily I say unto you, **I would that ye should always remember, and always retain in your minds what those gifts are, that are given unto the church.** For all have not every gift given unto them; for there are many gifts, and to every man is given a gift by the Spirit of God. To some is given one, and to some is given another, that all may be profited thereby. To some it is given by the Holy Ghost to know that Jesus Christ is the Son of God, and that he was crucified for the sins of the world. To others it is given to believe on their words, that they also might have eternal life if they continue faithful. And again, to some it is given by the Holy Ghost to know the differences of administration, as it will be pleasing unto the same Lord, according as the Lord will, suiting his mercies according to the conditions of the children of men. And again, it is given by the Holy Ghost to some to know the diversities of operations, whether they be of God, that the manifestations of the Spirit may be given to every man to profit withal. And again, verily I say unto you, to some is given, by the Spirit of God, the word of wisdom. To another is given the word of knowledge, that all may be taught to be wise and to have knowledge. And again, to some it is given to have faith to be healed; And to others it is given to have faith to heal. And again, to some is given the working of miracles; And to others it is given to prophesy; And to others the discerning of spirits. And again, it is given to some to speak with tongues; And to another is given the interpretation of tongues. And all these gifts come from God, for the benefit of the children of God. (Verses 10-26, emphasis added.)

These are identified in scripture, just as the Seventh Article of Faith identifies the expected power of godliness, to provide to you the evidences this is the work which God still owns, still supports, and still has His Spirit operating within. They show to you God's fingerprints on this Church.

If you do not detect these gifts in your experience as a Latter-day Saint, then the fault does not lie elsewhere, it lies with you. You needn't rely upon others to bring the power of godliness into the Church. You should be bringing these gifts into the Church through your own faithfulness. We will discuss this principle later in some detail. But if you are alarmed by what you think is an absence of the Spirit in your experiences, then let the alarm work within you to bring yourself to a deeper commitment to the Gospel. It is not your neighbor's or your bishop's or your stake president's responsibility to provide spiritual evidences to you. It is YOUR responsibility to receive the power of the Holy Ghost in your own life. When hands were laid upon your head and you were both promised and admonished to "receive the Holy Ghost." That imposed upon you the duty to seek for and find the Spirit for your life. Stop looking to others to provide this for you. It is not even the responsibility of the President of the Church to cause these gifts to be present in the Church. Do not be like those whom Joseph Smith described as "depending on the Prophet, hence were darkened in their minds, in consequence of neglecting the duties devolving upon themselves." (DHC 5: 19.) This duty devolves upon you. It is your duty, and it is your right to participate in a faith which has both the form and the power of godliness in it.

Christ taught the Church would be largely unprepared at His

coming. That, of course, is our day.[117] With respect to His return, which He likens to the "wedding" of the Church and the Bridegroom, He tells us the awaiting and expecting "virgins" are unprepared.[118] Five of the ten are dressed in the appropriate wedding attire, and are awaiting His arrival, but they lack "oil" in their lamps.

"Oil" has always been a symbol for the Holy Spirit. The kind of oil which Christ uses here is not something which can be shared. Each person must acquire that kind of "oil" or spiritual preparation for themselves. As Spencer W. Kimball taught in *Faith Precedes the Miracle*, p.255-256, "This was not selfishness or unkindness. The kind of oil that is needed to illuminate the way and light up the darkness is not shareable. How can one share obedience to the principle of tithing; a

---

[117]See, e.g., Spencer W. Kimball, *Faith Precedes the Miracle*, p. 253-254. "I believe that the Ten Virgins represent the people of the Church of Jesus Christ and not the rank and file of the world. All of the virgins, wise and foolish, had accepted the invitation to the wedding supper; they had knowledge of the program and had been warned of the important day to come. They were not the gentiles or the heathens or the pagans, nor were they necessarily corrupt and reprobate, but they were knowing people who were foolishly unprepared for the vital happenings that were to affect their eternal lives." (Kimball, Spencer W. *Faith Precedes the Miracle*. Salt Lake City: Deseret Book Company, 1972.)

[118]The parable is found in the beginning verses of Matt. 25: "Then shall the kingdom of heaven be likened unto ten virgins, which took their lamps, and went forth to meet the bridegroom. And five of them were wise, and five were foolish. They that were foolish took their lamps, and took no oil with them: But the wise took oil in their vessels with their lamps. While the bridegroom tarried, they all slumbered and slept. And at midnight there was a cry made, Behold, the bridegroom cometh; go ye out to meet him. Then all those virgins arose, and trimmed their lamps. And the foolish said unto the wise, Give us of your oil; for our lamps are gone out. But the wise answered, saying, Not so; lest there be not enough for us and you: but go ye rather to them that sell, and buy for yourselves. And while they went to buy, the bridegroom came; and they that were ready went in with him to the marriage: and the door was shut. Afterward came also the other virgins, saying, Lord, Lord, open to us. But he answered and said, Verily I say unto you, I know you not. Watch therefore, for ye know neither the day nor the hour wherein the Son of man cometh." (Vs. 1-13.)

mind at peace from righteous living; an accumulation of knowledge? How can one share faith or testimony? How can one share attitudes or chastity, or the experience of a mission? How can one share temple privileges? Each must obtain that kind of oil for himself." (Kimball, Spencer W. *Faith Precedes the Miracle*. Salt Lake City: Deseret Book Company, 1972.) It is up to each person. As Christ is telling us here, you cannot borrow other people's obedience. You alone must follow the process to obtain oil.

The Apostle Paul spoke about gifts in the Church. He taught: "Now ye are the body of Christ, and members in particular. And God hath set some in the church, first apostles, secondarily prophets, thirdly teachers, after that miracles, then gifts of healings, helps, governments, diversities of tongues. Are all apostles? are all prophets? are all teachers? are all workers of miracles? Have all the gifts of healing? do all speak with tongues? do all interpret? But covet earnestly the best gifts." (1 Cor. 12: 27-31.) Paul tells us within the Church the first and foremost office is the Apostle. It is the senior Apostle who presides as President of the Church. That senior Apostle's preeminence in the Church is reaffirmed in the revelation to Oliver Cowdery (about Hiram Page's 'revelations') previously referred to. Only the senior Apostle is to receive revelation for the whole Church. Without the foundation of the Apostles, the Church would be adrift and chaotic. Through their ministries, the Church has stability and a center. Therefore, any criticism or complaint about the Apostle's role comes from a lack of understanding and appreciation of the vital position they hold.

The gospel is and must be and can only be taught by the gift of the Holy Ghost. That gift is given to us as the Saints of the Most High and to none others. We stand alone and have a power the world does not possess. Our views on religious and spiritual matters are infinitely better than theirs because we have the inspiration of heaven.

This is the reason the call to teach, the call to be a teacher- and I speak now of teachers of both sexes-is the third greatest position in the Church. Truly Paul said: 'God hath set some in the church, first apostles, secondarily prophets, thirdly teachers, after that miracles, then gifts of healings, helps, governments, diversities of tongues' (1 Cor. 12: 28). Apostles, prophets, teachers-in that order. Then the moving of mountains and the raising of the dead.

Apostles and prophets are also teachers, and what greater commission can anyone have from the Lord than to stand in his place and stead, saying what he would say if he personally were present, and doing it because the words uttered flow forth by the power of the Holy Ghost? (*The Bible—A Sealed Book*, Church Education Symposium, BYU, 17 August 1984; reprinted in *Sermons and Writings of Bruce R. McConkie* , © 1989 Bookcraft, p. 294-295.) (McConkie, Bruce R. *Sermons and Writings of Bruce R. McConkie.* Salt Lake City: Bookcraft, 1989.)

These gifts (or at least one of them) should be present in your life. If you find they are not, then you need to do as Paul says, and seek after them. Remember the example of Nephi, whom we first looked at as an example in these materials. He writes: "...I, Nephi, was desirous also that I might **see, and hear, and know of these things**, by the power of the Holy Ghost, which **is the gift of God unto all those who diligently seek him**, as well in times of old as in the time that he should manifest himself unto the children of men." (1 Ne. 10: 17, emphasis added.) Nephi wrote this to instruct all who read it. He wrote it for you.

Each person has the responsibility and right to live their own life and be accountable for what they are willing to receive. The scriptures speak in terms of what we are "willing to receive."[119] Although this may seem an odd way to put the matter, it is remarkably apt.

You can affect the nature of your own resurrection right up to the moment you die. The choices you make define you. After death most people will covet just one day back in mortality, if they have not given heed to the invitation from Christ while here. On the other hand, others will be filled with joy and rejoicing in their memory of having lived the

---

[119]D&C 88: 32: "...they shall return again to their own place, to enjoy that which they are willing to receive, because they were not willing to enjoy that which they might have received."

commandments during mortality. Section 88 has this description of the resurrection:

> Your glory shall be that glory by which your bodies are quick-ened. Ye who are quickened by **a portion of the celestial glory** shall then receive of the same, even a fulness. And they who are quickened by **a portion of the terrestrial glory** shall then receive of the same, even a fulness. And also they who are quickened by **a portion of the telestial glory** shall then receive of the same, even a fulness. And they who remain shall also be quickened; nevertheless, they shall return again to their own place, **to enjoy that which they are willing to receive, because they were not willing to enjoy that which they might have received**. For what doth it profit a man if a gift is bestowed upon him, and he receive not the gift? Behold, he rejoices not in that which is given unto him, neither rejoices in him who is the giver of the gift. (Vs. 28-33, emphasis added.)

Here in mortality you and I are living our lives in accordance with some law. Broadly, the laws we are living are Celestial, Terrestrial, or Telestial. None of us live the laws fully, but we do live at least a portion of the law for one of these kingdoms. If you live by a portion of the Celestial Law (and because you can repent it is possible for you to do so), then that is the law which will govern your resurrection.

The most exciting part of the Celestial Law is the portion that entitles the person living it to receive angels, entertain visions, obtain ordinances, oracles, receive the Spirit, and behold the face of God. How do you know for certain you are living a portion of the Celestial Law? The only way to know for certain is to obtain a witness from God. Christ obtained this when His Father declared concerning Him: "And lo a voice from heaven, saying, This is my beloved Son, in whom I am well pleased." (Matt. 3: 17.) You can know you are doing this when the gifts of the Spirit are unmistakably present in your life. You know God is with you because God's Spirit is with you.

Joseph Smith wrote an editorial on these things reproduced below. It was issued on Wednesday, June 15th, 1842. It deals with the Holy

Ghost and its gifts. Although it is lengthy, this important material needs to be included to also put these things into context:

> We believe in the gift of the Holy Ghost being enjoyed now, as much as it was in the Apostles-days; we believe that it [the gift of the Holy Ghost] is necessary to make and to organize the Priesthood, that no man can be called to fill any office in the ministry without it; we also believe in prophecy, in tongues, in visions, and in revelations, in gifts, and in healings; and that these things cannot be enjoyed without the gift of the Holy Ghost. We believe that the holy men of old spake as they were moved by the Holy Ghost, and that holy men in these days speak by the same principle; we believe in its being a comforter and a witness bearer, that it brings things past to our remembrance, leads us into all truth, and shows us of things to come; believe that "no man can know that Jesus is the Christ, but by the Holy Ghost." We believe in it [this gift of the Holy Ghost] in all its fullness, and power, and greatness, and glory; but whilst we do this, we believe in it rationally, consistently, and scripturally, and not according to the wild vagaries, foolish notions and traditions of men.
>
> The human family are very apt to run to extremes, especially in religious matters, and hence people in general, either want some miraculous display, or they will not believe in the gift of the Holy Ghost at all. If an Elder lays his hands upon a person, it is thought by many that the person must immediately rise and speak in tongues and prophesy; this idea is gathered from the circumstance of Paul laying his hands upon certain individuals who had been previously (as they stated) baptized unto John's baptism; which when he had done, they "spake in tongues and prophesied." Phillip also, when he had preached the Gospel to the inhabitants of the city of Samaria, sent for Peter and John, who when they came laid their hands upon them for the gift of the Holy Ghost; for as yet he was fallen upon none of them; and when Simon Magus saw that through the laying on of the Apostles' hands the Holy Ghost was given, he offered them money that he might possess the same power. (Acts 8.) These passages are considered by many as affording

sufficient evidence for some miraculous, visible manifestation, whenever hands are laid on for the gift of the Holy Ghost.

We believe that the Holy Ghost is imparted by the laying on of hands of those in authority, and that the gift of tongues, and also the gift of prophecy are gifts of the Spirit, and are obtained through that medium; but then to say that men always prophesied and spoke in tongues when they had the imposition of hands, would be to state that which is untrue, contrary to the practice of the Apostles, and at variance with holy writ; for Paul says, "To one is given the gift of tongues, to another the gift of prophecy, and to another the gift of healing;" and again: "Do all prophesy? do all speak with tongues? do all interpret?" evidently showing that all did not possess these several gifts; but that one received one gift, and another received another gift—all did not prophesy, all did not speak in tongues, all did not work miracles; but all did receive the gift of the Holy Ghost; sometimes they spake in tongues and prophesied in the Apostles' days, and sometimes they did not. The same is the case with us also in our administrations, while more frequently there is no manifestation at all; that is visible to the surrounding multitude; this will appear plain when we consult the writings of the Apostles, and notice their proceedings in relation to this matter. Paul, in 1st Cor. 12, says, "Now concerning spiritual gifts, brethren, I would not have you ignorant; " it is evident from this, that some of them were ignorant in relation to these matters, or they would not need instruction.

Again, in chapter 14, he says, "Follow after charity and desire spiritual gifts, but rather that ye may prophesy." It is very evident from these Scriptures that many of them had not spiritual gifts, for if they had spiritual gifts where was the necessity of Paul telling them to follow after them, and it is as evident that they did not all receive those gifts by the imposition of the hands; for they as a Church had been baptized and confirmed by the laying on of hands – and yet to a Church of this kind, under the immediate inspection and superintendency of the Apostles, it was necessary for Paul to say, "Follow after charity, and desire spiritual gifts, but rather that ye may prophesy," evidently showing that those gifts were in the Church, but not enjoyed by all in their outward manifestations.

But suppose the gifts of the Spirit were immediately, upon the imposition of hands, enjoyed by all, in all their fullness and power; the skeptic would still be as far from receiving any testimony except upon a mere casualty as before, for all the gifts of the Spirit are not visible to the natural vision, or understanding of man; indeed very few of them are. We read that "Christ ascended into heaven and gave gifts unto men; and He gave some Apostles, and some Prophets, and some Evangelists, and some Pastors and Teachers." (Eph. 4).

The Church is a compact body composed of different members, and is strictly analogous to the human system, and Paul, after speaking of the different gifts, says, "Now ye are the body of Christ and members in particular; and God hath set some in the Church, first Apostles, secondarily Prophets, thirdly Teachers, after that miracles, then gifts of healing, helps, governments, diversities of tongues. Are all Teachers? Are all workers of miracles? Do all speak with tongues? Do all interpret?" It is evident that they do not; yet are they all members of one body. All members of the natural body are not the eye, the ear, the head or the hand– yet the eye cannot say to the ear I have no need of thee, nor the head to the foot, I have no need of thee; they are all so many component parts in the perfect machine– the one body; and if one member suffer, the whole of the members suffer with it: and if one member rejoice, all the rest are honored with it.

These, then, are all gifts; they come from God; they are of God; they are all the gifts of the Holy Ghost; they are what Christ ascended into heaven to impart; and yet how few of them could be known by the generality of men. Peter and John were Apostles, yet the Jewish court scourged them as impostors. Paul was both an Apostle and Prophet, yet they stoned him and put him into prison. The people knew nothing about it, although he had in his possession the gift of the Holy Ghost. Our Savior was "anointed with the oil of gladness above his fellows," yet so far from the people knowing Him, they said He was Beelzebub, and crucified Him as an impostor. Who could point out a Pastor, a Teacher, or an Evangelist by their appearance, yet had they the gift of the Holy Ghost?

But to come to the other members of the Church, and examine the gifts as spoken of by Paul, and we shall find that the world can in general know nothing about them, and that there is but one or two that could be immediately known, if they were all poured out immediately upon the imposition of hands. In I. Cor. 12., Paul says, "There are diversities of gifts yet the same spirit, and there are differences of administrations but the same Lord; and there are diversities of operations, but it is the same God which worketh all in all. But the manifestations of the Spirit is given unto every man to profit withal. For to one is given, by the Spirit, the word of wisdom, to another, the word of knowledge by the same Spirit; to another faith, by the same Spirit; to another the gifts of healing, by the same Spirit; to another the working of miracles; to another prophecy; to another the discerning of spirits; to another divers kinds of tongues; to another the interpretation of tongues. But all these worketh that one and the self same spirit, dividing to each man severally as he will."

There are several gifts mentioned here, yet which of them all could be known by an observer at the imposition of hands? The word of wisdom, and the word of knowledge, are as much gifts as any other, yet if a person possessed both of these gifts, or received them by the imposition of hands, who would know it? Another might receive the gift of faith, and they would be as ignorant of it. Or suppose a man had the gift of healing or power to work miracles, that would not then be known; it would require time and circumstances to call these gifts into operation. Suppose a man had the discerning of spirits, who would be the wiser for it? Or if he had the interpretation of tongues, unless someone spoke in an unknown tongue, he of course would have to be silent; there are only two gifts that could be made visible – the gift of tongues and the gift of prophecy. These are things that are the most talked about, and yet if a person spoke in an unknown tongue, according to Paul's testimony, he would be a barbarian to those present. They would say that it was gibberish; and if he prophesied they would call it nonsense. The gift of tongues is the smallest gift perhaps of the whole, and yet it is one that is the most sought after. (*DHC* 5: 27-30.)

Some of these gifts are not always outwardly observable. But they are all inwardly detectable. If you have not experienced this, and cannot relate to these descriptions, then you should seek, pray, ponder and ask. Follow Nephi's example. That is why he wrote it. If you have not had or are not having these kinds of spiritual experiences, you should ask yourself why that is the case? Today is the day in which the Spirit is to be poured out on all flesh.[120]

The Notion That It Is Reserved To Men:

Interestingly, some people question whether women in particular are entitled to these gifts. The answer is "yes," and one further illustration may be helpful, although there are many others which might also be cited. Recall the incident involving Hagar. She was Egyptian, the handmaiden of Sarah, and sent away with Ishmael into the wilderness. As she "lift[ed] up her voice, and wept" (Gen. 21: 16), we read that "the angel of God called to Hagar out of heaven, and said unto her, What aileth thee, Hagar? fear not; for God hath heard … And God opened her eyes, and she saw a well of water," from which hers and her son's lives were spared. (Gen. 21: 17, 19.) God calling to her, by name, and providing water through which life is restored to both her and her son, shows God's broad willingness to minister to all. He is liberal to all. It is only us who would make Him less so.

The Notion That It Is Reserved To Leaders:

There is a notion among some Saints that these things are reserved for Church leaders holding high office. That false notion is so widespread it deserves special notice here. Anything that wrong and pervasive deserves mention in its own right.

It is unclear where this notion began. Perhaps it originates with the charge given by Oliver Cowdery to the original Quorum of the Twelve Apostles. That charge has been given anew to subsequently ordained Apostles. It is found in the History of the Church, and has been referred to earlier in these materials. An excerpt from that charge is given again

---

[120]You will recall Moroni's quoting of Joel 2: 28: "And it shall come to pass afterward, that I will pour out my spirit upon all flesh; and your sons and your daughters shall prophesy, your old men shall dream dreams, your young men shall see visions:" which we have previously discussed.

here because of its importance. Oliver charged the first Quorum of Twelve with these words:

> You have been indebted to other men, in the first instance, for evidence; on that you have acted; but it is necessary that you receive a testimony from heaven for yourselves; so that you can bear testimony to the truth of the Book of Mormon, and that you have seen the face of God. That is more than the testimony of an angel. When the proper time arrives, you shall be able to bear this testimony to the world. When you bear testimony that you have seen God, this testimony God will never suffer to fall, but will bear you out; although many will not give heed, yet others will. You will therefore see the necessity of getting this testimony from heaven.
>
> Never cease striving until you have seen God face to face. Strengthen your faith; cast off your doubts, your sins, and all your unbelief; and nothing can prevent you from coming to God. Your ordination is not full and complete till God has laid His hand upon you. We require as much to qualify us as did those who have gone before us; God is the same. If the Savior in former days laid His hands upon His disciples, why not in latter days?" (*DHC* 2: 195-196.)

This charge gives members of the Quorum of the Twelve a special commission to seek for the Second Comforter.[121] However, it does not

---

[121]President Joseph F. Smith, in a General Conference talk given April 6, 1916 (found in Improvement Era 19: 646-652, May, 1916; and also in volume 5 of the *Messages of the First Presidency*, complied by James Clark) affirmed: "For instance, these twelve disciples of Christ are supposed to be eye and ear witnesses of the divine mission of Jesus Christ. It is not permissible for them to say, I believe, simply; I have accepted it, simply because I believe it. Read the revelation. The Lord informs us they must know, they must get the knowledge for themselves, it must be with them as if they had seen with their eyes and heard with their ears, and they know the truth. That is their mission, to testify of Jesus Christ and him crucified and risen from the dead and clothed now with almighty power at the right hand of God, the Savior of the world. That is their mission, and their duty; and that is the doctrine and the truth, that is their duty to preach to the world, and see that it is preached to the world." (*Messages of the First Presidency of The Church of Jesus Christ of Latter-*

say it is inapplicable to others, or is reserved to the Twelve alone. The extension of this charge into the notion it is an exclusively identified and limited body who is entitled to receive these things, if that is where the notion originated, has come gradually. But today it is a commonly held view by many Saints and even finds its way into written materials from prominent LDS authors.

A good example of a recent text contending for exclusivity, but by no means the only recent place to suggest it, discusses Nephi's desire to know the mysteries of God[122] and makes a comment on this as follows: "It is significant to me that Nephi specifically says here that he desired 'to know the mysteries of God' (1 Nephi 2: 16). While all are invited to seek and all are promised knowledge (1 Nephi 15: 8; Matthew 7: 7; Moroni 10: 4-5), **this is not an open invitation for all men and women to seek 'mysteries' beyond the declarative words of the prophets.**" (*Glimpses of Lehi's Jerusalem*; Provo, Utah: FARMS, 2004; at p. 435, emphasis added.) The author[123] cites no authority for this limiting and elitist assertion. How seeking knowledge or mysteries has been limited to "the declarative words of the prophets" is unexplained. The author has apparently confused the limitation on revelation for the whole Church (which is restricted) with personal revelation and witness (which is unrestricted).

In contrast to this limiting and exclusivist assertion, the Prophet Joseph Smith taught: "it is your privilege to purify yourselves and come up to the same glory, and see for yourselves, and know for yourselves. Ask, and it shall be given you; seek and ye shall find; knock, and it shall be opened unto you." (*TPJS*, p. 13.) Joseph did not envy the Saints

---

day Saints, 6 vols. Compiled by James R. Clark. Salt Lake City: Bookcraft, 1965-75.)

[122]Referring to 1 Ne. 2: 16; which we discussed earlier in this text.

[123]This particular article in the book was authored by John Welch. He is not unique in this view, however, and is reflecting a widespread notion rather than advancing a position uniquely his. So he does not deserve to be singled out as a proponent for he is only one of many who do so.

receiving revelation for themselves. Instead, he encouraged it. Many of his instructions to the Saints were to assist them in seeking and receiving their own revelations.

In another place, while trying to help the Saints grow to the point where they could receive the Second Comforter, Joseph taught:

> The Spirit of Revelation is in connection with these blessings. A person may profit by noticing the first intimation of the spirit of revelation; for instance, when you feel pure intelligence flowing into you, it may give you sudden strokes of ideas, so that by noticing it, you may find it fulfilled the same day or soon; (i.e.) those things that were presented unto your minds by the Spirit of God, will come to pass; and thus by learning the Spirit of God and understanding it, you may grow into the principle of revelation, until you become perfect in Christ Jesus. *(TPJS*, p. 151.)

This helpful instruction was intended to assist any Saint in their quest to receive the Second Comforter. It was not limited to a particular position or Quorum of the Church. It was universal in its application.

In another sermon to the Saints, Joseph exhorted the Saints to receive their calling and elections made sure in these words: "Then I would exhort you to go on and continue to call upon God until you make your calling and election sure for yourselves; by obtaining this more sure word of prophecy, and wait patiently for the promise until you obtain it." *(TPJS*, p. 299.)

Furthermore, the teaching of Alma on the subject of receiving "mysteries" has no limitation on who can receive, or what can be received. The limitation is not as to person or subject. Rather, it is limited because of obedience and faithfulness on the part of the one receiving. Look again at Alma's words we considered earlier:

> It is given unto **many** to know the mysteries of God; nevertheless they are laid under a strict command that they shall not impart only according to the portion of his word which he doth grant unto the children of men, according to the heed and

diligence which they give unto him. And, therefore, he that will harden his heart, the same receiveth the lesser portion of the word; and **he that will not harden his heart, to him is given the greater portion of the word**, until it is given unto him to know the mysteries of God until he know them in full. And they that will harden their hearts, to them is given the lesser portion of the word until they know nothing concerning his mysteries... (Alma 12: 9-11 emphasis added.)

There is no limitation on who can receive, based upon office. Rather, the limitation is based upon the hardness of each individual's heart. You are as welcome to come up to the principle of revelation and partake as anyone who has ever obtained these things. But they are to be received in accordance with certain principles. They are not obtained apart from the conditions which universally apply to all mankind. If you are willing to abide the conditions to receive them, by giving "heed and diligence" to the requirements, then you are welcome to come and receive them for yourself.

The notion some exclusive or limited body alone holds the right to receive these things is false. There is a true doctrine limiting who may declare new doctrine to the Church. But **no** such limit exists applicable to who may learn, or see, or know, or experience, or witness the glory and mysteries of God.

Moroni (quoting his father) asks: "[H]ave miracles ceased? Behold I say unto you, Nay; neither have angels ceased to minister unto the children of men. For behold, they are subject unto him, to minister according to the word of his command, showing themselves unto them of strong faith and a firm mind in every form of godliness. And the office of their ministry is to call men unto repentance, and to fulfil and to do the work of the covenants of the Father, which he hath made unto the children of men, to prepare the way among the children of men, by declaring the word of Christ **unto the chosen vessels** of the Lord, that they may bear testimony of him. And by so doing, the Lord God prepareth the way **that the residue of men may have faith in** Christ, that the Holy Ghost may have place in their hearts, according to the power thereof; and after this manner bringeth to pass the Father, the covenants which he hath made unto the children of men." (Moroni. 7: 29-32, emphasis added.) Some have read this passage to mean that the "chosen vessels" are a limited number of Church leaders. Similarly, the "residue of men" are the balance of the Church. However, this limited interpretation is precluded by Alma's teaching about the scope of angels' ministry. They have never come exclusively to leaders. They come to all. As Alma teaches: "And now, he imparteth his word by angels unto men, yea, not only men but women also. Now this is not all; little children do have words given unto them many times, which confound the wise and the learned." (Alma 32: 23.) Accordingly, the proper definition of "chosen vessel" is not a Church office, but, rather, whoever is visited. Whether the person is a "man" (as in the case of Paul when he held **no** Church office at the time and yet was visited on the road to Damascus) or "woman" (as in the case of the first one to receive the Second Comforter outside His tomb on the morning of His resurrection) or "child" (as in the case of the Nephite visit, discussed in the next chapter), the term "chosen vessel" applies to anyone and everyone to whom Christ ministers as Second Comforter. It will apply to you when you receive Him.

So if you are black or white, bond or free, male or female, young or old, so long as you are living , you are entitled. Joel prophesied of it. Moroni said it was shortly to come to pass. Joseph taught it. Christ wanted us to have more than just a form of godliness lacking power. All things point to your entitlement to these things. Ask! Seek! Knock! Receive! Have it opened to you! See His face and know that He lives! It is your right as a Latter-day Saint. That right belongs to us all. The "keeper of the gate"[124] is not a Church leader, political figure, college

---

[124] 2 Ne 9: 41: "O then, my beloved brethren, come unto the Lord, the Holy One. Remember that his paths are righteous. Behold, the way for man is narrow, but it lieth in a straight course before him, and the keeper of the gate is the Holy One of Israel; and he employeth no servant there; and there is none other way save it be by the gate; for he cannot be deceived, for the Lord God is his name."

professor or someone with a professional credential. The "keeper" is our Lord, and He welcomes us all as we abide His conditions.

Chapter Eight

SELF SELECTION

As a first year law student at BYU, I had the Torts class in a large section taught by Professor Carl S. Hawkins. He co-authored the text for the class,[125] and we assumed he was an absolute authority on the subject. He disagreed with Professor Prosser's[126] approach of teaching "proximate cause" analysis, and instead taught a conceptual framework involving "duty-risk" analysis.

In law school only a single exam is given in a class. A student attends the entire semester without any clue as to whether or not the subject is being understood; then a final exam accounts for the entire

---

[125]*Cases on the Law of Torts, Second Edition*; West Publishing Company, © 1977, by Leon Green, Willard Pedrick, James Rahl, Wayne Thode, Carl Hawkins, Allen Smith and James Treece.

[126]Prosser's text: "Prosser, *Law of Torts* (3d Edition), was a competitive text teaching a different form of analysis. Prosser's was the majority approach in law school teaching. His methods were criticized during our classes for their analytical failings and general incoherence.

grade. If the subject was not understood, then this is discovered when the exam is failed. So getting some security during the semester comes from cooperative feedback among students as they grope about in the dark together.

Professor Hawkins' class was particularly mystifying. We studied cases in which the judges wrote their opinions in terms of "proximate cause," but our professor would convert that into language of "duty-risk" analysis. It was like taking German and using a Spanish text.

As the semester progressed there was an increasing fog over the entire subject. Among the students there was near universal panic and confusion. This was one of the mandatory subjects, and you couldn't graduate without passing it.

The cases seemed to talk in contradiction to our professor's instruction. And what our professor did was alien to other classes, as well. The Socratic Method, used generally in law school was not employed in this class. Instead, Professor Hawkins would lecture and illustrate by example. On occasion, a student would be asked to recite a case, but instead of being asked to defend the case's holding or rationale, the Professor would take over and give his analysis. It seemed as though the course materials were going to scratch our eyes out.

It was the last few weeks of the class, and we were satisfied with our progress everywhere but in Torts. There only darkness and confusion reigned. Some of us discussed talking with Dean Lee[127] and asking for his intervention. Just at the time of this greatest alarm, things changed.

Professor Hawkins was proceeding in a manner which he had refined and perfected over a career of teaching the law. Just as the

---

[127]Rex E. Lee, Dean of the J. Reuben Clark Law School at BYU, and later Solicitor General of the United States. He was the founding Dean of the Law School and taught Constitutional Law during my time there.

closing weeks were brought together, so, too, the materials came together. It was semi-miraculous how the class ended with a flood of light on the subject. The confusion and difficulty, which had scratched our eyes out, now scratched them in again. The text materials which had previously seemed so alien, now took on a harmony and coherence putting it into magisterial construct of harmony, subtlety and nuance. Instead of the disharmonious cacophony that had reigned earlier, we now heard the music. Professor Hawkins was a brilliant educator and taught Torts with such effectiveness that now, over thirty-two years later, his words still echo in the minds of those lucky enough to have been his students.

Carl Hawkins is not the Lord. The Lord is a far better educator, and knows much better how to scratch our eyes out, and then scratch them in again. What I finally learned was that Professor Hawkins prepared me to pass a much more difficult exam.

The Gospel has a similar vagueness to its precepts as you press into them further and further. Things seem to fly apart as you look at them most carefully. How can you be a sinner, utterly reliant upon grace to save you, and also be required to be "perfect" as Christ demanded? How can we be judged according to our works, as we are reminded by Christ and John the Revelator, and yet have our "goodness" likened by Isaiah to "filthy rags?" We can covenant to live the Law of Consecration, but we don't even attempt to implement it in the Church. Even if you are most sincere and devout, you are reminded again and again that you aren't good enough and you aren't going to be good enough without a considerable borrowing from Christ's Atonement to cure your deficiencies. These things can and are read by observant students of the Gospel as disharmonious. The cacophony reigning at one level, must precede hearing the music.

At least this is required in our Western minds. Perhaps an Eastern mind may bypass it. But our culture imposes this difficulty upon us. Our culture "wants" us to go through this. And so we do.

In the aftermath of Christ's crucifixion, the American continent experienced a great upheaval. The earth itself mourned the Savior's death.[128] The Nephite record records the tempests and earthquakes began "in the first month, on the fourth day of the month." (3 Ne. 8: 5.) This calamity lasted for about three hours.[129] It was followed by three days of darkness.[130] Thereafter, the Nephite record is silent for approximately 11 months.

The record, which after the seventh day of the year (the calamities begin on the fourth day of the year, and last for three days) then resumes eleven months later.[131] When it resumes, there is an account of the people who have migrated to Bountiful to celebrate the season's festivals. This is the year end. Although life has not quite resumed

---

[128]The sentience of the earth is attested to in Moses 7: 48: "And it came to pass that Enoch looked upon the earth; and he heard a voice from the bowels thereof, saying: Wo, wo is me, the mother of men; I am pained, I am weary, because of the wickedness of my children. When shall I rest, and be cleansed from the filthiness which is gone forth out of me? When will my Creator sanctify me, that I may rest, and righteousness for a season abide upon my face?"

[129]3 Ne. 8: 19: "And it came to pass that when the thunderings, and the lightenings, and the storm, and the tempest, and the quakings of the earth did cease – for behold, they **did last for about the space of three hours**; and it was said by some that the time was greater; nevertheless, all these great and terrible things were **done in about the space of three hours…**" (Emphasis added.)

[130]3 Ne. 8: 23: "And it came to pass that it did last for the space of three days that there was no light seen; and there was great mourning and howling and weeping among the people continually; yea, great were the groanings of the people, because of the darkness and the great destruction which had come upon them."

[131]3 Ne. 10: 18: "And it came to pass that **in the ending of the thirty and fourth year**, behold, I will show unto you that the people of Nephi who were spared, and also those who had been called Lamanites, who had been spared, did have great favors shown unto them, and great blessings poured out upon their heads, insomuch that soon after the ascension of Christ into heaven he did truly manifest himself unto them—" (Emphasis added.)

normalcy, there is a band of pilgrims who come to Bountiful to celebrate the season despite the difficulty they encounter in the process.

We know they are pilgrims to the area because of their reaction to the changes. As the record recounts: "And now it came to pass that there were a great multitude gathered together, of the people of Nephi, round about the temple which was in the land Bountiful; and they were marveling and wondering one with another, and were showing one to another the great and marvelous change which had taken place." (3 Ne. 11: 1.) If they were residents of Bountiful, these great changes would have become less noteworthy over the preceding eleven months. Since they had only recently returned to Bountiful, however, these changes were exceptional to them and they were pointing them out to each other. All these things had changed since their last visit to the Temple town.

What is about to happen at the Temple in Bountiful is one of the greatest events of all history. These people are about to see the risen Lord and record the most extended account of the Second Comforter's visit available. Perhaps there have been other visits similar in scope. This is the greatest account we have any record of, however. But before looking at the event itself, it is important to note just **who** was involved in the events.

There were certainly local residents of Bountiful who would be among the witnesses of the Lord's appearance. But for the most part, the people appear to be comprised of those who had weathered the difficulties of coming to Bountiful to celebrate the festival season of the year's end. These people were from other places and newly arrived. The participants were so recent that, as we noted above, they were showing each other the landscape changes that had occurred since their last visit. They had come to the Temple precinct to be present at the year's end for some worthy observance. This original purpose is neglected in the record, because of what is about to happen.

This audience for Christ's coming is interesting to contemplate. It is comprised of people who self-selected. They came to observe their normal religious duties. And as a result of that intention and commit-ment, they are present for a much greater event.

Doing the Lord's everyday work is more important than it may seem at times. This example from the Lord's visit with the Nephites illustrates the point wonderfully. By routinely going to the Temple and keeping some observance commanded of them, as the year ended, these faithful people are selected by the Lord for His personal visit. They become heirs of the Second Comforter. They chose themselves by choosing the Lord, and so the Lord chooses them.

There is a powerful lesson in this for all of us. How the Lord finds you spending your time is important to whether He can visit with you or not. Had they not come to Bountiful on this occasion, they would not have had an audience with the risen Christ.

Think about the two others who met the mortal Lord in the Temple. Simeon and Anna saw the Lord because they too went up to the Temple when He was to be there.[132] The right kind of life puts you in the right place at the right time to receive the Second Comforter. They are all related to each other. The harmony of time, place and

---

[132] "And he came by the Spirit into the temple: and when the parents brought in the child Jesus, to do for him after the custom of the law, Then took he him up in his arms, and blessed God, and said, Lord, now lettest thou thy servant depart in peace, according to thy word: For mine eyes have seen thy salvation, Which thou hast prepared before the face of all people; A light to lighten the Gentiles, and the glory of thy people Israel. And Joseph and his mother marvelled at those things which were spoken of him. And Simeon blessed them, and said unto Mary his mother, Behold, this child is set for the fall and rising again of many in Israel; and for a sign which shall be spoken against; (Yea, a sword shall pierce through thy own soul also,) that the thoughts of many hearts may be revealed. And there was one Anna, a prophetess, the daughter of Phanuel, of the tribe of Aser: she was of a great age, and had lived with an husband seven years from her virginity; And she was a widow of about fourscore and four years, which departed not from the temple, but served God with fastings and prayers night and day. And she coming in that instant gave thanks likewise unto the Lord, and spake of him to all them that looked for redemption in Jerusalem. And when they had performed all things according to the law of the Lord, they returned into Galilee, to their own city Nazareth." (Luke 2: 27-39.)

person are the product of right choices in our lives.

These people chose to come to the land of Bountiful. That is a universal truth applicable to every one who receives the Second Comforter. They all (including you) must choose. It is not the Lord alone who makes the choice. It is also the person being visited who chooses, as well. Faithfulness in a few things precedes receiving many things.[133]

The Book of Mormon is a deliberate record trying to teach us what we lack. It answers many questions in a clear and unmistakable way. We must be willing only to see what it is saying to receive its teachings. Here it is saying you should keep the commandments, the everyday commandments, so the Lord may find you doing what He has asked, and thereby reward you with His presence.[134]

The self-assembled group at Bountiful is present when the Father announces the Son. The Father speaks, but the crowd cannot hear Him. He speaks again, but again they are unable to receive what He is offering to them. He speaks a third time, and then the audience can understand.[135] The record states: "And again the third time they did hear

---

[133]Matt. 25: 21: "His lord said unto him, Well done, thou good and faithful servant: thou hast been faithful over a few things, I will make thee ruler over many things: enter thou into the joy of thy lord." Being faithful in attending religious observances (home teaching, visiting teaching, sacrament meetings, Temple attendance, and such things) is how you position yourself to be faithful over a few things. This faithfulness in a few things must come, as this teaching of the Lord's suggests, before you "enter into the joy of thy lord."

[134]Christ suggested this everyday obedience with His teaching of the unexpectedly returning master. "Therefore be ye also ready: for in such an hour as ye think not the Son of man cometh. Who then is a faithful and wise servant, whom his lord hath made ruler over his household, to give them meat in due season? Blessed is that servant, whom his lord when he cometh shall find so doing." (Matt. 24: 44-46.)

[135]This need to call us three times is consistent in the teachings of the Gospel ordinances. Anyone who has been through the Temple endowment will recognize the three times God calls to Adam. We have placed ourselves

the voice, and did open their ears to hear it; and their eyes were towards the sound thereof; and they did look steadfastly towards heaven, from whence the sound came." (3 Ne. 11: 5.) This difference between the first two calls from Father when they could not hear, to the third time when they do hear, is accounted for in the audience's **willingness** to hear. They "did open their ears to hear it." They elected to listen the third time.

Though we are separated three levels from our Father in Heaven, it is us, and not He, who determines when we are willing finally to listen and hear Him. God is in all things.[136] We elect to hear, or not to hear. Similarly, we elect to see or not to see. In that sense, we self-select whether we are among the "elect" by whether we are willing to receive what God is offering freely to us all. We have far more involvement than John Calvin ever imagined.[137]

---

three degrees of Glory from our Father. (See, e.g., D&C Section 76.) For that gulf which we have imposed, He must reach down three levels to reach us. And we, in turn, must reach up three levels to Him.

[136]"He comprehendeth all things, and all things are before him, and all things are round about him; and he is above all things, and **in all things, and is through all things, and is round about all things**; and all things are by him, and of him, even God, forever and ever." (D&C 88: 41, emphasis added.) We should be able to see Him in His handiwork. As it is explained in D&C 88: 45-49: " The earth rolls upon her wings, and the sun giveth his light by day, and the moon giveth her light by night, and the stars also give their light, as they roll upon their wings in their glory, in the midst of the power of God. Unto what shall I liken these kingdoms, that ye may understand? Behold, all these are kingdoms, and any man who hath seen any or the least of these hath seen God moving in his majesty and power. I say unto you, he hath seen him; nevertheless, he who came unto his own was not comprehended. The light shineth in darkness, and the darkness comprehendeth it not; nevertheless, the day shall come when you shall comprehend even God, being quickened in him and by him." Until you can see Him in these things, you are not ready to see Him in His person.

[137]One of Calvin's tenets was "irresistible grace" which meant God was responsible for electing us to salvation, not us. In this tenet he couldn't be more wrong.

First, you see with an "eye of faith" and then by the eyes themselves.[138] The faith to see precedes seeing. This is also true here in the account of the visit to the Nephites. Until they were willing to hear, they could not hear. And it is the same, too, for you.

The account of the Savior's visit among the Nephites is extensive and instructive in many ways beyond the scope of this work. Some of it relates directly to the subject, and will be covered here. But the entire account has many insights which are unavailable elsewhere and are worthy of your own careful and prayerful study. No commentary presently exists which develops the materials in their true light. The Book of Mormon remains largely a "sealed book" even after the better part of two centuries.[139] Perhaps you will be among those who will do something meaningful about that.[140]

---

[138]This is set out in the following passage: "And there were many whose faith was so exceedingly strong, even before Christ came, who could not be kept from within the veil, but truly saw with their eyes the things which they had beheld with an eye of faith, and they were glad." (Ether 12:19.) Development of the faith to see within the veil comes after having first seen "with an eye of faith."

[139]This is as was predicted by the Book, itself. 2 Ne. 3: 12: "Wherefore, the fruit of thy loins shall write; and the fruit of the loins of Judah shall write; and that which shall be written by the fruit of thy loins, and also that which shall be written by the fruit of the loins of Judah, **shall grow together**, unto the confounding of false doctrines and laying down of contentions, and establishing peace among the fruit of thy loins, and bringing them to the knowledge of their fathers in the latter days, and also to the knowledge of my covenants, saith the Lord." (Emphasis added.) This describes a process of growth, which inevitably involves time. Nothing about the Book of Mormon was intended to spring fully and completely to view at the start of the dispensation. Rather, it was predicted to take time as the process unfolded and the understanding "grew together" of these things. This work remains in front of us, and is still largely undone.

[140]At present; the primary effort by LDS commentators consists in the rather modest accomplishment of showing the book's antiquity. Many volumes of intense scholarly work aim at this rather mundane objective. What the Book of Mormon teaches, on the other hand, has been covered by only the most superficial of treatment.

The Lord appears after the Father's introduction of Him. The account from 3 Ne. 11: 6-8 reads:

> And behold, the third time they did understand the voice which they heard; and it said unto them: Behold my Beloved Son, in whom I am well pleased, in whom I have glorified my name – hear ye him. And it came to pass, as they understood they cast their eyes up again towards heaven; and behold, they saw a Man descending out of heaven; and he was clothed in a white robe; and he came down and stood in the midst of them; and the eyes of the whole multitude were turned upon him, and they durst not open their mouths, even one to another, and wist not what it meant, for they thought it was an angel that had appeared unto them. (vs. 6-8.)

This account shows that the audience finally hears what the Father was saying. They understood they were about to behold His Son. After this introduction, a person appears and descends from heaven. Yet, when the person appears, "they thought it was an angel that had appeared unto them."

Despite the introduction of the Son by the Father, the audience is not able to see Him as the Son of God at His appearing. There is nothing in the person which demands He be worshipped. Rather, His countenance is so unremarkable to them they conclude He is an angel.

This is consistent with the Lord's humility in showing Himself to others, elsewhere.[141] He does not demand He be accepted by the glory

---

[141] The account of the Lord's appearing to the disciples on the road to Emmaus tells of His appearing there while not displaying any glory or reason for worship. Instead, He appears as any man would, with His identity hidden by their eyes being "holden." The account reads, in relevant part: "And, behold, two of them went that same day to a village called Emmaus, which was from Jerusalem about threescore furlongs. And they talked together of all these things which had happened. And it came to pass, that, while they communed together and reasoned, Jesus himself drew near, and went with them. But their eyes were holden that they should not know him. And he said unto them, What manner of communications are these that ye have one to another, as ye walk, and are sad? And the one of them, whose name was

of His personage.[142] Rather, He commands worship by the content of His teachings. In this He is perfectly consistent with the standards which He expects us to follow. We, like Him, should not expect others to accept what we say or teach based upon our status or standing.[143]

Cleopas, answering said unto him, Art thou only a stranger in Jerusalem, and hast not known the things which are come to pass there in these days? And he said unto them, What things? And they said unto him, Concerning Jesus of Nazareth, which was a prophet mighty in deed and word before God and all the people: And how the chief priests and our rulers delivered him to be condemned to death, and have crucified him. But we trusted that it had been he which should have redeemed Israel: and beside all this, to day is the third day since these things were done. ... Then he said unto them, O fools, and slow of heart to believe all that the prophets have spoken: Ought not Christ to have suffered these things, and to enter into his glory? And beginning at Moses and all the prophets, he expounded unto them in all the scriptures the things concerning himself. ... And it came to pass, as he sat at meat with them, he took bread, and blessed it, and brake, and gave to them. And their eyes were opened, and they knew him; and he vanished out of their sight. And they said one to another, **Did not our heart burn within us, while he talked with us** by the way, and while he opened to us the scriptures?" (Luke 24: 13-21, 25-27, 30-32, emphasis added.) The Lord in this appearing does not display anything to the senses to convert or impress the disciples. Rather, it is what He teaches them that makes their hearts burn within, as a witness to them that He speaks the truth.

[142]The Lord can certainly appear in a form distinctly recognizable as a Being of Glory. He did this in the Kirtland Temple, where it is recorded about Him that: "We saw the Lord standing upon the breastwork of the pulpit, before us; and under his feet was a paved work of pure gold, in color like amber. His eyes were as a flame of fire; the hair of his head was white like the pure snow; his countenance shone above the brightness of the sun; and his voice was as the sound of the rushing of great waters, even the voice of Jehovah," (D&C 110: 2-3.) He can, if He chooses, appear "above the brightness of the sun." But there is nothing which requires Him to do so. The fact that He elects not to do so is a powerful revelation about Him. He intends for us to accept Him on the basis of what He teaches, and not merely to cower before Him.

[143]As He directs the priesthood, the presiding authority in His Church: "No power or influence can or ought to be maintained by virtue of the priesthood, only by persuasion, by long-suffering, by gentleness and meekness,

Rather, it is the content of the Spirit within the message we teach which determines whether we have anything of worth to offer.[144]

The Nephites watch this person who has descended to them, without knowing who, or indeed what, He was. As they watch and listen, He speaks to them and defines who He is: "And it came to pass that he stretched forth his hand and spake unto the people, saying: Behold, I am Jesus Christ, whom the prophets testified shall come into the world. And behold, I am the light and the life of the world; and I have drunk out of that bitter cup which the Father hath given me, and have glorified the Father in taking upon me the sins of the world, in the which I have suffered the will of the Father in all things from the beginning." (3 Ne. 11: 9-11.) Here is Christ's definition of who He is. In two short verses He defines Himself using "the Father" three times. He drank out of the bitter cup "the Father" gave to Him. He glorified "the Father" in taking upon Him the sins of the world. And He suffered the will of "the Father" in all things from the beginning. This is how the Lord defines Himself. It is a pretty good definition of what He would like us to be as well, with the obvious exception of taking the world's sins upon us.[145]

At His introduction, the Nephites realize at last who it is speaking to them. They then worship Him. However, the worship at this point is described merely as "the whole multitude fell to the earth." (3 Ne. 11: 12.) This is in stark contrast to their worship which is to follow in a few moments. It begins with recognition. It turns into shouts for joy. He is,

and by love unfeigned;" (D&C 121: 41.)

[144]D&C 42: 14 contains this injunction to teachers in the Church: "And the Spirit shall be given unto you by the prayer of faith; and if ye receive not the Spirit ye shall not teach." Unfortunately, this is oftentimes ignored by people who teach without the Spirit. They, of course, will ultimately be called into account for that by the Lord. (See, e.g., Alma 12: 14.)

[145]However, even there we are expected to show "charity" and not to judge. This requires us to be types of Him in this respect, as well. This is discussed further, below, as we cover "Types of Christ in Our Lives."

despite what others may have told you, a most joyful countenance to behold.

He bids them to arise. He directs: "Arise and come forth unto me, that ye may thrust your hands into my side, and also that ye may feel the prints of the nails in my hands and in my feet, that ye may know that I am the God of Israel, and the God of the whole earth, and have been slain for the sins of the world." (*Id.*, v. 14.) In response, "the multitude went forth, and thrust their hands into his side, and did feel the prints of the nails in his hands and in his feet; and this they did do, going forth one by one until they had all gone forth, and did see with their eyes and did feel with their hands, and did know of a surety and did bear record, that it was he, of whom it was written by the prophets, that should come." (*Id.*, v. 15.)

He tells them to come, one by one, to feel the wounds in His side, and hands, and feet. "One by one" is how He directs. No person who is present is to have this witness through another. All of them are to be equally qualified as witnesses of Him. There is nothing vicarious about this meeting.[146] They are asked to perform a ceremony of recognition and witnessing. They first feel His side. To do this they must embrace the Lord, for you cannot feel His side without embracing Him. Embracing Him is an essential part of the ceremony of recognition. Ceremony and holiness are connected with each other. Recognize you are reading about a ceremony, as all encounters involved with God are in one way or another.

---

[146]Every person will be given this same experience at some point. As the scriptures record in 2 Ne. 9: 41: "O then, my beloved brethren, come unto the Lord, the Holy One. Remember that his paths are righteous. Behold, the way for man is narrow, but it lieth in a straight course before him, and the keeper of the gate is the Holy One of Israel; and he employeth no servant there; and there is none other way save it be by the gate; for he cannot be deceived, for the Lord God is his name." This statement by Nephi concerns the final judgment. But it needn't be delayed. He is the One through whom salvation comes. And He employs no servant to do these things. This encounter can be here, now, in mortality.

Having embraced the Lord and felt His side, the witnesses are asked to take a step back and feel His hands. Feeling the Lord's hands is also a part of this ceremonial process. At an arm's length, holding His hands, you feel the marks of the nails.

Then, having touched these sacred emblems of the Atonement, you are permitted to kneel, and feel the prints in His feet. This part of the ceremony is the easiest for men to observe. For kneeling at His feet is the natural position for anyone who has witnessed for themselves the price He paid on their behalf and feels the love within Him.

This is ceremony, and this is ritual, but it employs such rich witnesses in the body of the Lord as to be convincing beyond all doubt that He is the Christ, the Anointed One, the Deliverer, and the Holy One of Israel!

The Nephite record continues: "And when they had all gone forth and had witnessed for themselves, they did cry out with one accord, saying: Hosanna! Blessed be the name of the Most High God! And they did fall down at the feet of Jesus, and did worship him." (3 Ne. 11: 16-17.) No mere kneeling this! Now we have a form of worship in contrast to the kneeling before. Here is enthusiasm and gratitude indeed! Here is worship indeed! Accompanied by the Hosanna Shout, given in spontaneous reaction to Our Lord!

The purpose of this is to let the people know Christ. They "did see with their eyes and did feel with their hands, and did know of a surety and did bear record" of Christ. (*Id.*, v. 15.) This is eternal life, you see. "And this is life eternal, that they might know thee the only true God, and Jesus Christ, whom thou hast sent." (John 17: 3.) Christ is making eternal life possible for these people in the record. More importantly, however, the record is a universal appeal to all to come and partake of eternal life. It is not just a description of things long ago involving people long since dead. It is a description of what, how and who we worship now.

Every one of this Nephite audience was personally involved in this testimony and experience. Every one of them was individually brought to this knowledge. This involved more than two-thousand five-hundred people.[147] Significantly, it involved men, women and children.[148] All are invited. All are equal before the Lord.[149] You are as welcome as any who have received these things. And you are equally entitled,[150] provided you abide by the conditions which apply to these things.

Why were these twenty-five hundred witnesses of Christ chosen? The answer is they were where they should be (in Bountiful, near a surviving Temple) doing what they should be doing (preparing to celebrate the year end festivals). They chose themselves by doing what they should be doing, where they should be doing it. It is not the Lord who makes arbitrary choices. It is His children who elect to be and do what they are asked, and thereby qualify themselves. All are alike to God. But some abide the conditions and the rest do not. Anyone could abide the conditions. Only a few decide to do so. Those who do are self-selecting themselves to receive the things being offered to all of us.

This encounter has a good deal more to offer us in understanding worship of God. After the first day ends, Christ ascends to heaven. He returns for a second day, and people have now been gathering overnight to join those who had been there for His first appearance. In the second day's visit, the Lord enacts a sacred ceremony before the assembled throng which reveals much about true worship and passing through the veil to the presence of the Father.

---

[147]3 Ne. 17: 25: "And the multitude did see and hear and bear record; and they know that their record is true for they all of them did see and hear, every man for himself; and they were in number about two thousand and five hundred souls; and they did consist of men, women, and children."

[148]*Id.*

[149]"...he inviteth them all to come unto him and partake of his goodness; and he denieth none that come unto him, black and white, bond and free, male and female; and he remembereth the heathen; and all are alike unto God, both Jew and Gentile." (2 Ne. 26:33.)

[150]D&C 38: 16: "...all flesh is mine, and I am no respecter of persons."

During the first day, Christ taught His Sermon. In the New Testament it is called the Sermon on the Mount. In the Book of Mormon it is called the Sermon at Bountiful. They differ somewhat from each other,[151] but the differences are not relevant, here. This sermon had been recorded by the Lord's chosen twelve disciples overnight,[152] and they each taught that sermon to the assembled multitude the second day.

After teaching the multitude, the disciples separated themselves from the multitude and went into the water. The Nephites already practiced baptism, probably from the time Lehi was originally in Jerusalem. When Lehi expounded on his vision of the tree of life, he elaborated to include a prophecy about the one who would go before Christ and baptize Him.[153] This passing mention of the coming baptism

[151]The Sermon at Bountiful is plainly superior. The differences are worth study but cannot be addressed here.

[152]The disciples taught the very same words to the crowd. 3 Ne. 19: 8: "And when they had ministered those same words which Jesus had spoken – nothing varying from the words which Jesus had spoken – behold, they knelt again and prayed to the Father in the name of Jesus." This seems to indicate they had labored to record the sermon during the night, and were thereby equipped uniformly to teach the same words, "nothing varying" in their texts. To view this account otherwise would require an interpretation which involved almost superhuman memory, or a Divine intervention to accomplish the feat. And such Divine intervention would have been unnecessary had the disciples collaborated on preserving the text by their own labors. The Lord rarely (if ever) does for us what we are able to do for ourselves. Therefore, the most likely meaning is that the disciples had worked together overnight to get the text recorded by their applied collective efforts and then each one used that text to teach the sermon the following day.

[153]Nephi recorded that his father said, concerning John the Baptist; "Yea, even he should go forth and cry in the wilderness: Prepare ye the way of the Lord, and make his paths straight; for there standeth one among you whom ye know not; and he is mightier than I, whose shoe's latchet I am not worthy to unloose. And much spake my father concerning this thing. And my father said he should baptize in Bethabara, beyond Jordan; and he also said he should baptize with water; even that he should baptize the Messiah with water. And after he had baptized the Messiah with water, he should behold and bear

of Christ is made without elaboration or explanation of the ordinance. Given how casually the mention is made, it appears there was nothing unfamiliar with the rite, even at the time of Lehi. The practice is clearly familiar by the time we get to 1 Ne. 20: 1, where the verse from Isaiah Chapter 48 is rendered: "Hearken and hear this, O house of Jacob, who are called by the name of Israel, and are come forth out of the waters of Judah, or **out of the waters of baptism,**[154] who swear by the name of the Lord, and make mention of the God of Israel, yet they swear not in truth nor in righteousness." (Emphasis added.) This suggests familiarity with the ordinance of baptism goes back in Israelite history at least as early as the Isaiah period. While beyond the scope of this work, it is interesting to note.

The record of Nephi has one of the great arguments for baptism for every person. Nephi gives us this explanation: "Wherefore, I would that ye should remember that I have spoken unto you concerning that prophet which the Lord showed unto me, that should baptize the Lamb of God, which should take away the sins of the world. And now, if the Lamb of God, he being holy, should have need to be baptized by water, to fulfil all righteousness, O then, how much more need have we, being unholy, to be baptized, yea, even by water!" (2 Ne. 31: 4-5.) Numerous other examples exist throughout the record of the Nephite practice of baptism going back to the original period of Lehi's lifetime.

It is extremely unlikely, therefore, that these disciples had not been previously baptized. However, they are baptized **anew** on this occasion and that fact has symbolic meaning in this context here. This ordinance is performed by Nephi "on those whom Jesus had chosen." (3 Ne. 19:

---

record that he had baptized the Lamb of God, who should take away the sins of the world." (1 Ne. 10: 8-10.)

[154]The phrase "or out of the waters of baptism" was not in the first edition, but added by Joseph Smith after the first printing. However, that should not change the effect of the reference, given that Joseph was clarifying the meaning by this addition.

12.) That is, the rites were administered for the twelve disciples and not upon the multitude, who were observing these events.[155]

This baptism is a form of preparatory washing for the ceremonies which are underway in this part of the Book of Mormon. It is consistent with the higher ordinances of the Gospel, and with what the record is about to reveal happened on this second day of Christ's ministry among the Nephites. So the ceremonial baptism here is best regarded as a form of ceremonial washing of the twelve disciples who participated in them.

The washing of these chosen twelve is immediately followed by an anointing of the Spirit.[156] These disciples are now washed, anointed and prepared for an endowment from on-high. Now that the twelve are prepared by these first cleansing rites, Christ returns to minister further rites to them. "Jesus came and stood in the midst and ministered unto them. And it came to pass that he spake unto the **multitude**, and commanded them that they should kneel down again upon the earth, and also that his **disciples** should kneel down upon the earth." (3 Ne. 19: 15-16,[157] emphasis added.) There are two distinct groups here in the narrative.

---

[155]The text clearly differentiates between the "disciples" or the ones Jesus had "chosen" on the one hand, and the "multitude" on the other hand. This distinction must be recognized to catch the import of what is being taught or shown in the account.

[156]3 Ne. 19: 12-13: "And he came up out of the water and began to baptize. And he baptized all those whom Jesus had chosen [i.e., the twelve disciples]. And it came to pass when they were all [i.e., the twelve] baptized and had come up out of the water, the Holy Ghost did fall upon them [again the twelve], and they were filled with the Holy Ghost and with fire."

[157]Note here again the record distinguishes between the "disciples" on the one hand, and the "multitude" on the other hand. The disciples are going to participate in, while the multitude is going to watch, the ceremony which is about to take place.

The twelve are now assembled in a circle[158] by the Lord. He is in the center of the circle, as a fixed point about which the circle is drawn. He is the point by which a compass can draw a perfect round. This is a ceremony unfolding in the record. You must understand this to understand the record. The disciples are then commanded to pray.[159] This is a prayer circle, familiar to anyone who attends the Temple.

While the disciples pray in a circle, the Lord then knocks at the veil three times. You will recollect the earlier mention of the three degrees of separation between God and man. As God reached downward, He called three times the day before. Now, when reaching upward, there is a three-fold petition at the veil to bring a response.

The first knock at the veil is set out in full in verses 20-23. The second is also set out in full in verses 28-29. The final knock is described, without quoting the words used, in verse 32. Anyone who has been to the Temple will immediately recognize the ceremonial setting of this account. These events are not just haphazard or un-scripted. They are part of ceremonial worship which is required of any person who will conform to heaven's patterns.

The Lord's disciples are assembled in a circle, in prayer. They are praying in unison.[160] The final ceremonial preparation comes as they are clothed in white.[161] Sacred clothing is an important part of ceremonial

---

[158]The fact that "Jesus came and stood in the midst" (3 Ne. 19: 15) means that they were around or surrounding Him. He stood in the middle. This requires a circle. Which is consistent with what is about to occur.

[159]*Id.*, v. 17.

[160]"…they did not multiply many words, for it was given unto them what they should pray, and they were filled with desire." This giving unto them of the words to use in prayer requires praying in unison. (3Ne. 19:24.)

[161]*Id.*; v. 25, 30: "And it came to pass that Jesus blessed them as they did pray unto him; and his countenance did smile upon them, and the light of his countenance did shine upon them, and behold they were as white as the countenance and also the garments of Jesus; and behold the whiteness thereof did exceed all the whiteness, yea, even there could be nothing upon earth so

preparation for receiving the Father. Christ taught that without a proper "wedding garment" people are not permitted into the wedding feast.[162] Sacred clothing is a part of appearing before God and having your shame removed.[163] It is an essential part of the true faith. It is, therefore a part of the ceremony recounted here.

Now that the disciples have been washed, anointed, clothed in white garments, and otherwise instructed so as to prepare them to receive further light and knowledge through the veil, the veil is parted. This point of the ceremony, however, has its own veil extended over it in the record. "And tongue cannot speak the words which he prayed, neither can be written by man the words which he prayed. And the multitude did hear and do bear record; and their hearts were open and they did understand in their hearts the words which he prayed. Nevertheless, so great and marvelous were the words which he prayed that they cannot be written, neither can they be uttered by man." (*Id.*, v. 32-34.) And so it is with these things. They can be learned, but they cannot be taught. Those who are willing to receive them, however, will receive them. But only when they are prepared to respect the limits which should always separate the sacred from the profane.

Putting jewelry on pigs is no more appropriate today than it was when Christ advised against it. When entrusted with sacred things, you must respect them. If you cannot respect their sacred nature, you are not a candidate to receive them. The Temple is a qualifying ceremony to prepare you for the real thing. If you cannot see the Temple's proper

---

white as the whiteness thereof. ... and behold they were white, even as Jesus."

[162]Christ illustrated in a parable this principle: "And when the king came in to see the guests, he saw there a man which had not on a wedding garment: And he saith unto him, Friend, how camest thou in hither not having a wedding garment? And he was speechless. Then said the king to the servants, Bind him hand and foot, and take him away, and cast him into outer darkness; there shall be weeping and gnashing of teeth. For many are called, but few are chosen." (Matt. 22: 11-14.)

[163]See, e.g., Gen. 3: 21; 2 Ne. 9: 14; Rev. 3: 18.

context and give it the respect it is due, then you are not yet prepared to receive the real thing.[164] Honor the type, and you prove you will honor the reality. Dishonor the type, and you prove you are not worthy of the reality. God will not be mocked in large measure by keeping the mockers away from His presence. The nature of their forfeiture is far greater, and takes place far earlier than they suspect. They forfeit here and now the chance to receive the Second Comforter.

If you fail to respect a covenant made with God to keep ceremonial Temple knowledge sacred and apart from the world, then you cannot hope to receive sacred knowledge from God through revelation and visitations. The Temple is the qualifying test. The Temple needs to be seen in its true, sacred light. The Lord provides a unique and brilliant form of qualifying rite in the Temple. For those with eyes to see what is being given there, the very substance of the most sacred things offered by God to man are portrayed with clarity in the Temple.

This process must first be seen with the eyes of faith, as pointed out earlier. Unless you see these things through the eyes of faith as a necessary first step, you cannot behold the real thing. The one qualifies for the other. The one is a necessary precondition for the other. God has so constituted us as mortals that we must progress in these things, from grace to grace, before we can receive the fullness. If we cannot first see the "type" in faith, nothing doubting, then there is no reason for the Lord to send the real thing. That would be sending a "sign" to produce faith, rather than having the sign follow faith. When you accept the "type" as the real thing, and drain from it all of its symbolic meaning, then there is no reason to withhold the real thing any longer. Then you will see signs following faith. That is the process irrevocably

---

[164]Though it is well beyond the scope of this work, the notion that Joseph Smith copied another ordinance or another rite in restoring Temple worship is laughable. The Book of Mormon account is written in 1829. Joseph would not begin to restore the Temple rites until 1842. Nothing in Joseph's words or statements in 1829 even remotely suggest he anticipated Temple ceremonies. Though Joseph had no idea where the Restoration was headed in 1829, the Lord did.

decreed before the foundation of the world. If you conform to it and receive the types in faith, then you grow from grace to grace.

The Book of Mormon is a sacred text. It contains a fullness of the Gospel of Jesus Christ. It is a tool provided by God which can be used to prepare any person seeking God's presence. The Book of Mormon and the Temple are the primary means by which God has chosen to prepare us for the return to God and our redemption from the Fall. In the visit of Christ recorded in 3 Nephi we see these two tools merge together. The Risen Lord's ministry to the Nephites is a Temple text. It is best understood in its ritual setting. There is a clear ceremonial path being depicted which is intended to instruct you in the mysteries of godliness. But it must be seen through the eyes of faith. Then, having seen it through those eyes of faith, you can qualify to see the underlying reality it is trying to help you believe exists. This Book of Mormon text is trying to bring you through the veil. If you will heed its instructions, then you will be moved closer to that event.

Earlier we described it as bringing through the veil the things of the Spirit by obeying in a material world the commandments of the Spirit. Here, there is a concrete example of this occurring among a group of faithful Saints numbering in the thousands. It has already happened before. It is happening still. It can happen with you, as well. The Book of Mormon intends to teach each of us how to receive these things. In ways which are clearly superior to the Biblical record, the Book of Mormon is a masterwork of prophetic instruction in higher knowledge about God. It is a monument of truth, and the most correct book ever written on these things. If you want to get closer to God, the Book of Mormon is the best text available for tutoring you.

Chapter Nine

HOW THIS FAITH IS OBTAINED

After dropping my children off at school one morning, I was returning south to go to work. Buttercup Drive passed by the then new Sandy Library, and was a steep incline to 1300 East. This particular morning a fellow driving a pick-up pulling a trailer with a stack of sheetrock on the trailer was stopped across from the library. The sheetrock had dislodged while going down Buttercup Drive's incline and had slid forward into the back of the pickup towing the trailer. The fellow with the predicament was standing beside his trailer on the roadside, and as I drove by I noticed the difficulty. He was in distress and I felt for his problem. "I would not want to be that guy," I thought.

As I turned onto 1300 East, I had a feeling I ought to return and help him solve his dilemma. It would require two people to correct the situation. The sheetrock needed to be removed in order to be restacked and then secured back onto the trailer. He could not do it alone without great difficulty, if at all. If he had help from even a single additional person, it would be relatively easy to resolve. I was in a suit and wasn't dressed appropriately to move sheetrock, I thought. I drove on to work.

The nagging impulse to help the man persisted, and I persisted in ignoring it. Ultimately, I turned onto 11000 South, toward my office, and concluded too much time had gone by and I was now too far away. Surely someone had stopped to help him and I could continue on with my day and ignore the problem.

From time to time the rest of the day I felt I had failed this man, and more importantly, I had failed the Lord by not helping someone in need. That "golden rule" of treating others like we would want to be treated kept recurring to me. Had I been in his shoes, I would have wanted anyone's help. And I certainly would have been grateful for anyone's help, no matter how they were dressed.

The prompting I had ignored returned as a conviction I should have helped. I had let both that man and the Lord down by failing to respond. That evening I prayed about the matter and asked I be forgiven for failing to follow the prompting. The sense that I had failed in a significant way persisted, and prayer had no effect on removing it. It continued to trouble me. This seemed more serious a matter than I had first expected. I couldn't shake the impression I had failed a significant test that morning, driving by the man in need.

Some days later, I got the clearest of answers to my continued prayer on this troubling matter. The man with the difficulty had himself been praying over his problem. He needed the Lord's help, and he had asked for it. The Lord was answering his prayer when I had the prompting to help him. It had not just been a man in distress whom I had failed. It was the Lord. The Lord intended to answer him. He sent me and I refused to go. Rather than honoring the Lord and obeying His prompting, I had failed Him, and failed His petitioning and faithful child as I drove by. What was worse, I had not been heedless. I had elected to reject, ignore, and even argued the point *rather than respond. It was a serious matter and I had treated it lightly at the time.*

That happened many years ago. I still recall the incident, and wish I had behaved otherwise that morning. The Lord answers prayers to be sure, but His answers sometimes require those who are willing to follow Him to be His answer for others. I realize now that these opportunities are fleeting, and when we fail Him in one assignment, it is unreasonable to expect Him to trust you immediately with another.

Promptings are given to us as a sacred trust. When I violated that trust and failed to respond, it caused an injury to a man in need, but more importantly it injured me. I do not know if his faith was affected or not. I wish there were some way to let him know now the Lord heard his prayer, and attempted to answer it. I wish there were some way to let him know it was I who failed to respond when God heard him. I don't know if that would matter to him, but letting him know would at least make me feel better. Who knows but what someone else more willing to serve others did help. Perhaps even someone faithless but who had charity in their heart rose to the occasion. There are such people, and they are oftentimes better than the religious and proud. Ultimately, my role in it was a failure. The Lord may have solved the problem successfully and without any need to resort to me.

The scriptures claim faith is a gift from God.[165] It is received like all other things from God: in response to the conditions outlined before

---

[165]See, e.g., Rom. 12: 3: "For I say, through the grace given unto me, to every man that is among you, not to think of himself more highly than he ought to think; but to think soberly, according **as God hath dealt to every man the measure of faith**." (Emphasis added.)

the foundation of the world,[166] and like most gifts, it is merited and must be willingly received by the person choosing to receive it.[167] One of Joseph Smith's greatest contributions to understanding grace and faith is his revelation linking blessings, gifts and even faith to an established set of laws. Unlike the mystical and incomprehensible theologies of the religionists of his day (and our own), Joseph set out in simplicity that all blessings are obtained in obedience to laws set from before the foundation of the world.

Joseph saw no great mystery in the process of receiving grace. What kept most of mankind from great spiritual blessings was not unwillingness but ignorance. Joseph realized mankind needed to be brought out of ignorance. In explaining this need, Joseph taught, "A man is saved no faster than he gets knowledge, for if he does not get knowledge, he will be brought into captivity by some evil power in the other world, as evil spirits will have more knowledge, and consequently more power than many men who are on the earth. Hence it needs revelation to assist us, and give us knowledge of the things of God." *DHC* 4: 588. If mankind is to be saved, it will be through their acquisition of knowledge. Put otherwise, it is stupidity which damns us; it is knowledge which saves us.

Joseph linked blessings with knowledge. He linked knowledge with obedience to laws. Section 130: "And if a person gains more knowledge and intelligence in this life through his diligence and obedience than another, he will have so much the advantage in the world to come. There is a law, irrevocably decreed in heaven before the foundations of this world, upon which all blessings are predicated – And **when we obtain any blessing from God, it is by obedience to that law upon which it is predicated.**" (Vs. 19-21, emphasis added.) If we want a

---

[166]"There is a law, irrevocably decreed in heaven before the foundations of this world, upon which all blessings are predicated"— (D&C 130: 20.)

[167]"For what doth it profit a man if a gift is bestowed upon him, and he receive not the gift? Behold, he rejoices not in that which is given unto him, neither rejoices in him who is the giver of the gift." (D&C 88: 33.)

blessing, we must find the law upon which the blessing is predicated, and then follow that law. If we do, we get the blessing. There is a majestic simplicity to this orderly procedure.

It is from such an understanding Joseph authoritatively declared God was no respecter of persons. Joseph's declaration made profoundly more sense than what other religionists were teaching. Joseph made this whole process of gaining blessings through knowledge a natural one which grew out of conformity with natural law. Of course, God ordained that natural law. It was such a revolutionary notion, it still is underappreciated. It turns God's "whimsy" into a predictable, reliable and obtainable program all mankind can uniformly follow. It also revolutionizes the understanding of truth, and undercuts the falsity of Luther's and Calvin's views on grace.

People who accept Joseph as a Prophet should be the most eager of all to search the scriptures to learn what the laws are governing blessings. We should study the scriptures to learn the commandments. We learn the commandments to obey them. We obey the command-ments to obtain light and truth. These things all proceed in accordance with established law. When the law is followed, the results come for anyone and everyone. It flows as a natural consequence and comes as a result of God's grace. For God ordained the law to bring these blessings. Then God, in His mercy, revealed the laws to mankind so they could follow Him and obtain this grace He is so willing to grant unto them.

Joseph prepared a series of lectures to the School of the Prophets in Kirtland, Ohio. That series was contributed to by others, as well. But since Joseph presided in the Church and in the School, the Lectures became his product.

Much of the effort of the *Lectures on Faith* is devoted to conveying the relationship between sacrifice on the one hand, and receiving faith, on the other. One passage dealing with this says the following:

Let us here observe, that a religion that does not require the sacrifice of all things never has power sufficient to produce the faith necessary unto life and salvation; for, from the first existence of man, the faith necessary unto the enjoyment of life and salvation never could be obtained without the sacrifice of all earthly things. It was through sacrifice, and this only, that God has ordained that men should enjoy eternal life; and it is through the medium of the sacrifice of all earthly things that men do actually know that they are doing the things that are well pleasing in the sight of God. When a man has offered in sacrifice all that he has for the truth's sake, not even withholding his life, and believing before God that he has been called to make this sacrifice because he seeks to do his will, he does know, most assuredly, that God does and will accept his sacrifice and offering, and that he has not, nor will not seek his face in vain. ... It is in vain for persons to fancy to themselves that they are heirs with those, or can be heirs with them, who have offered their all in sacrifice, and by this means obtained faith in God and favor with him so as to obtain eternal life, unless they, in like manner, offer unto him the same sacrifice, and through that offering obtain a knowledge that they are accepted of him... From the days of righteous Able to the present time, the knowledge that men have that they are accepted in the sight of God is obtained by offering sacrifice. ... Those, then, who make this sacrifice, will have the testimony that their course is pleasing in the sight of God; and those who have this testimony will have faith to lay hold on eternal life, ... and through the knowledge thus obtained their faith became sufficiently strong to lay hold upon the promise of eternal life, and to endure as seeing him who is invisible; ... But those who have not made this sacrifice to God do not know that the course which they pursue is well pleasing in his sight; for whatever may be their belief or their opinion, it is a matter of doubt and uncertainty to their mind; and where doubt and uncertainty are there faith is not, nor can it be. For doubt and faith do not exist in the same person at the same time. (*Lectures, Sixth Lecture*, paragraphs 7-12, pp. 58-59.)

This explanation is so good a statement, and so directly on point, it is quoted at length. Joseph understood how faith was acquired. His life had been a practical study in faith. As the Prophet-teacher, he wanted to share with the Saints how they could similarly obtain an effective, powerful and saving faith. He is explaining here how anyone can receive faith.

The authority for such statements lies in the fact that Joseph was the one who, after over a millennia and a half of the heavens being sealed, received a visitation from God and shattered the long silence. Therefore, it is safe to conclude even if Joseph knew little about "men and things,"[168] he still knew a great deal about faith. Perhaps in all history there has been no person outside of Father Abraham who had comparable faith. He is the authority to be most trusted on this subject. He blazed a trail which all others must follow if they want to receive the blessings restored by God through Joseph to the earth.

If you trust Joseph's teaching on this subject, it leads you to the realization sacrifice is directly related to faith. And obtaining faith requires sacrifice. It can be had in no other way.

What Joseph didn't say in the quote, but is self-evident, is you can sacrifice without obtaining faith. When sacrifice is an end in itself, it produces nothing. Sacrifice must be directed toward the correct end, or it fails to produce faith. If sacrifice were in itself an end, then self-denial, and self-abuse, even the most extreme practices of asceticism, would be noble. They are not. They are instead self-centered and selfish. There is nothing noble about these extremes. None of them ever produced great faith.

From Moses to Jesus Christ there was sacrifice performed daily as a rite in Jerusalem (excepting only temporary interludes including the Babylonian captivity). Despite the daily sacrifices, the people most directly involved had no visitations from angels, had no revelations, received no audience with God and performed no miracles. When Christ came to fulfill the law of sacrifice, the ones performing the

---

[168]JSH 1: 8.

sacrifices were the least willing to accept Him. The sacrifices they had and were performing, had no faith-producing effects for them.

Sacrifice must, therefore, be connected with a proper understanding of how it relates to something higher. Sacrifices are not intended to teach you to sacrifice; they are trying to teach you another underlying truth. If there is no understanding of the underlying truth, then the act of sacrifice can become a meaningless end in itself. Almost any principle of the Gospel can become a misleading end in itself. The Gospel is a harmony of principles correctly weighed and measured. It is a symphony, and not a single bloated and distorted note.

The underlying truth sacrifice teaches is simple. All great truths are simple. If they were not, then they could not be obtained by the weak, simple, and childlike among us. And, of course, it was and is to such persons the Gospel has always been primarily directed.

What is that underlying truth sacrifice teaches, and which can be obtained through no other means? Christ addressed that underlying truth in simple statements about the heart and treasures. He said:

> Lay not up for yourselves treasures upon earth, where moth and rust doth corrupt, and where thieves break through and steal: But lay up for yourselves treasures in heaven, where neither moth nor rust doth corrupt, and where thieves do not break through nor steal: **For where your treasure is, there will your heart be also.** The light of the body is the eye: if therefore thine eye be single, thy whole body shall be full of light. But if thine eye be evil, thy whole body shall be full of darkness. If therefore the light that is in thee be darkness, how great is that darkness! **No man can serve two masters: for either he will hate the one, and love the other**; or else he will hold to the one, and despise the other. Ye cannot serve God and mammon. (Matt. 6: 19-24, emphasis added.)

You cannot be both spiritual and materialistic. What do you treasure? Sacrifice is a means of proving to yourself and to God that you treasure Him and His above all the things of this world. It is a way of changing your heart from things here on earth to the greater things in heaven. Eventually, if you are materialistic and you begin to sacrifice, you will begin to change. Sacrifice is a tool given to us to change our hearts and realign them to being less materialistic and more spiritual.

You have only "one light" you can let in. We are so constituted we are able to focus on only one thing at a time. We necessarily choose between all other things and that one thing. Christ is teaching us we have to choose God above all else. Sacrifice allows us to show by our choice whatever we lay upon the altar is not more treasured to us than God's will for us.

By laying ourselves and our emotional needs on the altar and sacrificing the things this world values, we are saying and proving we choose the other world to this one. We value the things of the Spirit above the material things of this existence. It is another affirmation that we would prefer to have our existence filled with things of the Spirit, rather than filled with the materialism of this world.

It was as a result of this relationship that Christ taught: "And he that taketh not his cross, and followeth after me, is not worthy of me. **He that findeth his life shall lose it: and he that loseth his life for my sake shall find it.** He that receiveth you receiveth me, and he that receiveth me receiveth him that sent me." (Matt. 10: 38-40, emphasis added.) If you want to find life, lose it. If you lose your life, *i.e.* you give your time, talents, and everything which God has given to you to His service and will, then you find a new life. That new life is connected with God, because it is lived in conformity with His will.

You will recall that Christ utterly lost His life in obedience to the Father. His explanation of how He lived His life was summarized briefly by Him: "And behold, I am the light and the life of the world; and I have drunk out of that bitter cup which the Father hath given me, and have glorified the Father in taking upon me the sins of the world, in the which **I have suffered the will of the Father in all things from the beginning.**" (3 Ne. 11: 11, emphasis added.) Christ was the most fulfilled, most intelligent, and most obedient person who ever lived. He was all these things because He obeyed the Father. Anyone who will obey Him will receive light and truth as a result.[169] Light and truth are "intelligence."[170] Christ was the most intelligent[171] because He was the most obedient. This is a simple concept, yet it holds profound implications. It suggests obedience is something much greater than might first be expected. Obedience brings intelligence, and unlocks mysteries. Far from being oppressive or confining, it turns out obedience is liberating and enlightening. How false have been the criticisms directed at obedience!

In another place He taught; "Then said Jesus unto his disciples, If any man will come after me, let him deny himself, and take up his cross, and follow me. **For whosoever will save his life shall lose it: and whosoever will lose his life for my sake shall find it.** For what is a man profited, if he shall gain the whole world, and lose his own soul? or what shall a man give in exchange for his soul?" (Matt. 16: 24-26, emphasis added.) The trade-off is again put succinctly. If you want life, real life, alive in God, then you need to obey Him. Lose yourself, your pride, self-will and meaningless individuality in something much greater. Become connected to the Father by obedience to His ordained laws, and follow His commandments and find yourself growing in light, truth and intelligence. It is a simple formula which anyone can follow. But for some reason only the humble are willing to submit to the process. The proud and vain will never climb that mountain and, therefore, will never receive a view of the things on the other side.

All these things go together. They are all the same subject. If we want to obtain the kind of faith needed to draw aside the veil and behold the things of God, then we must draw aside that veil by our

---

[169]D&C 93: 28: "He that keepeth his commandments receiveth truth and light, until he is glorified in truth and knoweth all things."

[170]D&C 93:36 "The glory of God is intelligence, or, in other words, light and truth."

[171]Abr. 3: 19: "I am the Lord thy God, I am more intelligent than they all."

sacrifice of this world for that world. We have to lose the connection here to gain the connection there. Without doing that through our sacrifices, we cannot develop the necessary faith. This was what Joseph was telling us with the quote from the *Lectures on Faith*, earlier. It is an indisputable truth that "a religion that does not require the sacrifice of all things never has power sufficient to produce the faith necessary unto life and salvation; for, from the first existence of man, the faith necessary unto the enjoyment of life and salvation never could be obtained without the sacrifice of all earthly things." So if we want to develop this faith, we must be willing to sacrifice all earthly things. How is this possible? We don't die for religion in most cultures of the world today. Living in an affluent, Western society, as many Saints do today, how is the sacrifice of all earthly things even possible? How, in particular, can you be like those who have offered their all in sacrifice to obtain approval from God? If you can have only a hope to receive a like portion of faith by doing a like form of sacrifice, how is this to be done?

All great truths are simple. Nephi assured us (as we covered earlier), God gives us no commandments unless He prepares a way for us to obey them. So, God must have provided a way for us to accomplish what He commands of us.

The answer may seem at first superficial. It is not. This process is not a single giant step. It is many small steps. When explaining the process of exaltation, Joseph stated you grow into exaltation: "from one small degree to another, and from a small capacity to a great one; from grace to grace, from exaltation to exaltation, until you attain to the resurrection of the dead and are able to dwell in everlasting burnings, and to sit in glory." (*DHC* 6: 306.) In that same talk he said, "When you climb up a ladder, you must begin at the bottom, and ascend step by step, until you arrive at the top; and so it is with the principles of the gospel — you must begin with the first, and go on until you learn all the principles of exaltation." (*Id.*, p. 306-307.) Here again, Joseph is connecting growth to knowledge and obedience. Again he is making this process openly democratic and universally applicable. And he is telling us this is a gradual process of increasing obedience in conformity to increasing knowledge.

So how, then, do the small steps leading to the growth in light and truth begin? The beginning of the answer lies in Church service. All of those irritating, sometimes grating things asked of you because you are a member of the Church are opportunities for sacrifice. The callings we receive, the home teaching and visiting teaching assignments we are given, and all the troubles and difficulties which come from holding a calling and serving others are opportunities for sacrifice. They are gifts from God, given as a part of His program for our exaltation. There is a genius to this program, and God is behind it. He offers to us the beginning of learning right inside His Church. Of course, it should not stop there, as we will presently see.

To be most meaningful, sacrifice by one person should bless and benefit another person. When Isaiah taught the highest principles and aspirations of the law of the fast, he linked it to blessing others. This is exactly what the Church's fast offering program allows the Saints to do. Isaiah wrote:

Wherefore have we fasted, say they, and thou seest not? Wherefore have we afflicted our soul, and thou takest no knowledge? Behold, in the day of your fast ye find pleasure, and exact all your labours. Behold, ye fast for strife and debate, and to smite with the fist of wickedness: ye shall not fast as ye do this day, to make your voice to be heard on high. Is it such a fast that I have chosen? A day for a man to afflict his soul? Is it to bow down his head as a bulrush, and to spread sackcloth and ashes under him? wilt thou call this a fast, and an acceptable day to the Lord? Is not this the fast that I have chosen? to loose the bands of wickedness, to undo the heavy burdens, and to let the oppressed go free, and that ye break every yoke? **Is it not to deal thy bread to the hungry, and that thou bring the poor that are cast out to thy house? when thou seest the naked, that thou cover him;** and that thou hide not thyself from thine own flesh? (Isa. 58: 3-7, emphasis added.)

Here He is teaching the difference between meaningless sacrifice as a hollow religious observance, in contrast to relieving the suffering of others through your fasting (and sharing abundance). Helping and blessing others is the highest form of sacrifice. When you act to relieve the burdens of others, you are acting as Christ would. You are rising to another level of living where angels themselves dwell. You are becoming a "type" of Christ. It is not merely asking yourself "what would Jesus do?" but rather it is doing what Jesus did and commanded you to do. Action in conformity to commandments brings light into your life. You follow His path and you will be walking up that same mountain in which you, too, will be transfigured.

What is needed, however, is not just a change in perception, but a change of heart. You can't change the heart without then changing the perception. In the Sermon on the Mount, Christ set out standards which should transform a person. The standards there ask us to change from merely avoiding physically harming others, as was required in the Law of Moses, to loving them instead. He even asks you to love them when they despitefully use and abuse you. Apparently impossible standards are being asked of us by the Lord.

Progress in anything involves going from a smaller degree to a greater one. You don't get to the point where you can run a mile until after you have first learned to run 100 yards. Physical things are intended to teach us about, and testify of, spiritual truths.[172] So stretching and improving in physical and mental efforts are intended to prove to you that this is also possible in spiritual things.

The process of developing the attributes Christ asks of us in the

---

[172]We sometimes forget this principle, but it nevertheless is true. "And behold, all things have their likeness, and all things are created and made to bear record of me, both things which are temporal, and things which are spiritual; things which are in the heavens above, and things which are on the earth, and things which are in the earth, and things which are under the earth, both above and beneath: all things bear record of me." (Moses 6: 63.) There is enough to testify of God in your daily, physical life that you should become acquainted with Him, assuming you are willing to see Him in the things which He has provided to you.

Sermon on the Mount begins in Church service. These fellow Saints are given you to help you grow and develop patience, love and charity. Some of our fellow Saints are lovely and loving. They are easy to show a Christ-like love to because they return your kindness, either in like measure or in greater measure. We all know Saints like that. But they don't stretch us into improvement.

It is that unlikable bishop, or the unworthy and uninspired high councilman, or the abrasive and unlikable semi-heretic, complaining every Gospel Doctrine class about some pet project or issue who provides us the greatest opportunities to begin to develop charity. These people are there as gifts from God to help us become more like Him. Having unlikable Saints about us is exactly as it should be. Having leaders who fail in their callings is also just as it should be. These things are a gift to you, to provide you a chance to return love and charity to those who need it, and probably will never recognize the gifts you are developing through their shortcomings.

Praying for the unlikable and unworthy is a part of the Christ-like attributes which both Nephi and Lehi display in the First Book of Nephi. Lehi makes intercession for the condemned residents of Jerusalem.[173] Nephi makes intercession for his unbelieving older brothers.[174] Both are showing the kind of charity that makes you like Christ. Christ was the Great Intercessor. In like measure, you must make intercession for those who fall short in your life. You should thank God for the opportunity which they give to you to show that charity. It may seem odd to do this when you start. But prayer and grace go together. You will find you are able to pray with sincerity for those in your life after you have spent time on your knees on their behalf. Grace begets grace.[175] Do it, and you will grow as a result.[176] The Saints

---

[173]1 Ne. 1: 5, *supra.*

[174]1 Ne. 2: 18, *supra.*

[175]Speaking of Christ, the Great Example, it is written: "And he received not of the fulness at first, but continued from grace to grace, until he

and your calling in the Church is the place where you begin this process. The offensive and failing Saint has not been given to you to judge, condemn or belittle. They are given to you as a gift from God, to allow you to serve, uplift, pray for and show love to as God's own son or daughter. They are your greatest opportunities. You should love them for this.

It does not end, of course, with service and kindness to your fellow Saint. You must also learn to serve the "Samaritan," and to heal and care for them. If it ends with mere Church service, you have not yet overcome xenophobia. It is the "other," the "outsider," and the "stranger and foreigner" through whom sacrifice is perfected. The unlovely and even the persecutor is where Christ's commandments lead us at last. We must develop love for those who persecute us, or despitefully use and abuse us to reach what Christ taught. He really meant it. And He really wants us to get there. When we do, we find ourselves standing on holy ground. For that ground was sanctified by His own blood, shed in His own sacrifice, when He poured out the last full measure of devotion to His Father's will. When you hear His words echoing in your own voice, "forgive them for they know not what they do," then you will begin to see the Master in the mirror. His image will appear to you there first. Your countenance will look more like His:

---

received a fulness;" (D&C 93: 13.)

[176] As Alma explained it: "But behold, if ye will awake and arouse your faculties, even to an experiment upon my words, and exercise a particle of faith, yea, even if ye can no more than desire to believe, let this desire work in you, even until ye believe in a manner that ye can give place for a portion of my words. Now, we will compare the word unto a seed. Now, if ye give place, that a seed may be planted in your heart, behold, if it be a true seed, or a good seed, if ye do not cast it out by your unbelief, that ye will resist the Spirit of the Lord, behold, it will begin to swell within your breasts; and when you feel these swelling motions, ye will begin to say within yourselves – It must needs be that this is a good seed, or that the word is good, for it beginneth to enlarge my soul; yea, it beginneth to enlighten my understanding, yea, it beginneth to be delicious to me. Now behold, would not this increase your faith? I say unto you, Yea..." (Alma 32: 27-29.)

more humble, more contrite, more obedient and filled with more light than you are right now.

King Benjamin was teaching us this principle. He said:

And also, ye yourselves will succor those that stand in need of your succor; ye will administer of your substance unto him that standeth in need; and ye will not suffer that the beggar putteth up his petition to you in vain, and turn him out to perish. Perhaps thou shalt say: The man has brought upon himself his misery; therefore I will stay my hand, and will not give unto him of my food, nor impart unto him of my substance that he may not suffer, for his punishments are just – But I say unto you, O man, whosoever doeth this the same hath great cause to repent; and except he repenteth of that which he hath done he perisheth forever, and hath no interest in the kingdom of God. For behold, are we not all beggars? Do we not all depend upon the same Being, even God, for all the substance which we have, for both food and raiment, and for gold, and for silver, and for all the riches which we have of every kind? And behold, even at this time, ye have been calling on his name, and begging for a remission of your sins. And has he suffered that ye have begged in vain? Nay; he has poured out his Spirit upon you, and has caused that your hearts should be filled with joy, and has caused that your mouths should be stopped that ye could not find utterance, so exceedingly great was your joy. And now, if God, who has created you, on whom you are dependent for your lives and for all that ye have and are, doth grant unto you whatsoever ye ask that is right, in faith, believing that ye shall receive, O then, how ye ought to impart of the substance that ye have one to another. And if ye judge the man who putteth up his petition to you for your substance that he perish not, and condemn him, how much more just will be your condemnation for withholding your substance, which doth not belong to you but to God, to whom also your life belongeth; and yet ye put up no petition, nor repent of the thing which thou hast done. I say unto you, wo be unto that man, for his substance shall perish with him; and now, I say these things unto those who are rich as pertaining to the things of this world. (Mosiah 4: 16-23.)

If you have **any** ability to relieve the suffering of another person, it is your responsibility to do so. The undesirable beggar, the foreigner who does not belong, is the one we tend to judge. The beggar whose language and customs are strange to us is easy to dismiss. He "deserves" this condemnation, we think. Yet that thought is the very thought King Benjamin is warning us about.

Outside the Salt Lake Temple are beggars who regularly put up their petition in vain to those passing into and out of the Temple. It is unlikely the Temple patrons could not spare something to relieve the suffering of the beggars. That location is one which allows Saints daily to demonstrate they have heard and are willing to obey, the principles of sacrifice.

I used to think having the right heart must precede action to be of any worth. What I have found instead is that action can lead the heart. Christ's Sermon on the Mount is a call to action. Do the things asked by Him, and the heart will follow. The mind can lead the heart. The heart does not always have to go first.

After a season of praying for the Saints, you will find your attitude toward them is less judgmental and more compassionate. Charity toward them will follow. Begin with the Saints, and you will find showing charity toward the world becomes a greater possibility. Loving the world, with all its failings and idolatry is perhaps not a possibility as a first step. But it becomes possible as you first develop charity toward the Household of God. Start at home, among the Saints.

In 3 Ne. 27: 27, Christ poses this question, and gives this answer: "Therefore, what manner of men ought ye to be? Verily I say unto you, even as I am." Christ came to save men, not to condemn them.[177] We must learn to be like Him.[178] If He forgave men frankly and freely, then

---

[177]John 3: 17: "For God sent not his Son into the world to condemn the world; but that the world through him might be saved."

[178]Joseph taught this principle in these words: "Here, then, is eternal life — to know the only wise and true God; and **you have got to learn how to be gods yourselves**, and to be kings and priests to God, **the same as all**

why should we believe ourselves justified when we judge, condemn and belittle them? How then can we obtain a hope or faith that we can inherit the same position with the exalted? It is by offering sacrifice in our daily lives and subordinating what we do to a higher purpose.

This may seem daunting. Perhaps it is when viewed as a single undertaking. Try viewing it as a state of being rather than as a list of things to accomplish. Whatever it is you do, do it for the sake of others. If you baby-sit, approach it as a servant serving the welfare of the children. Love them and care for them, and recall Christ taking the children and blessing them.[179] If you repair plumbing, do it to serve and bless others. Take time to show them the individual attention and care that you would show them if you were their elder brother. If you wait on tables, do it with the goal of showing compassion and care for those you serve. There is not a trade, profession or calling which cannot be viewed as an opportunity to care for and bless others. Western societies tend to reduce all business to its starkest fiscal terms. Don't do that. Remember the people who you serve.

Christ was a carpenter until He began His ministry. He undoubtedly developed His attributes during the season in which He served others as their carpenter. As JST-Matt. 3: 24-26 reports: "And it came to pass that Jesus grew up with his brethren, and waxed strong, and waited upon the Lord for the time of his ministry to come. And he served under his father, and he spake not as other men, neither could he be taught; for he needed not that any man should teach him. And after many years, the hour of his ministry drew nigh." Christ "waited" while fully prepared to act in His ministry as the Messiah. And while

---

gods have done before you, namely, by going from one small degree to another, and from a small capacity to a great one; from grace to grace, from exaltation to exaltation, until you attain to the resurrection of the dead, and are able to dwell in everlasting burnings, and to sit in glory, as do those who sit enthroned in everlasting power. And I want you to know that God, in the last days, while certain individuals are proclaiming His name, is not trifling with you or me." (*DHC* 6: 306, emphasis added.)

[179]See, e.g. Matt. 19: 13-15.

doing so, He "needed not that any man should teach him" because He was already fully prepared. This persisted for "many years" before His ministry began. While waiting in this fully prepared state, "he served under his father," as a carpenter. Just how do you imagine He would serve under Joseph as a carpenter? When you have decided how He would do that, you go and do likewise in whatever trade or profession you serve.

Whatever pains you have to bear, or difficulties you have to overcome, or burdens you have to put up with in helping others, do it as a sacrifice to God. There are infinite opportunities to do so. They are all around us. If you elect to treat these sacrifices as opportunities to grow and develop, and show compassion to others while subordinating your own self-interests in the bargain, you are doing what Joseph instructed in the *Lectures on Faith*. You are becoming like the ancients who gave their lives to God. But you are doing so in small, daily increments. That is how such sacrifices are best made. After all, the daily sacrifices in the Temple were designed to teach a principle. That principle of daily effort and on-going devotion to God through continual sacrifices over a lifetime is how Christ became the Only Begotten. He suffered His Father's will in all things from the beginning. It was not just a single, heroic act in Gethsemane and on the cross. It was devotion paid daily. He is our great example.

Don't drive by the man in need. Take the few minutes to stop and help. Such is the stuff from which faith to move mountains is made. Whether you move a mountain, or move yourself to climb over a mountain, the movement is the same. On the other side, everything will have been transfigured. Because you will have to be transfigured in order to move to that place.

These things are simple. But they are true and indispensable. Christ taught them to simple people living simple lives. They can be lived by anyone.

You have to be willing to obey and to sacrifice if you want to get there. But this sacrifice and obedience should not be performed in a hollow, rigid and meaningless way. The sacrifices you offer should be to bless others and undertaken with a sense of joy. They should be the same "type" which Christ offered, and intended to serve, bless and benefit others.

Chapter Ten

CEREMONY AND KNOWING GOD

Law school, children and post-graduation professional responsibilities overtook my life. When the ninth year approached, I had forgotten about it until just before its arrival. As I recalled the promise, I wondered if I had prepared for the ministry adequately. I wasn't certain, and didn't know of any way to be certain. So I awaited nervously the coming day.

At length, the day arrived. It had been nine years since my baptism, and it was now the first day of the third month. And I wondered what this day would involve. When I went to bed that night, it had involved nothing more than the usual activities and responsibilities. Nothing else. Not much of a "ministry" I thought. Perhaps I hadn't prepared adequately. Or maybe I was somehow mistaken in what was originally meant. But, then again, it was as if it had happened yesterday. I can still recall the event with such clarity, all of it was unmistakable. So the problem must have been some failing in me. With that, I let the thought die.

A year later, on the first day of the third month, the Bishop and the Sunday School President visited that evening and asked me to teach the Gospel Doctrine class. It was not until sometime after they left I realized I had miscalculated. The baptism (in September) was not the time I had been given the promise. Rather, it was some later date in the following year. I had been off by a year. The event had occurred as promised and now it was time for my "ministry" to begin.

Beginning then, and lasting for another twenty-one years thereafter, I taught Gospel Doctrine in six different wards in four different stakes in Pleasant Grove, Alpine, and Sandy, Utah. During this time I also taught for three years at BYU Education Week and for two years a graduate Institute class on the Book of Mormon to law students at the University of Utah.

As we move along in this path, there are some subjects which focus us on the tools God has given to prepare for the Second Comforter. These tools are extremely useful, but almost alien to modern culture. In this chapter we are going to look at the ceremonial tools God has given us to bring us closer to Him. They are useful tools to reshape our thinking and bridge the gap between us and Him. This will prepare us for later discussions.

For significant events or life changes, ceremony comes naturally to mankind. From marriage to death, all cultures have ceremonial celebrations to sanctify or dignify the great events of life. Mankind is naturally drawn into commemoration and celebration through ceremony. Across time and culture, ceremony is the stuff from which society is made and united.

Electing a President of the United States is not enough to confer the office. For that, he must be inaugurated. The ceremonies of inauguration are not dissimilar in intent from earlier enthronement ceremonies for monarchs through the ages. Although the Americans rejected a monarchy and the President holds office for a limited time, the process of assuming office is marked by a national observance and a ceremony intended to confer dignity and honor upon the new President.

People in all nations expect to have their highest office assumed and held by someone who has been installed in office through a commemorative ceremonial process. Without the legitimacy of the ceremony, the holder's claims to office are suspect or lacking in almost every society, including those regarded by some as primitive.

The forms of ceremony tell much about the people involved. From primitive to elaborate, ceremonies bespeak the traditions and the culture of the people involved.

Ceremonies allow the participants and observers to convey a broad spectrum of information and meaning through a limited symbolic observance. By using ceremony, the hallowed events of time past are brought back to mind in a meaningful and emotional way, but it is accomplished in a limited time frame condensing meanings into gestures, alignments to the compass, recitation of oaths, conferral of clothing or other hallmarks of authority and meaning. The meanings of the ceremony are condensed into symbolic communications, thereby allowing a great deal to be passed along in a gesture or label. It is the label's ability to contain a host of information in a small way that makes labeling a convenient communicating tool. Understanding the power of ceremony and its ability to communicate is a great asset in obtaining the meanings contained in the ordinances of the Gospel. It is also vital in order to grasp what the scriptures are attempting to communicate as well.

The culture behind the veil is very different from existing mortal cultures. The heavens resound with ceremonial events, intended to convey and celebrate the deepest of eternal meanings. When the Gospel is brought to mankind in its fullness, it is brought in largest part through ceremony and ordinance to reflect the heavenly culture from which it originated. Egypt was perhaps the culture in history to best convey in its everyday life the kind of symbolism and ritual reflecting culture beyond the veil. After all, the first Pharaoh made a conscious attempt to imitate the original culture of mankind which, in turn, was based upon the culture of heaven.[180] Egypt's preoccupation with ceremony and symbolism resulted in even their architecture testifying of higher things.

Just like Egypt's culture was an echo of things that went before and ultimately was an echo of heaven itself, so, too, the ceremonies from all cultures have an echo of higher meaning in them. Ceremonial rites are man's attempt to bring a part of heaven here to earth. The restored Gospel has rites which are far closer to heaven than any rites anywhere else. To appreciate the great value of our restored rites, we are going to look at other rites in this chapter, then return to explore our own, to help show the value of our sacred ceremonies.

What follows as an illustration of ceremonial meaning is an extended description of the ceremonial coronation of Louis XVI, as written by Jacques Barzan. Its details should remind any Latter-day Saint of sacred things we are familiar with from our own rites:

> Here is a description, abridged, of the crowning of the last of the Bourbons, Louis XVI, in 1774. In symbolism and drama it is no less elaborate and effective than the enthronement of the Venetian doge or the Vicar of Christ at the Vatican.
>
> The sacre takes place at the Cathedral of Reims, where it is supposed that in 496 the Germanic chieftain Clovis was baptized a Christian with his 3,000 warriors and accepted as the first king of a region called France. The Clovis story is pure legend, but so potent that the anniversary of that event was officially celebrated in France in 1996 and sanctified by the presence of the pope (776>). Reims is the chosen place because the holy oil (or chrism), which came from heaven to anoint Clovis, is kept there for all time. It is indispensable to making

---

[180]Abraham 1: 26: "Pharaoh, being a righteous man, established his kingdom and judged his people wisely and justly all his days, seeking earnestly to imitate that order established by the fathers in the first generations, in the days of the first patriarchal reign, even in the reign of Adam, and also of Noah, his father."

the king sacred. By it he becomes another person. (Similarly, the king of Madagascar changes his name on gaining the throne.) In 1774, for Louis XVI, the canons of the cathedral went to it at dawn, soon followed by the higher clergy, who set the scene. The archbishop puts on the altar the crown, the spurs, the "hand of justice," and the garments of purple silk embroidered in gold and of priestly cut.

By then, all the high orders – civil, military, and religious – have been mustered and arrive in procession to attend mass and witness the unction (anointing) of the king. He is not yet in sight. He has to be fetched from behind a closed door by delegation of notables. They knock on the door. "What do you want?" asks the king's chamberlain without opening, "We want the king." "The king is asleep." Challenge and response are gone through twice again – in vain. The highest ecclesiastical peer then calls for the particular king: "We want Louis XVI whom God has given us king."

The door opens and the king is borne in on a litter richly draped. The prelate then delivers a harangue: "Almighty and eternal God, who hast raised Thy servant Louis to be king, grant that he shall secure the good of his subjects and that he shall never stray from the path of justice and truth." The king is lifted bodily by two bishops and brought into the main aisle of the church, the choir all the while singing prayers. He is led toward a group of lay lords whom the king has appointed to hold the ampulla of oil. They have sworn on their lives, and vowed moreover to be hostages, to ensure that no harm shall come to that holy vessel until its present use is over.

Before Louis can receive the ointment, he must swear to protect the church and to exterminate heretics. Thereupon he is presented to the assembly and asks for its consent to the act that will make him king. This is given by a moment of silence. The primate hands the king the Holy Scriptures for him to take the oath of office. The words state particulars such as enforcing the prohibition of dueling. Sworn in, he is handed the sword of Charlemagne. Prayers follow, calling for prosperity to reach all classes of the nation during the reign. For the seven unctions administered to the king, he lies facedown toward the altar; one drop of the holy oil has been mixed with the ordinary kind. He is anointed on the chest; shoulders, top of the head, middle of the back, and inside each elbow.

During and between the main phases of the ceremony, choral music resounds. There follows another harangue by the archbishop, who enjoins on the king charity to the poor, a good example to the rich, and the will to keep the nation at peace. Yet he also recommends that the king not give up his claims to "various kingdoms of the north." Last comes the clothing of the king, from the shirt to the coat of purple velvet lined with ermine. He is then led to the throne. The archbishop doffs his mitre, bows, and kisses the sovereign, exclaiming in Latin, "May he live forever!" The doors of the church open and the people rush in." (Barzun, Jacques. *FROM DAWN TO DECA-DENCE: 500 Years of Western Cultural Life*. New York: Harper Collins, 2000, pp. 351-353.)

This ceremony contains elements familiar to Latter-day Saints who have attended the Temple. From anointing with oil to sanctify the king, to the clothing with holy or empowering clothing, to the taking of a new name, there are elements in this ceremony which date back to times and reasons so distant they drift from history into myth and mythology. The necessary door and the knock repeated three times before the king emerges from behind the door veiling him is also a familiar symbol to Latter-day Saints. The French were trying to confer power and office through this ceremony. These things are intended to make the king a person above his peers and to dignify his person and the office held by him elevated above the commonplace. Through it he became sacred or holy. These rites attach to the person a ceremonial cleansing through the anointing which makes him of a greater dignity, and thereby entitled to respect and awe from his subjects.

This ceremony to make King Louis XVI sacred is not dissimilar in intent (or in some particulars, for that matter) from that Biblical ceremony which involved Aaron assuming the sacred office of high priest. The account of Aaron's empowerment is found in Exodus, Chapter 29: 4-9:

And Aaron and his sons thou shalt bring unto the door of the tabernacle of the congregation, and shalt wash them with water. And thou shalt take the garments, and put upon Aaron the coat, and the robe of the ephod, and the ephod, and the breastplate, and gird him with the curious girdle of the ephod: And thou shalt put the mitre upon his head, and put the holy crown upon the mitre. Then shalt thou take the anointing oil, and pour it upon his head, and anoint him. And thou shalt bring his sons, and put coats upon them. And thou shalt gird them with girdles, Aaron and his sons, and put the bonnets on them: and the priest's office shall be theirs for a perpetual statute: and thou shalt consecrate Aaron and his sons.

Here again are washings, anointing, clothing and sanctifying of the person as he assumes an official status.

The purpose of this ceremony was to make a public acknowledgment that Aaron was to be regarded as something out of the ordinary, and elevated as a result of the ceremony into a new and higher form of both personal and public life. It was designed to impress observers as well as Aaron. He was to take his office more seriously as a result of his consecration. He was to be taken more seriously by those he ministered to as well.

This inclination to have ceremony is not limited by time, nationality, culture or continent. The pervasiveness of the practice of ceremony suggests it is an echo of something more innate in humanity than mere coincidence.[181] It is an echo of an earlier and more permanent culture which lies behind the veil. The compulsion to engage in ceremony is rooted in a culture now hidden to us, from which our primordial spirits came, and where they feel most at home. This is why we feel the need, across language and time, space and culture, to celebrate events and passages with ceremonies to mark their passing. Therefore, it should be expected the fullness of the Gospel of Jesus Christ would also convey deep truths through ceremonial rites. And, of course, that is the case.

---

[181]Numerous anthropological studies have been made of this phenomena but they are beyond the scope of this work.

The scriptures contain abundant evidence of ceremonies from heaven. The visions recorded there all have ceremonial content. We tend to overlook them, but the scriptures are filled with examples. We are going to take a look at a few examples to show how these heavenly ceremonies have been witnessed by those who have had an opportunity to see into heaven. Knowing this should help prepare you, as well. You can anticipate what you will be shown by what has been shown to others before you.

Nephi gives an account of his father's first view into the heavens in these words found in 1 Ne. 1: 8: "And being thus overcome with the Spirit, he was carried away in a vision, even that he saw the heavens open, and he thought he saw God sitting upon his throne, surrounded with numberless concourses of angels in the attitude of singing and praising their God." John Welch takes this recitation and fits it into the scholarly tradition of the divine council.[182] That is not a bad scholarly view. However, it ought to occur to any reader that "the attitude of singing and praising" in that setting has decidedly ceremonial context as well. Lehi is seeing and describing what goes on behind the veil. What he describes is steeped with ceremony and celebration. God is seen in the vision, sitting on a throne, with praise going on all the while. You might ask yourself whether this vision of God and the worship of Him is a continuous event, and if so whether heaven itself might be a rather boring and "churchy" place. It was this notion which inspired Mark Twain to make his sardonic tale of Captain Stormfield's visit to heaven.[183]

---

[182]See *The Calling of Lehi as a Prophet*, found in *Glimpses of Lehi's Jerusalem, op. cit.*, pp. 427-438 and citations found there.

[183]There Stormfield is told, with respect to his preliminary singing and harp playing: "People take the figurative language of the Bible and the allegories for literal, and the first thing they ask for when they get here is a halo and a harp, and so on. Nothing that's harmless and reasonable is refused a body here, if he asks it in the right spirit. So they are outfitted with these things without a word. They go and sing and play just about one day, and that's the last you'll ever see them in the choir. They don't need anybody to tell

There must be more to what Lehi is seeing and telling us, and it must have deeper meaning than the scholars attribute to it. We tend to make very superficial use of this vision of Lehi's. After all, it took some effort to record it, preserve it, and etch it into metal plates. And that process was so very deliberate and selective[184] Nephi must want us to appreciate its significance. He addresses this text to his descendants and to a latter-day audience. He wants us to "get it," and so we should make an attempt to do so.

The setting of God's throne tells us we are looking at the pinnacle. This is the seat of power. We see here a throne setting. It is "surrounded" or in a middle. The point from which the compass draws a true circle must be fixed by the center point. God is that center point. It is in the middle. He is that fixed, central position from which all creation arises. "Surrounding" it are the "numberless concourses" of angels. That is, the center of the infinite is God. From Him all blessings flow. From Him all sustaining power and authority rises. The surrounding concourses, infinite in number, are all engaged in "singing and

them that that sort of thing wouldn't make a heaven — at least not a heaven that a sane man could stand a week and remain sane. That cloud-bank is placed where the noise can't disturb the old inhabitants, and so there ain't any harm in letting everybody get up there and cure himself as soon as he comes.

"Now you just remember this — heaven is as blissful and lovely as it can be; but it's just the busiest place you ever heard of. There ain't any idle people here after the first day. Singing hymns and waving palm branches through all eternity is pretty when you hear about it in the pulpit, but it's as poor a way to put in valuable time as a body could contrive. It would just make a heaven of warbling ignoramuses, don't you see? Eternal Rest sounds comforting in the pulpit, too. Well, you try it once, and see how heavy time will hang on your hands. Why, Stormfield, a man like you, that had been active and stirring all his life, would go mad in six months in a heaven where he hadn't anything to do. Heaven is the very last place to come to *rest* in, -- and don't you be afraid to bet on that!" (Twain, Mark. *Extract from Captain Stormfield's Visit to Heaven*; *The Complete Short Stories of Mark Twain*. New York: Bantam Book, 1958.)

[184] 1 Ne. 6: 6 "Wherefore, I shall give commandment unto my seed, that they shall not occupy these plates with things which are not of worth unto the children of men."

praising" Him. Here the ceremony is designed to communicate to the mind of Lehi (and in turn to our own minds) the notion of God's central position and fixed center-point, from which glory proceeds and to which all praise and thanks should be returned. The setting and the information are ceremonial and symbolic. They tell us something. They try to teach us, with the setting and brief description of events, about higher things. They use simple words describing a ceremonial scene from heaven, to tell us something about sacred things from above. They can communicate powerful things to us, if we will let them. They teach us about God's role in creation and His continuing, presiding position to which we, as well as heaven itself, turn for light and power. They tell us God is worthy in heaven of being praised and thanked. If they praise Him in Heaven, how much more worthy is He of our praise and thanks on earth. If they praise Him, given their position of glory and light, how much more ought we to do so. If they accept His central role and power, how much more confidence ought we to have in Him.

In another altogether separate vision given to Alma, he reports seeing the same kind of ceremonial celebration in heaven. Alma 36:22: "Yea, methought I saw, even as our father Lehi saw, God sitting upon his throne, surrounded with numberless concourses of angels, in the attitude of singing and praising their God; yea, and my soul did long to be there." He uses almost identical language as Lehi had used earlier in Nephi's written account. Therefore, Alma must have had a similar view of the events going on behind the veil. What was it that singing, praising and interaction with God caused Alma to long to be there and join in the celebration? (He sees what is going on and he tells us he longs to be there.) It is something so familiar, so compelling, so comforting and inviting that Alma wants to leave this earth and join in the celebration and songs there. This isn't just a "Churchy" event. It's great fun! It's a wonderful time! A party! And Alma is saying he wants to join in so badly that his very soul "longs" to be there. It is a higher thing than Captain Stormfield witnessed. It is much more fulfilling. It is informative, stabilizing, edifying and celebrating. It is holy. Ceremonies can give us a better grasp of profound truths in a few moments than we can get from study for a lifetime. Indeed, if you could gaze into heaven for five minutes, you would put many things into a new perspective. Alma did and as a result Alma longed to be there and join in the celebration.

In the familiar account of the announcement of Christ's birth, there are clear ceremonial overtones, as well.[185] Though we pass over it without much thought, the text clearly indicates a ceremonial event witnessed by the shepherds who were abiding in the fields, keeping watch over the lambs. In the still of the evening, a multitude appears dressed in white, and they break forth into anthems of praise. The heavens resound with the sound of celebration and commemoration because the birth of Christ is a long-awaited event fulfilling the promises made from before the foundation of the earth. They are delighted at His birth, and that delight results in their public songs of praise. It makes us wonder how long they practiced for that one night's chorus, and whether that performance was ever to be repeated again. Probably not. This one show was such a sacred event it got its own single command performance. Heaven's excitement is pouring forth to an audience of a few shepherds in a field. Such is the stuff of which visions are made. Ceremony is the common fare of heaven!

In another vision of Christ's birth, Enoch gives us another view into heaven and the birth's great ceremonial meaning. Enoch knew of the promises made to mankind of a coming Savior. He saw mankind's wickedness and ached over it. He wanted to see the promise realized bringing about mankind's redemption from the fatal rupture between God and man. "And it came to pass that Enoch looked; and from Noah, he beheld all the families of the earth; and he cried unto the Lord, saying: When shall the day of the Lord come? When shall the blood of the Righteous be shed, that all they that mourn may be

---

[185]The account is from Luke 2: 12-14: "And this shall be a sign unto you; Ye shall find the babe wrapped in swaddling clothes, lying in a manger. And suddenly there was with the angel a multitude of the heavenly host praising God, and saying, Glory to God in the highest, and on earth peace, good will toward men."

sanctified and have eternal life?" (Moses 7: 45.) This coming of a Redeemer was what Enoch longed for; and Enoch's impatience and ache for the promise to be fulfilled mirrors the anticipation on the other side of the veil for this same event. Enoch was on the other side of the veil when he asked the question. In the Luke account the heavens cannot conceal their joy and celebration at the announcement of Christ's birth. Anthems are raised and voices unite in ceremonial shouting and outpouring. Similarly, Enoch witnessed the event on the other side of the veil and celebrated there.[186] But spoken words alone are not enough. This particular triumph needed a deeper meaning, reflected by ceremonial observances, on both sides of the veil. It required song and celebration. A party is going on here! No one is standing still. Things are in motion and gestures, waving, singing and shouting all combine in a beautiful and rhythmic chorus that would make anyone beholding it say to themselves afterwards: "Let us now go even unto Bethlehem, and see this thing which is come to pass, which the Lord hath made known unto us." (Luke 2: 15.) Similarly, the excitement produced such enthusiasm that: "And they came with haste, and found Mary, and Joseph, and the babe lying in a manger." (Luke 2: 16.)

If you gazed into heaven for five minutes you would also long to be there. You would hasten your step to go and see what they celebrated. You would catch the fire that burns in heaven for the sacred events which occur here below. You would see and feel more deeply the profound truths which have been restored to us here.

Creation, fall, redemption, a Savior, covenants, return to God's presence, escape from the adversary, and clothing of the Saints in robes of righteousness all call for the adoption of ceremony to teach and commemorate the entire sweep of the vast plan of God for mankind.

---

[186]Moses 7: 47: "And behold, Enoch saw the day of the coming of the Son of Man, even in the flesh; and **his soul rejoiced, saying: The Righteous is lifted up, and the Lamb is slain from the foundation of the world**; and through faith I am in the bosom of the Father, and behold, Zion is with me." (Emphasis added.)

Such things cannot be conveyed in a single phrase or verse. They require celebration and ceremony and Saints joining each other in rites and rituals to adequately capture the notions of holiness, wisdom and joy associated with these things. It is no wonder the rites of the Temple capture these themes. The greatest wonder of this process is how little use we make of it to pour meaning into our lives here.

This notion of ceremonial holiness is also contained in the Psalms. For example, in the 119th Psalm there is an ascension canticle originally written to be sung while ascending the steps to the Temple. It holds the notion of increasing holiness as you approach the Holy Place. These words appear in verses 18-20 of the Psalm: "Open thou mine eyes, that I may behold wondrous things out of thy law. I am a stranger in the earth: hide not thy commandments from me. My soul breaketh for the longing that it hath unto thy judgments at all times."

It recognizes we are strangers and sojourners here in this mortal estate, and we belong somewhere else. While singing and ascending to the Temple, the process of ascension is accompanied by this thought of being alien here, and finding a home where there are wondrous things to be gained as our association with God is renewed. That event of reunification with God is symbolized in the Temple. The Temple is God's House. This song is sung as you go up to His House. You are going up physically to celebrate going upward spiritually. When you get to the Temple you find ceremony originating from, and relating us back into, that other culture behind the veil. The Temple experience in any age is intended to take the participant and convey them into another, higher reality. It is intended to transport you into the culture of heaven, and remove you from the earth.

When you attend the Temple, you should recognize while this is an alien environment to the earth, it is one in which your spirit finds a familiar home. This is the culture from which your spirit originated. Within the Temple, the ceremonies of heaven are presented to the view of man again, and the themes of God's wonder are renewed. Deep truths are conveyed by symbol, by gesture and by word. Layers of symbolic truths are folded over onto each other. It is a process celebrating the entire sweep and majesty of God's works, power and intelligence.

The greatest wonder of God is His creation of this earth. That theme has always been a Temple theme, even during the First Temple era. Writing about the First Temple period, Methodist scholar Margaret Barker states on page 47:

> That creation rituals should be performed by the Lord is hardly surprising. If the Lord had bound the creation at the beginning with the great covenant which kept the forces of chaos in their place and gave security to his people, any covenant renewal ceremony must have involved the Lord performing these acts. Atonement rituals repaired the damage to the created order caused by sin through which 'wrath' could have broken in with such disastrous consequences. Again *The Jewish Encyclopedia* makes an interesting observation: 'But while, according to Scripture, the high priest made atonement, *tradition transferred the atoning power to God.* ... The *d'bir*, the holy of holies, was the place of the Lord's throne, but the *hekal*, the great hall of the temple, was the Garden of Eden. The decorations of the temple were those of Eden (trees, pomegranates, lilies, cherubim), the seven-branched lamp was described in later tradition as the tree of life, a bronze serpent was removed from the temple by Hezekiah, and Ezekiel saw the river of life flowing from the temple. Just as the *d'bir* represented heaven ('represented' is a concession to our way of thinking), so the *hekal* represented the completed creation. This again suggests that the rituals of the temple were creation rituals." (Barker, Margaret. *The Great High Priest, The Temple Roots of Christian Liturgy.* New York: T&T Clark Ltd, 2003.)

She is putting the creation back into First Temple rites. Latter-day Saints find this comfortable. Some of Margaret Barker's scholarly peers find her assertions controversial. She sees through the eyes of the scholar what Latter-day Saints believe to be true. She arrived there through the scholar's tools (and an abundance of candor), and not by following latter-day revelation. It is little wonder she has attracted a Latter-day Saint following. But her research puts the First Temple, like the Latter-day Saint restored Temple rites, squarely in the Garden of Eden celebrating the creation and God's purposes through ceremony and ritual. The House of God has always served the same end and taught the same lessons.

Apocalyptic visions also contain ceremonial details. Even though the Apocalypse of John is not popular reading, it still has profound ceremonial details which get overlooked. Bear with it as we look at an excerpt because there are some good things here. We get this description in Rev. 4: 2-6,10-11:

> And immediately I was in the spirit: and, behold, a throne was set in heaven, and one sat on the throne. And he that sat was to look upon like a jasper and a sardine stone: and there was a rainbow round about the throne, in sight like unto an emerald. And round about the throne were four and twenty seats: and upon the seats I saw four and twenty elders sitting, clothed in white raiment; and they had on their heads crowns of gold. And out of the throne proceeded lightnings and thunderings and voices: and there were seven lamps of fire burning before the throne, which are the seven Spirits of God. And before the throne there was a sea of glass like unto crystal: and in the midst of the throne, and round about the throne, were four beasts full of eyes before and behind... The four and twenty elders fall down before him that sat on the throne, and worship him that liveth for ever and ever, and cast their crowns before the throne, saying, Thou art worthy, O Lord, to receive glory and honour and power: for thou hast created all things, and for thy pleasure they are and were created.

This description has a setting reminiscent of the breastplate of Aaron to be used in the Holy Place of the Temple.[187] The twenty-four seats are

---

[187]The symbol in the breastplate harkens forward to the Celestial Kingdom, and the vision of the ceremony in Revelation harkens back to the attire worn in the Holy Place of the First Temple, and both point to eternity and Celestial glory. We see in this one eternal round of symbol pointing

backward and reality pointing forward. Exo. 39: 1-31: "And of the blue, and purple, and scarlet, they made cloths of service, to do service in the holy place, and made the holy garments for Aaron; as the Lord commanded Moses. And he made the ephod of gold, blue, and purple, and scarlet, and fine twined linen. And they did beat the gold into thin plates, and cut it into wires, to work it in the blue, and in the purple, and in the scarlet, and in the fine linen, with cunning work. They made shoulderpieces for it, to couple it together: by the two edges was it coupled together. And the curious girdle of his ephod, that was upon it, was of the same, according to the work thereof; of gold, blue, and purple, and scarlet, and fine twined linen; as the Lord commanded Moses. And they wrought onyx stones enclosed in ouches of gold, graven, as signets are graven, with the names of the children of Israel. And he put them on the shoulders of the ephod, that they should be stones for a memorial to the children of Israel; as the Lord commanded Moses. And he made the breastplate of cunning work, like the work of the ephod; of gold, blue, and purple, and scarlet, and fine twined linen. It was foursquare; they made the breastplate double: a span was the length thereof, and a span the breadth thereof, being doubled. And they set in it four rows of stones: the first row was a sardius, a topaz, and a carbuncle: this was the first row. And the second row, an emerald, a sapphire, and a diamond. And the third row, a ligure, an agate, and an amethyst. And the fourth row, a beryl, an onyx, and a jasper: they were enclosed in ouches of gold in their enclosings. And the stones were according to the names of the children of Israel, twelve, according to their names, like the engravings of a signet, every one with his name, according to the twelve tribes. And they made upon the breastplate chains at the ends, of wreathen work of pure gold. And they made two ouches of gold, and two gold rings; and put the two rings in the two ends of the breastplate. And they put the two wreathen chains of gold in the two rings on the ends of the breastplate. And the two ends of the two wreathen chains they fastened in the two ouches, and put them on the shoulder pieces of the ephod, before it. And they made two rings of gold, and put them on the two ends of the breastplate, upon the border of it, which was on the side of the ephod inward. And they made two other golden rings, and put them on the two sides of the ephod underneath, toward the forepart of it, over against the other coupling thereof, above the curious girdle of the ephod. And they did bind the breastplate by his rings unto the rings of the ephod with a lace of blue, that it might be above the curious girdle of the ephod, and that the breastplate might not be loosed from the ephod; as the Lord commanded Moses. And he made the robe of the ephod of woven work, all of blue. And there was an hole in the midst of the robe, as the hole of an habergeon, with a band round about the hole, that it should not rend. And they made upon the hems of the robe pomegranates of blue, and purple, and surrounding the throne, the throne forming the center and the twenty-four seats a circle about it. A form of circle or eternal round is depicted in this ceremonial setting. Just as before, the center point must be fixed to use a compass to draw a circle. The center point in this ceremonial setting is again the throne of God. God is always the sure place, the certain fixed point, from which all truths are to be derived.

The throne scene here has the elements of thunder and lightening, the symbols of heavenly power here on earth. Voices, too, come from the throne, where communication goes to and from God, who is in control of all things and from whom all prayers are heard and answered. These things of nature (thunder and lightning) are things of power. The things of man and angels (voices) are things of intelligence and truth. The ceremonial details are conveying to us a clear picture of power, glory, might, dominion, majesty, intelligence and authority. They are the very things of which exaltation is composed.[188]

The seven lamps of the Menorah are there in the Apocalypse, too, symbolically tying this vision's setting to the Holy Place of the earthly Temple, as well. Temple and throne, heaven and earth, are put together

---

scarlet, and twined linen. And they made bells of pure gold, and put the bells between the pomegranates upon the hem of the robe, round about between the pomegranates; A bell and a pomegranate, a bell and a pomegranate, round about the hem of the robe to minister in; as the Lord commanded Moses. And they made coats of fine linen of woven work for Aaron, and for his sons, And a mitre of fine linen, and goodly bonnets of fine linen, and linen breeches of fine twined linen, And a girdle of fine twined linen, and blue, and purple, and scarlet, of needlework; as the Lord commanded Moses. And they made the plate of the holy crown of pure gold, and wrote upon it a writing, like to the engravings of a signet, HOLINESS TO THE LORD. And they tied unto it a lace of blue, to fasten it on high upon the mitre; as the Lord commanded Moses."

[188]See, e.g., D&C 132:19 which states the Saints who receive a fullness of the ordinances here "shall inherit thrones, kingdoms, principalities, and powers, dominions, all heights and depths – ... and they shall pass by the angels, and the gods, which are set there, to their exaltation and glory in all things, as hath been sealed upon their heads, which glory shall be a fulness and a continuation of the seeds forever and ever."

in ceremony and symbol in this vision. The elders in the circle of seats cast their crowns down in worship of the God of all, in a ceremonial reaffirmation of God's rule over all. And if that symbolic act is not clear enough, the elders then proceed to acknowledge God's right to rule over all creation because He is the author of all creation, as they recite in unison the words of a worshipful prayer in their heavenly prayer circle.

These scenes shown to John are steeped in ceremonial meaning and ambiance. This is the culture of heaven, where joy over God's creative acts and gratitude over what He has done for all His creation are best acknowledged in a ceremonial rite of celebration. They are, therefore, filled with Temple typology. In the Temple the rites of heaven are celebrated. And in heaven the Temple symbolism is found in its truest and most complete ceremonial form. The one pointing to the other, and the other pointing to the One.

When words are inadequate to proclaim what is felt, it is ceremony that gets used to capture the awe and reverence for the thing. Ceremony is the way joy and rejoicing are proclaimed in heaven. We are given glimpses of that from time to time, to affirm the true order of this higher culture to mankind. It is, therefore, altogether appropriate we should try and find a heavenly setting and deeper meaning within the Temple's rites. It is in the Temple's ceremony, which was given to us by Heaven, where Heaven attempts to inculcate in us an otherworldly culture and setting. Do not think that the Temple needs to be refined to fit into your culture. Rather, it is you who must change to see another world through it. Seeing that power in the Temple setting is part of being prepared to view other things beyond the veil.[189]

---

[189]Think of the ceremonial details found in Rev. 19: 1-9: "And after these things I heard a great voice of much people in heaven, saying, Alleluia; Salvation, and glory, and honour, and power, unto the Lord our God: For true and righteous [are] his judgments: for he hath judged the great whore, which did corrupt the earth with her fornication, and hath avenged the blood of his servants at her hand. And again they said, Alleluia. And her smoke rose up for ever and ever. And the four and twenty elders and the four beasts fell down and worshipped God that sat on the throne, saying, Amen; Alleluia. And a

Before we leave scriptural examples of this phenomena we will look at three other examples of visions with ceremonial details in the scriptures: Dan. 7: 13-16: "I saw in the night visions, and, behold, one like the Son of man came with the clouds of heaven, and came to the Ancient of days, and they brought him near before him. And there was given him dominion, and glory, and a kingdom, that all people, nations, and languages, should serve him: his dominion is an everlasting dominion, which shall not pass away, and his kingdom that which shall not be destroyed. I, Daniel was grieved in my spirit in the midst of my body, and the visions of my head troubled me. I came near unto one of them that stood by, and asked him the truth of all this. So he told me, and made me know the interpretation of the things." In this account Daniel sees a vision of worship and coronation. The ceremonial vesting of titles, power and glory is shown, but he is lost in the amazement of this otherworldly setting and scene. He asks another angelic bystander to help in the explanation of these things, for they made Daniel's head spin. This kind of display of holy beings in ceremonial celebration and acknowledgment of eternal glory is too much for Daniel. He needs a guide. The wonder and glory of it all is dizzying. Ceremony is intended

---

voice came out of the throne, saying, Praise our God, all ye his servants, and ye that fear him, both small and great. And I heard as it were the voice of a great multitude, and as the voice of many waters, and as the voice of mighty thunderings, saying, Alleluia: for the Lord God omnipotent reigneth. Let us be glad and rejoice, and give honour to him: for the marriage of the Lamb is come, and his wife hath made herself ready. And to her was granted that she should be arrayed in fine linen, clean and white: for the fine linen is the righteousness of saints. And he saith unto me, Write, Blessed are they which are called unto the marriage supper of the Lamb. And he saith unto me, These are the true sayings of God." Celebration and praise are coupled with the Hosanna Shout, and tied to a Temple wedding setting, where eternal marriage is foreshadowed and affirmed. Sacred and clean vestments are incorporated into this ceremonial setting, as well. Writing and testimony of the truthfulness of these things are also depicted here. It is a chorus of symbolic and ceremonial truths being put onto display. John is being allowed to show some of the culture of the heavens to us. We should not miss the meaning of these things.

to be awe-inspiring. It has accomplished its purpose here, with Daniel, for Daniel is struck by its awe and splendor.

This vision is full of Temple typology as well. Conferring or endowment of power and glory are clearly tied to Temple rites. This is so much so that the name given to the largest portion of the Temple rites in our day is the "endowment."

A second example of this form of vision is taken from 1 Kgs. 22: 19-23:

> And he said, Hear thou therefore the word of the Lord: I saw the Lord sitting on his throne, and all the host of heaven standing by him on his right hand and on his left. And the Lord said, Who shall persuade Ahab, that he may go up and fall at Ramoth-gilead? And one said on this manner, and another said on that manner. And there came forth a spirit, and stood before the Lord, and said, I will persuade him. And the Lord said unto him, Wherewith? And he said, I will go forth, and I will be a lying spirit in the mouth of all his prophets. And he said, Thou shalt persuade him, and prevail also: go forth, and do so. Now therefore, behold, the Lord hath put a lying spirit in the mouth of all these thy prophets, and the Lord hath spoken evil concerning thee.

Here we see a setting for deliberation and counsel among a host in heaven. They are on the right and on the left, no circle among these hosts, unlike the examples before. They are arraigned in this vision in a setting where sides have been taken. No circle, and therefore they are not "one," but in a divided and ceremonially polarized setting. One spirit here offers to act the part of the adversary, in much the same way Satan has functioned throughout history.[190] The setting conveys the

---

[190]The account in Job of Satan's challenge in a council is typical of Satan's role in mankind's Second Estate: "Now there was a day when the sons of God came to present themselves before the Lord, and Satan came also among them. And the Lord said unto Satan, Whence comest thou? Then Satan answered the Lord, and said, From going to and fro in the earth, and from walking up and down in it. And the Lord said unto Satan, Hast thou considered my servant Job, that there is none like him in the earth, a perfect

nature of the deliberation and decision. Through this heavenly setting showing division, the ceremony is passing along deeper meaning. Think about the Temple prayer circle, on the one hand, and a Stake Church disciplinary council, on the other. In the one, there is harmony and united purpose. In the other, there is conflict and conflict resolution. Someone is before the disciplinary council to resolve their disharmony with the Church. As a consequence, the council is ceremonially divided[191] to render a decision. These two kinds of assemblies have different purposes and therefore different forms for gathering. The scriptures show us similar things go on behind the veil.

In Isa. 6: 1-13 we find this final example to use here:

> In the year that king Uzziah died I saw also the Lord sitting upon a throne, high and lifted up, and his train filled the temple. Above it stood the seraphims: each one had six wings; with twain he covered his face, and with twain he covered his feet,

and an upright man, one that feareth God, and escheweth evil? Then Satan answered the Lord, and said, Doth Job fear God for nought? Hast not thou made an hedge about him, and about his house, and about all that he hath on every side? thou hast blessed the work of his hands, and his substance is increased in the land. But put forth thine hand now, and touch all that he hath, and he will curse thee to thy face. And the LORD said unto Satan, Behold, all that he hath is in thy power; only upon himself put not forth thine hand. So Satan went forth from the presence of the LORD." (Job 1: 6-12.)

[191]The procedure for a Church disciplinary council is set out in relevant part in D&C 102: 15, 17 – 18: "The accused, in all cases, has a right to one-half of the council, to prevent insult or injustice. ... Those councilors who draw even numbers, that is, 2, 4, 6, 8, 10, and 12, are the individuals who are to stand up in behalf of the accused, and prevent insult and injustice. In all cases the accuser and the accused shall have a privilege of speaking for themselves before the council, after the evidences are heard and the councilors who are appointed to speak on the case have finished their remarks." The division of the council is a reflection of the division of interests between the person who is before the council as opposed to the Church. Though this is for the benefit of the person, and its purpose is to reclaim and not to punish, this setting is a good illustration of a Church setting in which division is a part of the event.

and with twain he did fly. And one cried unto another, and said, Holy, holy, holy, is the Lord of hosts: the whole earth is full of his glory. And the posts of the door moved at the voice of him that cried, and the house was filled with smoke. Then said I, Woe is me! for I am undone; because I am a man of unclean lips, and I dwell in the midst of a people of unclean lips: for mine eyes have seen the King, the Lord of hosts. Then flew one of the seraphims unto me, having a live coal in his hand, which he had taken with the tongs from off the altar: And he laid it upon my mouth, and said, Lo, this hath touched thy lips; and thine iniquity is taken away, and thy sin purged. Also I heard the voice of the Lord, saying, Whom shall I send, and who will go for us? Then said I, Here am I; send me. And he said, Go, and tell this people, Hear ye indeed, but understand not; and see ye indeed, but perceive not. Make the heart of this people fat, and make their ears heavy, and shut their eyes; lest they see with their eyes, and hear with their ears, and understand with their heart, and convert, and be healed. Then said I, Lord, how long? And he answered, Until the cities be wasted without inhabitant, and the houses without man, and the land be utterly desolate, And the Lord have removed men far away, and there be a great forsaking in the midst of the land. But yet in it shall be a tenth, and it shall return, and shall be eaten: as a teil tree, and as an oak, whose substance is in them, when they cast their leaves: so the holy seed shall be the substance thereof.

Here the worship of God in the vision is accompanied by shaking the pillars of the doorpost. These are the main structural members of the Temple. If they move, the Temple will fall. Yet here they shake, to remind Isaiah that there is One greater than the Temple, itself. It is that One who makes the Temple holy, because it is His house. So He can shake the foundations, and yet He can keep it from falling. His glory and might are greater than the Temple itself.

Isaiah needs Divine grace and forgiveness to qualify as a suitable messenger for the words from God. This problem is approached as a ceremonial issue in the vision. In this First Temple setting, the coals come from the altar of incense before the veil of the Temple, where incense symbolizes the prayers of the faithful ascending to God. The coal from this altar is taken and touched to Isaiah's lips, making them clean and removing all guilt and sin. This ceremonial cleansing is enough, coming as it is from God, to qualify Isaiah to now speak the words of God to Israel. Deeper truths and lessons are condensed into ceremonial acts. The words of the prophet's mouth are tied to the altar of incense and prayers to God. It conveys meaning through rites and symbol.

Fire or coals as a purgative for Isaiah's lips are linked to prayer to God. Linking them together is a form of communication through symbol that is intended to inspire awe and worship, along with the excitement of understanding God's hidden meanings. The altar and prayer are ways for anyone to cleanse their lips from the impurity of living in this world to the purity of speaking God's message. These are powerfully expressive symbols, put into the vision to teach and elevate our thoughts. They come from a culture beyond the veil where such ceremonial rites are the common substance of communications, because so much can be and needs to be condensed into so few acts and words.

God hides most truths in plain sight. He awaits your willingness to see them. That will come from within you. When you are ready to see, however, the truths are staring you right in the face. By using ceremony, He gives us a great deal to think about, pray about and meditate upon. We can look at the visions over and over and find new meanings. The visions begin to expand the longer you reflect upon them.

You will probably need to adopt a different cultural outlook before you can see these things for the rich form of communication they offer. But if you do, they will begin to flood in upon you. Leave Babylon and come to Zion. Though it involves a slight elevation in thought and action, it results in a view that is panoramic and ageless.

We are going to address these things in the coming chapters. However, this subject is important and needed to be considered as a separate chapter. The ordinances of the Gospel of Jesus Christ are more than hollow gestures and rituals. They are deeply communicative and expressive rites. They prepare people for the visions of eternity. Contained in them is the substance of what you will see behind the veil. Therefore, they should become the subject of reverence and prayerful consideration.

It is for the reasons set out in this chapter the scriptures report: "And this greater priesthood administereth the gospel and holdeth the key of the mysteries of the kingdom, even the key of the knowledge of God. Therefore, in the ordinances thereof, the power of godliness is manifest. And without the ordinances thereof, and the authority of the priesthood, the power of godliness is not manifest unto men in the flesh; For without this no man can see the face of God, even the Father, and live." (D&C 84: 19-22.) These rites and ceremonies are necessary for anyone to be able to see the face of God. They are an indispensable prerequisite to the veil parting. In fact, they are the ceremonial equivalent to having the veil part.

First you must see these things for the truths they contain. When you can accept them for what they are in symbolic meaning and ascribe to them the holiness and virtue they are intended to convey, then you are prepared to encounter the reality which they reflect. This is the process described in Ether 12: 19, which tells us of those "who could not be kept from within the veil, but truly saw with their eyes the things which they had beheld with an eye of faith, and they were glad." First you see with the eyes of faith. Then you see the reality which your eyes of faith had witnessed first.

Promises and covenants precede the reality. Reality follows the promises and covenants. The one comes from above to below and then points upward. The other comes from above to the person who, while living below, has been prepared for citizenship above. Preparation for citizenship above is through the ceremonies of the Priesthood.

Chapter Eleven

BECOMING AS A LITTLE CHILD

I have learned the Lord intends to answer every prayer *ever uttered by any of His faithful children. There are no exceptions. But the time frame is His and not ours. There came a point when every prayer I had uttered had been answered, a point when I realized every promise given to me in blessings, or in covenants, or by the voice of inspiration had been realized. It was not always apparent this was the case.*

It was only in hindsight I realized the Lord was answering the prayers all along. But what was asked in haste or impatience expecting a quick response was answered over time by His patient providence.

I was often unprepared for what I asked to receive and therefore the necessary developmental experiences had to come first. There is always a time of necessary testing and proving which precedes the blessing. Spencer W. Kimball's thought captured in the book title Faith Precedes the Miracle *is not just a catchy title, but a truism. If you want a miracle, you have to receive faith equivalent to the thing sought first.*

Inspired by a Patriarchal Blessing which held out the promise of an audience with the Father, my prayers knew no limit to what I asked. Although my hopes reached the heavens, my character and inner-self remained decidedly earth-bound. You have to be careful what you ask for, because what you seek may require much more than just rearranging your schedule. It may require (as it did with me) a wholesale change of mind, thought, self-perception, ambition, ego and heart. If you are willing, and will follow Him, He can lead you there. The trek will be traumatic, difficult to bear and sometimes searing to the soul.

If it is humility you lack, then the required humiliation needed to acquire humility will be given. The losses of marriage, of children and association, of status and property, and the crippling insecurity I needed were all secured for me through the wisdom of God and my own personal failings.

The Lord set about immediately to answer the prayers I offered Him. It took me, however, over two and a half decades of preparation to be ready for the final answer to the greatest requests. The intermediate steps needed for my own development came line upon line, precept upon precept, experience upon experience, loss upon loss, challenge upon challenge, failure upon failure, apparent defeat upon apparent defeat and real success upon success. Life itself gave me all the needed encounters, events and personalized experiences to gain what I lacked. And what I lacked most was the inner character to be fit for the thing asked.

You get what you ask for, and if you are anything like me, what you are asking for is going to require many changes. I hardly recognize myself from where I started. There are so many scars and wounds to the heart and mind that I cannot look back upon myself without a profound sense of disappointment at what I was and gratitude for what the Lord has made of me.

At last, as the journey progressed, the pride of accomplishment was replaced by the humility to accept. Eagerness in pushing the Lord into acting on my own will was replaced by the defeats which brought patience to accept His will. The desire and ambition to be something more was replaced by the contentment to accept what I was. Defeat and triumph merged into one. I found rest.

The patriarch's blessing to me stated I should have "the blessings of being satisfied with the things that you are able to do...." Early on I resented this notion. I wanted much more. How could anyone ever be satisfied they had gotten enough, done enough, seen enough, and obtained enough? It seemed to me being satisfied was more of a character flaw than a blessing.

After being driven to my knees from personal failings and losses, however, the universe of possibilities contracted enough that I realized I had to be content with less. Then I grew grateful for what I had. Then I grew satisfied that getting back up after falling so many times along the path was how progress was made. And I had made progress.

Children fall a lot before they learn to cooperate with gravity and walk. I saw my children suffer through bruised knees, bloody noses, hurt hands and chipped teeth as they struggled against gravity trying to walk. One of my children has a life-long scar under his eye from a fall as a child. He later became a cross-country track runner in high school.

After years of being oblivious to the lesson in front of my eyes, at last I realized the simple truth: If my children fight back after every fall, and every injury, and every pain to overcome and learn to walk, then I needed to do the same. Comparatively, I was little more than an infant myself and had a long way to go before I could "walk" before God and be content.

The Gospel includes all truth, wherever the truth is found. As Brigham Young said:

> 'Mormonism,' so-called, embraces every principle pertaining to life and salvation, for time and eternity. No matter who has it. If the infidel has got truth it belongs to 'Mormonism.' The truth and sound doctrine possessed by the sectarian world, and they have a great deal, all belong to this Church. As for their morality, many of them are morally just as good as we are. All that is good, lovely, and praiseworthy belongs to this church and kingdom. **'Mormonism' includes all truth. There is no truth but what belongs to the gospel.** It is life, eternal life; it is bliss; it is the fullness of all things in the gods and in the eternities of the gods. (*JD* 11: 375, emphasis added.)

This thought was echoed by Wilford Woodruff, who taught: "The building up of the Zion of God in these latter days includes, I may say of a truth, every branch of business, both temporal and spiritual, in which we are engaged. **We cannot touch upon any subject which is lawful in the sight of God and man, that is not embraced in our religion. The Gospel of Jesus Christ which we have embraced, and which we preach, includes all truth.**" *JD* 15: 77, emphasis added. Similarly President Spencer W. Kimball said: "The gospel is true beyond all questioning. There may be parts of it we do not yet know and fully understand, but we shall never be able to prove it untrue for **it includes all truth, known and unknown**, developed and undeveloped." (*Teachings of Spencer W. Kimball, The.* Edited by Edward L. Kimball. Salt Lake City: Deseret Book Company, 1982, p.24, emphasis added.)

The Thirteenth Article of Faith ends with the sentence: "If there is anything virtuous, lovely, or of good report or praiseworthy, we seek after these things." This Article of Faith is consistent with these later declarations from Church Prophets and Apostles.

When we look to find understanding, we should be willing to consider truth from any source. Brigham Young cut to the heart of the matter, as he was wont to do so very often, and proclaimed:

We say, are you willing to receive more? If so, here is more for you. So far as your faith in Christ goes, and your morality, we say, amen. But here is something more. "Ah," say they, "we have got enough, we don't want any of your Mormonism." Well, now they do, if they only knew it. I had a conversation recently with a prominent minister of a church in the East and he said, I do not agree with you in your peculiar views. I answered, are you not for the truth, the whole truth and nothing but the truth? If you are, so am I. How is it possible to get up an argument? I will make a bargain. I will compare my religion with yours. We will start out with the Bible alone, taking it as the standard. All that the Bible teaches for doctrine and practice we will take for our guide. **If I have an error I will part with it. Will you do the same? If you can find that you have a truth that I have not, and that I have an error, I will trade ten errors if I have them for one truth.** (*JD* 16: 43, emphasis added.)

We should be willing to trade truth for any errors we have in ourselves. This is so commonsensical, to say it is to be persuaded of it. Yet saying it and conducting life according to it are two very different things. We tend to be jealous of what truths we are willing to accept. We tend to want to have a presumptive "bona-fide" source to rely upon, and to screen out truths offered from elsewhere. Setting a narrower view may screen out errors, but it will also screen out great volumes of truths.

In His historic context and setting, Christ was not a "bona-fide" source for truth. He was the "carpenter's son" and not the son of a great rabbi. He had no learning or social position. There was nothing in Him that His contemporaries should desire.[192] Even when He spoke words of grace and truth, the common reaction was described: "And when he was come into his own country, he taught them in their

---

[192]Isa. 53: 2-3: "he hath no form nor comeliness; and when we shall see him, there is no beauty that we should desire him. He is despised and rejected of men; a man of sorrows, and acquainted with grief: and we hid as it were our faces from him; he was despised, and we esteemed him not."

synagogue, insomuch that they were astonished, and said, Whence hath this man this wisdom, and these mighty works? Is not this the carpenter's son? Is not his mother called Mary? And his brethren, James, and Joses, and Simon, and Judas? And his sisters, are they not all with us? Whence then hath this man all these things? And they were offended in him." (Matt. 13: 54-57.) Accepting this carpenter's son, this unlikely man of truth, this astonishing claim from one so obscure, required more than some could give. It required the humility to accept truth, although its proponent was not sitting in a position of authority among the chief priests, scribes, Pharisees and rabbis. It required of them in their day the same thing which Section 121 asks you to listen for, from a teacher in our day.

What this modern revelation specifically tells you NOT to do is to accept someone merely because of position. If it were status alone that mattered, the contemporaries of Christ's day would have properly rejected Him. They had to listen for the voice of truth. It is the same in our day. We must also listen for the voice of truth, whether it comes from unlikely sources or not.

It is always true that "many are called, but few are chosen. No power or influence can or ought to be maintained by virtue of the priesthood." (D&C 121: 40-41.) If your sole source of what you regard as "bona fide" knowledge is the authorities in a priestly group, or in a scholarly discipline, or a philosophical school of thought, then you would be among those who would have rejected the carpenter's son. He came without rank, position or authority. He came with nothing more than the truth. He came with exactly what He asks you to follow now, armed only with the tools of "persuasion, ... long-suffering, ... gentleness and meekness, and ... love unfeigned; By kindness, and pure knowledge, which shall greatly enlarge the soul without hypocrisy, and without guile—." (*Id.*, vs. 41-42.) He came as He comes now. It is a test. It has always been a test. The test is no different now than it was then. Do you hear Him? Do you listen to Him? His voice resonates in the words of His true disciples. They do not resonate in the words of the pretenders and the faithless. His voice cannot be faked. The voice of inspiration cannot be breathed into the lifeless words of a false or faithless or disobedient disciple.

The first place to look for the Master's voice is, of course, among the presiding authorities of the Church of Jesus Christ of Latter-day Saints. But they are not entitled to anyone's blind trust. They are ordained to speak with the voice of inspiration, however, and they should be listened to carefully. As the scriptures inform us: "And, behold, and lo, this is an ensample unto all those who were ordained unto this priesthood, whose mission is appointed unto them to go forth — [193] And this is the ensample unto them, that they shall speak as they are moved upon by the Holy Ghost. And whatsoever they shall speak when moved upon by the Holy Ghost shall be scripture, shall be the will of the Lord, shall be the mind of the Lord, shall be the word of the Lord, shall be the voice of the Lord, and the power of God unto salvation." (D&C 68: 2-4.) The inspired leaders of the Church of Jesus Christ of Latter-day Saints are assigned by the Lord to lead His Saints in these latter-days. They are entrusted with keys and authority which is necessary for salvation. If you want to make personal covenants with God, you must do so through His established system for allowing that. And those who are chosen by Him to preside in His Church are entitled to receive the voice of inspiration to assist them in the process. When they do speak with the voice of inspiration, you should hear them as the "voice of the Lord." But, this relates to those times when their voice is inspired by the Holy Ghost. It is possible for any man to err. Joseph Smith confessed his numerous faults and shortcomings, as we have discussed earlier. Certainly no mortal is free from error. Therefore, it is up to you to distinguish between moments of inspiration and the rest.

Brigham Young cut to the core of this when he cautioned:

---

[193]This section is speaking specifically about the leaders of the Church of Jesus Christ of Latter-day Saints.

What a pity it would be if we were led by one man to utter destruction! Are you afraid of this? I am more afraid that this people have so much confidence in their leaders that they will not inquire of themselves of God whether they are led by Him. I am fearful they settle down in a state of blind self-security, trusting their eternal destiny in the hands of their leaders with a reckless confidence that in itself would thwart the purposes of God in their salvation, and weaken that influence they could give to their leaders, did they know for themselves, by the revelations of Jesus, that they are led in the right way. Let every man and woman know, by the whispering of the Spirit of God to themselves, whether their leaders are walking in the path that the Lord dictates, or not. This has been my exhortation continually. (*JD* 9: 150.)

He also exhorted the Saints to listen to the Holy Ghost, and not men, because if it was only men they followed they would inherit a Telestial kingdom.[194] He tells us:

Now those men, or those women, who know no more about the power of God, and the influences of the Holy Spirit, than to be led entirely by another person, suspending their own understanding, and pinning their faith upon another's sleeve, will never be capable of entering into the celestial glory, to be crowned as they anticipate; they will never be capable of becoming Gods. They cannot rule themselves, to say nothing of ruling others, but they must be dictated to in every trifle, like a child. They cannot control themselves in the least, but James, Peter, or somebody else must control them. They never can become Gods, nor be crowned as rulers with glory, immortality,

[194]His teachings on this come from scripture, where in Section 76 it is revealed: "And the glory of the telestial is one, even as the glory of the stars is one; for as one star differs from another star in glory, even so differs one from another in glory in the telestial world; For these are they who are of Paul, and of Apollos, and of Cephas. These are they who say they are some of one and some of another – some of Christ and some of John, and some of Moses, and some of Elias, and some of Esaias, and some of Isaiah, and some of Enoch; But received not the gospel, neither the testimony of Jesus, neither the prophets, neither the everlasting covenant." (vs. 98-101.)

and eternal lives. They never can hold scepters of glory, majesty, and power in the celestial kingdom. Who will? Those who are valiant and inspired with the true independence of heaven, who will go forth boldly in the service of their God, leaving others to do as they please, determined to do right, though all mankind besides should take the opposite course. (*JD* 1: 312, also found in *Discourses of Brigham Young*, Young, Brigham. *Discourses of Brigham Young*. Selected and arranged by John A. Widtsoe. Salt Lake City: Deseret Book Company, 1973, p. 382-3.)

George Q. Cannon also expressed concern over following men, rather than the voice of the Spirit. He put it in this way: "Put trust in no man. Do not, brethren, put your trust in man though he be a Bishop, an Apostle or a President; if you do, they will fail you at some time or place; they will do wrong or seem to, and your support be gone; but if we lean on God, He never will fail us. When men and women depend on God alone and trust in Him alone, their faith will not be shaken if the highest in the Church should step aside. They could still see that He is just and true, that truth is lovely in His sight and the pure in heart are dear to Him." (Cannon, George Q. *Gospel Truth: Discourses and Writings of President George Q. Cannon*. Selected, arranged and edited by Jerreld L. Newquist. Salt Lake City: Zion's Book Store, 1957, p.249.)

When men speak as men, no matter their role in society or church, they are not entitled to your faith. If you give it to them, you are an idolater and following a Telestial standard. When prophets speak by the voice of inspiration, then it is the voice of inspiration you follow. We are disciples of the Master and not of the Master's servants. Brigham Young, once again, made the distinction most clear:

> How... are we to know the voice of the Good Shepherd from the voice of a stranger? Can any person answer this question? I can, it is very easy. To every philosopher upon the earth, I say, Your eye can be deceived, so can mine; your ear can be deceived, so can mine; the touch of your hand can be deceived, so can mine; but the Spirit of God filling the creature with revelation and the light of eternity, cannot be mistaken – the

revelation which comes from God is never mistaken... When an individual, filled with the Spirit of God, declares the truth of heaven, the sheep hear that, the Spirit of the Lord pierces their inmost souls and sinks deep into their hearts; by the testimony of the Holy Ghost light springs up within them, and they see and understand for themselves. This is the way the Gospel should be preached by every Elder in Israel, and by this power every hearer should hear; and if we would know the voice of the Good Shepherd, we must live so that the Spirit of the Lord can find its way to our hearts." (*JD* 16: 74-75.)

So you see it is you who are responsible for these things. You cannot defer them to another. Even trusted others cannot be the ones you rely upon for exaltation. Following Christ is a rugged and individual responsibility each must shoulder for him or herself. If you elect to defer to another for your source of truth, then you cannot hope to rise above a Telestial inheritance, for you are among those who "are of Paul, and of Apollos, and of Cephas. These are they who say they are some of one and some of another – some of Christ and some of John, and some of Moses, and some of Elias, and some of Esaias, and some of Isaiah, and some of Enoch; But received not the gospel, neither the testimony of Jesus, neither the prophets, neither the everlasting covenant." (D&C 76: 99-101.) We must follow the Father and not the messengers of the Son, even if they are truly sent by Him. Worship of anyone or anything other than the true God is idolatry; and, therefore, worthy only of Telestial beings.

The Gospel requires us to proceed carefully, to be sure. We are required to find the voice of the Spirit for ourselves. Every Saint must become, in their own right, a prophet or prophetess. Not to lead others, but themselves. For each must choose for him or herself to find and follow the Master's voice in his or her life. The only sure rock upon which salvation remains to be found is that same rock of revelation which Christ assured Peter was secure to trust.[195] If you follow President

---

[195]Peter's testimony about Christ as the Father's Son resulted in Christ's declaration: "And Jesus answered and said unto him, Blessed art thou,

Hinckley solely because he is the President of the Church of Jesus Christ of Latter-day Saints, you are following a man. But if you follow President Hinckley because you hear the Master's voice in his counsel and teaching, then you are following the Lord, and not a man. There is a great difference between the two. One honors the Lord and leads to exaltation. The other misses the mark and makes such followers Telestial. This distinction is pivotal to salvation itself. It is not merely rhetorical, but of such substance if you fail to understand it you fail in the test of mortality itself. This is what we signed up for in coming to mortality. We accepted this challenge and expected it. Now it confronts us. So the test is afoot and must be taken with caution and humility.

Christ commands us: "Except ye be converted, and become as little children, ye shall not enter into the kingdom of heaven." (Matt. 18: 3.) This "except" seems to preclude from the kingdom of heaven, altogether, anyone who is unwilling to become as a little child. Given the importance, therefore, of this requirement, defining what 'becoming as a little child' means takes on new and greater significance.

The scriptural explanation in Mosiah 3: 19 says every person must "become[…] as a child, **submissive, meek, humble, patient, full of love, willing to submit to all things which the Lord seeth fit to inflict** upon him, even as a child doth submit to his father." (Emphasis added.) This list and its implications are as follows..

"Submissive" denotes acceptance of the Father's will in preference to your own. It does not say you should submit to men. There is nothing about following a man in the concept of "submission." As used here, submission is not just an unanchored term, abstractly applied to anyone or anything. It is submission to God. Christ best exemplified this trait as He defined who He was in His introduction to the Nephites. There He proclaimed that He had "suffered the will of the Father in all things from the beginning." (3 Ne. 11: 11.) He did not submit to the

---

Simon Barjona: for **flesh and blood hath not revealed it unto thee, but my Father which is in heaven**. And I say also unto thee, That thou art Peter, and **upon this rock I will build my church**; and the gates of hell shall not prevail against it." (Matt. 16: 17-18, emphasis added.)

rabbis, or the scribes and Pharisees. Though He taught their position warranted respect,[196] He did not submit to them in the sense used here. Rather He challenged them and provoked their ire. Ultimately, He so offended them, they had Him killed. And so following "the will in all things from the beginning" does not ever require anyone to submit to the rule or command of a man, even in marriage. All things are predicated on first hearkening to the Lord.

"Meek" is a word Christ used in the Sermon on the Mount, telling us that the meek will inherit the earth. Meekness denotes, among other things, a conscious effort to avoid harming or offending others. It requires an absence of pride or self will. It is not insistent upon being recognized or applauded. It denotes a willingness to suffer without complaint. Others may never recognize the meek, because meekness does not vaunt itself, nor demand notice. They are "satisfied with things they are able to do." There is a great freedom in meekness. It relieves the meek from the burden of seeking their acclaim. It gives them the security of feeling God's approval for their course of living. It is private.

"Humble" is the word we use for a most remarkable trait. If you have children, you see immediately they are by nature more humble than adults. They not only do not have a good working knowledge of practical skills, they are keenly aware of their own ignorance. As a result, children are inquisitive. They search relentlessly for greater understanding, and pester their parents for the "whys" and "hows" and "whens"of life. As a result, children are willing students and eager to be taught. They not only don't know, they **know they don't know**, and want to be given the chance to learn. They "seek" and "ask" and "knock." Children do by nature just as Christ bids us to do.

In contrast, adulthood is where we find the arrogant and the unwilling. Pride and the refusal to search for knowledge is the typical adult reaction to any new knowledge. Particularly, this hostility is toward

---

[196]Matt. 23: 1-3: "Then spake Jesus to the multitude, and to his disciples, Saying, The scribes and the Pharisees sit in Moses' seat: All therefore whatsoever they bid you observe, that observe and do; but do not ye after their works: for they say, and do not."

knowledge that is obtained in a foreign way, which we will discuss further. Nephi wrote a lament typifying the adult mind, stating: "I am left to mourn because of the unbelief, and the wickedness, and the ignorance, and the stiffneckedness of men; for they will not search knowledge, nor understand great knowledge, when it is given unto them in plainness, even as plain as word can be." (2 Ne. 32: 7.) The most eager students are the young. The older the person, the less likely it is they will accept instruction from others with humility. Older people, like the proverbial old dogs, do not willingly accept new "tricks" in their lives. Hence the need for all of us to become as little children again.

The child's patient waiting is not readily apparent. Most children have little impulse control and do not want to wait for anything. "Patience" as used here does not mean what you typically think. Rather it refers to the child's "patience" to grow into adulthood. They have many years ahead before reaching adulthood. There is nothing the child can do to change that. Nor do they attempt to do so. Most adults have many years ahead of them before they become fit for the Second Comforter. Just like you cannot rush from childhood into adulthood but must progress by degrees through the many long months into many years, so, too, we must progress from a smaller degree to a much larger one. Going back, like going forward, involves effort, as we shall presently see. Perhaps it takes decades to develop as necessary to receive an audience with Christ. Children persist in waiting, growing and maturing. Their progression into adulthood is gradual. But that process is relentless and marches on through two decades of development and maturity. That is the patience spoken of here. You will have to grow, mature and progress gradually by degrees to receive the Second Comforter.

Being "full of love" is what the 13th chapter of 1 Corinthians is all about. Charity is the "pure love of Christ." This childlike attribute comes from a natural disposition to share love which children enjoy by their native status. As we progress into adulthood and experience the disappointments of other's failings, we become less willing to love others. We suspect their motives. We distrust their worthiness to be loved. We guard against their potential for causing us mischief. These are learned fears. Little children are "too trusting" because they find it easier to love than to fear. We all found it easier to love when we were children.

The final quality of being "willing to submit" again reminds us of Christ. His knee bent to the Father in all things. And although every knee will ultimately submit to Him, many of those kneeling at the last day will do so from fear or regret, although most will do so from gratitude. Submitting to Him now, when there is no great persuasion to do so and all of the world may be aligned against His ways, stands as proof you really are willing to submit.

Christ asked: "And why call ye me, Lord, Lord, and do not the things which I say?" (Luke 6: 46.) Calling Him Lord is not enough. Willingness to submit requires a willingness to be inconvenienced.

How does the disciple become "childlike?" How does the adult return to the status of their former, childlike mind?

In the Pulitzer Prize winning book *Godel, Escher, Bach: An Eternal Golden Braid*, there are some interesting glimpses of how some of these things can be be fit together.[197] The Crab is a recurring character in the book. The Crab is speaking about its movement on page 200: "It's in our genes, you know, turning round and round. That reminds me – I've always wondered, 'Which came first – the Crab or the Gene?' That is to say, 'Which came last, the Gene or the Crab?' I'm always turning things round and round you know. It's in our genes, after all. When we walk backwards, we move forwards." (Hofstadter, Douglas R. *Godel, Escher, Bach: An Eternal Golden Braid*. New York: Basic Books, Inc, 1979.) You see, for a crab to walk on dry ground, the weight of its forward arms is so great that they must be drug along the ground. They cannot push them by going forward. Instead, that requires the crab to walk back-wards. To go forward, it must walk backwards. Since all things testify of

---

[197]The whole of the book is a chiasm, although its author refers to his discussion in terms of "loops."

God and His ways, the crab is also a testimony of some truth. It tells us by its movement that to go forward we must go backward.

An illustration on page 201, Figure 43, has this commentary: "Here is a short section of one of the Crab's Genes, turning round and round. When the two DNA strands are unraveled and laid out side by side, they read this way:

....TTTTTTTTTCGAAAAAAAAA...AAAAAAAAAGCTTTTTT TTT.....

Notice that they are the same, only one goes forwards while the other goes backwards. This is the defining property of the form called 'crab cannon' in music. It is reminiscent of, though a little different from, a palindrome, which is a sentence that reads the same backwards and forwards. In molecular biology, such segments of DNA are called 'palindromes' – a slight misnomer, since 'crab cannon' would be more accurate. Not only is this DNA segment crab-canonical – but moreover its base segment sequence codes for the Dialogue's structure." (*Id.*) Interesting how this forward/backward movement goes right to the level of the crab's DNA. The sequence reminds us of chiasmus.[198] The crab's DNA is a chiasm.

Later, on page 661 of *Godel, Escher, Bach* there is a discussion regarding Bongard[199] problems, also relevant to the child's mind: "I still have a certain faith that Bongard problems depend on a sense of simplicity... our notion of simplicity is universal, for what matters is not any of these individual objects, but the fact that taken together they span a wide space." (*Id.*) When I read this the first time, I performed a

---

[198]Chiasmus is an ancient sentence structure in which the pattern reaches a central point, then reverses. The pattern can be summarized by the example: ABCDCBA; where the concept in "A" appears in the first and again in the last sentence. Similarly concept "B" repeats in the second to the first and second to the last sentence, and so on.

[199]Bongard developed a series of tests involving patterns and shapes. The discussion uses Bongard's tests to demonstrate analytical and reasoning issues relevant to the text. They depend upon abstract reasoning, but also require an ability to find the simple patterns within a complex set of problems.

test using the Bongard problems. I saw no pattern. They seemed too random to my mind. I showed them to my wife, and they eluded her, too. However, when I showed them to my children, they recognized patterns in the sequences which eluded me. The children reduced the problems to such a basic and simple level, they could see the matching patterns which the adult complex mind could not see. The author was right. Bongard problems do depend upon a sense of simplicity. They are greatly aided by seeing them in a simple way with a simple mind. The child's view is infinitely superior to the adult's in seeing the patterns because children can see things simply.

This leads us back to the ancient word form of chiasmus. As John Welch[200] has written about chiasmus, he has not related it to the question of *why* this form of writing was developed in the first place. Writers, including Welch, have suggested it points to the central theme of the writing and emphasizes the thought found there. While this may be true, viewing it in light of the observations made in *Godel, Escher, Bach* make it useful to look at it more simply. In chiasmus the first of the pattern repeats at the last. What came first is repeated in the end. It is a literary way of depicting "the last shall be first, and the first shall be last."

That same pattern appears in the Menorah. The seven lamps have arms which connect the first to the last.[201] If you were to set the lamp stand out in the same form using "ABC" the pattern would look like:
A-B-C-D-C-B-A.

---

[200]It was John Welch who discovered chiasmus in the Book of Mormon while a missionary in Germany. He has written about the subject, including *Chiasmus in Antiquity*. Edited by John W. Welch. Provo: The Foundation for Ancient Research and Mormon Studies, 1981. One of the longest examples of a chiasm in the Book of Mormon is found in Chapter 36 of Alma. The entire chapter is a lengthy form of this pattern of writing.

[201]See Exo. 25: 32: "And six branches shall come out of the sides of it; three branches of the candlestick out of the one side, and three branches of the candlestick out of the other side."

The arms of the Menorah are also a chiasm. The first is also the last. The pattern is the same from beginning to middle and from middle to end, the one being a mirror image of the other. So we have a Temple article containing, by its form, a symbol which mirrors the ancient word form of chiasmus. The pattern seems to have a meaning.

We have a description of the Urim and Thummim from Lucy Mack Smith. She described it as follows: "[On the morning of September 22, after Joseph had returned from the hill, he placed] the article [the Urim and Thummim] of which he spoke into my hands, and, upon examination, [I] found that it consisted of two smooth three-cornered diamonds set in glass, and the glasses were set in silver bows, which were connected with each other in much the same way as old fashioned spectacles." (Taken from *Eyewitness Accounts of the Restoration* by Milton V. Backman, Jr., p.73. Backman, Milton V., Jr. *Eyewitness Accounts of the Restoration.* Salt Lake City: Deseret Book Company, 1986.)

One of these "two smooth three-cornered" stones pointed upward. The other pointed downward. This pattern of two triangles pointing in opposite directions is what the Star of David is made from. One pointing up, and the other pointing down. It, too, is a kind of chiasm. Progression and regression set in a side-by-side pattern. The Urim and Thummim is a chiasm. The Star of David was modeled on the Urim and Thummim, and is also a chiasm.

In ceremony, we move what was on the left side to the right side. The orientation of clothing changes from the one side to the other, forming a mirror image of progression and regression. As husband and wife kneel between the mirrors of the sealing room, facing each other, the right side of the one matches the left side of the other. As the dialogue at the veil concludes, the one acting as proxy speaks words of blessing vicariously for an ancestor, who in turn blesses descendants including the one acting as proxy. The images and symbols fold over upon each other in a repeating pattern of chiasms. Symbol and meaning merge into patterns intended to suggest to the mind a deeper level of meaning.

What do we make of these symbols? These imbedded messages seem to return to a theme. Whatever other meanings as may be contained in these forms, patterns and types, it necessarily includes the notion that to go forward you must go backward. Perhaps this meaning reigns supreme over all the other symbolic meanings of the pattern.

This pattern also reminds us anew of the Lord's injunction: "Except ye be converted, and become as little children, ye shall not enter into the kingdom of heaven." (Matt. 18: 3.) Returning to the mind of a child is necessary as a precondition, according to Christ's words, for us to be able to enter His kingdom.

What is it about the mind of a child that makes him or her more suited to following Christ? Is it innocence? Certainly a child's mind is more innocent than the adult's. But innocence also accompanies the willingness or even the necessity to imagine things. Children are able to hold out the possibilities for Santa and tooth-fairies and Peter Pan. To a child these things are possible. It requires failures and disappointments to form an adult mind. Those failings and disappointments make the adult mind skeptical, and unbelieving. Things once held in honor by the childish mind become impossible to believe in adulthood.

After a parable about camels and the eye of a needle making salvation seem unlikely, the disciples exclaimed it wasn't possible for such men to be saved. "But Jesus beheld them, and said unto them, With men this is impossible; but with God all things are possible." (Matt. 19: 26.) Men do not believe enough. Children do.

This feature of the child's mind needs to be reclaimed. Hard though it may be, the opening up for yourself of the possibility you, too, may receive these things must come first. You will not receive until after you have been first proven. And you will not be up to the test if you are unwilling to believe it is possible for you to receive these things.

Even more fundamental is a discussion in 2 Nephi. After paraphrasing Isaiah chapter 29 in 2 Ne. 27, Nephi gives an extended commentary about the latter-days. He is speaking directly to us. He is speaking about us, as well. His analysis includes the following:

For it shall come to pass in that day that the churches which are
built up, and not unto the Lord, when the one shall say unto the
other: Behold, I, I am the Lord's; and the others shall say: I, I
am the Lord's; and thus shall every one say that hath built up
churches, and not unto the Lord – And they shall contend one
with another; and their priests shall contend one with another,
and they shall teach with their learning, and deny the Holy
Ghost, which giveth utterance. And they deny the power of
God, the Holy One of Israel; and they say unto the people:
Hearken unto us, and hear ye our precept; for behold there is
no God today, for the Lord and the Redeemer hath done his
work, and he hath given his power unto men; (2 Ne. 28: 3-5.)

This is our day. The defects of our day include "teaching with their
learning" and consequently "denying the Holy Ghost."

The adult mind likes "learning," and rather prefers the world's way
of learning to the Holy Ghost. The Holy Ghost is always
unpredictable.[202] Scholars are much more predictable. Requiring
authority and citing precedent allows even the most uninspired of
teachers to get away with being an authority. At one level, scholarship
is a fake and a substitute for the authority of the Spirit. You can't fake
inspiration. You either have it or you do not. But you can become a
fake authority by appealing to an extensive bibliography and citing those
who agree with you.

You also can't fake is spiritual power. Healing and visions,
prophecy and revelation cannot be faked. You either experience it, or
you do not. No amount of bibliography can substitute for having
spiritual experiences.

The Gospel is not anti-intellectual. But neither is it controlled by
scholars. Christ didn't call the Rabbis to be His chosen twelve. Rather,
He chose fishermen and common laborers. These simple men were
rather more prepared to see the Gospel than were the educated and

[202]"The wind bloweth where it listeth, and thou hearest the sound
thereof, but canst not tell whence it cometh, and whither it goeth; so is every
one who is born of the Spirit." (John 3: 8.)

intellectual. It was the best and brightest who opposed Christ and ultimately conspired to kill Him. It is the educated and sophisticated who seem to struggle most with the notions of inspiration and being led by the Holy Ghost.

In this dispensation, God came to a fourteen-year-old boy, and one, who came from an environment steeped in folk magic.[203] Joseph was not a scholar and did not live long enough to become one. Rather, in all things which mattered most he was one whose mind was educated from on high. That suited the Lord's purpose much better than the formal education the ministers of his day possessed.[204] There is a powerful and sobering lesson in that. You should choose your teachers

---

[203]See, Quinn, Michael D. *Early Mormonism and the Magic World View.* Salt Lake City: Signature Books, 1987. Quinn notes the phenomenon but fails to see its real utility for preparing Joseph Smith to be a prophet of God. This cultural condition fitted Joseph's mind to receive with simplicity and trust the revelations of God. Quinn thinks it a handicap reflecting poorly on Joseph. He has the right data about the environment, but reaches the wrong conclusions. We need to be more like Joseph and less like Quinn, if we are going to receive the Second Comforter. This phenomenon is noted also in Richard Bushman's latest work *Rough Stone Rolling.* He makes a more reasonable allowance for the possibility that Joseph was prepared for greater things through his experiences with folk magic. One of Bushman's observations is worth repeating: "After 1828, Joseph could no longer see that magic might have prepared him to believe in a revelation of gold plates and translation with a stone. It did not occur to him that without magic his family might have scoffed at his story of Moroni, as did the minister who rejected the First Vision. Magic had played its part and now could be cast aside." (Bushman, Richard Lyman. *Joseph Smith Rough Stone Rolling*, New York: Alfred A. Knopf, 2005, at p. 69.) While this gets close to the mark, it ignores the possibility that a different mindset was possessed by Joseph which allowed the development of a form of faith which we, holding a different mindset cannot attain. The full import of this as it relates to Joseph is beyond the scope of this work and worthy of some treatment in its own right. However, the implications for us need to be dealt with here.

[204]Joseph said: "Could you gaze into heaven five minutes, you would know more than you would by reading all that ever was written on the subject" (*TPJS*, p. 324.)

carefully.[205] Avoid what Nephi says will occur in our day from those who "teach with their learning, and deny the Holy Ghost, which giveth utterance. And they deny the power of God." (2 Ne. 28:4.) The "utterance" (teaching) should come from the Holy Ghost. Church authorities should speak by the power of the Holy Ghost. For "no power or influence can, or ought, to be maintained by virtue of the priesthood" according to Joseph.[206] That is, the office someone holds never entitles them to power or influence, only the Spirit with which they teach. "If ye receive not the Spirit, ye shall not teach." (D&C 42: 14.) That command, of course, does not deter all teachers who ought to not be teaching. But whether it deters an uninspired teacher or not, it should act as a caution to you in evaluating and accepting teachers.

Nephi continues: "Yea, and there shall be many which shall say: Eat, drink, and be merry, for tomorrow we die; and it shall be well with us. And there shall also be many which shall say: Eat, drink, and be merry; nevertheless, fear God – he will justify in committing a little sin; yea, lie a little, take the advantage of one because of his words, dig a pit for thy neighbor; there is no harm in this; and do all these things, for tomorrow we die; and if it so be that we are guilty, God will beat us with a few stripes, and at last we shall be saved in the kingdom of God." (2 Ne. 28: 7-8.) Here we have the notions "we shouldn't try and be

---

[205]This does not mean insipid, faith promoting stories are better than intellectual studies. They are not. But you should be able to tell the difference between someone teaching with the power of the Holy Ghost and a mere scholar. Some teachers offer emotional stories in lieu of the Spirit. Emotional storytelling is certainly no better than intellectual ruminations. Teaching by the power of the Holy Ghost is something different from either of these. If you cannot tell the difference, you should consider fasting, prayer and scripture study to aid you. Encounters with the Spirit are not merely emotional, they are enlightening. They can be felt, and they increase the intellect, enliven your understanding, and bring more light to you. They do not merely leave you with your emotions touched.

[206]D&C 121: 41, see also verses 36-42. Mere authority or office is no substitute for speaking by the voice of inspiration. Indeed real authority comes only **from the Spirit** and not from ordination.

devoted to any teachings which limit you, curtail your misconduct or personal indulgences, or require you to rein in your appetites." "There is no absolute standard which God intends to hold you to." When, in reality, the Lord has told us to the contrary He "cannot look upon sin with the least degree of allowance." (D&C 1: 31.) This life is serious stuff. Now is the time to prepare for the judgment. Every moment of this life is precious. Every moment of this life, including the thoughts of your heart, will require an accounting.[207]

Nephi continues in his discussion of us:

> Yea, and there shall be many which shall teach after this manner, false and vain and foolish doctrines, and shall be puffed up in their hearts, and shall seek deep to hide their counsels from the Lord; and their works shall be in the dark. And the blood of the saints shall cry from the ground against them. Yea, they have all gone out of the way; they have become corrupted. Because of pride, and because of false teachers, and false doctrine, their churches have become corrupted, and their churches are lifted up; because of pride they are puffed up. They rob the poor because of their fine sanctuaries; they rob the poor because of their fine clothing; and they persecute the meek and the poor in heart, because in their pride they are puffed up. (2 Ne. 28: 9-13.)

False, vain and foolish doctrines are going to be taught in our day. Any of the teachers among the Saints who are puffed up in their hearts are unworthy of your discipleship. You should not buy their books, attend their lectures, or listen to their tapes. They offer you nothing, but charge you for doing so. Choose your teachers carefully. Some of them will poison your mind and retard your progress because they are not on higher ground and therefore cannot lead you to higher ground. They are like the Scribes and Pharisees about whom Christ warned they "neither go in [themselves], neither suffer them that are entering to go in." (Matt. 23: 13.) You can't follow a false teacher and find heaven at the end of

---

[207] Alma 12: 12-15.

the trail. You are accountable for measuring all teachings against the scriptures and against the voice of the Spirit. You cannot rely upon others and blame them for your own responsibilities. You cannot even push this responsibility onto the Prophet.[208]

Now we get to the alarming warnings of verse 14: "They wear stiff necks and high heads; yea, and because of pride, and wickedness, and abominations, and whoredoms, **they have all gone astray save it be a few, who are the humble followers of Christ; nevertheless, they are led, that in many instances they do err because they are taught by the precepts of men.**" (2 Ne. 28: 14, emphasis added.) This inspired warning about our day should trouble any faithful Saint. We have "all gone astray." Not just some belonging to false, apostate Christianity where the Restoration has not been accepted. This chapter speaks prophetically about *our* day and specifically mentions "Zion" in the same discussion. Nephi does not use the term "Zion" to mean anyone other than *us*. So including Zion within the Chapter requires us to include Zion within the "all" in our day who have these problems. It was meant to personalize this message. It was meant to make us reevaluate ourselves. We should be shaken by the warning and reevaluate our own conduct and beliefs.

If that is not enough, the Doctrine and Covenants warns the members of the Church directly: "And your minds in times past have been darkened because of unbelief, and because you have treated lightly the things you have received – Which vanity and unbelief have brought the whole church under condemnation. And this condemnation resteth upon the children of Zion, even all. And they shall remain under this condemnation until they repent and remember the new covenant, even

---

[208]Joseph said to the Relief Society, "they were depending on the Prophet, hence were darkened in their minds, in consequence of neglecting the duties devolving upon themselves." (*TPJS*, p. 238.) Further, the explanation in D&C 121:34-42 places decided limits upon the kind of deference that a person in authority in the priesthood should receive. Implicit in this Section is unless the authority actually does persuade you by the Spirit, then they are as other men and not entitled to any greater deference than any other man.

the Book of Mormon and the former commandments which I have given them, not only to say, but to do according to that which I have written — " (D&C 84: 54-57.) President Ezra Taft Benson reiterated that this warning remains in effect, and the Saints remain under this condemnation[209] still today.

Simplicity marks the child's mind. Things are much clearer to a child than they are to an adult. Craftiness and cunning develop in the maturing adult mind and are alien to the child's mind. Part of the process of developing involves learning people can be mean, cunning and manipulative. Adults can generally recall specific events in their childhood when they felt betrayed for the first time. All of that is a part of the mortal curriculum because we have come here to receive knowledge of good and evil.

Adult cynicism and skepticism, however, ill-serves us as we seek higher things. The Lord was teaching a profound principle in telling us we must become as little children if we wish to enter His kingdom. It is a requirement. We will need to explore this further.

For this chapter, what we need to realize is to go forward we must go back. We must return to what we were in a more innocent time.

---

[209]"As I participated in the Mexico City Temple dedication, I received the distinct impression that God is not pleased with our neglect of the Book of Mormon. The object of studying the Book of Mormon is to learn from the experiences of those who have gone before us that blessings come by keeping the commandments of God and that tragedy is the result of disobedience. By learning from the lessons of the past, mistakes need not be repeated in our own lives. You will gain a firm and unshakable testimony of Jesus Christ and the absolute knowledge that the origin of the Book of Mormon, as described by Joseph Smith, is true. Reading and pondering the Book of Mormon and other scriptures brings spiritual-mindedness. The Lord has instructed: "Let the solemnities of eternity rest upon your mind" (D&C 43:34), and "treasure up in your minds continually the words of life" (D&C 84:85)." (*Lord, Increase Our Faith*, Ezra Taft Benson, Provo Utah Tabernacle Rededication, 21 September 1986.) "In our day, the Lord has revealed the need to reemphasize the Book of Mormon to get the Church and all the children of Zion out from under condemnation – the scourge and judgment (see D&C 84:54-58). This message must be carried to the members of the Church throughout the world." (CR April 1986, *Ensign* 16 [May 1986]: 78.)

Because of our individual "Fall" in the "Garden of Eden" of our youth, we need to regain God's presence in our lives. That childlike innocence we all came with, including believing, trusting, wanting, hoping, and accepting, must be found again.

Our minds are more of an impediment than an asset in this struggle. Margaret Barker's comments about the early Christian worldview of evil are relevant here, and a good point to end with. Speaking of the Christians at the time of Christ she writes: "They had a picture of a vast conspiracy of evil actively engaged in a struggle against humankind, working to corrupt and destroy the creation. People needed protection against this onslaught, and help to overcome its effects. They were not hampered by our sophisticated attitudes, which have come to terms with evil forces by saying that they do not exist, or by turning them into a form of late-night entertainment. Our Christian ancestors in the time of Jesus would have recognized this ploy. The devil, they knew, acted through the human mind, where man was most proud and therefore most vulnerable. To convince a thinking man that evil forces did not exist was indeed a triumph." (Barker, Margaret *THE LOST PROPHET: The Book of Enoch and its Influence on Christianity*. Sheffield: England, 2005, p. 36.)

Chapter Twelve

IN THE ORDINANCES THEREOF

I took the first 11 names of my male ancestors to the South Jordan Temple on August 30, 2000. No one other than myself, in all prior generations of my family, had been a member of the Church. This was the day on which the work for my ancestors began. The restoration to my kindred dead commenced!

I took 11 names with me that day. I did the baptisms and confirmations, and then went to my truck to put my towel and extra garments away. Since I had never done the ordinances before, I hadn't known the Temple supplied these things for you.

As I left the Temple, I was accompanied by the spirits of these 11 brothers who had been permitted to come on the occasion of their baptism to witness their work being done. One of them spoke to me saying: "But we have not yet been clothed." I replied: "Don't worry, I'm just putting my things in the truck. I intend to return to take care of that."

They then said: "We form a quorum."

I thought about it for a moment and replied: "What do you mean you form a 'quorum'? There are only 11 of you."

Came the reply: "But with you we are twelve."

The smallest and first priesthood quorum you join in the Church is the Deacon's quorum, which consists of 12 members. If these brothers regarded me as one of them, then we were 12. I was touched by their rejoinder.

I returned and completed the washings and anointings for these 11 ancestors. As I was preparing to leave the Temple they confronted me and petitioned again: "But we have not yet received the robes of righteousness." I replied: "I've been here all day, and can't stay longer. I'll take care of it, but can't do so now." They were unhappy, but I could not remain longer that day.

When I got home later my wife asked me how it was. I replied: "They are just like my kids." She didn't ask me what I meant by that, but I meant that they, like my children, were always asking for more and rarely content with what I had already done for them. I didn't explain that to her, but that was what I meant. I saw in this a distinct family trait.

The scriptures hold many keys. One great key to understanding the process of receiving the Second Comforter comes in the following passage from D&C 84: "And this greater priesthood administereth the gospel and holdeth the key of the mysteries of the kingdom, even the key of the knowledge of God. Therefore, in the ordinances thereof, the power of godliness is manifest. And without the ordinances thereof, and the authority of the priesthood, the power of godliness is not manifest unto men in the flesh; For without this no man can see the face of God, even the Father, and live." (vs. 19-22.) This verse is misread by many. We need to take it apart a bit to understand what it is saying and what it is not saying. Misreading it has led to confusion by some people into thinking there is a presumptive superiority to those holding priesthood authority in seeing the face of God.

It does **not** say a person must hold priesthood. Rather, it says, "in the ordinances" of the priesthood people are prepared to see God's face. If holding priestly authority was required for these promises, then the promise made elsewhere that "he denieth none that come unto him, black and white, bond and free, male and female; and he remembereth the heathen; and all are alike unto God, both Jew and Gentile" (2 Ne. 26: 33) would be wrong. Holding the priesthood is not required. Receiving the ordinances is what is required. **Someone** needs to hold the priesthood and to minister the ordinances. But the effect which is described here is an effect on the person **receiving** the ordinance, not on the one **administering** the ordinance. Receiving the ordinance is the preparation, not performing the ordinance for someone else. All are alike in receiving the ordinances. These verses are describing the power extended to all, male and female, young and old, bond and free, when they receive the ordinances of the Gospel.

No one, from the President of the Church to the youngest infant receiving a blessing, lays their hands on their own head. The priesthood is needed by someone administering the ordinances for you. But the promises in these verses are made to the person receiving the ordinances. Whether the recipient has or does not have priestly authority, the ordinances deliver to him or her the promises which give the power of godliness. Whether the person is a male or female, the ordinances deliver to them the same promises and therefore the same qualification. All are equal in receiving the ordinances.[210] To focus on

---

[210]Some women have been misled by this wrongheaded interpretation of the scripture. They believe they are not entitled to receive the "mysteries" because they do not hold priestly office. It is not the office, but rather the ordinances which make the difference. The Relief Society sisters were once rebuked by Joseph Smith for their dependence upon revelation from the Prophet and neglecting their own gifts, as we have previously discussed. This rebuke remains appropriate even today. "In Doctrine and Covenants 84:64-66, he had already clarified the familiar verses from the Gospel of Mark, emphasizing that 'every soul who believeth upon your words, and is baptized

the administrator,as many Saints do, is to be distracted from the real meaning. The ordinances have little to offer the officiator outside of an opportunity to serve. The power of the ordinances is offered to the recipient. The misreading of the verse comes from pride, envy and competitiveness. It should stop.

How, then, do the ordinances qualify one to "see the face of God, even the Father, and live?" A passing phrase from Ether helps connect these things together: "Wherefore man must hope, or he cannot receive." (Ether 12: 32.) The ordinances deliver to us the reason for hope. They also uncover to the receptive mind, the things God is willing to permit us to receive and how they are to be received. The ordinances are a blueprint for the actual event.

Baptism and laying on of hands for the Gift of the Holy Ghost are indispensable foundational ordinances to receiving a remission of sins. Even Christ, who was sinless, required baptism.[211] If this is an issue for you, then this book is not really addressed to you. You cannot obtain what is offered by God through ordinance and covenant unless you willingly accept the ordinances. Without obedience to Christ's Gospel, you cannot expect to receive what Christ promises through His Gospel. If you are not willing to accept this, then there is no basis for you to develop the required faith to receive any of the blessings He has offered to the obedient.

---

by water for the remission of sins, shall receive the Holy Ghost,' with signs and 'many wonderful works' following 'them that believe.' 'No matter who believeth,' Joseph now added, 'whether male or female.'" (*Women of Covenant: The Story of Relief Society*, p.44, by Jill Mulvay Derr, Janath Russell Cannon, and Maureen Ursenbach Beecher.) Yet, such revelations are their private matter and not for public display. "A woman has no right to found or organize a church – God never sent them to do it." (*TPJS*, p. 212.) So it is the same with the sisters as with the brothers: Mysteries can be received, but they cannot be taught. All are equal and alike.

[211]Matt. 3: 15. See also 2 Ne. 31: 5, where it is taught: "And now, if the Lamb of God, he being holy, should have need to be baptized by water, to fulfill all righteousness, O then, how much more need have we, being unholy, to be baptized, yea, even by water!"

The ordinances are not hollow rites. They are powerful tools. God ordained them for your personal benefit and development. Through them you come in contact with His power. They prepare you, empower you, and confer reason for hope upon you.

After the initial rite of baptism, however, approaching God requires an added measure of grace and holiness. You have removed sin from your life, but you are not yet holy. Approaching the presence of God requires you to become "like Him," and therefore, requires you also become holy. The required grace and holiness is recognized, and then obtained, by following the ordinances of Christ's Gospel.

Joseph Smith received anew through revelation the ordinances of washing and anointing. At the time of their restoration, these rites were apparently original with him. However, he claimed only to be restoring what was always a part of Christ's Gospel. St. Cyril, writing in the Third Century, taught "Christians" were called "Christian" because they had been "Christened." That is, the name of Christ is derived from being anointed or christened by oil. And those who followed Him (the Anointed One) should themselves become anointed.

St. Cyril wrote lectures explaining Church practices and doctrine. In his *Twenty-First Lecture, On Chrism*, St. Cyril wrote the following:

> And as Christ was in reality crucified, and buried, and raised, and you are in Baptism accounted worthy of being crucified, buried, and raised together with Him in a likeness, so is it with the unction[212] also. As He was anointed with an ideal oil of gladness, that is, with the Holy Ghost, called oil of gladness, because He is the author of spiritual gladness, so ye were anointed with ointment, having been made partakers and fellows of Christ. But beware of supposing this to be plain ointment. For as Bread of the Eucharist, after the invocation of the Holy Ghost, is mere bread no longer, but the body of Christ, so also this holy ointment is no more simple ointment, nor (so to say) common, after invocation, but it is Christ's gift of grace, and, by advent of the Holy Ghost, is made fit to

---

[212]"Unction," an archaic word, means anointing.

impart His Divine Nature. Which ointment is symbolically applied to the forehead and thy other senses; and while thy body is anointed with the visible ointment, the soul is sanctified by the Holy and life-giving Spirit. And ye were first anointed on the forehead, ... Then on your ears; that ye might receive the ears which are quick to hear the Divine Mysteries... Then on the nostrils ... Then on your breast... Having been counted worthy of this Holy Chrism, ye are called Christians, verifying the name also by your new birth." (St. Cyril, *Lecture 21, On Chrism*, explaining 1 John 2: 20-28; paragraphs 2-5.)

From this explanation of early third-century "Christian" practice, it is apparent the name of "Christian" is clearly identified with a practice of anointing the followers of Christ with a "holy anointing." These rites were once a part of the early Christian movement, but had been lost by the time they were restored through Joseph Smith. Joseph was not inventing something, but was restoring what was lost.

These rites originally belonged to Christianity to help men and women become closer to God. They are restored to provide additional power, assistance and encouragement to Saints seeking God's presence. These rites stem from antiquity, and were original with Christ and belong to His Gospel.

When you are washed and anointed, you are brought closer to God by a rite which communicates notions of cleanliness and purity. God is saying to you in a symbolic act that He is washing you and cleaning you up. He is applying through the ordinance the cleansing and purifying power which He alone possesses in full measure. If He is saying you are clean, then a person of faith can accept God's work and feel clean. God, of course, has the power to clean us, forgive us, and make us holy. If He applies His power to our person by an ordinance in which He covenants to make us clean, then our confidence in Him should allow us to accept our derivative cleanliness.

The notion of taking a sinful, fallen body back into God's presence is a frightening thing to contemplate. When Isaiah was in the Temple and brought into God's presence, he reacted with fear and horror. The gulf between "Man of Holiness"[213] and our un-holiness compels us, when granted an audience with the Man of Holiness, to cry out for relief. It becomes apparent He is greater than we are. We can see and feel the gap between what He is and what we are. He is Holy, and we are not. We are viewing Holiness itself, and can for the first time fully appreciate the great gulf between what He is and radiates, and what we are. Which is exactly how Isaiah relates the experience: "Then said I, Woe is me! For I am undone; because I am a man of unclean lips, and I dwell in the midst of a people of unclean lips: for mine eyes have seen the King, the Lord of hosts." (Isaiah 6: 5.) This is not a contrived reaction by Isaiah, nor mere rhetorical or literary form. It is an actual description of an unholy being beholding the presence of a Holy Being and his deepest feelings at the moment of the experience. It is Isaiah's spontaneous reaction.

In 2 Ne. 9: 14, the explanation of how our individual meeting with God will go is explained: "Wherefore, we shall have a perfect knowledge of all our guilt, and our uncleanness, and our nakedness; and the righteous shall have a perfect knowledge of their enjoyment, and their righteousness, being clothed with purity, yea, even with the robe of righteousness." In another passage explaining the discomfort of coming into God's presence Moroni explains:

> Behold, will ye believe in the day of your visitation – … in that great day when ye shall be brought to stand before the Lamb of God – … Do ye suppose that ye shall dwell with him under a consciousness of your guilt? Do ye suppose that ye could be happy to dwell with that holy Being, when your souls are racked

---

[213]Moses 6: 57, explains: "Wherefore teach it unto your children, that all men, everywhere, must repent, or they can in nowise inherit the kingdom of God, for no unclean thing can dwell there, or dwell in his presence; for, in the language of Adam, Man of Holiness is his name, and the name of his Only Begotten is the Son of Man, even Jesus Christ, a righteous Judge, who shall come in the meridian of time." And in Moses 7: 35 it says: "Behold, I am God; Man of Holiness is my name; Man of Counsel is my name; and Endless and Eternal is my name, also."

with a consciousness of guilt that ye have ever abused his laws? Behold, I say unto you that ye would be more miserable to dwell with a holy and just God, under a consciousness of your filthiness before him, than ye would to dwell with the damned souls in hell. For behold, when ye shall be brought to see your nakedness before God, and also the glory of God, and the holiness of Jesus Christ, it will kindle a flame of unquenchable fire upon you. O then ye unbelieving, turn ye unto the Lord; cry mightily unto the Father in the name of Jesus, that perhaps ye may be found spotless, pure, fair, and white, having been cleansed by the blood of the Lamb, at that great and last day. And again I speak unto you who deny the revelations of God, and say that they are done away, that there are no revelations, nor prophecies, nor gifts, nor healing, nor speaking with tongues, and the interpretation of tongues; Behold I say unto you, he that denieth these things knoweth not the gospel of Christ; yea, he has not read the scriptures; if so, he does not understand them. For do we not read that God is the same yesterday, today, and forever, and in him there is no variableness neither shadow of changing? (Mormon 9: 2-9.)[214]

In each of these accounts, the people feel unworthy before God. They speak in terms of panic and pain at seeing a Holy Being, while keenly aware of personal un-cleanliness. This reaction in both passages is contrasted with the reaction of others who are prepared to be in God's presence. Those others are not taken aback by their "nakedness" because they have been given "robes of righteousness."

---

[214]This passage is speaking about the Second Coming and the conditions of the Millennium. However, they are an apt description of what anyone will encounter when receiving an audience with the Man of Holiness. And they are made more applicable by Bruce R. McConkie's reminder that, "And in this connection, be it known that **it is the privilege of the saints today** to separate themselves from the world and to receive millennial blessings in their lives. And any person who today abides the laws that will be kept during the Millennium will receive, here and now, the spirit and blessings of the Millennium in his life, even though he is surrounded by a world of sin and evil." (McConkie, Bruce R. *Millennial Messiah*. Salt Lake City: Deseret Book Company, 1982, p. 682, emphasis added.)

So we begin to see through the Book of Mormon's authoritative teachings on this subject, that washing, anointing, clothing and endowing the Saints is not merely a hollow ceremonial act. It can result in the proper case with the proper recipient, in preparing them for God's presence. The juxtaposition of "nakedness" with being "clothed with the robes of righteousness" is again, not just a hollow literary form. It is describing an actual, physical endowment of power which some have received (and thereby become prepared) and some have not. Those who receive it are comfortable in God's presence, and those who have not are in pain.[215]

The washing, anointing and clothing of the Saint through ordinance and ritual is intended to have deep meaning to the recipient. These rites are supposed to be received in faith. If they are received with faith, then you can see from them God has promised to wash away your iniquity. He has also anointed you with oil, which makes you "christened" or holy. The anointing makes you like "Christ" whose very name means "anointed one." The anointing makes all who receive it "like Him." These rites make John's teachings in his letters all the more clear and meaningful. He writes in 1 John 3:2: "Beloved, **now are we the sons of God**, and it doth not yet appear what we shall be: but we know that, when he shall appear, **we shall be like him**; for we shall see him as he is." (Emphasis added.) The power underlying these ceremonies makes us like Him. We obtain holiness through His

---

[215]Christ also alluded to this in His parable containing these cautionary words: "And when the king came in to see the guests, he saw there a man which had not on a wedding garment: And he saith unto him, Friend, how camest thou in hither not having a wedding garment? And he was speechless. Then said the king to the servants, Bind him hand and foot, and take him away, and cast him into outer darkness; there shall be weeping and gnashing of teeth. For many are called, but few are chosen." (Matt 22: 11-14.) Here the "king" and the "wedding" are symbols of Christ's return. The "wedding garment" is a reference to the ceremonially conferred "robes of righteousness" received in the Temple.

Atonement, and become holy through His power. His Gospel has been restored to bring again the power of godliness to mankind.

These ceremonies are what Section 84 is alluding to when it says: "in the ordinances thereof, the power of godliness is manifest. And without the ordinances thereof, and the authority of the priesthood, the power of godliness is not manifest unto men in the flesh; For without this no man can see the face of God, even the Father, and live." (84: 20-22.)

Un-cleanliness is washed away. Spirit is conferred upon the very person of the prepared individual through anointing with oil. The oil is a symbol of the Holy Ghost. The Holy Ghost is a purifying and cleansing agent. The purity and cleanliness imparted allows the recipient to come "boldly unto the throne of grace, that we may obtain mercy, and find grace to help in time of need." (JST-Heb. 4: 16; taken from *Joseph Smith's New Translation of the Bible, Original Manuscripts*. Edited by Scott H. Faulring, Kent P. Jackson and Robert J. Matthews. Provo: Religious Studies Center Brigham Young University, 2004; p. 531.)

Instead of a lament and fear, you have "a perfect knowledge of [your] enjoyment, and [your] righteousness, being clothed with purity, yea, even with the robe of righteousness." (2 Ne. 9: 14.) A robe of righteousness covers you with the Atonement. Instead of your "nakedness," which implies shame and fear, you have derivative cleanliness given you by a covering to take away that shame and fear. These are symbols of deeper truths. God is trying to teach you these things in a ceremonial vesting of gifts or an endowment from on-high.

If God removes your sins, then they are removed. It is only left for you to have faith in His promise that your sins are removed. Faith in His promise of the removal of your sins comes directly from obedience to His commandments, as we have seen earlier. If you obey Him, you will have that faith, and your sins will be removed.

Similarly, if God has granted to you a covering which He calls the "robes of righteousness," then you can trust the garment will cover (through the Atonement of Christ) your sins and thereby remove your shame. All of these things are intended to bring you "confidence in the presence of the Lord."[216]

The ordinances 1) bathe you and return you from the watery grave, as a symbol of being born again. Then they 2) confer upon you a Spirit presence to accompany and guide you. This Spirit revives the dead body you lived in before and provides to you a connection to Heaven, anew. You are put into contact with a member of the Godhead. Weekly, the ordinances have you 3) eating and drinking the symbols of Christ's great sacrifice, making your body incorporate into its very elements the symbols of Christ. These are to have you remember Him that you may always have His Spirit to be with you. Then the ordinances 4) wash you anew to cleanse you from the world. Then you are 5) anointed with oil, to symbolize and confirm that you, too, are anointed or christened, as was Christ. You become a Christ-type by mimicking Him. You receive derivative holiness from His true holiness. Then the ordinances 6) confer upon you sacred knowledge and key symbolic understanding. These are symbols of real knowledge. They are entrusted to you as a test to see if you can be trusted with sacred knowledge. If you hold them sacred, as you covenant to do, then you are able to qualify for the real sacred knowledge that comes in the same way as depicted in the ceremonial rites. Then the ordinances 7) take you symbolically back to the presence of the Father.

The whole process can be briefly summarized in these few words: We are to be prepared in all things to receive further light and knowledge by conversing with the Lord through the veil. That is what the ordinances teach. That is what the ordinances symbolize. They all point to this final act of redemption from the Fall.

Actually conversing with the Lord through the veil requires you to first receive its sacred type and shadow through ceremony and promise.

---

[216]See D&C 121: 45: "Let thy bowels also be full of charity towards all men, and to the household of faith, and let virtue garnish thy thoughts unceasingly; **then shall thy confidence wax strong in the presence of God**; and the doctrine of the priesthood shall distil upon thy soul as the dews from heaven." (Emphasis added.)

First comes the type and shadow, then comes the real thing. Covenant and obligation with the Lord comes first, then the patient Saint lives in conformity with the promise on her end, and at length, when the Lord has proven her,[217] He steps out from behind the veil and confers in reality what was first a matter of promise and faith. Joseph taught that the Lord will "try" and will "prove" the faithful "in all things...even unto death" (D&C 98: 12-14.) The Prophet Joseph Smith taught that before one could have his calling and election made sure, he must be "thoroughly proved"; he must demonstrate that he is "determined to serve [God] at all hazards" (TPJS, p. 150.) You first receive the covenant, and only later when you have been proven, will the Lord fulfill the promise He made to you.

If you will not receive the ordinance, you cannot receive the real thing. If you receive the ordinance and then trample it underfoot, you cannot hope to receive the real thing. For God will not permit Himself to be trampled underfoot again.

The promises made to you in the Temple include within their scope the promise you are to receive sacred knowledge. Sacred knowledge requires you, by covenant, to keep it from the world. You profane it when you let others who are not going to receive it as holy, to have it for their amusement and contempt. Joseph taught: "The reason we do not have the secrets of the Lord revealed unto us, is because we do not keep them but reveal them; we do not keep our own secrets, but reveal our difficulties to the world, even to our enemies, then how would we keep the secrets of the Lord?" (TPJS, p. 195.) The Temple is a formalized way of revealing to each Saint who will come and receive the endowment presented in the form of a selection of sacred knowledge. The things received come through a covenant. The Lord promises to bless the individual, but requires them to promise not to reveal the sacred knowledge which He gives to us there.

---

[217]In using the feminine here there is no attempt at "political correctness" being employed. Rather it is out of respect of the person who was first to receive the Second Comforter, on the morning of His resurrection. She becomes the original whom we seek to follow in this sacred act.

In the life of Adam, he received sacred knowledge and was tested, tried and proven. Only after he passed the test of remaining true and faithful to the things he received from God, was Adam then given further light and knowledge. Similarly, we are asked to do the same. The path of Adam's return to God's presence is the same path we must follow to return to God's presence. This symbolic journey is a ritualized return to God, which is then to result in the actual return to God by honoring the symbol as if it were the reality.

The Temple gives sacred knowledge. For those who are interested in receiving more, they must keep the sacred things given first in the Temple. It is not possible for a person to defy the Lord, forsake his promises to God, abandon his covenant with God, and then receive further light and knowledge from Him.

It does not matter if every other Latter-day Saint who ever went to the Temple breaks their covenants. It doesn't matter if Sandra and Jerald Tanner publish the endowment ceremonies on the Internet. The only thing which matters is that you, as a person in direct covenant with God, remain true to the promises you made to Him. Though people all around you may abandon what they promised to Him, if you remain true, you will receive the blessings promised to you by Him. No one but you can break your covenant with God. If you honor the covenant you are allowed to make with Him in His Temple, then He will honor you for doing so.

Interlopers do not gain blessings from God. Those who think publication of the Temple rites accomplishes something are mistaken. They have only proven themselves unworthy of the blessing of receiving more. They disqualify themselves from receiving further light and knowledge by conversing with the Lord. You mustn't do that. You must remain true and faithful to your God and the promises you made to Him. It is only in that way you can receive more.

Those who attempt to gain sacred knowledge by secretly spying on the rites and publishing them have gained nothing. The symbol is not the real thing. It is ritual to prepare the faithful to receive the real thing.

Without faith, real intent, and seeing the underlying higher reality which the rites symbolize, they have gained nothing. Sacred knowledge cannot be stolen. It is unavailable that way. No-one ever gained anything of value by spying on the rites of the Temple. They have done themselves perhaps an infinite injury by disqualifying themselves from higher knowledge. But they have not gained a blessing. Blessings are never gained by dishonesty or entering the wrong way.

The Temple is a sacred place for those who are prepared to receive sacred things. But it is just another place in the world for those who are worldly. Either the person brings with them personal worthiness and personal holiness or they do not. The Temple provides a place for their personal holiness to develop. But those who bring only worldliness with them are not able to flee from that internal worldliness by merely entering the Temple. For them it is much the same as the Temple of Herod where the scribes and Pharisees entered into a "den of thieves." And, in the same structure at the same time, Christ entered into a "house of prayer."[218] It was the same place. But for Christ, who had holiness within Him, the house was sacred. For the proud and sinful, it remained a den of thieves.

Sacred knowledge kept sacred makes the one holding it a vessel of righteousness. There is a notion of things which are "most holy" in Judaism. It is beyond the scope of this work to fully examine that subject. But things "most holy" have the capacity to impart to the recipient holiness. Things given in the Temple to the one being endowed are "most holy." They can impart holiness to the one who receives them. By receiving these sacred and most holy things the recipient is made holy by holding them within her person. When they are profaned, however, and covenants are disregarded, they then condemn the person who treats the things of God lightly.

When you begin to see the ceremonies of the "ordinances thereof" as the power of godliness in your life, you begin to approach the final

---

[218]Matt. 21: 13: "And said unto them, It is written, My house shall be called the house of prayer; but ye have made it a den of thieves."

preparation needed to experience the real thing. First comes the type, then the reality. Passing through the ordinances and seeing them as God's word to you, prepares your mind to go further.

The scriptures explain: "But, behold, faith cometh not by signs, but signs follow those who believe."(D&C 63:19.) You are not going to receive the Second Comforter to advance your faith. Instead, you receive Him to confirm the existing faith you already have, and to give your mind and heart reason to rise further in desire and aspiration to follow God.

The ordinances of the Gospel were given to you by God to help you prepare for His presence. They are intended to both motivate you, and confirm to you that God's promises are assured to you. He wants you to individually obtain the covenant status that will inspire confidence in you to proceed further.

The Temple covenants include the sealing of the man and woman together as an eternal family unit. This is what Paul spoke of when he taught in I Cor. 11: 11: "Nevertheless neither is the man without the woman, neither the woman without the man, in the Lord." It is the sealing of the two which brings together again what was originally intended as the completion of man. Adam was incomplete without his female counterpart. Gen 2: 18: "And the Lord God said, It is not good that the man should be alone; I will make him an help meet for him." Man is created in God's image which necessarily requires a female counterpart. When the scriptures speak of the "image of God," the male/female counterparts are both present.[219] The rites of the Temple

---

[219]See, e.g., Moses 2:27: "And I, God, created man in mine own image, in the image of mine Only Begotten created I him; male and female created I them." Moses 6:9: " In the image of his own body, male and female, created he them, and blessed them, and called their name Adam, in the day when they were created and became living souls in the land upon the footstool of God." And Gen 1:27: "So God created man in his own image, in the image of God created he him; male and female created he them." God's "image" requires both the male and female to be coupled, for only then do either of them become infinite. Without the other, both are lacking a vital part of God's image in their countenance.

culminate in the establishment by covenant and ordinance of another creation, in God's image, involving both the male and female in an eternal union.

In the Salt Lake Temple, the ordinances of washing and anointing begin at the lower level of the Temple. As the endowment begins, the level on which the presentation begins is higher. As the endowment progresses, each room is elevated from the one before, and throughout the endowment the participants are moving upward in a symbolic elevation of the endowed Saints' rise in glory toward God's presence. When the ceremony ends, the final transition into the Celestial Room again involves elevating from the floor of the Terrestrial Room to the floor level of the Celestial Room. This final room symbolizes the return to God the Father's presence.

Off of the Celestial Room in the Salt Lake Temple are the sealing rooms. These are also elevated above the Celestial Room. This final step upward in the ordinances of the Temple involves the symbolically highest rites available. They provide the eternal relationship which makes the man and woman like God.

As the scriptures tell us:

> And again, verily I say unto you, if a man marry a wife by my word, which is my law, and by the new and everlasting covenant, and it is sealed unto them by the Holy Spirit of promise, by him who is anointed, unto whom I have appointed this power and the keys of this priesthood; and it shall be said unto them – Ye shall come forth in the first resurrection; and if it be after the first resurrection, in the next resurrection; and shall inherit thrones, kingdoms, principalities, and powers, dominions, all heights and depths – then shall it be written in the Lamb's Book of Life, ... it shall be done unto them in all things whatsoever my servant hath put upon them, in time, and through all eternity; and shall be of full force when they are out of the world; and they shall pass by the angels, and the gods, which are set there, to their exaltation and glory in all things, as hath been sealed upon their heads, which glory shall be a fullness and a continuation of the seeds forever and ever. Then

shall they be gods, because they have no end; therefore shall they be from everlasting to everlasting, because they continue; then shall they be above all, because all things are subject unto them. Then shall they be gods, because they have all power, and the angels are subject unto them. (D&C 132: 19-20.)

They are now whole, whereas before they were only a fragment. They are now self-sustaining, and can produce the infinite through their family life, whereas before they were finite and apart.

This creation of the new creators through covenant and promise is intended to elevate the participants into a relationship which is holy. Through that relationship here in mortality, the souls of mortals are brought into the second estate. Through it the man and woman learn to love; first each other, then their children. The highest form of life is the life led in service to others. In no relationship is the opportunity to develop through service to others perfected as it is in the family unit. In it mere men become fathers. In it mere women become mothers. The status of father and of mother is sacred and trusted to the offspring born of them. Faithful fathers and mothers can demonstrate to the children they love the very attributes of godliness. They can begin to practice here, in mortality, the highest and holiest of character traits.

It is in the highest of the Temple ordinances just as it is in the others. Each provides a forum for individual growth and holiness to the participants. The rites can confer righteousness, but not without the efforts of the ones involved. The Temple rites can be hollow forms, if the participants do not receive them in faith and follow their meaning. There is nothing automatic about the personal growth involved. The rites give you opportunities. Your obedience and faithfulness gives to the rites the power of godliness. Without obedience and harkening to the Temple teachings and instructions, the Temple is not going to elevate you. Personal choice remains the thing which activates the promises given to you in the Temple covenants. If you choose, you can become holy through them. If you choose not to do so, then nothing will happen.

When you see God within the ordinances, and your faith allows you to seize upon the words of the officiators as the words of God, then you are approaching God Himself. When your faith in His ordinances is secure enough that seeing Him will produce no further conviction of His word, no greater confidence in Him and no additional confirmation than what you have already, you are prepared to receive Him. When at last you say to Him in earnest, "It is enough" because you have seen Him in His ordinances and promises, and scriptures, and blessings in your life, then He is able to step out from behind the veil and show His face to you. He will not do that to produce faith, but will do so to confirm existing faith.

But if, instead, you want Him to come to you to confer upon you faith in Him which you do not already have, you are not yet ready. As Joseph put it: "The Lord cannot always be known by the thunder of His voice, by the display of His glory or by the manifestation of His power; and those that are the most anxious to see these things, are the least prepared to meet them, and were the Lord to manifest His power as He did to the children of Israel, such characters would be the first to say, 'Let not the Lord speak any more, lest we His people die.'" (*DHC* 5: 31.)

If your faith would increase because of this experience, you are not ready for it. The Second Comforter comes to confirm the faith which already resides in a person, not to produce that faith.

The ordinances are a blueprint to return to God. They are not the actual return. They point the way and confirm the path. When you see them as God's personal invitation to return to Him, then you have a glimpse of the truth. Let that glimpse grow in you. It will lead, ultimately, to you standing at the veil between God and man, knocking three times and reaching upward to God. He, in turn, will meet you, reaching downward three degrees to where you are. In ceremony and sacred embrace, you will find that the rites of the Temple are a wonderfully accurate preparation for the real event. The ceremony of the Temple and the ceremony of recognition will fold over onto each other in such harmony you will want to exclaim the wonder, majesty and glory of God and His wisdom in providing to mankind in His mercy, the rites of the Temple.

The power of godliness has returned to the earth. There are again, here on earth, people who hold the keys in which the fullness of Christ's Gospel is practiced anew. The key to returning to God through the veil is found in the rites of the priesthood. For without them, no one can return to God's presence and see the face of God. But with them, any faithful follower of the covenants He has provided can return to Him. Through them every covenant-holder is invited to do so.

Chapter Thirteen

CHARITY, LOVE, INTERCESSION

In a drawer in my roll-top desk I have a bundle of checks written to me from a man owing a substantial debt to me. The checks are dated one month apart, and go on for more than two years. Each one was for hundreds of dollars. They were given to me to settle a debt. The account on which they were written has been closed for years. None of them, including the first, ever cleared the bank.

I have represented people in law suits for over two decades. I have seen people under tremendous stress as a result of their litigation problems. People respond to this in a variety of ways, few of them really noble. One client, however, repaid an unjust debt when my counsel, and the counsel of my partner, was to avoid paying, by filing for protection through the bankruptcy court. Rather than file for bankruptcy, he paid the debt in full, despite tremendous personal sacrifices. He refused to use the legal system to avoid the payment of this unjust obligation. He rejected all counsel to do otherwise. He was a singular example of personal integrity.

In addition to the worthless checks, there are many others who owe me money, from whom I have no hope of being repaid. In hindsight, it has been bad for business, but good for the soul.

I believe the man who wrote the worthless checks thought he was going to repay me when he wrote them. It would have been good for him had he done so. But he had a wife and young children, and I think he got into financial troubles from a lack of foresight and wisdom. Perhaps it was something more malevolent. But I think it benign. He couldn't afford to pay me, and at the time, I couldn't afford to absorb the loss. I've since recovered financially, and no longer need to have payment to make my circumstances tolerable.

Neither this man, nor any other, is my concern. I am my concern. I have a short season here to live, and then will pass, as have all others before, into the grave. At that point, my record is complete, and nothing further can be done to change my eternal state. Only in the few moments in this life am I able to develop the capacity to forgive and wish others well. In one way of looking at it, I should thank these men for giving me these experiences. I do thank my client for his example of integrity in a time of great personal stress. Some people have integrity that falls apart under stress. This client weathered personal financial crises and still kept his integrity.

It is a wonder to me Joseph Smith could say he died with a conscience void of offense toward his fellow man. I am certain I have offended others. I have some hate-mail kept in my journal to prove it. I have attempted to forgive my offenders. Perhaps there is some hope for me in that. But then again, I have kept the old worthless checks in the roll-top desk, haven't I? So why do I still have them? I expect my client who repaid his unjust debt would have thrown them away by now.[220]

---

[220]The subject addressed here is broader than this material will be able to cover. This chapter is intended to add to your thinking about these matters, and not to exhaust the subject. You could benefit from a good deal more

As we know from both the New Testament[221] and the Doctrine & Covenants, Christ visited the Spirit World during His time in the grave. Although Peter alludes to it in his first epistle, written two millennia ago, it was not until 1918 that any significant knowledge about this part of Christ's ministry was restored.

In the Vision of the Redemption of the Dead, President Joseph F. Smith saw the nature of Christ's mission to the world of departed spirits.[222] President Smith wrote:

> . . . the eyes of my understanding were opened, and the Spirit of the Lord rested upon me, and I saw the hosts of the dead, both small and great. And there were gathered together in one place an innumerable company of the spirits of the just, who had been faithful in the testimony of Jesus while they lived in mortality; And who had offered sacrifice in the similitude of the great sacrifice of the Son of God, and had suffered tribulation in their Redeemer's name. All these had departed the mortal life, firm in the hope of a glorious resurrection, through the grace of God the Father and his Only Begotten Son, Jesus Christ. (D&C 138: 11-14.)

Here we have a description of those spirits whom Christ visited while He was in the grave. They had been 1) faithful in the testimony of Jesus while they lived. They had 2) offered sacrifice in the similitude of the great sacrifice of Christ's. And as a consequence, they 3) departed this life firm in the hope of a glorious resurrection.

---

study of these matters apart from this limited chapter.

[221]Christ predicted His visit in John 5: 25: "Verily, verily, I say unto you, The hour is coming, and now is, when the dead shall hear the voice of the Son of God: and they that hear shall live." Peter confirmed it had occurred in 1 Peter 4: 6: "For for this cause was the gospel preached also to them that are dead, that they might be judged according to men in the flesh, but live according to God in the spirit."

[222]Now found as Section 138 of the Doctrine and Covenants.

Being faithful in the testimony of Jesus was required for those who saw Him during this part of His ministry. It is not enough to have a testimony. You must be faithful to that testimony. Those who are not faithful to their testimony cannot inherit the Celestial Kingdom, as the revelation on the afterlife has confirmed. Doctrine and Covenants 76:79 says, with respect to those who inherit the Terrestrial Kingdom: "These are they who are not valiant in the testimony of Jesus; wherefore, they obtain not the crown over the kingdom of our God." A testimony alone is not enough.[223] Nor is "confessing Jesus" enough as some evangelical sects falsely contend.[224] It is through doing the things commanded of a disciple, people become Saints and members of the household of God.

The statement that these spirits had been faithful to the testimony of Jesus while they lived is, therefore, a significant acknowledgment of personal character. They were not just observing hollow religious forms while alive. They penetrated to the underlying meaning. They lived their religion.

What does it mean that these people had offered sacrifice in the similitude of the great sacrifice of Christ? We have earlier discussed the need for sacrifice. Here we need to develop it further. The "great sacrifice of Christ's" was the Atonement itself. He offered Himself as a ransom for mankind. He paid a price and healed mankind from the

---

[223]Even devils have testimonies, as James 2: 19 confirms: "Thou believest that there is one God; thou doest well: the devils also believe, and tremble." A testimony alone, therefore does not amount to much. It is living consistent with the testimony which accounts for something.

[224]Christ spoke of those who would confess His name and attribute their salvation to that name-dropping. He said of them: "And why call ye me, Lord, Lord, and do not the things which I say? Whosoever cometh to me, and heareth my sayings, and doeth them, I will shew you to whom he is like: He is like a man which built an house, and digged deep, and laid the foundation on a rock: and when the flood arose, the stream beat vehemently upon that house, and could not shake it: for it was founded upon a rock. But he that heareth, and doeth not, is like a man that without a foundation built an house upon the earth; against which the stream did beat vehemently, and immediately it fell; and the ruin of that house was great." (Luke 6: 46-49.)

effects of the Fall. He further made reconciliation between God and mankind possible. That reconciliation was an accomplishment almost beyond description. Think of the gulf it repaired: On the one hand God has said: "For I the Lord cannot look upon sin with the least degree of allowance." (D&C 1: 31.) And on the other hand: "all have sinned, and come short of the glory of God," (Rom. 3: 23.) This statement of opposites makes it impossible for us to return to God's presence. We have all sinned and God cannot tolerate sin. Therefore God cannot tolerate us in our sinful state. We all merit outer darkness without Christ's intervention. Christ's Atonement repairs that and makes our return to a sinless state possible. So when we read this account, we are left asking how we can do something which would result in us offering sacrifice in similitude to this great act?

Christ's Atonement was an act of intercession by Him on our behalf. We are barred from God the Father's presence. Christ made it possible for us to overcome that barrier and return to Him. He made mercy possible by satisfying the demands of justice. Alma 34: 14-16:

> And behold, this is the whole meaning of the law, every whit pointing to that great and last sacrifice; and that great and last sacrifice will be the Son of God, yea, infinite and eternal. And thus he shall bring salvation to all those who shall believe on his name; this being the intent of this last sacrifice, to bring about the bowels of mercy, which overpowereth justice, and bringeth about means unto men that they may have faith unto repentance. And **thus mercy can satisfy the demands of justice**, and encircles them in the arms of safety, while he that exercises no faith unto repentance is exposed to the whole law of the demands of justice; therefore only unto him that has faith unto repentance is brought about the great and eternal plan of redemption. (Emphasis added.)

In one sense, it is not possible for us to satisfy justice by providing mercy for ourselves. But in another sense, we certainly can do so for others. We cannot atone for other's offenses. But, we can forgive other's trespasses against us. Christ provided the way for us all to be forgiven. But He also taught we should forgive others. He said, ". . . forgive us our trespasses as we forgive those who trespass against us." (JST Matt. 6: 13; taken from *Joseph Smith's New Translation of the Bible, Original Manuscripts.* Edited by Scott H. Faulring, Kent P. Jackson and Robert J. Matthews. Provo: Religious Studies Center Brigham Young University, 2004; p. 247.) Forgiving others is our duty. Our own forgiveness is dependent upon it. Within our limited capacities, we must also provide mercy to others just as Christ provided mercy to us all. We, in our sphere, must act just as Christ did in His much greater sphere.

Remember we must become "types" of Him whom we follow. To do so we must mimic Him to acquire His attributes. When we have acquired His attributes, He has claim upon us as one of His own.

We all suffer offenses caused by others. From childhood we are all hurt, ignored, offended and belittled at one time or another. There are those who have offended you without trying. And worse still, there are others who have intentionally offended you, even those who enjoyed being cruel. No one grows to adulthood without experiencing the cruelty of others.

Against this common experience for all mortals, Christ taught us to forgive our attackers. In the Sermon at Bountiful, He commanded us:

> And behold, it is written, an eye for an eye, and a tooth for a tooth; But I say unto you, that ye shall not resist evil, but whosoever shall smite thee on thy right cheek, turn to him the other also; And if any man will sue thee at the law and take away thy coat, let him have thy cloak also; And whosoever shall compel thee to go a mile, go with him twain. Give to him that asketh thee, and from him that would borrow of thee turn thou not away. And behold it is written also, that thou shalt love thy neighbor and hate thine enemy; But behold I say unto you, **love your enemies, bless them that curse you, do good to them that hate you, and pray for them who despitefully use you and persecute you;** That ye may be the children of your Father

who is in heaven; for he maketh his sun to rise on the evil and on the good. (3 Ne. 12: 38-45, emphasis added.)

These are extraordinary standards for us to follow. Not resisting those who are determined to do evil to us presents such a formidable barrier to living that all of us recoil at its implications. Giving the unjust litigant all that he demands, and more, seems impossibly hard. Loving our enemies, blessing those who curse you, and doing good to those who hate you are astonishing hurdles to contemplate. Yet, there it is! Christ asking us to overcome and leave behind our pride, our tendency to defend ourselves and our need for approval.

Christ meant these things. Not only that, He led the way in actually doing them. As proof of His commitment to these standards of self-conduct Christ forgave the men who crucified Him. He said, as they were in the act of killing Him: "Father, forgive them; for they know not what they do. And they parted his raiment, and cast lots." (Luke 23: 34.) He did not resist those who were not only despitefully using Him, but who were determined to kill Him. He did not resist the one who would sue Him for his cloak. He permitted them to part His entire wardrobe among them without complaint. These teachings may have been rejected by most of the audience He taught, but they were not rejected by Him. He did what He asks us to do. If you accept Him as the guide and example to follow then you must accept this part of His example as well.

Remember Nephi's assurance: "I know that the Lord giveth no commandments unto the children of men, save he shall prepare a way for them that they may accomplish the thing which he commandeth them." (1 Ne. 3: 7.) That promise has no limit on it. If we are asked to do these things, and we are determined to follow God in doing them, then the Lord will provide a way for you to be able to accomplish it. However difficult this proposition may seem to be, it is something within your reach. Trust in that, and have the faith to reach out trying to follow Him. His yoke, you will find, is easy after all.

Ask yourself : Why is it necessary for this standard to be adopted by you? What exactly does it have to do with offering an acceptable sacrifice? The answer to those questions puts a different light on the entire matter:

Joseph Smith taught in *DHC* 4: 445: "If you do not accuse each other, God will not accuse you. If you have no accuser you will enter heaven, and if you will follow the revelations and instructions which God gives you through me, I will take you into heaven as my back load. If you will not accuse me, I will not accuse you. If you will throw a cloak of charity over my sins, I will over yours - for charity covereth a multitude of sins." This notion of accusing one another is an important principle. Joseph is explaining something directly relating to obtaining salvation.

Accusing someone is Satanic. One of the titles for Satan is "the accuser of the brethren."[225] Satan's accusations are not said to be unwarranted or unsupported. He is not necessarily accusing his victims unjustly. It is probable some if not all of the accusations were, or are, just. If any of us were measured by an absolute standard of obedience,

---

[225]Rev. 12: 10: "And I heard a loud voice saying in heaven, Now is come salvation, and strength, and the kingdom of our God, and the power of his Christ: for **the accuser of our brethren** is cast down, **which accused them before our God** day and night." (Emphasis added.) See also Job 2: 1-5 where Satan accuses Job of being loyal to God only because Job is favored by God: "Again there was a day when the sons of God came to present themselves before the Lord, and Satan came also among them to present himself before the Lord. And the Lord said unto Satan, From whence comest thou? And Satan answered the Lord, and said, From going to and fro in the earth, and from walking up and down in it. And the Lord said unto Satan, Hast thou considered my servant Job, that there is none like him in the earth, a perfect and an upright man, one that feareth God, and escheweth evil? and still he holdeth fast his integrity, although thou movedst me against him, to destroy him without cause. And Satan answered the Lord, and said, Skin for skin, yea, all that a man hath will he give for his life. But put forth thine hand now, and touch his bone and his flesh, and he will curse thee to thy face." Here Satan is accusing Job of being loyal to God only because of God's favor toward him. In essence, Satan is accusing Job of being a phony follower whose loyalty has been bought by God's favors.

faithfulness, or virtue, we would all necessarily fail. Satan does not need to use an unfair standard to accuse and condemn us. We are assured that "all have sinned, and come short of the glory of God." (Rom. 3: 23.) So if you want to condemn any of us, you need only look at our actual deeds and you will find sufficient reason to accuse us. Yet the negative and condemned role of accusing belongs to Satan. Those who take it upon themselves to do the condemning are acting the part of Satan. What Christ has asked us to do is forgive each other. Or, as Joseph put it, we are asked not to accuse each other.

The Lord is serious about our forgiving each other. Christ meant it when He taught "Verily, verily, I say unto you, Judge not, that ye be not judged. For with what judgment ye judge, ye shall be judged; and with what measure ye mete, it shall be measured to you again." (3 Ne. 14: 1-2.) This teaching is an integral part of the salvation of yourself and mankind. If you are not accused by your fellow man, Satan's accusations alone will not be sufficient to condemn you.

The incident in John 8: 10-11 illustrates the Lord's approach to judgment and mercy: "When Jesus had lifted up himself, and saw none but the woman, he said unto her, Woman, where are those thine accusers? hath no man condemned thee? She said, No man, Lord. And Jesus said unto her, Neither do I condemn thee: go, and sin no more."[226] Here the woman had violated the law prohibiting adultery. She was brought to Christ to find out His reaction to this breach of the law. In spite of clear guilt, Christ found a way to avoid accusing her. This incident shows the lengths to which the Lord will go to avoid becoming

---

[226] As Dean of the J. Reuben Clark Law School, Rex Lee pointed out to his Constitutional Law students that the woman was guilty. There was no question about her violation of the law. But since there was no accuser, and the law required two accusers for conviction, there was a technical procedural defect in condemning the woman. Without this technical requirement being met, the woman would stand uncondemned under the Mosaic Law. Dean Lee used this example to explain the concept of "procedural due process" to his students.

the accuser. His title: "Our Advocate with the Father"[227] is the antithesis of the role of the "accuser." The Advocate helps defend us against accusations. Even accusations properly brought, as was the one against the woman taken in adultery. He will seek whatever reason or even excuse as may exist to warrant forgiveness for our mistakes and failings. This role of Advocate He has adopted for Himself, is the role of Mercy itself.

The Lord also revealed, "I, the Lord, will forgive whom I will forgive, but of you it is required to forgive all men." (D&C 64: 10.) Here we are admonished to forgive all. Without regard to the justice of your claims against others, you are to forgive. Certainly there are others who have offended you. Certainly you have just complaints about others. You are justified in finding fault with your fellow man, because your fellow man is weak, sinful, error prone and ignorant. Christ is saying to forgive them anyway. No matter how right your complaint is against them, forgive them anyway. No matter how little they deserve your forgiveness, forgive them anyway. It is required of you to forgive all men.

Society does not do this. Society exacts vengeance and retaliates. Socially, if retaliation was not expected, we would not have a legal industry, a prosecutor for every city, county, state or district in America and for similar political subdivisions throughout the world. The world wants vengeance. But Christ tells us that *you* should not. We are discussing you, and not society, in this chapter.

In the great Day of Judgment, men will have to face their accusers. The standard by which mankind will be judged in that great day will be perfection. For us to pass that test, we must not accuse our offenders. It does not matter who will accuse you. What matters is whether or not you will accuse another. If you do not accuse anyone, then the

---

[227]John the Beloved called Him this in 1 Jn 2: 1: "My little children, these things write I unto you, that ye sin not. And if any man sin, we have an advocate with the Father, Jesus Christ the righteous. He also calls Himself this in D&C 110: 4: "I am the first and the last; I am he who liveth, I am he who was slain; I am your advocate with the Father."

accusations against you will fail. But if you accuse anyone, then you set a standard for judgment against which you will fail.

Satan is not mortal, and has no body. All of the actions in the second estate involve the actions of fellow physical beings toward or with each other. Satan can whisper to us, but he cannot control us, here. He does not reside here. He is a shadow without substance or standing. He has no position to bring an accusation, since he has no part in the physical world. We, on the other hand, suffer physically by the actions or inactions of each other. We do have standing to accuse each other because we have caused each other's sufferings. And we immeasurably complicate the Lord's work when we insist upon judging each other, and accusing each other. We create a barrier to forgiveness for each other when we accuse each other.

If we show mercy to our fellow man, we merit mercy from Our Lord. If we show love to our fellow man, we merit love from Our Lord. With what measure we measure, it will be measured again to us; pressed down and overflowing.[228]

This is serious business. We are living in a brief, temporary and probationary state. It is going to pass by as if a dream, and end sooner than any of us imagine. When it does, if we have left a record of forgiving our fellow man, loving them, and refraining from returning evil for evil, we will have filled the measure of what God has asked of us. He will be able to excuse our sins, because we have adopted a standard by which we can be forgiven. Our mercy shown to others is really mercy being shown to ourselves. We set the standard for our own judgment. Christ's counsel pleads for us to set that standard mercifully low for others, so we can meet that standard ourselves. His perspective takes a larger view into account. If you will follow Him and accept His teachings, when you arrive at life's end, you will proclaim the wisdom

---

[228] See Luke 6: 38: "Give, and it shall be given unto you; good measure, pressed down, and shaken together, and running over, shall men give into your bosom. For with the same measure that ye mete withal it shall be measured to you again."

and mercy of the Lord. He will have prepared you for that day by helping you set the standard for your own forgiveness.

If you forgive greater offenses by others than you have committed against others, you will surely pass the test. If the standard of tolerance and kindness shown by you to your fellow man is broader than the one which you have demanded that they show you, you will be forgiven.

It is in this sense that Joseph taught, "A man is **his own tormentor and his own condemner.**" Hence the saying, 'They shall go into the lake that burns with fire and brimstone.' The torment of disappointment in the mind of man is as exquisite as a lake burning with fire and brimstone. I say, so is the torment of man." (*DHC* 6: 314, emphasis added.) This self-condemnation may come about in a different way than you might first imagine. Don't think of this explanation by Joseph as you damning yourself out of guilt for your misdeeds. Rather, think of it in terms of having set a standard by judging others which you cannot meet when that standard is used against you.[229] The accusation you bring against yourself will be the criteria you have set for others. It is "just" to use that standard against you. It is "merciful" to judge you by a tolerant standard which showed greater leniency to others beyond what you asked for yourself. All of these things interrelate and are the substance of what Christ is trying to teach us. He is trying to make of us something much better than we are now. To accomplish this, you will have to adopt His standards for dealing with the unjust, the unmerciful and the cruel. The bread cast upon the water returns to you.[230]

---

[229]Remember the earlier discussion about Laban condemning Lemuel of being a robber, and then passing the sentence of death upon him. This made Nephi's later killing of Laban just, under the standard of judgment Laban had set. We do not condemn others by our judging of them; rather we condemn ourselves to be judged by a standard we must be willing to meet. This is why we should apply our standards internally to measure our own conduct, and not externally to judge and condemn others.

[230]Eccl 11: 1: "Cast thy bread upon the waters: for thou shalt find it after many days."

Help others face God without the guilt of offenses they have caused you. Let them go free. Let the prison open and all who have ever caused you injury walk in the light of freedom free from any accusation you could bring against them. Forgive them for this because when they did so, they knew not what they did. Forgiving them will not just liberate them, but it will liberate you, as well. Letting go of the just accusation will not only let them out of their prison, but it will let you out of yours. Take down the bars on your own home's windows, and open the windows to the air outside. Remove the locks and bars you have erected on your own home, and change it from the prison you have made it. Locking the world out has ultimately locked you in. When you set your own tormentors free, you will set yourself free.

Most of the offenses we harbor have been inflicted on us long ago. The perpetrators are long since gone out of our lives. It is our own choice keeping their offense with us, still. Forgiving lets you drop the burden of carrying that offense alive. Without your effort, it will die. So let it go and move on with life.

This matter does not end there, however. Christ tells us to pray for those who abuse and misuse us. Odd as this may sound, it is what He did. It is one of the things that allows us most to emulate Him. Though it may seem out of character, you should try doing it. You can't sincerely pray for another person without losing your anger toward them. This act of intercession with God for those who have committed offenses is directly related to making sacrifice in the similitude of the great sacrifice of Christ. Lehi did this, as recorded in 1 Ne. 1: 5: "Wherefore it came to pass that my father, Lehi, as he went forth prayed unto the Lord, yea, even with all his heart, in behalf of his people." These people had the judgments of God about to fall upon them. Rather than join in condemning them, Lehi prayed to God about them. He showed mercy to them.[231]

---

[231]Only after being commanded did Lehi begin to warn them and repeat God's (not his) judgments against them. (See 1 Ne. 2: 1 "...because thou hast been faithful and declared unto this people the things which I commanded thee, behold, they seek to take away thy life.")

Nephi similarly showed mercy and made intercession for his elder brothers. In 1 Ne. 2: 18 it is recorded: "But, behold, Laman and Lemuel would not hearken unto my words; and being grieved because of the hardness of their hearts I cried unto the Lord for them." Nephi's act of showing mercy, refraining from judging, and praying in intercession for brothers who rejected him, made Nephi a "type" of Christ. Meaning that Nephi's example conformed with the later message and ministry of the One who made intercession for all mankind. Christ did it for real. Nephi did it in imitation of Him. We can do it as an imitation as well. That imitation of Him is required to qualify us for the Second Comforter. If we are unwilling to accept these standards and imitate these acts, we are not qualified to receive the Second Comforter. Without resonating at the same frequency as He, we are not going to be moving where we can see Him.

Charity is one subject that has been given a great deal of treatment by the Saints. Numerous books exist. One of the best is *Bonds that Make us Free: Healing Our Relationships, Coming to Ourselves.* (Warner, C. Terry The Arbinger Institute, Inc., Salt Lake City: Shadow Mountain Press, 2001.) In it Professor Warner not only discusses charity, but does so in a remarkably readable way. It is a book worth studying. In it he reaches into the nature of sin itself and demonstrates how charity can cure it.

Many Church authorities have spoken on charity, as well. The subject is amply treated elsewhere, and does not need to be discussed at length here. But there is an aspect of charity we need to discuss. We do not think of it as a lack of charity. It is a defect only charity can cure, though it is not often thought of in that context.

Criticism of fellow Saints has almost become a cottage industry. There is a widely held attitude the Saints should be better than they are, and that attitude has led to open criticism of the Saints by the Saints. Semi-apostate writings pass as good social commentary. Mildly adopting the role of accuser is considered by some to be sophisticated and intelligent. Some think that being a little critical of the Saints, and the

Church and the presiding authorities, shows that you have "independence of thought."

This is wrong. The Saints are just as they should be. They are human, frail, weak and vulnerable. They need your example and your encouragement. They do not need your criticism and judgment piled on top of the other discouragements facing them as Latter-day Saints living in the latter-days. These times are tough. No one has it easy. Saints struggle. That is as it should be. You are here to help them, not to condemn them. Christ said He came into the world to save the world, not to condemn it. Imitate Him. Do something to avoid condemning His Saints. He doesn't condemn them, so why should you? The Saints deserve your mercy.

The rhetorical criticism seems to raise a notch when some pseudo-intellectual Saints speak about the presiding authorities of the Church. The Brethren who preside over the Church of Jesus Christ of Latter-day Saints deserve your support, prayers and confidence, not your judgment and criticism. If they fail or err, forgive them and sustain them with your prayers. You fail. You err. If you want to be forgiven of that in your life, then forgive them for their failings and errors.

You may think you could do a better job than your bishop or stake president. You might be right. But they were called, not you. When they were called you were asked to sustain them. If they fail in their calling, that is their stewardship to report on and be held accountable for. You will not have to answer for any of their shortcomings.

But you will have to account for how you behaved toward the presiding authorities. You will have to justify how you "sustained" them when they presided over you. A good deal, if not all, of a presiding officer's deficiencies can be covered by a faithful quorum, society, group, ward, or stake. You are accountable for you. If you can help them succeed, then you should do so. Support them the way you would want to be supported if you had the calling. This is what Christ taught.[232] If you want to receive an audience with Him, it will come only as you do as He has taught and shown you how to act.

The seriousness of this issue is reflected in the Temple covenants. Refraining from "evil speaking of the Lord's anointed" should be given its broadest possible application. Included within the broadest of the definitions of the "Lord's anointed" would be any Saint who had received their Temple anointings. If you have covenanted to refrain from speaking evil of them, then that covenant should be honored by keeping your tongue when speaking of your fellow Saint. And all the more so when speaking of the presiding authorities who have a double claim on your speaking about them. For they not only are anointed in the Temple as all Saints who receive those rites are, but they are further "anointed" by your sustaining vote and by ordination to office as a General Authority in the Church.[233]

It is a serious matter, therefore, to treat your fellow Saint and the presiding authorities with critical and judgmental disregard. They deserve better. More importantly, however, you covenanted to give them better. The failure to do that is more serious a failing than you

---

[232]Matt: 7: 12: "Therefore all things whatsoever ye would that men should do to you, do ye even so to them: for this is the law and the prophets."

[233]A good indication of how important this issue is in this dispensation is found in a letter from the First Presidency dealing with recommends for second anointings written to a Stake President. The letter includes, in relevant part: "They should be men of good report, men whose faith has never been shaken, whose integrity to **the Lord and his servants** has been beyond question, men who have been valiant for the truth, men **who have either defended the servants of the Lord or would do so at all hazards should circumstances require** it at their hands. They should be men who have done what they could whether in preaching or working or **otherwise helping their file leaders in the building up of** Zion, and who are ever ready and willing to labor in the interests of Zion at home or abroad." Joseph F. Smith and Anthon H. Lund to William C. Partridge, 23 Oct. 1911, (Joseph F. Smith Papers, LDS archives; reprinted in part in *The Mysteries of Godliness.* Buerger, David John. San Francisco: Smith Research Associates, 1994, at p. 120, emphasis added.) This strongly suggests the folly of belittling and dismissing the presiding authorities, whether General or local.

may have realized. Treat them charitably and repent, if need be, of evil speaking about them.

It is within us all to live a charitable life. If you do, the rest of these things will take care of themselves. Be content with the challenges you already face in your life. Calling Church authorities into question is an unnecessary distraction from the issues you should be dealing with. Work on the things in your life that need attention. Criticism of Church leaders or members from afar is just not one of the things you need to crowd into your life. Let them go in peace, and without your judgment and censure. Support them with your prayers. They will do better with your charity than they will with your complaints.

As Alma taught us, while wishing he could do more: "But behold, I am a man, and do sin in my wish; for I ought to be content with the things which the Lord hath allotted unto me." (Alma 29: 3.) That's it, you know. You "ought to be content." Both content with your own life and with the lives of others who are trying to live the Gospel.

Christ wisely taught us: "He that findeth his life shall lose it: and he that loseth his life for my sake shall find it." (Matt. 10: 39.) "For whosoever will save his life shall lose it: and whosoever will lose his life for my sake shall find it." (Matt. 16: 25.) Helping others without regard to their "worthiness" is liberating.[234] Supporting Church leaders without

---

[234]King Benjamin was not just dispensing good advice when he taught: "And also, ye yourselves will succor those that stand in need of your succor; ye will administer of your substance unto him that standeth in need; and ye will not suffer that the beggar putteth up his petition to you in vain, and turn him out to perish. Perhaps thou shalt say: The man has brought upon himself his misery; therefore I will stay my hand, and will not give unto him of my food, nor impart unto him of my substance that he may not suffer, for his punishments are just – But I say unto you, O man, whosoever doeth this the same hath great cause to repent; and except he repenteth of that which he hath done he perisheth forever, and hath no interest in the kingdom of God. For behold, are we not all beggars? Do we not all depend upon the same Being, even God, for all the substance which we have, for both food and raiment, and for gold, and for silver, and for all the riches which we have of every kind?" (Mosiah 4: 16-19.) He was also telling his subjects how to find happiness.

regard to their individual talents is liberating, as well. More importantly, it is one of the necessary steps to receiving the Second Comforter.

The purpose of these teachings is not to start a debate over the "highest good" or the "meaning of life." It is far more practical than that. Christ did not offer us theology, but a way of conduct. He offers a way of living.

Truth and light are not acquired by study alone.[235] If they were, the scholars would be the greatest among us. Scholars are often rebellious, proud, contrary and discontent. They question truth, but rarely find it. You can find scholars among the least content people in the Church. Apostates include many scholars among their ranks. Scholars in our own day include Dallin Oaks of the Quorum of the Twelve on the one hand, and D. Michael Quinn on the other hand -- the one a teacher of righteousness, the other excommunicated. If scholarship alone could confer truth and light, we would not see this gross dichotomy. So scholarship is no guarantee of greater enlightenment. Often it is the guarantee of the opposite.

Truth and light are acquired by living a life in tune with the things Christ has asked us to do. The commandments are themselves revelations of God and His nature. By obeying them, you begin to resonate at the same frequency as He resonates. You begin to find harmony in His teachings. You begin to "see" things as they really are.

It is an odd thing, but it really works. The process is marvelously democratic. Anyone can receive the same results. All they need do is follow the same steps. Light and truth come to even the most uneducated, if they will heed Christ's commandments.

The view into heaven is as thin as the razor's edge. You must be

---

[235]When D&C 88:118 says: "And as all have not faith, seek ye diligently and teach one another words of wisdom; yea, seek ye out of the best books words of wisdom; seek learning, even by study and also by faith." It is **not** (as commonly taught) commending study as the first source of light. It is saying since there is a general inability to receive light the right way (by faith), then study and teaching is a secondary way to acquire it. But even then, faith is still needed, as the final phrase indicates.

perfectly perpendicular to this world to see through that narrow opening. But when you are, eternity itself opens to your view. It is a veil, and not a wall, to make it possible to pass through. It is you that must change and align yourself to the opening if you want a view of what is to be seen there. You cannot readjust the opening. You can only realign yourself.

Charity is not an option. It is a requirement. When you meet that requirement, you will conform to another of the things which are required by Him to see His face and know that He lives.

Show charity to the Saints. Give it to the Church authorities. Rather than judge or dismiss them, pray for, sustain and support them. It will please God and relieve you of yet another difficult, self-imposed test that might prevent you from surviving the Day of Judgment.

Chapter Fourteen

KEEPING THE COMMANDMENTS
(Reprised)

I t occurred to me that although I was "living" the teachings of the Church as expected, there had to be more to Gospel obedience than the criteria the Church uses to evaluate "activity." The institution needs some kind of feedback, and counting home teaching percentages, Sacrament Meeting attendance, Temple recommend holders among adults, and other measurable things is the only practical way to measure what is going on within the population. So it makes sense there must be some kind of counting going on. But it made equal sense that getting "counted" in the "active" column could never be an adequate measure of my heart.

Do these activity-measuring criteria really measure the individual? Does it really measure me? After all, holding a Temple recommend does reflect on whether I am paying tithing, supporting the authorities, complying with the Word of Wisdom and other basic *rules of conduct. So it does indicate something about me, but I could do all these things and still not be a particularly good person.*

As I reflected on this I concluded it would be possible to pass scrutiny in a recommend interview and be allowed to attend the Temple, and still be lacking. The inner heart is a thing so private and so difficult to measure, no interview can disclose it. In the end, it is only the individual and the Lord who know what lies within any given human heart.

As for my heart, there were many things I resented, doubted and questioned. There were many things I had not yet resolved for myself, despite years of Church membership. When being objective (to the extent anyone can be objective about themselves), I was "converted" but still lacked conviction about many things that probably needed resolving before I could say I unhesitatingly accepted the Church in its fullness.

I could see a difference between Church culture and true faith, between traditions and presumptions governing many people's conduct, and the things taught or commanded in scripture. I could see that the scriptures themselves discouraged me from applying an outward measuring rule against others, while they encouraged the need to confine my judgment using the scriptural standards, internally, and only against myself. Many of the criticisms and resentments I held were there because of this looking outward, and failing internally to apply the same standard of judgment against myself.

I determined I needed to accept others, or at least attempt to do so, no matter what they did, thought, said or failed to do. I would attempt simply to accept them and leave it to them and God to decide what they ought to be doing. As for me, faith would be applied as an internal measure for deciding what I should do, should not do, and should change. Religion was, I determined, to be applied only internally, and not for external application.

I feared this new approach would be confining. I feared it might make me neurotic and insecure. Instead, I found it liberating. It was like dropping a great weight when I no longer needed to evaluate others. And when I applied it to myself, I found some things that troubled me before were petty and superficial and did not merit further consideration. Cultural things may be significant to others, but that is their concern. The real work that needed doing was within my heart. There was so much amiss, so little overall harmony, so little delight, that this faith of Christ's which had been so joyful at first had become a joyless burden. I could still recall the joy I felt as I converted. I remembered the excitement of new discovery and new learning through those first couple of years of membership. That was now lacking in my life.

I needed to recapture what was right in the Faith. To do so, I needed to return to where I was when I first joined the Church. I needed to go back to anxiously seeking for light and truth, wherever it was to be found, and without regard for the opinions of others. That was the happiest time in my life. Every day was alive with the new discoveries being made about the connections between Gospel concepts and doctrines.

I enrolled in a Know Your Religion class and found an instructor who was a marvel. I hadn't had a Church teacher who taught me anything for over a decade and a half. Now I had found someone who had something to contribute. He was an answer to prayer. For two years I eagerly attended class. I didn't miss a class. I always sat on the back row.

After a year he told us he was considering ending his class because of heavy responsibilities he had elsewhere. The class complained and asked him to stay. Against his better judgment, he remained for another term.

At the end of two years he announced he could no longer teach, and was ending his class because of the press of family and work responsibilities which could no longer be ignored. That last evening I came up after the last class and told him how much I had appreciated him these past two years. I said, "I've been sitting on the back row all this time, so you probably haven't noticed me. But I've been regular in attending and appreciate all you have done."

He looked me in the eyes and replied, "For the last year I have only remained because of the back row." I believed that to be true. I needed him and somehow he sensed it. He was a lifeline to heaven, as all great teachers are. We need more like him.

If you have read this far, you must be actually interested in this process. You actually want practical help in receiving the Second Comforter. The discussion in this chapter is related to the gate for entry itself. What will most prepare you (or alternatively entitle you[236]) to receive the Second Comforter is keeping commandments. It is not optional in the process. It is required. We have spoken about that already, but we need to return and reexamine the subject here, because anyone seeking this must return and reexamine their life on this same subject. What you have been doing so far has not been enough. What you need is to return to these fundamental, basic principles to relearn them for yourself. Relearn them in the context of actually applying the teachings in your daily, even hourly, life.

---

[236]"Entitled" is really not a good term but is used to illustrate the point. This whole process is a gift from God. He set the bounds and terms by His grace. D&C 130: 20-21 makes it clear this process of receiving the Second Comforter is, like all other blessings, obtained in accordance with "law, irrevocably decreed before the foundations of this world." To obtain any blessing you must obtain it "by obedience to that law upon which it is predicated." So if we elect to abide those conditions we are entitled to receive the grace He promises. It remains a gift throughout, however, even when we abide the conditions. King Benjamin explained this process of keeping commandments, receiving blessings and remaining in God's debt in Mosiah 2: 20-25. But I use the term "entitle" here to make the point that once you've done your part, He will do His. You will not go down the road only to find it closed at the end. He keeps His promises.

You can gain a command of many skills in this life by study and formal education. You can acquire wealth by effort and care. Skills in sport come from practice and good coaching. But an increase in light and truth is acquired through keeping the commandments and in no other way. Light and truth do not come by study alone, nor by effort, practice, coaching or tutoring. Light and truth come to you from above, as you keep the commandments in your life. You must obey to obtain.

The commandments are a revelation to you of God's nature. By keeping them, you obtain from God light and truth as a by-product of obedience to them. They reveal to you, in a very personal way, what the mind of God is for your life. It is intensely personal because it is all internal. You cannot measure, count or tally it. You must become something new through this process.

In a formula we have already read from D&C 93:1, the Lord outlines the means for obtaining the Second Comforter: "Verily, thus saith the Lord: It shall come to pass that every soul[237] who forsaketh his sins[238] and cometh unto me,[239] and calleth on my name,[240] and obeyeth

---

[237]Note the universal application here, as we have previously pointed out. This is not limited to any office, sex or familial connection. **Any** soul, including you, qualifies.

[238]*I.e.* through repentance and baptism, which is the only means God has ordained to forsake your sins.

[239]*I.e.* through conforming to His terms to come to Him, through the ordinances and covenants He has restored in the Church of Jesus Christ of Latter-day Saints. It is through this process that you obtain a covenant with God for yourself. You must obtain these ordinances in your own name through the restored Church or you are not able to "come unto" Him. As Joseph Smith explained: "And though we cannot claim these promises which were made to the ancients for **they are not our property, merely because they were made to the ancient Saints**, yet if we are the children of the Most High, and are called with the same calling with which they were called, and embrace the same covenant that they embraced, and are faithful to the testimony of our Lord as they were, **we can approach the Father in the name of Christ as they approached Him and for ourselves obtain the same promises**. These promises, when obtained, if ever by us, will not be because Peter, John, and the other Apostles, with the churches at Sardis,

my voice,[241] and keepeth my commandments,[242] shall see my face and know that I am." This process builds. (You should read this paragraph's footnotes if you have not already done so.) From baptism and receiving the remission of sins, to obeying His ordinances, to personal prayer and developing a revelatory relationship in which you become acquainted with hearing the "still small voice" of God, to then responding and doing what you are inspired to do in answer to your own prayers, this process builds one precept upon the next. But the final step in this building process requires you to reconcile yourself to God by the requirement to "keep His commandments." This is perhaps as perplexing a requirement to some people as has ever been given. The whole argument between works and grace resurfaces here.[243]

Pergamos, Philadelphia, and elsewhere, walked in the fear of God and had power and faith to prevail and obtain them; but it will be because we, ourselves, have faith and approach God in the name of His Son Jesus Christ, even as they did; and **when these promises are obtained, they will be promises directly to us, or they will do us no good**. They will be communicated for our benefit, being our own property (through the gift of God), earned by our own diligence in keeping His commandments, and walking uprightly before Him. If not, to what end serves the Gospel of our Lord Jesus Christ, and why was it ever communicated to us?" (*TPJS*, p. 66, emphasis added.)This process begins with baptism, and matures through the other ordinances made available through the Melchizedek Priesthood.

[240]I.e. through prayer; which is immediately connected with the next phrase.

[241]*I.e.* through following those things directed to you through the Spirit or personal revelation received in response to the prayers offered in the immediately preceding phrase.

[242]This is what we are focusing upon in this chapter.

[243]The Apostle Paul did not, as is argued by the proponents of "saved by grace without works" theorists, teach that obedience to commandments was unnecessary. See, e.g.: Rom. 6: 16: "Know ye not, that to whom ye yield yourselves servants to obey, his servants ye are to whom ye obey; whether of sin unto death, or of obedience unto righteousness?" Heb. 5: 9: "And being made perfect, he became the author of eternal salvation unto all them that

But we are going to by-pass that argument (since it is off the subject) in favor of trying to see Gospel harmony. We are going to look for the harmony. It would probably serve you well to spend a couple of decades (as I did) trying to keep the commandments before reading this chapter. You would grow immeasurably if that could be achieved.[244]

As in all matters in the Gospel, Christ is the Great Example in this one, as well. John the Baptist left his written testimony about Christ, which is no longer extant. But we have a portion of that testimony restored to us in the verses which follow in Section 93 of the D&C. His testimony begins with:

> And he bore record, saying: I saw his glory, that he was in the beginning, before the world was; Therefore, in the beginning the Word was, for he was the Word, even the messenger of salvation -- The light and the Redeemer of the world; the Spirit of truth, who came into the world, because the world was made by him, and in him was the life of men and the light of men. The worlds were made by him; men were made by him; all things were made by him, and through him, and of him. And I, John, bear record that I beheld his glory, as the glory of the Only Begotten of the Father, full of grace and truth, even the Spirit of truth, which came and dwelt in the flesh, and dwelt among us. (D&C 93: 7-11.)

John is telling us Christ had a preeminent role before the earth was created, and He was directly responsible in the creation itself. In the

---

obey him;" 2 Cor.10: 5; "Casting down imaginations, and every high thing that exalteth itself against the knowledge of God, and bringing into captivity every thought to the obedience of Christ;" The "grace without works" proponents ignore Paul in these and other passages, yet base their arguments on Paul's teachings.

[244]This can be viewed as the "Pharisee Phase" because of the potential rigidity this process can bring with it. Although ultimately you must grow beyond it, going through this effort is actually very worthwhile and produces its own benefits in increasing your understanding. I went through that. While there, I was devoted to religion, but not a very good Latter-day Saint.

pre-earth life, before creation and before we came into mortality, we all looked to Christ as the One to follow. Things repeat themselves, and we find ourselves situated here as we were situated there. It is to Him we look for the way to live this second estate. His example is the continuous source of light to which we look to see the way we must go.

John then tells us some remarkable doctrine contained nowhere else in scripture.[245] He explains of the Lord: "And I, John, saw that he received not of the fullness at the first, but received grace for grace. And he received not of the fullness at first, but continued from grace to grace, until he received a fullness; And thus he was called the Son of God, because he received not of the fullness at the first." (D&C 93: 12-14.) Christ was not given a full endowment of knowledge or grace from birth in mortality! Similarly, He was not given a full endowment in the preexistence, either. In the preexistence and in mortality, He led by example. The example was going from less to more through obedience. He kept the commandments of the Father, and as a result He grew in light and truth. He proved the truthfulness of the Father's promises by obeying the Father's commandments. We witnessed it there and witness it again here. He received the fullness in the preexistence by obedience. He received the fullness in this life by obedience. He is our example of what happens when you obey the commandments of the Father.

He came to mortality with potential, as we all do. But He did not have the fullness from the start. He grew and struggled through the veil until He was once more the Son of God. Just as He led us by His example in the pre-earth life, He leads us by example here.

Just as Christ did, we should also become sons and daughters of God, but not by virtue of our pre-earth heritage on the other side of the veil. We come here as children of earthly parents. However, we need to become reborn here, and through that rebirth, readopted into God's

---

[245]Paul alludes to this doctrine, but does not explain it, in his passing remark: "Though he were a Son, yet learned he obedience by the things which he suffered;" (Heb. 5: 8.) John's restored testimony in Section 93 goes well beyond this comment to explain the underlying reality of Christ's actual limited beginnings and progress in mortality.

family. Even though we are living as mortals, we are asked to become members of the Father's family again. That was what Christ showed by His example. All of us can become sons and daughters of God by following His lead.

In the pre-existence, Christ grew from a lesser to a greater degree until He was filled with light and truth. He **became** the Son of God, the Firstborn, and the Lamb Slain from the Foundation of the World. He was the "fullness" because of what He chose to do with his free will and how He obeyed there. He so exemplified what the Father commanded, He literally became the "Word" of God. It was He who showed that following the Father would actually result in fulfilling the promises made by the Father in the lives of all who obeyed Him. He was the Father's "Word" because what the Father said to do, Christ did. He obeyed whatever the Father commanded in pre-earth life. As a result, while there He was "like unto God."[246]

Here on earth He did the same. He grew from a lesser degree until He was filled with light and truth as a mortal. On earth, He again became the Son of God, the Only Begotten in the Flesh, the Lamb of God. He so exemplified the Father's will, that once again, He became the living example of the Word of God. That is what He wants us to do as well. That is why His Gospel teaches us to follow commandments. They are not a burden. They are the path to higher knowledge. They provide the experiences which change us, mold us and develop us. They do not confine, but liberate.

Christ defined Himself as the fulfillment of God's commandments. When introducing Himself to the Nephites He explained, "behold, I am the light and the life of the world; and I have drunk out of that bitter cup which the Father hath given me, and have glorified the Father in taking upon me the sins of the world, in the which **I have suffered the will of the Father in all things from the beginning**." (3 Ne. 11: 11, emphasis added.) He is glorious and worthy of worship, possessing

---

[246] Abraham 3: 24: "And there stood **one among them that was like unto God**," (emphasis added).

powers, principalities, dominions, kingdoms and thrones because He did what the Father commanded Him to do. The effect of obeying the Father was to fill Him with light and truth. By doing what the Father commands, **anyone**, including you, can qualify to receive the same things. Christ was unique in that He alone has done it perfectly. Because of Him, however, we can do it imperfectly and be forgiven of our sins and errors. His perfection in this undertaking allows us to become a perfect similarity, through His Atonement.

There is no magic, though. There is nothing given to us effortlessly. Christ paid the price to allow us to repent. But it is up to each person to choose for themselves the amount of truth and light they are willing to receive. That light and truth you are willing to receive is dependent upon your obedience. How much light and truth are you willing to receive?

John the Baptist is testifying to us about these things in his restored testimony in Section 93. In turn, John is offering the possibility we can receive the fullness, as well.

Christ gives us these sayings from John to help us see this potential applies not to Him alone, but also to all of the Saints. He says: " I give unto you these sayings that you may understand and know how to worship, and know what you worship, that you may come unto the Father in my name, and in due time receive of his fullness." (D&C 93:19.) So Christ gives us these sayings to teach us "how to worship." This is no idle statement. In this is the essence of what we must do to worship the Father. We worship Him by keeping His commandments. We keep His commandments to follow the example of His Son. That example allows us to go from grace to grace. Eventually, having grown from grace to grace by keeping His commandments, we, too, can receive a fullness. D&C 93:20: "For **if you keep my commandments you shall receive of his fullness**, and be glorified in me as I am in the Father; therefore, I say unto you, you shall receive grace for grace." (Emphasis added.)

Keeping commandments is not keeping statistics. Nor is it to attract notice from others. It is not to finish some check-list of questions in an interview. It has a deeper meaning and serves a much higher purpose.

Would you like to proceed from a lesser to a greater degree of grace? Would you like to receive a fullness of what God offers to mankind in mortality? Then you must worship the Father in this way. He wants you to worship Him by keeping the commandments and growing thereby in light and truth and grace. D&C 93: 27-28: "And no man receiveth a fulness unless he keepeth his commandments. **He that keepeth his commandments receiveth truth and light, until he is glorified in truth and knoweth all things**." (Emphasis added.)

This cuts the matter squarely. Acquiring this – getting the fullness -- is not done by study, or theological courses. It is not the province of the scholar. Nor is it the academic who commands this fullness. It is acquired exclusively by those who are willing to keep the commandments and thereby qualify to receive light and truth as a by-product of following this path. This is the way Christ became the Son of God. This is the way any son or daughter of God will qualify to be a part of His eternal family. There is no other way.

You could spend a lifetime of study and not obtain these things. Generations have done that already. You can read the works of the academics, even those who are good and devoted disciples, without securing for yourself anything other than merely learning through the arm of flesh. Paul described such activity as "Ever learning, and never able to come to the knowledge of the truth." (2 Tim. 3: 7.) Joseph put it into context by saying: "Could you gaze into heaven five minutes, you would know more than you would by reading all that ever was written on the subject" (*TPJS*, p. 324.) The promise is not that you become academically qualified, but you will "know all things."[247] This is something more secure than mere learning of skills or training.

---

[247]Joseph commented: "But I am learned, and know more than all the world put together. The Holy Ghost does, anyhow, and he is within me, and comprehends more than all the world; and I will associate myself with him." (*DHC* 6: 308.) This is the way anyone can receive a fullness of truth and light.

Knowledge of all things comes from knowledge of God. If you know Him, you do know "all things." At least you will know all things of eternal importance. Everything else is transitory and will change or fade away.

This process of gaining light and truth by keeping the commandments is no small thing. Acquiring light and truth is acquiring "intelligence" in the scriptural meaning of the term. It is explained in these words: "The glory of God is intelligence, or, in other words, light and truth." (D&C 98: 36.) Here we see how significant these things are. Light and truth, or intelligence, are the same thing. They are also synonymous with the glory of God. These are acquired through keeping the commandments. God wants us to have light and truth. He wants to give it to us. The way He can and does give it to us is through the commandments He has provided. We accept that invitation and keep the commandments, then we accept God's offering to us. We receive what He offers. We get light and truth. This is a simple process and God has made it universally available. Whether or not you have access to a good school, you have access to light and truth. Whatever language you speak, or circumstance you live in, you have access to light and truth. It is available to all.

This principle is explained further: "That which is of God is light; and he that receiveth light, and continueth in God, receiveth more light; and that light groweth brighter and brighter until the perfect day." (D&C 50: 24.) This is another way of describing the same growth in grace. From a lesser to a greater degree you progress in light and truth as you obey the commandments. That growth increases the brightness of the light in the mind of the obedient "until the perfect day." Think about what is implied by this phrase. A perfect day would be bright, clear, warm and at the zenith of the summer solstice. If you were trying to find a metaphor for being in God's presence, you would use such a phrase. That is what receiving the Second Comforter is like; the Perfect Day, in which there is no longer shadow, darkness or clouds. There is clarity, vision and warmth. To get there you must keep the commandments.

There is an opposition to getting there. You must face an adversary who is committed to keeping you from receiving light and truth. He knows very well how this process works. Unlike you, he has no doubts about this process. So the adversary directs his efforts to keep you from closing the distance between you and God. Interestingly his role in this process is described with perfect clarity in the scriptures as well: "And that wicked one cometh and **taketh away light and truth, through disobedience**, from the children of men, and because of the tradition of their fathers." (D&C 93: 39, emphasis added.) The Adversary is trying to keep you from gaining light and truth. He understands how to do that: Get you to disobey the commandments.

You think you are just struggling with a problem or weakness. You think you are having some temptation that drives you to distraction. The criticism, complaint or weakness you have that challenges your faith is not that at all. It is your enemy working on taking light and truth away from you. This is the balance in which you find yourself. Choose the light.

And I now give unto you a commandment to beware concerning yourselves, to give diligent heed to the words of eternal life. For you shall live by every word that proceedeth forth from the mouth of God.[248] For the word of the Lord is truth, and whatsoever is truth is light, and whatsoever is light is Spirit, even the Spirit of Jesus Christ. And the Spirit giveth light to every man that cometh into the world; and the Spirit enlighteneth every man through the world, that hearkeneth[249] to the voice of the Spirit. And every one that hearkeneth to the

---

[248]"Every word" includes not only the written commandments in scripture, but also the words you receive through the voice of inspiration, as D&C 93:1 refers to.

[249]Enlightenment and hearkening to the voice of the Spirit are related. Hearkening to the voice of the Spirit, and not other methods such as study and philosophy, is what produces enlightenment.

voice of the Spirit cometh unto God, even the Father.[250] And
the Father teacheth him of the covenant which he has renewed
and confirmed upon you,[251] which is confirmed upon you for
your sakes, and not for your sakes only, but for the sake of the
whole world. And the whole world lieth in sin, and groaneth
under darkness and under the bondage of sin. And by this you
may know they are under the bondage of sin, because they
come not unto me. For whoso cometh not unto me is under the
bondage of sin. And whoso receiveth not my voice is not
acquainted with my voice, and is not of me.[252] And by this you
may know the righteous from the wicked, and that the whole
world groaneth under sin and darkness[253] even now. And your
minds in times past have been darkened because of unbelief,
and because you have treated lightly the things you have
received – Which vanity and unbelief have brought the whole
church under condemnation. And this condemnation resteth
upon the children of Zion, even all. And they shall remain

---

[250]If you listen to the voice of the Spirit you will inevitably come to
the Father. That is where it leads you.

[251]This is what Joseph was speaking of when he said: "if we are the
children of the Most High, and are called with the same calling with which
they were called, and embrace the same covenant that they embraced, and are
faithful to the testimony of our Lord as they were, we can approach the Father
in the name of Christ as they approached Him, and for ourselves obtain the
same promises. These promises, when obtained, if ever by us, will not be
because Peter, John, and the other Apostles, with the churches at Sardis,
Pergamos, Philadelphia, and elsewhere, walked in the fear of God and had
power and faith to prevail and obtain them; but it will be because we,
ourselves, have faith and approach God in the name of His Son Jesus Christ,
even as they did; and when these promises are obtained, they will be promises
directly to us, or they will do us no good. They will be communicated for our
benefit, being our own property (through the gift of God), earned by our own
diligence in keeping His commandments, and walking uprightly before Him.
If not, to what end serves the Gospel of our Lord Jesus Christ, and why was
it ever communicated to us?" (*TPJS*, p. 66.)

[252]He offers His voice, but we must be willing to receive it.

[253]Even if we do not connect "sin" with the loss of light and truth or
"darkness" the scriptures consistently do so.

under this condemnation until they repent and remember the new covenant, even the Book of Mormon and the former commandments which I have given them, not only to say, but to do according to that which I have written, – (D&C 84: 43-57.)

The Book of Mormon contains the fullness of the Gospel of Jesus Christ. More than any other volume of scripture it holds the greatest amount of light and truth for us. If you follow its teachings, it will lead you to the perfect day. But you must be willing not only to say you believe in the book, but also to follow and obey what it is telling you to do. This process is natural and follows laws ordained before the foundation of the world. It works for anyone who follows it. It will work for you.

Christ warned and taught:

And why call ye me, Lord, Lord, and do not the things which I say? Whosoever cometh to me, and heareth my sayings, and doeth them, I will shew you to whom he is like: He is like a man which built an house, and digged deep, and laid the foundation on a rock: and when the flood arose, the stream beat vehemently upon that house, and could not shake it: for it was founded upon a rock. But he that heareth, and doeth not, is like a man that without a foundation built an house upon the earth; against which the stream did beat vehemently, and immediately it fell; and the ruin of that house was great. (Luke 6:46-49.)

Hearing alone is not enough. It has never been enough. Confessing you believe is not enough and never has been. Nor is it enough to argue over the scriptures in a Gospel Doctrine class. A wide ranging knowledge of doctrine is not enough. It is the "doing" that is needed. If you want to get light and truth from the scriptures, it comes from obeying what they teach.

The commandments get viewed by the immature disciple as a kind of necessary evil. They are something to follow in order to belong to the

Church. That kind of approach makes the commandments confining and even suffocating. It misses the point.

The commandments are the roadway to greater light and truth. They can be liberating. They can elevate you and teach you. They can be used as stepping stones taking you to greater heights. We don't follow them to fit in with other people or to pass an interview. If that is all they mean to you, then you are not getting what they really offer you. They can bring you to such great light and truth, that you pass through the veil and back to God's presence.

Christ links keeping the commandments with love. He taught: "If ye love me, keep my commandments." (John 14: 15.) "If ye keep my commandments, ye shall abide in my love; even as I have kept my Father's commandments, and abide in his love."(John 15: 10.) You say that you love Christ. You can know if you really do by the degree to which you keep His commandments. The commandments can be an extension of your love and devotion to Christ, **if** you live them that way.

Describing the exalted, John the Revelator wrote: "Here is the patience of the saints: here are they that keep the commandments of God, and the faith of Jesus." (Rev. 14: 12.) Patience and keeping God's commandments are linked together. So we find patience, love, light and truth all connected with keeping His commandments. It is an interesting intersection of things all found in keeping the commandments. The scriptures are plain in telling us how these things work. But they only work as you actually keep the commandments.

The wonder of the process is that it works. But it works within its own context and through its own proofs. Light and truth come from obeying the commandments. Looking at it without keeping the commandments will never result in greater understanding, even though it may be a lifetime's study. What seems vague, ill-connected and difficult to grasp with the mind, becomes clear, reasonable and understandable through obedience. There is an emerging clarity as you follow this process. Without following it, there is an almost vaporous fog to it. God hides most truths in plain sight. But developing the vision to see them comes only one way. People who are willing to follow the commandments and obey God will find greater light and truth. Skeptical people who retain some distrust of God, or who believe His Church is just trying to control people's lives, hold back. But what they hold back is light and knowledge from themselves. Rather than losing themselves, they insist on finding themselves. Christ taught that will never work.[254] By filling our lives with God's commandments, we fill it with light and truth.

There is only one way to get it right. There are many ways to get it wrong. There is an infinite number of errors you can make. As King Benjamin was concluding his teachings, he observed: "And finally, I cannot tell you all the things whereby ye may commit sin; for there are divers ways and means, even so many that I cannot number them. But this much I can tell you, that if ye do not watch yourselves, and your thoughts, and your words, and your deeds, and observe the commandments of God, and continue in the faith of what ye have heard concerning the coming of our Lord, even unto the end of your lives, ye must perish. And now, O man, remember, and perish not." (Mosiah 4: 29-30.) Despite these nearly countless ways of erring, the point is there is a way to get it right. That is the good news. In a world filled with sin and error, you can still get it right, but not without following the commandments.

You should know the errors you are committing. You know your own heart and know clearly the sins and weaknesses which plague you. That is where you should go and what you should work to fix. Repent of the sins you labor with, and move on to something much better and far nobler. It is fun. Finding truth and light are the most rewarding, most exciting and most edifying opportunities in life. Knowing it is possible and that you, too, can qualify is half the battle. That knowledge can steel your determination if you let it.

If you are a convert, return to those beginning days when keeping

---

[254]Christ said: "For whosoever will save his life shall lose it: and whosoever will lose his life for my sake shall find it." (Matt 16:25.)

the commandments was fun. A time when every day was a new adventure in gaining greater understanding from following the Gospel. If you have been a lifelong member, realize the Gospel offers you exciting and rewarding insights. There is nothing more enjoyable than getting greater light and truth. Although this may seem like a vague process, it is not. As you keep the commandments you gain light and truth. Experience will be your guide. It works. If you find this odd or difficult to grasp, keep the commandments and you will find it becoming increasingly easy to understand. You will get light and truth as you follow the process. Do it and see it unfold for you.

This is the way in which Christ grew from grace to grace. This is how He received the fullness. It is also the way you can get greater grace, greater light and truth. It is the way you will obtain the fullness of light and truth.

Assuming you are at this point, satisfied that keeping the commandments is necessary, this then leads to a discussion of what it means to keep the commandments. Does it require you to become a new form of modern "Pharisee?" Do you need to become rigid and sanctimonious? How, exactly do you keep the commandments? That requires another discussion about the difference between "doing" on the one hand and "being" on the other.

Chapter Fifteen

DOING AND BEING

I could not escape the thought that if *"no other success could compensate for failure in the home,"*[255] *my divorce signaled for me the greatest of all personal failings. I feared it meant I had irreparably limited my chances for God's approval, both in this life and in the next. It represented first of all a failure to my children who were entitled to have a secure home life to spend their youth in. It also was a failure of a covenant made in the Temple which was intended to endure not only this life, but all eternity. It collapsed an eternal institution, and was the most grave of failures I could conceive of at the time. It also meant the forfeiture of promises made in the Temple covenant. I lost everything.*

Divorce is the most painful emotional experience I can imagine

---

[255]This is a reference to a 'truism' from President David O. McKay. In General Conference, April 1964, President McKay reminded parents that "No other success can compensate for failure in the home." (IE 67 [June 1964]:445). That statement had become a well-known catch phrase among the Saints by the time of my baptism in 1973.

for a Latter-day Saint. Marriage, particularly one solemnized in the Temple, has a life greater than that of the direct participants. When it ends in divorce, that greater life dies. Though the members may continue on and live separate lives thereafter, there has been a death when the marriage ends.

While in the depths of this self-doubt, I wrote the following in my journal on the night of August 25, 1989:

I am alone.

I had children, and books, tables, rugs and other things. (I thought you never lost children, as you lose other things.)

In a day, they are all gone.

I am alone.

Frankly Lord, your promises of a better future and suggestions of hope do little for the pain....

Will you hold me?

Will you put your hand on my back to comfort me?

Or, will you only whisper, instead, as you are wont to do?

You sent an angel to announce the Blessed Birth, and choruses to sing... Messengers of warning to prophets....

But they are always aloof.

Except for the angel who wrestled with Israel, Isaiah's who touched a coal to his lips, and Nephi's who shook his brothers, your messengers don't really <u>do</u> much.

They just talk.

And right now I am but a child.

And alone... and in pain.

I could use a touch, a caress, a hand of help...

It is not right to force me to look to my fellow-man exclusively for comfort....

They have all failed me.
Except for my children.
And my wife keeps them away during this divorce.

I am alone.
Yes, You whisper to me.
Yes, I know there will be days of joy ahead.
But now I am alone. And your intrusion into my thoughts does not bring the comfort that a supporting hand on my back would give.

...What? ...You are frustrated too?
Now, that's a curious thing to me.
You, too, would love to hold and help?
..... I'm sorry, I didn't understand that.

You too feel the pain, and despair.... Lonely for us, bitter with us....
Eager for our joy... impatient for our pain.
Frustrated by this veil.
...I hadn't thought that possible, Lord.

...I am sorry....
I'll accept your promises.
I can handle this.
There will be a new season of joy, and I know it will come.

No, I am not alone.
Nor, Lord, are you.
Thank you for your concern....
It's not easy for either of us having this veil.

This plan, with its frustrations, and limitations, is still a good one.

I'll get over this...

And thank you, Lord, for being there when no-one else was.

It's a hard lesson – but You (and only You), are always to be trusted.

Of all the concepts discussed in this book, this one is the most difficult to articulate, and about which the least has been written by Latter-day Saints. Yet it remains a pivotal part of the changes required to get you where you want to be.

Christ ministered to the least members of society. He was at home among the outcasts and misfits. He was not at home, accepted or honored among the "chief priests" and public leaders. There is a reason for that, of course. But it is a reason you need to contemplate for yourself.

Harlots, publicans, the maimed, halt, poor, and lower castes of society know in this life they have nothing much to offer. They were (and are) humiliated when they compare themselves to the great ones of the day. They have broken hearts and contrite spirits because they know so keenly they are not great. They are the least, and they know it. No one defers to them. And the chief seats are never surrendered to them.

These were the people who accepted Christ. They were willing to see the Great Light because of their own keen desire to have their outcast and demeaned station replaced by a hope for a better world. They were open to the possibility of Christ being their Deliverer because they wanted so much to be delivered.

In our own day and cultural setting, comparable groups are the part-member family, the divorced, the uneducated and those who have never been considered "leadership material." They include today's blue-collar workers who attend services in a Church led by white collar, middle-management types. Many of those most attracted to this message of hope are those whose circumstances have not been that of the stereotypical LDS life. Anyone who does not quite "fit into the mold," fits the personality type Christ preferred. He preferred them because their hearts were broken.[256]

You should never conclude that a lack of conformity equates to a lack of worthiness. That assumption is unjustified in the truest of sense. As Brigham Young once remarked: "There is too much of a sameness among our people. . . . I do not like stereotyped Mormons; away with stereotyped Mormons!" (JD 8: 185; quoted in *The Incomparable Christ: Our Master and Model*, at p.119. Featherstone, Vaughn J. *The Incomparable Christ: Our Master and Model*. Salt Lake City: Deseret Book Company, 1996.) There is a great value to every Saint, no matter how unique their life's circumstances.[257] But what is relevant here, and so very important, is that these feelings of inadequacy do have great value. Feelings of inferiority, or of not quite belonging, or of being less than you should be, all lead to the essential humility needed for the next step.

---

[256]Christ's parable of Lazarus and the Rich Man, as well as His comments in the Sermon on the Mount, suggest that receiving your reward, here, prevents receiving a full reward in the afterlife. These are not idle comments from the Great Teacher, but disclosure of a profoundly insightful reality: Not many of those whom the world regards as "great" are great in the eyes of God.

[257]Actually there is not just great value, but it is an essential part of the Church. Without regular introduction of convert members in large numbers, the Church would acquire a staleness that would cripple its spiritual power. The Gospel is ill-transferred from generation to generation without on-going missionary work to increase its numbers, not only by the converts themselves, but through the missionary experience it affords to the descendants of families who have belonged for many generations. Hugh Nibley wrote, "To quote one of the greatest of leaders, the founder of this institution, 'There is too much of a sameness in this community. . . . I am not a stereotyped Latter-day Saint and do not believe in the doctrine . . . away with stereotyped "Mormons!"' Good-bye, all. True leaders are inspiring because they are inspired, caught up in a higher purpose, devoid of personal ambition, idealistic, and incorruptible." (Nibley, Hugh. *Brother Brigham Challenges the Saints*. Salt Lake City: Deseret Book Company, 1994, p. 498.)

Remember, these kinds of people were better able to see Christ as the Redeemer when He walked among us than were the leaders, the wealthy, and the great ones of His day.

Feelings of inferiority and need also come to people whose lives have been marred by disease or illness. Serious sickness or injury often results in feelings of inadequacy. Feelings that you do not measure up and cannot be as useful to the Lord as you would have liked to be are humbling.

Sooner or later everyone reaches a point when their lives become humbled by age, disease, infirmity and loss of function. Measured by this world's standards, such things are difficult burdens, even injustices. Measured by the criteria for exalting us, however, these things are gifts from God. It is a rare person who can come to the point of a broken heart and contrite spirit without some profound weakness or serious failure in life given to them as a gift from God. "And if men come unto me I will show unto them their weakness. **I give unto men weakness that they may be humble**; and my grace is sufficient for all men that humble themselves before me; for **if they humble themselves before me, and have faith in me, then will I make weak things become strong** unto them." (Ether 12: 27, emphasis added.) (Without a crushing personal failure of my own, this book could not have been written.)

Because of the great value to advancing the human soul through suffering from great infirmity, weakness or personal ill-ease, the Lord has chosen His servants carefully. The program of the Lord in providing successors to the office of President of the High Priesthood is to have the longest ordained Apostle succeed to the office upon the death of his predecessor. This guarantees the Saints the one holding this office will be elderly and oftentimes in ill health. Such people will have vanity and self-pride at an all-time low as a result of declining health and advancing age. Their circumstances in this life fit them uniquely and wonderfully, to give heed to the Lord's promptings and to find little worth in acclaim from the world. An approaching veil into the next life is certain to bring with it a sensitivity to the Lord which the very same man may not have had even ten or twenty years earlier.

Who among us, for example, could not feel the deep humility of President Kimball as he first assumed the office of President. That small, hoarse-voiced, infirm, elderly man was carefully refined for the office. It took suffering and infirmity to bring him to that height. That is a part of the Lord's program. He takes similar care with all of us. If we will allow our weaknesses to do so, they can bring us to Him. As the verse previously quoted in Ether reminds us, it is not just possessing the weakness that refines us, but "if men come unto me I will show unto them their weakness. ... for if they humble themselves before me, and have faith in me, then will I make weak things become strong unto them." Rather than producing resentment, envy, anger or bitterness, you should allow these things to produce humility. Through a profound sense that relief can only come from God, people become prepared to approach Him with the kind of humility, awe and reverence that moves aside the veil.

Proverbs 8:13 states: "The fear of the Lord is to hate evil: pride, and arrogancy, and the evil way, and the froward mouth, do I hate." The Lord's revulsion at our pride has produced carefully tailored experiences in mortality to remove it. Setbacks and failures are wonderfully suited to refining and honing our character. They advance us even as we think they hold us back.

Keeping these things in mind, we need to paint a picture to try and get the concept right:

The pit and the mountain:

Imagine a deep and dangerous pit in the center of your community. Your community has been given the commandment to stay out of the pit. Assuming no other commandment is given, it is the nature of almost all mankind that this one commandment would result in almost everyone falling into the pit sooner or later. Curiosity, rebellion, peer pressure, pride or some other vanity would lead to risk-taking around the pit and inevitable falling in. That is the nature of most of us during the teenage years, and many of us right into adulthood.

Those disposed to being "protectors of virtue" (i.e., busybodies) would post signs nearby to try to prevent people from falling into the pit. Yet while posting signs, such "protectors of virtue" oftentimes fall into temptation themselves, and many of them would fall, too. Of course, later, the "protectors" would add a handrail. Other precautions would follow. But these would do no good, for if the only commandment is a "thou shalt not," then the failings would follow, while the precautions taken would invite further curiosity by the unconvinced, or rebellious, or curious. Precautions at one end invite further risks at the other, since it appears safer to take the risk.

The only sure way to prevent you from falling into the pit would be to give you something positive to do that will take you in another direction. Climbing a mountain would keep you so far from the pit there is no danger of falling. If you are headed away from the pit, you can never fall into it.

This basic notion underlies many of the commandments. The "thou-shalt-nots" get accompanied by positive commandments, as well. The Sermon on the Mount/Sermon at Bountiful is filled with positive injunctions to action. This positive approach toward what the Lord wants of you is not only more satisfying to the soul, it is also the only way to avoid the "thou-shalt-nots." Trying merely by force of will to avoid some particular weakness or transgression will generally result in failure. Ask any addict how they overcame addiction. None of them will tell you they just managed to stop. They had to get involved in some wholesome, replacement activity. That is how the commandments work. Go away and do something good somewhere distant from the temptation, and you will find you can overcome every weakness.

Weaknesses are, oddly enough, a gift from God as we mentioned earlier. Strange as a gift of weakness may sound, it is nonetheless so – as the verse from Ether says. Take your weaknesses and come to the Lord. Trade them for strengths. But you will find the trade is not direct.

It is indirect, and requires you to be willing to replace the weakness with some positive activity. Direct confrontation of a weakness is not usually successful at first. A reformed alcoholic sitting in a bar and praying for God to help her overcome the temptation is likely to fail. That same woman spending time volunteering to help others overcome their addictions will likely succeed. Going somewhere else and doing something positive makes the weakness irrelevant. Over time, it turns the weakness into nothing. Then it turns the weakness into strength as you have replaced the desire to sin with a desire to do good. It also makes you able to help others who suffer from your previous weakness. It isn't magic. It comes through application of effort and common sense. There is some struggle inherent in the process, but it develops and refines anyone willing to engage in the effort. It is how any sin, even serious sin, is overcome.

Great rivers start as small streams. That is true of sin, and it is equally true of strengths. Persistence in little acts develops character into towers of strength and virtue. There are no little sins. There are no little virtues. They accumulate over time. They become great mountains.

The Lord encouraged the Saints with this commandment:

> Wherefore, I give unto them a commandment, saying thus: Thou shalt love the Lord thy God with all thy heart, with all thy might, mind, and strength; and in the name of Jesus Christ thou shalt serve him. Thou shalt love thy neighbor as thyself. Thou shalt not steal; neither commit adultery, nor kill, nor do anything like unto it. Thou shalt thank the Lord thy God in all things. Thou shalt offer a sacrifice unto the Lord thy God in righteousness, even that of a broken heart and a contrite spirit. And that thou mayest more fully keep thyself unspotted from the world, thou shalt go to the house of prayer and offer up thy sacraments upon my holy day; For verily this is a day appointed unto you to rest from your labors, and to pay thy devotions unto the Most High; Nevertheless thy vows shall be offered up in righteousness on all days and at all times. (D&C 59: 5-11.)

Here we have the "thou-shalt-nots" accompanied with positive activities to keep you engaged. The Lord does not expect us to simply not do evil acts. He has provided in His mercy and wisdom a host of things which will permit us to replace every vice in our lives with some virtue. Go to Sacrament Meeting. Partake of the ordinance. Pay devotions to God. Take one day out of seven and devote it to meditation and reflection. Love your neighbors. Live in harmony with them. These injunctions to positive behavior are mixed with the "thou-shalt-not's."

There is a difference between doing and being. Alma 7: 23: "And now I would that ye should **be** humble, and **be** submissive and gentle; easy to be entreated; full of patience and long-suffering; **being** temperate in all things; **being** diligent in keeping the commandments of God at all times; asking for whatsoever things ye stand in need, both spiritual and temporal; always returning thanks unto God for whatsoever things ye do receive." (Emphasis added.) In the thirteenth Article of Faith we find: "We believe in **being** honest, true, chaste, benevolent, virtuous, and in **doing** good to all men; indeed, we may say that we follow the admonition of Paul – We believe all things, we hope all things, we have endured many things, and hope to be able to endure all things. If there is anything virtuous, lovely, or of good report or praiseworthy, we seek after these things." (Emphasis added.) "Being" and "doing" are both referred to in this statement of faith.

You can never **do** enough. But you can **be** enough. It isn't necessary for you to swallow the entire ocean. You can't do that anyway. It is only required that you function within your limited time and space in conformity to the things God asks of you. And this you can do.

There are many things in life which illustrate this principle. When you ski down a frozen mountain, you cannot be thinking of other responsibilities or taking your eye off the terrain. You must be consumed with the "now," and not looking or thinking of elsewhere. If you take your mind off the task for even an instant, you may catch an edge on your ski and go down. Skiing is very "childlike" in its demand you live in the instant and clear your mind of things that went on yesterday or the things you have to do tomorrow. One of the great joys of skiing is the need to live in the moment. It brings you back to childhood because it forces this approach upon you while you ski.

This physical process illustrates another spiritual process. No one starts out a great skier. They develop by degrees from novice to expert. You first learn technique and 'rules' to follow when skiing. However, when you finally become an accomplished skier you cannot ski aggressively and think about the rules of skiing. You must apply them with speed to accomplish the activity. You can't be reciting rules, or trying to keep the edges in an exact alignment. To ski well you must 'feel' the activity. You still follow the rules for the activity, but you do this subconsciously. It is more 'feel' than anything else. An experienced skier does not recognize where his legs end and the skis begin. They become one with the boards on their feet. The skis become an extension of the body. Until you become an accomplished skier, however, you must do the activity while keeping the fundamental rules in mind. You "do" in order to "become." But once you have become, you then do it because that is what you are.

When teaching someone to ride a motorcycle, the best way is to let them ride as a passenger behind an experienced rider. The experienced rider will tell them to lean when the rider leans, and keep their bodies aligned behind the driver. After enough miles in the seat, the rider will instinctively begin to "feel" the way to turn, how to lean, how to accelerate, how to shift, how to stop, and then will be ready to try it themselves. The experience of riding behind an accomplished rider imprints on the learners. After first learning the mechanical rules for riding, the learner eventually will duplicate the 'feel' of what was learned. When the feel is right, they are comfortable in riding. This method of teaching motorcycling produces not only a better rider, it produces them much more quickly than any other teaching method.

An experienced motorcyclist does not recognize where the bike begins and where they leave off. They become one. The motorcycle becomes an extension of the body. You "do" and then you "become."

When making a turn on a motorcycle, the experienced rider looks where she wants to go. The bike follows her sight as a natural extension of her thought. You drive down the road where you look. If there is an obstruction on the road you want to avoid, you mustn't fix your eyes on the obstacle or you will hit it. You look where you want the bike to go. To avoid the obstruction you look to the right or the left, and the bike will follow. Staring at a road obstruction is called "target fixation" and is a common problem with new riders. If you fixate on a target, even one you want to avoid, you will hit it. You go where you look.

Luke 11: 34-36: "The light of the body is the eye: therefore when thine eye is single, thy whole body also is full of light; but when thine eye is evil, thy body also is full of darkness. Take heed therefore that the light which is in thee be not darkness. If thy whole body therefore be full of light, having no part dark, the whole shall be full of light, as when the bright shining of a candle doth give thee light." Christ is the light. Look to Him. Keep your eyes away from the things you want to avoid. You cannot avoid them if you are fixated on them. The process of trading strength for weakness begins by looking away from the weaknesses and toward what it is you would like to become.

When you begin to play the drums, you count measures and notes. One-ee-an-da-Two-ee-an-da-Three Four, gives you quarter notes in the first half of the measure. Few things are less rhythmic than a beginning drummer counting notes as they pound away. Mercifully, beginners use rubber drum pads which make no sound. After years of effort, something clicks inside the drummer and the notes no longer get counted. They are heard instead. And when it sounds right, it feels right, and it is right. An accomplished drummer feels the music they play. They and the drums become one. It is difficult for the drummer to know where he leaves off and the drums begin, because the instrument becomes an extension of his body. A good drummer can listen to a record and then play the piece without music or practice. It is an experience stemming from a deeply imprinted feel for the instrument and how it sounds right. It is a kind of oneness between instrument and player that must be experienced to be understood. The mind of the drummer thinks and the sound follows, without any apparent intermediate effort.

Piano playing also progresses from counting and pounding to feeling and being. When you have mastered the instrument, it is a mental and even an emotional exercise, not something involving the fingering and counting of measures. It is harmony. It is music. It is beauty.

In all activities involving skill, you progress from a state of "doing" to a state of "being." Harmony and feeling for the activity replaces rules and exercises. Somewhere along the line, the fundamental rules of the activity are replaced by the music or harmony underlying the activity.

Nolan Ryan once remarked that after throwing 80,000 pitches any pitcher could throw a strike to any spot in the strike zone with his eyes closed. Good baseball pitchers begin by focusing on balance, alignment, arm movement, finger placement on the ball, seam alignment to the fingers, grip, release, leg stride and aim. But by the time a pitcher is accomplished, there is no longer an "aim" to their throwing. They see the object and hit it with the throw. There is no concentration on any mechanics or fundamentals. All of that has been replaced by "feel" and harmony of the activity.

Good cooks do not need a recipe, only their sense of taste. Bad cooks follow recipes and wonder, while doing so, how the end product will taste. Good framers do not need a detailed framing plan, for a floor plan is enough for their purposes. Jazz bands play without written music and feel their way through a musical fusion. Once the choreographer has finished teaching the movements, the performers take the rules of the performance and convert it into a thing of beauty, "felt" more than "done." The audience can feel it performed, too. There can be artistry to any activity. An accomplished surgeon, bricklayer, mechanic or finish carpenter can make their skills sing. Yet all these activities can be done poorly as well. They can be grudgingly done by people who are just marking time in a responsibility they find tedious. Some people think about retiring decades before retirement and never do acquire a profession that fulfills them.

The Gospel is similar. It begins as a rigid group of rules, but should evolve into something more. It can be music. It involves the highest aspirations of man, and the eager encouragement of a loving God. Men reach upward while God reaches downward in a chiasm of longing, fulfilling for both. Two interlocking triangles, one pointing upward and the other pointing downward, as the searching and longing soul is met by the loving and encouraging Father. It is an embrace between the lonely searcher/child and the eager Parent/God through a veil. Whereupon the son or daughter finally realizes this longing was mutual, and the need you have for God is equaled by the need God has for you. The emptiness which you have felt all along in mortality has its counterpart in a Parent whose longing for you exceeds your longing for Him. Bread and water coming as a gift from above, blessed to symbolize the sacrifices of a God for you, being consumed and becoming a part of your person. Harmony. Music. Love and feeling. Uniting and becoming One. It is mankind losing his sinful nature and receiving holiness by joining with a perfect and Holy Being. It is the final realization that this process is not complete for either you, as child, or God, as Parent, until your personal redemption from the Fall and return to God has been accomplished. Until then the longing remains mutual. We are drawn to Him, He is drawn to us, and we complete each other and form at last an eternal family. He is incomplete without us, just as we are incomplete without Him. We are a part of Him, just as He is a part of us.

You need to be something different and much more complete than you have been in the past. That state of 'being' is what you seek. It is not working to do something good in imitation of the Holy One, though that is what it begins with at the first. You must get behind the

Savior and ride along, feeling how it was that He (the only perfect example of progression directly from grace to grace) moved through His mortal estate. His most complete statement of His own approach to life's challenges is the Sermon on the Mount/Sermon at Bountiful. Follow that ride and you will be feeling His life, living His experience, and suffering His burdens. Keep His commandments to know Him. Keep them to love Him. Don't do it to try to follow a rigid set of rules. See the harmony underlying what He asks you to do. Work on these things until you finally begin to feel what He meant for you to feel. It requires you to accept a state of being and to rest in that state after it becomes second nature. It is entering into the "rest of the Lord."

At the end of the journey through the restored Gospel's ordinances, you pass through the veil into the Celestial Room in the Temple and there you are ceremonially 'at rest.' You are in the symbolic presence of God, and at a state of rest. This is the only room in the Temple where there is nothing to do except to rest and meditate. It is the symbol of the state of rest. It is the state of being. No "doing" is involved in this state or in this room symbolizing this state. You just "are" when you arrive there. It is a powerful reminder of a greater truth, and intended to convey to the mind of man the underlying concept of harmony and being. What you feel in that room is what you should feel in your life.

While in line at the grocery store, in traffic, or dealing with the evening news, this state of rest should be what you seek to feel. The Temple was given to you for a reason. It is a powerful teaching tool. Feel its meaning, then duplicate that feeling in your life.

There are times, even in the Temple, when the press of other patrons and the excitement of a new marriage entourage make meditation and contemplation difficult. Perhaps there are other places and times when you have felt particularly close to God. Sometimes in the woods or on a mountain there are moments of quiet and reflection that make the veil seem thin and God's presence palpable. You can use those experiences to draw on, as well.

There is a tree growing out of a granite cliff in the Sawtooth Mountains of Idaho. It has been twisted and contorted by the winds that whip around the granite outcropping. That yellow pine tree persisted in its upward reach, pointing to God who created it, despite the opposition of the wind and elements and the difficulty of growing out of a granite wall. These forces produced a spiral tree, twisted by opposition, yet still pointing upward to God. It preaches a sermon louder than words by testifying through its very being. Reflecting on this tree and its testimony of competing forces, God and persistence in life, brought me to a state of rest and meditation. You no doubt have something similar in your own experience. Some profound moment of insight and meaning that can be used to the same effect. The Celestial Room was intended for this purpose. But any moment of similar peace can be used in the same way. Remember such a feeling, and duplicate it when dealing with life's stresses and challenges. Try to feel your way back into that experience by pondering on it daily.

Quiet reflection and meditation will accomplish the same thing, whether in the Temple or in nature. God is in the Temple. He is in the redwoods, too. Having the Temple rites memorized and being in nature brings the Temple with you there. Temple reflections can flood the mind as symbol in ceremony is matched by symbol in creation. They overlap and point back upon each other, until the one prepares you for the other, and the other prepares you for the One.

When you feel this harmony and closeness, remember it. When you are in balance, in harmony and at rest, you can feel His presence. Feel it, follow it, lean when He leans, and you will learn quicker what it is you are trying to accomplish with your heart, might, mind, and strength. You've been keeping His commandments. Now try to feel the underlying state it was intended to bring you to. God did not give you a mere 'rule book.' He gave you something much greater. It is a harmony and symphony. But more of a feeling than a thought. It is an experience, and not just an analysis, which brings you into balance as thin as a razor's edge.

There is a description of Christ in Nephi's words: "Wherefore, redemption cometh in and through the Holy Messiah; for he is **full of grace and truth.**" (2 Ne. 2: 6, emphasis added.) We imagine that statement to mean He had all conceivable grace and all conceivable truth. It might instead mean His life was filled with such grace as was needed for it, and such truth as was required for it. Within His sphere and element, He attained perfection. But did He know calculus (to make an illustration)? Nothing indicates Christ had any need to know calculus. It wasn't that He couldn't learn it, of course, but it wasn't required of Him. There were many things which, in His context and day, in His culture and society, in His time and place, He had no reason to know. His message spoke of simple things to illustrate higher truths about love, kindness, Godliness, charity, and mercy. These are universal issues transcending time, culture, society, and place. These are the elements, therefore, which matter most for this second estate. He used wildlife, animals, plants, and weather to illustrate His messages. He used things relevant to His environment to teach truths which are still relevant across political, cultural and language boundaries two millennia later. But the focus of His teachings had nothing to do with practicing medicine, or computer programming, or calculus. Yet every doctor, programmer and mathematician would be morally benefitted by heeding Christ's teachings -- not to do their work better, but to live better lives. So when you read He was "full of light and truth," you needn't think of that as something beyond your level of understanding. You have a sphere and element, too. You are not required to live your life as if you were anything other than what you are, living where you are, among the people of your own family and neighborhood. Within your life's context, you too can be full of light and truth. You too can drink the cup given to you, without regard to attempting to swallow an ocean never given to you to drink. Theoretical and impractical challenges are not yours. You only have those challenges that will occur the next moment in your life. That moment can be confronted with the same rest you have as you sit in the Celestial Room of the Temple. Today's problems (and only today's) are your challenge. Feel the music and rhythm to this specific challenge given to you. Use the Gift of the Holy Ghost to confront these limited challenges. You can feel it when you do it right. Become one with the life you have. Rest from your worries and let the moment be filled with light and truth. You can be full of grace in your environment, just as Christ was in His.

The disappointments and failings of your life are no impediment to you. If they discourage you, then it is only for your own preparation for something much better and much greater. God is the perfect tutor. He is also individually preparing each of us. To make more room in our hearts, they must be broken and contrite. His is a kind and caring Parent. He is taking you somewhere. Do not fight against it. Find peace within it.

All of these things are for our good. The Lord's promise is that He will make all of these disappointments and apparent failures redound to our good. To Joseph in Liberty Jail the Lord said: "And if thou shouldst be cast into the pit, or into the hands of murderers, and the sentence of death passed upon thee; if thou be cast into the deep; if the billowing surge conspire against thee; if fierce winds become thine enemy; if the heavens gather blackness, and all the elements combine to hedge up the way; and above all, if the very jaws of hell shall gape open the mouth wide after thee, know thou, my son, that all these things shall give thee experience, and shall be for thy good."(D&C 122: 7.)

If you cannot see it in this light now, then rest assured the Lord will provide you satisfactory relief in the end. As is foretold in Rev 21:4, in the end: "And God shall wipe away all tears from their eyes; and there shall be no more death, neither sorrow, nor crying, neither shall there be any more pain: for the former things are passed away." He can do it for you now, if you permit it. Do not struggle against the process, but find the harmony within it. Rest from the fight and find peace and contentment in what God has given you for this estate. It is enough. It was carefully planned for you. We all live as a part of a well cultivated garden in which God is the gardener, and we are carefully placed to grow. Some of the growth involves necessary pruning as Hugh B. Brown spoke of not so long ago.[258] It is all for our good.

Rather than wait for the future day when God will make it clear to all of mankind how His hand has ruled over all of us, you can use these things *now* for their intended purpose. They are here to help you. Find your balance in spite of (or through) your unique circumstances. Do it so you can feel it. Become it, and find rest.

This dispensation opened when Joseph Smith inquired of God in response to a verse in James. "If any of you lack wisdom, let him ask of God, that giveth to all men liberally, and upbraideth not; and it shall be given him." (James 1: 5.) This verse still works. If you do not find the harmony in your mortal experience, ask God to help you find it. It does exist. There is a wise and caring God who governs in our lives. When Joseph was despondent in Liberty Jail, he asked and got God's assurance that 'all these apparently awful experiences were for his good.' Joseph was benefitted by them. You are benefitted by your own time in 'Liberty Jail.' The experiences should not be fought, but accepted.

Similarly, the commandments should not be fought. Work with them. Accept them. Let them change what you are, and find the harmony which the commandments can bring between you and God. They offer harmony to you as nothing else does. What you lack internally, can be filled as you feel your way back to God by keeping His commandments. They confer light and truth. Live the Gospel with the harmony and passion it was meant to evoke. Be as Christ was. His commandments will provide that for you, if you will permit them to do so.

---

[258]See Hugh B. Brown's talk *God is the Gardener* which is still available as an audio recording. The essential part of which can be found in *An Abundant Life: The Memoirs of Hugh B. Brown*, edited by Edwin B. Firmage, Salt Lake City: Signature Books, 1988 at pp. 49, 57.

Chapter Sixteen

FLEEING BABYLON

Two weeks after my remarriage, all of my children were returned to my custody. It was the greatest gift I could have hoped for. No matter the challenges, their return was a blessing.

A few years later, however, I could feel my oldest son slipping away from me. He and I had less and less in common as he went through the teenage years. Although I recalled my own teen years and knew what he was going through, I could not break through that teenage angst that was erecting a wall between us. I needed some common ground where we could meet and find a new relationship. At length I found the solution: I went to Clinton, Utah, and bought the new Softail® Harley from a fellow who had purchased it two weeks earlier. The demand for Harleys was so high at the time you had to wait nearly eighteen months to purchase one from the Utah dealers. So this was the way to get one in a hurry, provided you were willing to pay a premium.

Outfitted with saddle-bags and with a T-bag to handle our minimalist needs, my son and I traveled over the Western United States together. Our first trip to Sturgis, South Dakota for the Rally took us out through central Wyoming and the National Grasslands. The road was resurfaced with red aggregate, which made it look like a pink ribbon through the sage green grasslands. The sky overhead was the deep blue of early August. We passed through this scene with reverence for the majesty of the blend of vista, color, monotony and contrast. The prong-horned herds watched as the rumble of the Harley brought their gaze up briefly from the grass. It began to cloud over as we left a gas stop at Wright, Wyoming and headed toward Newcastle on the edge of the Black Hills.

We stopped in Newcastle to get a drink and eat an apple in the shade of a grocery store awning. Locals passed by us and no doubt thought us vagabond 'scooter-trash' as we very much looked the part. It's hard not to when you tour for days in the saddle of a motorcycle. That is part of its appeal: appearances begin to matter less.

As we entered the Black Hills, the clouds darkened. When we arrived near the top elevation it began to hail. We passed a group of bikers who had taken cover under an old barn awning. As we passed by I thought we could continue, but the hail began to hurt. Finally a hailstone hit my right hand with such force it felt like I'd been struck by a hammer. We made a u-turn and went back to join the crowd under the awning.

All the bikes were left out in the hail. Under the barn awning there was a packed group of bikers crowded under the shelter, waiting for the storm to pass. We joined them. Still others joined us. The hail intensified. The noise of the hail on the roof of the barn was a chorus of drumming like John Bonher, Ginger Baker and Keith Moon all in the throes of an unsynchronized solo competition with each other. It was a spectacular display of sight and sound with the lightning contributing to both.

While under the awning, the crowd began to pass among themselves a bottle of Jack Daniel's Whiskey. It went from person to person, as communal sharing and brotherhood would dictate. The bottle was passed to me, and I smiled as I passed it to my son who passed it to the next fellow. The guy next to me asked me why I hadn't taken a drink.

"I'm Mormon."

"Hey, man that's cool. I'd like me a dozen wives, too."

My son and I smiled.

While watching the storm pass in front of us, a large Miller Lite tractor-trailer came creeping through the storm on the road in front of our barn, then the trailer stopped in front of us, to our collective curious stares. The driver got out of his truck in the hail, went to the rear of his rig and retrieved two cases of beer. Amid the applause of the crowd under the awning, he came through the storm and gave the beer to the sheltered mass.

He shouted above the din of the hail-drum solo, "See you guys at the Rally!" And with continuing cheers he left through the storm back to his rig and went on his way. That no doubt produced a lasting brand loyalty from our compatriots. Gestures like that endure, even from a beer company.

As they were handed to us, my son and I helped pass around the beer. These people were part of a brother- and sisterhood, and among them we were their brothers, too. We were not the only teetotalers either, for some refused the beer not on moral grounds, but because they were conscious of bike safety and the risks of alcohol impairment. I wondered for a moment if it was morally superior to abstain for religious reasons or for safety reasons, but reached no conclusion.

The hail abated but the rain continued, and my son and I were the first to leave the shelter and our new friends. We'd never been to Sturgis and were anxious to make the final few miles' descent into the

Rally. As we left, we were wished the best by those who still wanted the light rain to stop before they would venture out. Or perhaps they were kept there by the remaining Miller Lite.

The road was covered by hail, but the little traffic which passed through had cut two tire paths through the accumulations, and I put the tires of the bike in a rut cut through the hail. We continued along in this manner until the accumulations ended and the full road was again available for us.

We descended from the canyon roads into the Rally as the rain ended and took our place among the over 250,000 people attending that year. It was odd, being in the majority for the first time. Motorcyclists are always the pitiful minority. Here, however, it was the "cagers" (i.e., people driving caged up in a car) who were in the minority. It felt much like a Latter-day Saint moving to Utah from the mission field in the East. Finally, here is where we predominate! Vindication! "We" can outvote "You" now! Biker heaven lives each August in the Black Hills of South Dakota.

After the rally we returned through Cody, Wyoming and through the Eastern Gate to Yellowstone Park. We passed along the Grand Tetons, Jackson Hole, Bear Lake, Idaho, through Logan, Utah and stopped at the Logan Temple. We still have the photos of us beside our Harley, the Logan Temple in the background. Then it was on to home, in Sandy, Utah.

It has been over a decade since that first trip to Sturgis. My son and I still talk about it.

He and I found common ground sharing the saddle of a Harley Davidson. The barriers of the teen years gave way to a friendship and commonality that has endured. He served a mission a few years later. During his mission he visited a Harley shop in New Hampshire and regaled them with tales of his trips to Sturgis. They had never been, and here was a Mormon missionary, with the nametag on and all, telling them of 'high and holy things' pertaining to their world. He was prepared to tell them of other things much higher and more holy as well.

Going to Zion requires us to flee from Babylon. These two stand as the polar opposites, the symbols of "the two ways." "Babylon" has become the symbol of the non-believing world in scripture. 1 Nephi 20: 20 warns us to: "Go ye forth of Babylon, flee ye from the Chaldeans, with a voice of singing declare ye, tell this, utter to the end of the earth; say ye: The Lord hath redeemed his servant Jacob." In this chapter we are going to look at how to flee. Christian and Jewish teachers have discussed this subject. But they contradict each other, and leave the subject in confusion. The confusion of theologians is cleared up through the Book of Mormon. From this we can see the necessity and profound relevance of the Book of Mormon for our day. We will look at the scholar's work to develop the Book of Mormon's greatest contribution to us. But we only do so for context and not for content.

Babylon's great influence begins at the time of Nebuchadnezzar. It conquered Jerusalem and took the Jews into captivity. So we need to return to that generation to know how Babylon remains among us still today. And we need to recognize Babylon today if we are to flee from her.

Daniel interprets King Nebuchadnezzar's dream in the second chapter of the Book of Daniel. The dream involved the great image of the being with a head of gold, arms of silver, and other metal body parts. Because of its importance we need to know how this vision applies to us now. It isn't just a dream filled with symbolism, but also a discussion of a latter-day obligation. We are the ones living in the time these things are unfolding. Prophecies do not 'just happen' without the efforts of people living as they are fulfilled. Therefore, we must follow the prophetic instruction given us. It is in the scriptures to help us realize our destiny. With that in mind, we turn to the prophetic dream.

The interpretation of the king's dream is given by Daniel to the king:

Thou art this head of gold. And after thee shall arise another kingdom inferior to thee, and another third kingdom of brass, which shall bear rule over all the earth. And the fourth kingdom shall be strong as iron: forasmuch as iron breaketh in pieces and subdueth all things: and as iron that breaketh all these, shall it break in pieces and bruise. And whereas thou sawest the feet and toes, part of potters' clay, and part of iron, the kingdom shall be divided; but there shall be in it of the strength of the iron, forasmuch as thou sawest the iron mixed with miry clay. And as the toes of the feet were part of iron, and part of clay, so the kingdom shall be partly strong, and partly broken. And whereas thou sawest iron mixed with miry clay, they shall mingle themselves with the seed of men: but they shall not cleave one to another, even as iron is not mixed with clay. And in the days of these kings shall the God of heaven set up a kingdom, which shall never be destroyed: and the kingdom shall not be left to other people, but it shall break in pieces and consume all these kingdoms, and it shall stand for ever. Forasmuch as thou sawest that the stone was cut out of the mountain without hands, and that it brake in pieces the iron, the brass, the clay, the silver, and the gold; the great God hath made known to the king what shall come to pass hereafter: and the dream is certain, and the interpretation thereof sure. (Dan., 2: 38-45.)

Volumes have been written about this by Jewish, Christian and Latter-day Saint commentators. Latter-day Saints have relied upon the prophecy as a proof text for the authenticity of the latter day restoration. But the implications of the vision also have relevance to the Second Comforter, so need to be addressed here.

Typical of Latter-day Saint treatment of this passage is this one written by Sidney B. Sperry: "We say that the kingdom never to be destroyed is the Church of Jesus Christ of Latter-day Saints, which was restored in the 'latter days' ([Dan.] 2:28) and is never to be taken from the people to whom it came, or left to another people. It shall, in God's hands, break in pieces and consume all other kingdoms, and stand forever. The stone that was 'cut out without hands,' which Nebuchadnezzar saw, is none other than the gospel of Jesus Christ restored under the leadership of the modern Prophet Joseph Smith. As the gospel spreads in the world under our missionary efforts, the remnants of worldly kingdoms will be swept away as chaff, and the 'stone' will fill the whole earth. (2:35, 45) That the stone is the gospel is made clear in a revelation given to Joseph Smith in October, 1831: 'The keys of the kingdom of God are committed unto man on the earth, and from thence shall the gospel roll forth unto the ends of the earth, as the stone which is cut out of the mountain without hands shall roll forth, until it has filled the whole earth.' (D. & C. 65:2)" (Sperry, Sidney B. *The Voice of Israel's Prophets.* Salt Lake City: Deseret Book Company, 1952, p. 247-248.) So the Church claims to be that promised latter-day stone. Latter-day revelation confirms this about the restored Gospel.[259] This claim is part of the justification for a restoration, and part of our claim to prophetic and Biblical promise of the Latter-day Church. But it means something more to us, too. It means something about receiving the Second Comforter.

We need to look at this vision for how it connects to the Second Comforter, for we must flee from Babylon if we hope to receive the Lord.

Interestingly, the vision makes the destruction of the "head of gold," or Babylon, a latter-day event. How can Babylon, which fell nearly two-and-a-half millennia ago still be "ground to dust" by this latter-day work? Similarly, the Medes, Persians, Greeks and Romans[260]

---

[259]See, e.g., the dedicatory prayer for the Kirtland Temple which also contains reference to this: D&C 109:72: "Remember all thy church, O Lord, with all their families, and all their immediate connections, with all their sick and afflicted ones, with all the poor and meek of the earth; that the kingdom, which thou hast set up without hands, may become a great mountain and fill the whole earth."

[260]For purposes of this work it is not important to debate the exact identities of the various contributions to the great image. Using these identifiers for the image's silver, bronze and iron is not intended to be any

have all passed into history long ago; yet according to the vision, they are to be ground to dust by this latter-day restoration, and it will occur in our day. How is this to work? What is it about Babylon that is still with us and needs now be ground to dust by the latter-day restoration of the Gospel?

Western Civilization has been influenced from top to bottom by the Bible. The history of the Bible is the foundational history of Western man. It is the origin of Judaeo-Christian traditions.

Briefly, during the Historic Christian movement, Catholicism claimed exclusive right to mediate between God and man by virtue of the contents of scripture for nearly 1500 years.[261] For generations the scriptures were claimed to be sacred, holy things to be used exclusively by the Roman Catholic clergy and not for private reading or interpretation. One of Martin Luther's great contributions was to translate the Bible from the antiquated language of Rome into the everyday language of the German people. What followed thereafter was translation and publication of the Bible into other common tongues, along with a Protestant reformation and splintering of Roman hegemony. Tyndale and then the King James' translators put the Biblical teachings into English, with the wisdom and literature which would forever alter the English-speaking world's thinking and language development as well. This epic story should be kept in mind. The Bible influenced Western Civilization and possession of it entitled the Roman Church to dominate political and economic life for over a millennium. When the Bible became the property of the common man, it influenced church movements and political developments, which directly influenced the thinking leading to evolving patterns in Europe, North and South America, Australia and indirectly in the rest of the world.

The Biblical content was based upon the history of the people who originally wrote it. Its contents were also impacted by the Babylonian

resolution of that debate, but only to conveniently refer to possible meanings.

[261]Although the division between the Orthodox Christian movement occurred at about 1,000 a.d., this fine a distinction is not really needed here.

captivity. Babylon engulfed the Jews for nearly three-quarters of a century. During that time Jewish custom, thought and records were altered. This was, unfortunately, so pervasive that the Biblical record itself did not escape Babylonian influence. The full extent of this influence is being studied by scholars who advance more alarming discoveries about this period each year. We do not need to develop this subject here, beyond mentioning its existence. But the Babylonian conquest of the Jews remains even today an influence which has infiltrated the Bible itself.

Those who copied scripture, and who preserved it after it left the prophets' hands, influenced its content much more than theologians have been willing to admit. Increasingly however, scholars are coming to the conclusion Babylon changed the Biblical trajectory, and introduced both changes to religious practices and to earlier records. What followed the Babylonian captivity was forever affected by the persistent lingering influence of Babylon.

It was not just the record after Babylon which was affected, however. Even the portions written before 600 BC had to be preserved by the post-Babylonian copyists and curators. Babylon influenced them, and they influenced the text.

Furthermore, throughout the post-Babylonian Israelite history, the writers and thinkers were unable to escape exposure to Babylonian culture, and it affected their thinking. All that was written after Babylon was influenced by their exile there. Even those few prophets who spoke after Babylon used that era in metaphor and parable to teach and warn. Babylon and the experiences there, including the changes to thought, have been inculcated into the scriptures at the "DNA level" and it cannot be removed at this point.[262] The Bible therefore must be studied

---

[262]Joseph's *New Translation of the Bible* is not an attempt to fully remedy that. It was more of an inspired commentary than a wholesale repair of it. Bruce R. McConkie commented: "No one has ever improved upon the King James Version of the Bible except the Prophet Joseph Smith as he was moved upon by the spirit of prophecy and revelation. As you know, 'We believe the Bible to be the word of God as far as it is translated correctly' (eighth article

with care to distinguish between its divergent influences. We make only brief mention of this here. Latter-day Saint commentators have dealt with this subject, and we are not going to repeat what can be found elsewhere.[263] We only note the Babylonian "head of gold" is with us

---

of faith); and as you also know, many 'plain and precious things,' and 'many covenants of the Lord,' were taken from this sacred record when it passed through the hands of that great church which is not the Lord's church (1 Ne. 13:26-29). As you also know, Joseph Smith restored many of these 'plain and precious things' in his New Translation, which is commonly called among us the Joseph Smith Translation. This version, as now published, accurately records the inspired corrections of the Prophet and can be used by us with great profit. It is in fact one of the great evidences of the divine mission of the greatest of our prophets." (McConkie, Bruce R. *Sermons and Writings of Bruce R. McConkie*. Salt Lake City: Bookcraft, 1989. p.267.)

[263]See, e.g., Hugh Nibley, *Approaching Zion*, p.152: "Nothing was more offensive in the teachings of Joseph Smith than the ideas of revelation and restoration. The Protestant doctrine was sola scriptura; the Catholic claim was that the only sources of revelation were (1) scripture and (2) tradition. But in our own generation both revelation and restoration have ceased to be naughty words; and Catholics and Protestants are exploiting them in a way that makes us forget how recently and how vigorously they were condemned as a peculiarly wild aberration in Joseph Smith." (Nibley, Hugh. *Approaching Zion.* Salt Lake City: Deseret Book Company, 1989.) Also, Stephen E. Robinson, *Are Mormons Christians?*, p.88: "The Latter-day Saints accept unequivocally all the biblical teachings on the nature of God, but they reject the extrabiblical elaborations of the councils and creeds. A doctrinal exclusion applied to the Latter-day Saints for rejecting the Nicene doctrine of the Trinity is invalid because that doctrine was not taught in the Bible or in the early Christian church. It is not found in the teachings of the Apostolic Fathers or those of the Greek Apologists. Even today Eastern and Western orthodoxies still disagree strongly over both the precise nature of God and the exact wordings of the major creed of Christianity (the filioque dispute). If in order to be a true Christian one must conceive of the Christian God in precisely the terms of Nicene orthodoxy, then all Christians who lived before the fifth century, and all those on at least one side of the filioque dispute since the eighth century, must be excluded as Christians as well as the Latter-day Saints. Moreover, it is contradictory for Protestants to insist on the doctrine of *sola scriptura*-that the Bible alone is sufficient for salvation-in one context, and then to turn around and add nonscriptural requirements for salvation, like acceptance of councils and creeds, in other contexts." (Robinson, Stephen E. *Are Mormons*

still, and to flee from it we need first to realize it remains an influence today. Without that recognition we cannot hope to "grind it to dust."

This is not all, however, as Daniel's vision warns us. The Post-Babylonian great world powers of the Medes and Persians, Greeks and Romans all brought their influences and thoughts to the people of the Bible and to the people of the world. Language, art, mathematics, science and culture itself all have their foundations in these prior ancient civilizations. We build over their ruins and accept their ways. The horse path of the Medes becomes the worn and widened road of the Greeks, and the cobblestone pathways of Rome, and our own paved highways today. We do what they did, and go where they went. Not just in our foot-traffic, but in our legislatures, art, and even in our minds..

Though these civilizations have long since passed from the world's center stage, while they occupied it they left an influence which persists today. From commerce to language, thought to dress, all these world-dominating cultures hold a continuing influence among the people of Western Civilization. Western Civilization in turn dominates the world.[264] Therefore, although these prior cultures may have ceased as

Christians. Bridgend: Seren Books, 1998.) And Joseph Fielding McConkie, *Here We Stand*, p.27-28: "Two primary concerns are raised by the doctrine of sola scriptura. First, the moment Luther claimed that the authority of the Bible superseded that of the tradition of the Church, he invited criticism because the selection of books that constitute the Bible were determined by nothing other than tradition! No revelation identifies them or even directs that they be gathered together. The church was the father of the Bible, not the child. That is to say, if there had been no church with its traditions, there would have been no Bible as Martin Luther knew it. The question then challenging Luther was how he could accept one line of tradition as inspired while rejecting the other. Second, the doctrine of *sola scriptura* makes Bible worshipers of its adherents. The Catholics claim an infallible pope; the Protestants counter with the claim to an infallible book. For them the scriptures, not God, are the Supreme Judge of all things." (McConkie, Joseph Fielding. *Here We Stand*. Salt Lake City: Deseret Book Company, 1995.)

[264]Though this is a sweeping comment, it is nonetheless warranted. "Mc-Culture" is a rallying cry against Western Civilization in general and Americanism in particular throughout the Islamic World and into China and

active world governmental powers, they remain alive and influential in mankind's thoughts and culture. They affect every aspect of our modern-day lives.

Daniel's interpretation of the king's dream promises in our day we will break free from these influences. Their accumulated influences are to be ground to dust and blown away by the wind. Some of us take pride in the Western traditions we have built upon. To some extent these traditions are very good. But they mix such error and arrogance, superstition and foolishness into our minds that loyalty to them can keep us from an appointment we need to keep. We need to follow a new pathway. The tried and familiar highway, with the cobblestones from the ancients still a foundation below our own pavement, must be abandoned. We need to follow a newly restored path. This is our future, and if we fail to embrace it we will retain these Babylonian influences. Since it is promised, and since it is to occur now, in our day, how is this to occur? How is Babylon's influence to be ground to dust among us? After all, we do not have a unique culture, freed from these influences. The collection of sometimes amusing essays by Hugh Nibley in *Approaching Zion*[265] demonstrates Babylon's continuing influence among the Saints. We have no economic life as Latter-day Saints apart from the larger world economy. The United Order and other restored but unpracticed laws which might have brought us rapidly away from "Babylon" are not being practiced. Yet here we are, living when the

---

India. Every corner of the world is influenced by Western Civilization. By saying this however, it should not be viewed as necessarily good or a permanent thing. Daniel's vision clearly foresees the end of this influence, as it is displaced by a "stone, cut out of the mountain without hands." The end of all nations, including the United States of America, is specifically foretold in D&C 87: 6, where the latter-day judgments of God are predicted to last "until the consumption decreed hath made **a full end of all nations**." (Emphasis added.)

[265]Nibley, Hugh. *Approaching Zion*. Salt Lake City: Deseret Book Company, 1989.

Babylonian influences are to pass away from among us, and then away from the earth itself.

Latter-day Saints are not alone in trying to locate Babylonian influences on the Bible and Israelite history. Non-LDS scholar Margaret Barker has made an extraordinary effort to reconstruct the First Temple theology of Israel. She relies upon a formidable and praiseworthy scholarly effort to accomplish this.[266] Other scholars have acknowledged these influences on Judaism which occurred as a result of the Babylonian exile, including the post-exile Deuteronomists.[267] It is clear that during the captivity in Babylon the trauma to Jewish faith was significant and resulted in significant changes to Judaism and Jewish thought as a result. Things were lost, things were added and things were kept but changed or viewed in a much different light. A recent LDS-published volume attempts to reconstruct the world of Lehi's Jerusalem using the scholar's tools.[268]

There is a form of Biblical analysis called "Higher Criticism" which seeks to find a way to unravel the Bible into earlier threads. Higher Criticism attempts to identify the varying influences and figure out the various schools of thought which contributed the varying views contained in our surviving scriptures. That whole line of academic

---

[266]See her works: Barker, Margaret. *The Great High Priest, The Temple Roots of Christian Liturgy.* New York: T&T Clark Ltd, 2003; Barker, Margaret. *The Great Angel: A Study of Israel's Second God.* Louisville: Westminser/John Knox Press, 1992; Barker, Margaret. *The Older Testament: The Survival of Themes from the Ancient Royal Cult in Sectarian Judaism and Early Christianity.* London: SPK, 1987.

[267]See, e.g., Doorly, William J. *Obsession with Justice: The Story of the Deuteronomists.* Mahwah: Paulist, 1994; and Friedman, Richard Elliott. *Who Wrote the Bible?* New York, Summit Books, 1987.

[268]*Glimpses of Lehi's Jerusalem.* Edited by John W. Welch. Provo: FARMS, 2004. Interestingly, Margaret Barker is a contributor to this volume. That work does not attempt to reconstruct the setting from the Book of Mormon, but instead attempts to understand the setting using the scholar's tools to recreate a background for the readers, who then are left to use the background to aid them in reading the Book of Mormon.

inquiry is interesting, but we only need to make passing mention. There are entire careers devoted to trying to figure out what preceded and contributed to what we know as "the Bible." This great search involving intense scholarly work has a simple solution provided to us through the restoration. We already have in our hands an accurate pre-exilic picture of Judaism. It was one of the very first things which God provided to us in this dispensation. It came to us even before the Church was restored.

Lehi's departure from Jerusalem at 600 BC was not happenstance. Its timing was precisely calibrated to result in a record which preserved an accurate picture of pre-exile Judaism. Lehi's family left approximately four years before Jerusalem's fall to Babylon. They took with them records and a tradition of faith which they then continued to preserve in a new land. That record and practice of faith were not influenced by the subsequent Babylonian captivity of the Jews. From the time of their departure, through the end of the Nephite record, the Book of Mormon was unaffected by Babylonian culture, thought, customs or language.

If you seek a clearer picture of pre-exile Judaism, the record of Lehi and his descendants is the best source for reconstructing what comprised that ancient faith and its practices.

Since the promise to Daniel was "the dream is certain, and the interpretation thereof sure," then we should expect there will be means provided through the restoration for us to reacquire a view of God which is purged from the influences of Babylon, the Medes and Persians, Greeks, Romans and modern corruptions as well. The Book of Mormon is the only pre-exilic document in existence today, that was transmitted by a prophet to a prophet, to publication and then to us. All other records have passed through hands (and minds) influenced to one degree or another by the Babylonians, Medes and Persians, Romans, and modern corruptions.

If you, therefore, want to read a record that will remove these influences, you must read the Book of Mormon. If you want your faith untainted by these past civilizations, you must go to the Book of Mormon to find it.

The Book of Mormon presents a very different picture of the ancient world from the one we find urged by the scholars. Christology or teachings about Christ in the Book of Mormon seem much more prominent than what they assure us should be expected. It is that feature which provoked early waves of criticism[269] of the Book of Mormon, and still forms the basis for many critics' greatest skepticism. But these critics rely upon the Babylonian, Greek, Roman, etc. influences contained in the Bible. They are trying to see backward through time, using a lens distorted by these prior cultures. Instead, they should be looking at the Book of Mormon as the clearest and most accurate lens from which to reconstruct antiquity.

Mormon abridged the work centuries after Christ's visit to the Americas, and some apologists argue he could easily have breathed greater Christology into the text as a result of his more perfect hindsight. However, the Book of Mormon will not permit that as a reason for this Christological material because Mormon had nothing to do with the contents of the Book from 1 Nephi through Omni, the first 143 pages. Those were taken from an unabridged set of plates prepared by Nephi, and appended without abridgement by Mormon. Nephi lived and wrote from about 620 BC through 544 BC. Therefore, his writings could not have been affected by a post-resurrection revision of the record. He wrote nearly six centuries before Christ. Mormon made no abridgment to Nephi's plates.

In these beginning books written by Nephi, the Christology is as prominent as in the later materials abridged by the post-Christian era Mormon. So it is not possible to dismiss the Christology as a later historical accretion by those who rewrote the history in light of later knowledge. Rather, the Book of Mormon insists you must accept this

---

[269]*Millennial Harbinger*, 7 February 1831, *Delusion,* by Alexander Campbell. Alexander Campbell wrote *Delusions* in the *Millennial Harbinger*, 7 February 1831, at p. 85-95, protesting there was too much of Christ in this pre-Christian book.

pre-exile view of Christ's prominence in Judaism rooted in 600 BC beginnings.[270] If you accept the Book of Mormon, you do violence to its claims of miraculous origins by dismissing these Christological features as something not a part of the authentic pre-exile Jewish faith.[271]

Critics ask why would something so startling be omitted from the record we have had handed down to us in the Bible from the same period? One reason is the loss of the Temple at Jerusalem was traumatic to Judaism in a way we now hardly appreciate. The expected deliverance of the "chosen people" by God was not forthcoming. The history of deliverance from Egypt, which gave Israel its bedrock identity, had been reversed in the conquest by Babylon. They were back where they were before: subjugated by a larger world power dependent upon the permission of their rulers even to practice their faith. Whatever historic vindication they had believed they had from God's prior deliverance from Egypt was now in tatters as this new historic development seemed to show God's abandonment of them as "chosen."

When Israel fell without a deliverer, Israel's Messianic expectations were dashed. Little wonder why the faith should suffer from trauma and be rethought in this setting. Little wonder, too, only a remnant should

---

[270]The only other way to excuse it is to attribute to Joseph Smith the insertion of a Christological world view through the translation process. However, the current state of that issue seems most strongly to demonstrate that Joseph didn't actually "translate" the work as we understand translation, but instead read it through miraculous means while the actual word by word content came through "the power of God." This interesting discussion is also outside the boundaries of this work.

[271]Scholars may, if given enough time to accomplish it, be able to construct a rationalization to support that notion. But a fair reading of the text imposes the view that this Christology is a part of the original faith transmitted by Lehi and his children, who hail from this 600 BC setting. Everything about the setting is otherwise authentic in a 600 BC setting from the unexpected name of "Ishmael" (c.f. 2 Kings 25: 25) for a faithful Jewish resident of Jerusalem to the desert Bedouin life of Lehi's family. This, too, is beyond the scope of this work but has been dealt with by numerous authors, including most recently, *Glimpses of Lehi's Jerusalem*, op. cit.

choose to return and the larger body of Jews would settle in Babylon, to mix bloodlines into the Arab world and spread the covenant with Abraham, Isaac and Jacob into the seed of Ishmael and Esau.[272] Little wonder the scriptural basis for expecting a Messiah should be reworked, since history had shown such deliverance had not happened.

When the post-Babylonian reworking was underway and the writers were trying to understand what went wrong, the issue of the Messianic "failure" would certainly require attention. One of the Deuteronomist's demonstrated efforts was the elimination of the "Second God" from Israel's records. Margaret Barker has ably demonstrated this in *The Great Angel: A Study of Israel's Second God*, (Louisville: Westminser/John Knox Press, 1992) and *The Great High Priest, The Temple Roots of Christian Liturgy*, (New York: T&T Clark Ltd, 2003), among other places. It is one of the great changes to Biblical texts, and was primarily through deletions, not additions, to the record.

Subsequent Greek philosophy about the definition of perfection and the one indivisible nature of God also affected Judaism and the Bible. These influences changed the beliefs of the Jews and the way the scriptures were transmitted by them.

Christ's ministry and work would launch yet another incentive for both the "Christian" and "Jewish" world to work on distinguishing the two faiths from each other. These efforts resulted in changes to scripture which the Higher Critics still are laboring to sort out.

However interesting a detour into these things may be, it is not our focus to sort all this out. Our focus is simply to demonstrate, by reference, the enormous and prophetic value of the Book of Mormon in restoring a way to get us beyond the influences of the "head of gold" (and the other body parts/cultural influences) of the great image. I do not believe this latter-day work of grinding the prior cultures' influences

---

[272]It is one of history's ironies that the modern Muslim populations of Iraq and Iran have within them the descendants of this larger body of Jewish exiles. They are heirs of the promises and will, in due time, receive their own restoration to the fold of covenant Israel, although that notion offends them greatly today.

to dust is the work of the scholars. The Lord does not need the "arm of flesh" to accomplish His designs. He means to put a fullness of salvation into the hands of the commonest of the Saints. Therefore, the answer to these inquiries must lie with the work He has commonly provided to us all and be within the power of the "least of the Saints."

The Book of Mormon's ability to do that is why Joseph Smith commented as follows: "I spent the day in the council with the Twelve Apostles at the house of President Young, conversing with them upon a variety of subjects. ... I told the brethren that the Book of Mormon was the most correct of any book on earth, and the keystone of our religion, and a man would get nearer to God by abiding by its precepts than by any other book." (*DHC* 4: 461.) It is that statement which relates to this issue. The truth of that statement has hardly been appreciated.

The Book of Mormon puts you into a world view purified from Babylonian influences because it begins pre-exile. The ensuing history develops among a people who have no direct or indirect contact with the subsequent governments and cultures of the "silver" or "bronze" or "iron" or "clay and iron" of the vision. From the record we have in the Book of Mormon you can more readily flee Babylon than through any other means or tool. And it is commonly available to any Latter-day Saint. It is written in plain, even simple language. Any Latter-day Saint child can read and understand the text. It is such an effective tool at undoing these past cultures' influences, it can literally "grind to dust" any one of them if you study it.

It is for this reason the Book of Mormon is the most correct book. It is for this reason you can get nearer to God through its pages than by any other source. Since we are attempting to get nearer to God in this work, and seek the companionship of the Second Comforter, it is from the Book of Mormon most of the scriptures used in this work are taken. The most underused tool in our possession is the Book of Mormon. We need to rediscover it. Or more correctly, we need to finally discover what it offers to us.

When condemning the Saints for their failings, the Lord picked out the neglect of the Book of Mormon as His indictment of the Saints: "And they shall remain under this condemnation until they repent and remember the new covenant, even the Book of Mormon and the former commandments which I have given them, not only to say, but to do according to that which I have written—" (D&C 84: 57.) We are now attempting to reconstruct what is required to "not only say, but do," in order to repent and remember the new covenant offered to us.

If you are going to flee from Babylon and its influences, you need to study the Book of Mormon. If you have any interest in reading the words of eternal life, they are to be found in their purest form in the Book of Mormon. Not only Joseph Smith, but President Ezra Taft Benson testifies: "It is that most correct book which, if men will abide by its precepts, will get them closer to God than any other book. It is the Book of Mormon." (Benson, Ezra Taft. *A Witness and a Warning: A Modern-Day Prophet Testifies of the Book of Mormon.* Salt Lake City: Deseret Book Company, 1988, p. 36.)

He said elsewhere, "These two great works of scripture then, become a major tool in the Lord's hand for preserving His people in the latter days. The Book of Mormon, written under the hand of inspiration for our day, preserved through the centuries to come forth in our time, translated by the gift and power of God, is the keystone of our religion. It is the keystone of our doctrine. It is the keystone of our testimony. It is a keystone in the witness of Jesus Christ. It is a keystone in helping us avoid the deceptions of the evil one in these latter days. Satan rages in the hearts of men and has power over all of his dominions. (See D&C 1:35.) But the Book of Mormon has greater power — power to reveal false doctrine, power to help us overcome temptations, power to help us get closer to God than any other book." (*Id.*, p. 27.)

So as we look to leave behind the world's accumulations of errors, we look to the Book of Mormon. We have hardly begun that process, though the book has been available for 175 years. Most commentaries are superficial or apologetic. The apologists endlessly attempt to show it to be an authentic ancient work by scholarly proofs. But if you already accept it as an authentic text, these works do little more than equip you for an argument. That doesn't convert nor edify.[273]

The real work is to uncover its content and then practice its faith. The greatest part of that work remains undone. Study it and perhaps you will contribute to that largely still undone work. More importantly, through it you prepare to receive Christ's greatest promised blessings. It contains, unlike any other volume of scripture, a fullness of the Gospel of Jesus Christ. Within its pages are the doctrines Joseph Smith would later teach. Every fundamental doctrine, from pre-existence to the Temple rites, has its foundations in the Book of Mormon. Someone, perhaps you, will eventually write a commentary which adequately begins to explore the Book of Mormon's deep spiritual and doctrinal content. In the meantime, if you want to flee Babylon, you should use the Book of Mormon to help you to get away.

---

[273] 3 Ne 11:29: "For verily, verily I say unto you, he that hath the spirit of contention is not of me, but is of the devil, who is the father of contention, and he stirreth up the hearts of men to contend with anger, one with another."

Chapter Seventeen

NECESSARY OPPOSITION

By the late 1990's, my reading and study had produced the question, yet again: Is this whole restored religion true? Well, hadn't I decided that years ago? What cause was there to be rethinking it now? Arguments were made by both sides, and I'd gotten well past them, hadn't I?

Fellow lawyer and my former fellow law student Paul Toscano had been excommunicated. He had been a tower of faith during law school, even working to convert a member of the law school faculty. Now he was no longer even a Latter-day Saint and was being vocal about his criticisms of the Church. This was troubling for many reasons, including the debt of gratitude I owed to him for his faithfulness and testimony during law school. Paul's very public personal crisis brought introspection of my own.

I had received answers to prayer, been visited by angels and witnessed miracles. I had been given the proofs promised by scripture. I knew my faith was directly connected to the powers of heaven, I had that personal witness. So, why should I doubt or question because of any author or critic? If Joseph was right and doubt and faith cannot co-exist in the mind at the same time, then I needed to choose faith and refuse doubt. That choice had to be made even if friends or admired others failed in their faith. The Gospel's truthfulness is independent of whether we believe it or not. And it is independent of other people's faith or skepticism. Paul's latest book, The Sanctity of Dissent, *was a combative, frontal attack on Elder Packer. Whatever goodness and grace Paul had shown me through his gracious and insightful comments in the past, it seemed to me this book was now trying to take away. In my opinion it attacked Church leaders, Church policy, and Church doctrine.*

I'd always read widely, including books from our critics. The work of critics, using strident, combative, and arrogant attacks was not what was needed, I thought. Reading these arguments made me feel a personal sense of loss for the authors. However the critics had gotten there, it was not where I wanted to go.

Yet there remained a gnawing feeling there had to be something more to the Gospel of Christ, but the route there did not lie in criticism or attacking the Church or its leaders. The scriptures spoke of greater things than I had received. Enough had already been given to me to hold out the possibility of all the rest. So what did I lack that would bring the rest? What remained undone? That was the real question. Not a question of belief or unbelief, for that had been long settled. The real question was why my own progress was on a persistent plateau?

There was certainly more to the Gospel, for I could read that in the scriptures. The defect in progress had to be internal. There was something lacking in me. That same feeling was probably why some former Saints lost their faith as they searched to find more. They made the mistake of looking past the mark.

Looking for deeper meaning does not get satisfied through criticism of the Lord's servants. That seems an easy outlet because men are always going to be flawed. What of that? Do we reject Peter or the New Testament Church because of Peter's failings? He denied Christ three times the night of Christ's trial. What of it? He fought with Paul over the Gentile question and was probably an excessive Judaizer, trying to make Gentile converts practice the Mosaic Law as Christians. This too after the vision of the blanket and unclean animals, which should have made him think better of the matter. What of that? If both strength and weakness coincided in Peter, are not the Lord's current leaders entitled to at least as much patience and tolerance for their strengths and weaknesses?

If doubt and faith cannot co-exist, then I must choose faith. Whenever an issue arose, I would choose to rely upon past proofs as the basis to trust that these new issues will be similarly resolved in the Lord's own time. They always had been, so why expect that to change. Actually, by having new questions arise, it is an opportunity for faith to grow and the only way in which it can. Until the answer is known, only trust and faith leads you along. But it is trust and faith based upon decades of prior experience. It is an informed and proven trust between the Lord and myself. Something like that deserves to be respected. It does not require much faith, given the past experiences.

I resolved to accept the Lord's programs, and to trust in Him. By providing to me in the past all the promised proofs, He has met His burden, and all doubts should be resolved in favor of faith in Him. It is the opposition who bears a heavy burden of proof, because they have been proven wrong so often before. I will drop that weight I have been carrying and will elect to trust and believe first, and require strict and demonstrable proof from the opposition -- proof from them that is equal to or greater than the decades of experience and light which the Lord has provided. I will doubt doubt itself.

It became apparent, however, that learning alone is not enough. The process of learning is linked to action, and action leads to stretching and discomfort. Light and knowledge are not gained in abstract reflection, but gained in battle in the trenches. Much of that battle for me is with my own internal failings and deficiencies.

You cannot simply learn. If mysteries are given to you, you are going to have to fight in the war.

Lehi taught his children that opposition is necessary in all things. Nephi records that Lehi instructed them (and us):

> For it must needs be, that there is an opposition in all things. If not so, my first-born in the wilderness, righteousness could not be brought to pass, neither wickedness, neither holiness nor misery, neither good nor bad. Wherefore, all things must needs be a compound in one; wherefore, if it should be one body it must needs remain as dead, having no life neither death, nor corruption nor incorruption, happiness nor misery, neither sense nor insensibility. (2 Ne. 2: 11.)

While opposition takes many forms, the primary opposition to receiving the Second Comforter lies in our faithlessness. It is this form of opposition we address here.

This "essential opposition" is not just a philosophical statement. It is a principle of what is encountered by all of us in this estate. There will always be opposition to the truth. No truth goes unchallenged. No event will be testified to without an alternative explanation of the event offered in opposition. Christ's status as Son of God will be opposed by those who challenge His witnesses, or the authenticity of the records relied upon as accounts of His life, or the practical acceptability of a man of miracles. Similarly, alternative explanations of Joseph Smith's ministry flood in upon the Saints in eager opposition to each other. These alternative explanations never agree among themselves why Joseph was not a true prophet. Rather, they offer a smorgasbord of choices, all of which agree on nothing except that Joseph was *not* a prophet. How they get there is of no real concern to their proponents. This opposition tries to catch you with one argument, and if it is unconvincing, they will offer you another, and yet another, until at last you will accept one. When you are ready to buy, they are ready to sell in whatever color, flavor, size or fabric, because they don't mind special orders. They only care that you be willing to buy.

This opposition is there to make you choose between faith and skepticism. To choose between accepting the truth or rejecting it. Without the opposition, there would be nothing worthy about belief. Acceptance of truth when it is unopposed is meaningless. But accepting it against opposition and in the face of controversy refines the character and develops the soul.

Because of these things the path to heaven runs through hell. You don't get the epiphany without confronting Satan. There is always a balance, because agency and the right (or obligation) to choose is part of God's plan.

How we exercise our right (or obligation) to choose defines who or what we are. If we choose goodness, and faith, and mercy for ourselves, we merit goodness, the gift of faith, and great mercy from God in return.

As you choose faith, you draw nearer to God and are entitled to greater grace as a result. Faith grows, or it shrinks. It is never static. Here in mortality, the one great constant is change. The Greek's noticed this long ago and developed a school of thought about the notion that change involves corruption and is inherently bad.[274] Change, for good or bad, is a part of mortality. As a result, you are changing and growing

---

[274]It was this notion which underlies the philosophical conclusion that since matter changes and is subject to decay and corruption, God could not be composed of matter because He is incorruptible, unchangeable and constant. Therefore, they reasoned, God must be immaterial. This notion affected the thinking of Augustine and Historic Christian thought, resulting in God's loss of body, parts and passions. In spite of Christ's injunction to the Apostles to "Behold my hands and my feet, that it is I myself: handle me, and see; for a spirit hath not flesh and bones, as ye see me have." (Luke 24: 39.)

toward God, or drawing away from Him. It is up to the individual to make the choices which move toward one way or the other.

Christ used the Holy Ghost to lead Him into all truth. As is explained in John 3: 34: "For he whom God hath sent speaketh the words of God: for God giveth not the Spirit by measure unto him." This is how Christ was able to live His life going from grace to grace till He received a fullness of light and truth. Through the Holy Ghost He was able to know all things.

This same instrument is also available to you. As is explained in Moroni 10: 4-5: "I would exhort you that ye would ask God, the Eternal Father, in the name of Christ, if these things are not true; and if ye shall ask with a sincere heart, with real intent, having faith in Christ, he will manifest the truth of it unto you, by the power of the Holy Ghost. And **by the power of the Holy Ghost ye may know the truth of all things.**" (Emphasis added.) This is no small promise. Contained in it is the possibility of knowing the truth of **all** things. Joseph Smith remarked: "I am learned, and know more than all the world put together. The Holy Ghost does, anyhow, and He is within me, and comprehends more than all the world; and I will associate myself with him." (*TPJS*, p. 350.)[275]

The acceptance of truth from this source is indispensable to acquiring the "feel" of being one with God. When you do it right, the Spirit is able to lead you to the truth of all things.

A recent Latter-day Saint writer has found this step to be beyond his reach. He insists upon rational and materialistic truths, and finds any

---

[275]The entire quote includes this explanation which expands and contradicts traditional Christian (and Jewish) doctrine: "Now, I ask all who hear me, why the learned men who are preaching salvation, say that God created the heavens and the earth out of nothing? The reason is, that they are unlearned in the things of God, and have not the gift of the Holy Ghost; they account it blasphemy in any one to contradict their idea. If you tell them that God made the world out of something, they will call you a fool. But I am learned, and know more than all the world put together. The Holy Ghost does, anyhow, and He is within me, and comprehends more than all the world; and I will associate myself with him."

spiritual witness to be unreliable.[276] Grant Palmer sets himself and his rational/faithless criteria as the proper measure of determining truth. He rejects the concept of the Holy Ghost as a guide to all truth, and instead proposes this kind of belief must be rejected in favor of what he regards as a "more objective, less unreliable" standard. His book illustrates well the teaching of Alma that mysteries are given to some, and withheld from others, based upon their willingness to accept the Lord's criteria for learning. "[H]e that will harden his heart, the same receiveth the lesser portion of the word; ... until they know nothing concerning his mysteries." (Alma 12: 10-11.) Mr. Palmer claims not to know of God's mysteries, and also claims to debunk them and substitute for them a more rational way of thinking about the

---

[276]Grant Palmer writes in *An Insider's View of Mormon Origins*, pages 130-131; 133: "When faced with this evidence, our first impulse is often to resort to personal inspiration as our defense of the Book of Mormon. This is a higher means of substantiating the book's antiquity, we assume. ... Most of us have felt this spiritual feeling when reading the Book of Mormon or hearing about Joseph Smith's epiphanies. What we interpret this to mean is that we have therefore encountered the truth, and we then base subsequent religious commitments on these feelings. The question I will pose is whether this is an unfailing guide to truth? ... The evangelical position of identifying and verifying truth by emotional feelings, which the Book of Mormon advocates, **is therefore not always dependable.** ... abundant evidence also demonstrates that **it is an unreliable means of proving truth.** Those who advocate the witness of the Holy Spirit as the foundation for determining the truthfulness of a given religious text need to honestly deal with these epistemological contradictions. ... When a person experiences the Spirit at a Protestant revival meeting or when reading the Book of Mormon, **it is not my belief that this feeling proves the truthfulness** of the doctrines taught, or read." (Emphasis added. Palmer, Grant H. *An Insider's View of Mormon Origins*. Salt Lake City: Signature Books, 2002.) Here Grant Palmer is advancing an argument which is diametrically opposed to the scriptures' teaching that the Holy Ghost is the way to learn truth. If you join in Palmer's approach, it will cost you the opportunity of learning greater truths which can be learned only through the Spirit. He has been unable to learn greater things through the Spirit precisely because of his lack of faith in the process itself. Those who join with him in this will, of course, receive similar results. In that respect the system is perfect, and lets each person choose what they are willing to receive.

Restoration.

For him, the "mysteries" become a part of an earlier frontier culture of folk-magic and imaginative "second sight." With that he dismisses the authenticity of God's hand in Joseph's work as Prophet. His book compiles and accepts uncritically, the widest range of alternative explanations for the Lord's Latter-day work, even when they are mutually exclusive and contradictory.[277] Such an approach has ill-served Palmer and similar skeptics. When it is faith that is necessary, the absence of faith will prevent progress in spiritual communications and experiences. Such people will always fall short of any hope of receiving the Second Comforter. They don't even believe such a thing is possible. So why would they expect to receive an audience with Him?

Palmer has been influenced in many of his views by D. Michael Quinn, whom he quotes often and cites for authority. Quinn's work, *Early Mormonism and the Magic World View*, is a study of the cultural setting in which Joseph Smith lived. While Quinn correctly identifies the setting and the features of the mind which developed within that setting, he misses the point. Quinn uses our standards to judge Joseph Smith's day and time, instead of reversing the comparison. We are not superior. Joseph is the one who had visions and witnessed angels. We

---

[277]When it serves his purposes, he quotes Emma Smith for the proposition that Joseph used the seer stone and his hat to accomplish the translation of the Book of Mormon. *(Id.,* p. 3.) But he rejects Emma's testimony that Joseph never used the Bible for translation because that would require almost miraculous abilities for Joseph, which no one ever assigned to him. *(Id.,* pp. 83-85.) (*Cf.* with Emma's testimony on this same issue as follows: "Question: Had he [Joseph] not a book or manuscript from which he read [when translating], or dictating to you? Answer: He had neither manuscript nor book to read from. Question: Could he not have had, and you not know of it? Answer: If he had had anything of the kind he could not have concealed it from me." (*Saints Herald* 26, no. 19 (1 October 1879) 289-290, Joseph Smith III, "Last Testimony of Sister Emma.")

Palmer's selective and inconsistent use of the sources he cites makes him a far less reliable source for determining the truth than the Holy Spirit which he denigrates for that purpose. He can't keep his use of authorities consistent as he bobs and weaves into unfair and inconsistent conclusions.

should be trying to recapture that kind of mind, not be condescending toward it as Quinn and Palmer are. Until we have similar visitations, visions, and experiences, we stand on lower ground. To use the lower ground to judge the higher is wrongheaded. We should be studying them and their time with a bit more humility, rather than just assuming we hold the best vantage point from which to judge all others. I do not quibble over Quinn's accounts of Joseph's time and setting. I reject, however, his conclusions. He allowed the material to take him to the wrong place, and he actively attempts to persuade others to go there with him.

In a study of myth, sexuality, history and meaning, William Irwin Thompson wrote these concluding remarks:

> Myth and religion, as the old ancestral heritage from the dark ages before the rise of the Technological Society, stand in the way, and so the social scientists have rewritten history to bring it under their control. The history of the soul is obliterated, the universe is shut out, and on the walls of Plato's cave the experts in the casting of shadows tell the story of *Man's* rise from ignorance to science through the power of technology. From the raising of children through the techniques of behavioral modification in the elementary schools to the philosophical indoctrination of students in graduate schools, a class of behavioral scientists has positioned itself at the strategic places of power in our secular society. As psychologists, they are our Thought Police; as professors, they are our Cultural Police; as consultants to government, they are the legislators who empower the Police. Small wonder that when these social scientists write history, they write only a history of economics and technology.
>
> The revisioning of history is, therefore, a revolutionary act. It challenges the legitimacy of a description of reality, and the class of scribes who write that description. If this sounds Marxist it is because I have kept the form of Marx's sociology of knowledge but turned the old man on his head, for in that position he can better converse with Hegel he himself turned upside down. In challenging the narrative of human origins

given to me by the socio-biologists, I am also challenging their narrative of the future of human civilization. At one edge of history or the other, I would prefer to show that the history of their construction is a Hollywood stage set; at either end of the street the ancient stars can be found marking the time the civilization has left before its two dimensional vanities collapse. (Thompson, William Irwin. *The Time Falling Bodies Take to Light: Mythology, Sexuality & The Origins of Culture.* New York: St. Martin's Griffin Edition, 1996, pp. 247-248.)

Good historians are usually candid about this. They know history is filled with philosophical indoctrination. Most historians write propaganda and not real history. But bad historians rarely will admit this to be the case. Who is objective and can escape their own biases, fears and limitations? When writers attempt to take an historic view of Joseph Smith, do they cast him in the light in which they think he belongs, or do they accept the light in which he casts himself? Who knows his setting better, they or he? He lived it, after all. Rex Bushman's contribution to the Library of Congress' Symposium on Joseph Smith discusses this. His paper is found in *The Worlds of Joseph Smith: A Bicentennial Conference at the Library of Congress*, BYU Press; Provo, 2006, at pp. 3-20, titled *Joseph Smith's Many Histories*.

From the time of Cain through Judas, if you were to ask the Biblical antagonists to tell the stories of the Bible you would have a far different record than we have now in scripture. Do you think Nephi would come across the same if you let Laman tell the account of First Nephi?

These thoughts of Thompson on myth and meaning capture the tension involved in any history. You should be careful about whom you trust to relate history to you. If you are going to err, you should elect to err on the side of accepting the words of prophets, rather than the adversaries and enemies of the prophets.

Continuing with Thompson's observations:

Technological Man has consciously excluded myth from his consciousness; this has brought him back under the sway of the collective unconscious. . .

In the classical era the person who saw history in the light of myth was the prophet, an Isaiah or Jeremiah; in the modern era the person who saw history in the light of myth was the artist, a Blake or a Yeats. But now in our postmodern era the artists have become a degenerate priesthood; they have become not spirits of liberation, but the interior decorators of Plato's cave. We cannot look to them for revolutionary deliverance. If history becomes the medium of our imprisonment, then history must become the medium of our liberation; (to rise, we must push against the ground to which we have fallen). For this radical task, the boundaries of both art and science must be redrawn. *Wissenschaft* must become *Wissenkunst*.

What I am talking about is the re-sacralization of culture and, in particular, the re-sacralization of scholarship. I am talking about a movement from ratio to Logos. Under the sway of ratio, a unit is uniform and capable of measurement and mass production; in the light of Logos, each being is unique and yet capable of universal expression. In *Wissenschaft* you train a neutral observer to read a meter with objectivity; all observers everywhere should see the same event and describe it in the same way. In *Wissenkunst* the historian, like the musical composer, creates a unique narrative of time and in this unique narrative the reader recognizes the universal truth of events. (*Id.*, p. 248-249.)

We will get a different story from the New York Times than we would get from Isaiah. We do not have prophets like Isaiah writing for popular news outlets. Therefore, if you are going to accept the modern, prevailing views as your guide in assessing things, you are not going to see them in the prophetic way. These views compete with and oppose each other. Whether you want to or not, you are forced to choose between these competing ways of thinking and of viewing events.

He continues:

To study myth one must go to a different kind of school
from our universities, but the ancient schools are long since
gone. Vibrating in another ether, the mystery schools are made
out of music, not matter. To go there to study myth, one has to
be drawn out of the body in sympathetic resonance with what
it is. If one has never floated out of the body in meditation or
sleep, then one should be disqualified from writing explanations
of Egyptian religion with its Khat, Ba, Ka, Sahu, and Khu. We
have built up a materialistic civilization that is concerned almost
exclusively with technology, power, and wealth, but the ancient
Egyptians built up an entire civilization concerned, almost
exclusively, with the psychic and the evolution of the human
body as a vehicle for Illumination... The states of
consciousness and the psychic experiences which are marginal
for us were central for them. What we repress or ignore as a
distraction from our proper attention on the physical, or as a
possible seductive diversion from our central task of the
conquest and domination of nature, or as a path to madness and
schizophrenia, was to the ancient Egyptians the *donnee* of the
human consciousness that had to be dealt with if humanity was
to understand its place in the cosmos. (Id., p. 249-250.)

We've mentioned Egypt before. Their society was based upon a
form which came down from the beginning of time. They lasted longer
than any other government in history. Israel and Israel's Redeemer had
connections with Egypt which ran deep. We are reminded of Egypt's
significance in the Book of Mormon (recorded in Reformed Egyptian)
and again in the Book of Abraham (with the facsimiles in Egyptian
hieroglyphs). Here it is suggested by Thompson our modern minds
would find their culture almost insane. Our "superior" culture is of
recent fabrication and is unstable, while their "inferior" culture lasted
over three millennia. We hardly have a chance of equaling them.

We breathe the smog of our times and culture. But what if, as
Thompson suggests, our cultural setting and time is not the best within
which to understand God? What if that smog has corrupted our minds
and cost us spiritual strength? Although we find such a possibility
troubling, we should be willing to consider it. If our era is marked by a

decline in the sacred and in spiritual experiences, then it is perhaps an indication there is something missing in our culture and in turn missing in us. Egypt was a culture marked by its stability and continuity. It lasted for more than 3,500 years, longer than any other civilization. Its core was mythical and oriented as Thompson observed, around psychic experiences and states of consciousness. Christ spent perhaps as many as seven years of His formative development in Egypt, waiting for Herod's death. His time in Egypt was a prophetic necessity for His development.[278] Perhaps there was more to that than a convenient place to dodge a murderous monarch. If Our Lord's development was benefitted by a season among Egyptian symbolism, then what benefits might we derive from a similar willingness to entertain a more mythical view of life? What could we gain if we were willing to look backward to an earlier and more mythical time for our own way of thought.

Joseph Smith's environment, steeped in folk magic, may not have been a defect after all. It may have been a blessing which enabled a young man to accept in faith the things needed to allow him to see within the veil. And we may be much better served by humbling ourselves and seeking to adopt a similar more mythical, more childlike view, than in condemning and arrogantly assuming our own superiority. Until we produce similar works of prophecy and visions, it seems self-evident we are not superior people. From Temples to universities to shopping malls,[279] our people have grown more materialistic and less mythical since the time of Joseph Smith. President Hinckley's urgent

---

[278]Matthew observed: "And was there until the death of Herod: that it might be fulfilled which was spoken of the Lord by the prophet, saying, 'Out of Egypt have I called my son'." (Matt. 2: 15.)

[279]Paul Toscano gave the graduation talk for the Class of 1978 at the J. Reuben Clark Law School, BYU. He used that comparison in the talk when he said: "Our grandfathers built temples; our fathers built universities; and we build shopping malls." (*Kings and Priest v. Secular Priests*. Student Convocation Speaker, J. Reuben Clark Law School Graduation 1978.) I am indebted to him for this thought. The J. Reuben Clark Law School library has provided a copy of this wonderful and insightful talk to me.

Temple building program is not merely an attempt to bring the ordinances to the Saints. It is also an attempt to reorient the Saints from this world to another, as we once were. As a prophet and seer, his example and ministry are both instruction and warning.

As one author put it: "Possibly the world of external facts is much more fertile and plastic than we have ventured to suppose; it may be that all these cosmologies and many more analyses and classifications are genuine ways of arranging what nature offers to our understanding, and that the main condition determining our selection between them is something in us rather than something external in the world."[280] Going on, he concludes: "the factors conditioning a selection between them [varying ways of interpreting the world] are to be found primarily in us who think about the world rather than the world we are thinking about." (*Id.*)

In a lament about the loss of mythical thought, Claude Levi-Strauss, one of our time's great anthropologists observed: "I think there are some things we have lost, and we should try perhaps to regain them, because I am not sure that in the kind of world in which we are living and with the kind of scientific thinking we are bound to follow, we can regain these things exactly as if they had never been lost; but we can try to become aware of their existence and their importance."[281]

In the earlier dispensation when Christ came into mortality, He taught His disciples about the fruits of the Spirit. His apostle Paul wrote: "But the fruit of the Spirit is love, joy, peace, longsuffering, gentleness, goodness, faith, Meekness, temperance: against such there is no law. And they that are Christ's have crucified the flesh with the affections and lusts. If we live in the Spirit, let us also walk in the Spirit." (Gal. 5: 22-25.) Connect up in your life the Spirit, the Temple ordinances which provide the "power of godliness" to you, faith, childlike approaches to

---

[280]Burtt, Edwin Arthur. *The Metaphysical Foundations of Modern Physical Science*, Revised edition. New York: Humanity Books, p. 307.

[281]Levi-Strauss, Claude. *Myth and Meaning: Cracking the Code of Culture.* New York: Schocken Books, University of Toronto Press, 1978, p. 5.

faith and belief, and see this call to "walk in the Spirit," as a call to view your life and the world differently.

The greatest part of the necessary opposition we find in our day consists of the cultural smog we breathe in and its hostility to faith. Christ taught in His opening words in this dispensation that we live among a people who have "a form of godliness, but they deny the power thereof." (JSH 1: 19.) Why is there no power to their form of godliness? It does not generate the faith necessary to receive power. It does not generate this faith because the principles of the Gospel of Jesus Christ are not believed, not obeyed, and not even understood among such people. You cannot shake together the philosophies of men mingled with scriptures and produce from that the power of godliness.

Levi-Strauss tells more about us than perhaps he realized when he discovered: "When I was writing the first version of *Mythologiques (Introduction to a Science of Mythology),* I was confronted with a problem which to me was extremely mysterious. It seems that there was a particular tribe which was able to see the planet Venus in full daylight, something which to me would be utterly impossible and incredible. I put the question to professional astronomers; they told me, of course, that we don't but, nevertheless, when we know the amount of light emitted by the planet Venus in full daylight, it was not absolutely inconceivable that some people could. Later on I looked into old treatises on navigation belonging to our own civilization and it seems that sailors of old were perfectly able to see the planet in full daylight. Probably we could still do so if we had a trained eye."[282] We live in our time among a people without eyes trained to see beyond the veil. You needn't accept their limitations and make them your own. If the capacity ever existed among the household of faith, then it can return. God insists He is the same yesterday, today and forever. Worship of Him includes, in times past as well as now, the promise of the Second Comforter.

---

[282]*Myth and Meaning, supra,* p. 18.

In a talk by John Taylor, we read:

There is something great and comprehensive associated with the plans and purposes of Jehovah in connection with the human family, which very few men care to take the trouble to investigate or reflect upon; and, as "No man can know the things of God, but by the Spirit of God;" and as very few place themselves in a position to obtain this spirit, the result necessarily is, that there is a large amount of ignorance in relation to the things of God and consequently a large amount of evil prevailing everywhere and which has existed in every age. I suppose, associated with these matters, there is a grand overruling destiny, and that it was necessary that this set of things should exist. There have always been two grand powers in juxtaposition, or rather in opposition to each other. There was in the heavens a conflict, and one-third of the angels, we are told, were cast out of there. That conflict has existed here upon the earth, and will continue to exist for a length of time yet to come, until, as we are told, Satan shall be bound. The conflict is between right and wrong, between truth and error, between God and the spirit of darkness, and the powers of evil that are opposed to Him; and these principles have existed in the various ages. ... It is not easy for men, without a knowledge of these principles, to comprehend those things of which I speak, for as I said before, and so say the Scriptures — "No man knows the things of God, but by the spirit of God;" and the Lord has revealed unto us, through very simple methods, the way whereby we can approach unto him. Who is there among men, with all their wisdom and intelligence, that can comprehend God? Who understands his laws and his doctrines? Who knows anything about his purposes and designs? Why, it is as high as the heavens, it is deeper than hell, it is as wide as the expanse of the universe, it circumscribes all subjects, and comprehends all intelligence. Who knows it? Nobody, but those who are enlightened by the spirit of revelation that proceeds from God. How did men in former times obtain a knowledge of these things? By obedience to the laws of God, by submitting to his authority, by taking up their cross and following him, and by searching diligently to obtain a knowledge of his laws. (*JD*

19: 79, John Taylor, July 29, 1877 (reported by Rudger
Clawson).)

The opposition in these things gives you the chance to choose. For
every argument for faith, there is another opposed to it. The arguments
require a choice. When the scales hang in equal balance, it is up to you
to put your finger on them and make the final tip in favor of faith or in
favor of agnosticism, disbelief or rejection of the Restored Gospel's
principles. Things are so ordered that this choice is left to you.

Never think you will arrive at a point where there is no counter-
argument. Grant Palmer was an instructor in the Church Education
System. He decided, however, to give the weight to Joseph Smith's
critics and to view our own Western Culture as clearly superior to a
culture of myth and meaning. His faith in the visions and visitations has
left him. Oddly, like many others, he sees no harm in retaining a belief
in the visions of others from distant times and more myth-ridden
cultures. He accepts the mission of Christ, though it is less well attested
than Joseph's mission. He accepts the scriptures from Christ's
Dispensation, though that time was decidedly more mythical than our
own. Again, his approach is internally inconsistent.

Grant Palmer's arguments ask us to forsake faith in God's ability
to do something in our day and only accept belief that God acted long
ago, among other people, and has finished His miraculous work among
us. He wants the Saints to abandon faith in a current system of
communication from Heaven, and to instead rely upon the revelations
given during the New Testament, thereby joining a broader coalition of
"Christian" pseudo-believers. He asks us to rejoin that same movement
which Christ said had a form of godliness but lacked the power of
godliness.

The words of Moroni weigh in on this subject and teach us that
revelation, visitations, ministering angels and the veil being rent are a
part of the essential faith in Christ for any people. Moroni asks:

...have miracles ceased? Behold I say unto you, Nay; neither have angels ceased to minister unto the children of men. For behold, they are subject unto him, to minister according to the word of his command, showing themselves unto them of strong faith and a firm mind in every form of godliness. And the office of their ministry is to call men unto repentance, and to fulfill and to do the work of the covenants of the Father, which he hath made unto the children of men, to prepare the way among the children of men, by declaring the word of Christ unto the chosen vessels[283] of the Lord, that they may bear testimony of him. And by so doing, the Lord God prepareth the way that the residue of men may have faith in Christ, that the Holy Ghost may have place in their hearts, according to the power thereof; and after this manner bringeth to pass the Father, the covenants which he hath made unto the children of men. And Christ hath said: If ye will have faith in me ye shall have power to do whatsoever thing is expedient in me. ... And now, my beloved brethren, if this be the case that these things are true which I have spoken unto you, and God will show unto you, with power and great glory at the last day, that they are true, and if they are true has the day of miracles ceased? Or have angels ceased to appear unto the children of men? Or has he withheld the power of the Holy Ghost from them? Or will he, so long as time shall last, or the earth shall stand, or there shall be one man upon the face thereof to be saved? Behold I say unto you, Nay; for **it is by faith that miracles are wrought; and it is by faith that angels appear and minister unto men; wherefore, if these things have ceased wo be unto the children of men, for it is because of unbelief, and all is vain.** For no man can be saved, according to the words of Christ, save they shall have faith in his name; wherefore, **if these things have ceased, then has faith ceased also; and awful is the state of man, for they are as though there had been no redemption made.** (Moroni 7: 29-33, 35-38, emphasis added.)

---

[283] As pointed out previously, the term "chosen vessel" means anyone who has received such a visit. The scope of such visits is covered in Alma 32: 23: "And now, he imparteth his word by angels unto men, yea, not only men but women also. Now this is not all; little children do have words given unto them many times, which confound the wise and the learned."

It is not up to someone else, some other time, to develop this faith. It is up to you, now. It is the heritage of the Saints and was the promise made in Joel and repeated by Moroni in his visit to Joseph Smith: "And it shall come to pass afterward, that I will pour out my spirit upon all flesh; and your sons and your daughters shall prophesy, your old men shall dream dreams, your young men shall see visions." (Joel 2: 28.) Sons, daughters, young and old are all involved in this prophetic promise concerning this latter-day faith being restored.

Joseph was sent as a prophet to restore faith in Christ. He was to restore an active, vibrant, and living faith. It was to be the kind of faith producing the ministering of angels and the opening of the heavens -- not the kind of faith that believes in a closed book of scriptures, hedges up heaven's ability to reveal new truths, and keeps the visions of heaven from rolling forth. There is no real difference between a belief that God only spoke in a closed cannon of scripture dating to the New Testament on the one hand, and a belief which renounces such gifts for the Saints today other than for a few leading authorities[284] on the other. Each shirks the duty to obtain a form of godliness that has power within it.

As the Gospel reaches into other societies, it will resonate with some "primitive" cultures with greater effect than in western, industrialized nations. Africa will seize and treasure things which France and the Netherlands disdain. Culture has predisposed some people with advantages we do not appreciate and with handicaps we view as

---

[284]Welch's position that Nephi's search into an understanding of the mysteries of God was not a general invitation to the Saints is similar in nature, if not a little broader in scope. You will recall his statement quoted earlier on page 153: "It is significant to me that Nephi specifically says here that he desired 'to know the mysteries of God' (1 Nephi 2: 16). While all are invited to seek and all are promised knowledge (1 Nephi 15: 8; Matthew 7: 7; Moroni 10: 4-5), this is not an open invitation for all men and women to seek 'mysteries' beyond the declarative words of the prophets." *Glimpses of Lehi's Jerusalem*. Edited by John W. Welch. Provo: FARMS; at p. 435. Leaving the responsibility to another, whether living or dead, departs from that faith in which "all are alike unto God." (2 Ne. 26: 33.) It also defeats the teachings of Joseph Smith and the Book of Mormon as set out throughout this work.

strengths. There are many ironies in this, though we often fail to see them.

The chorus above still sings. Herald angels still announce the Son of God. Those who ignore the opposition of a hostile and faithless culture will continue to hear these hymns of praise flowing from above. You can hear them, too, if you will recognize the necessary opposition for what it really is. Venus can still be seen among some people, as it was once seen among our own seafaring ancestors. Those who have sight to see can still see[285] the light in heaven, however unlikely such a thing may seem to those who have lost such abilities. Follow the commandments and you will see that light, too. It is not the amount of light in heaven which has changed, rather, it is ourselves as we walk about with our cultural sunglasses on, limiting our sight. We do not see because we do not want to or believe it is okay to see.

There were and are many ways to view Joseph Smith's history. How Joseph viewed it, after difficulty and struggle to get it right, was within a sacred narrative. God was at work in his life. He was chosen as God's Prophet. He was the restorer of ancient, lost truths. He was the one who brought back Divine authority. His failings and experience as a "money digger" were "foolish errors," not "serious sins." He acquired a hard-won awareness of God's unfolding plan for his life. And this hard-won awareness was what he testified to and proclaimed.

We all live sacred lives. God is at work in your life and in mine. See the sacred narrative in your own life. Allow faith to have a place in your life. There are no coincidences. The unfolding work of God in your life can be ignored, explained away, rationalized into nothing, or accepted with the eyes of faith. God did not just work in the lives of Moses, Isaiah, Nephi, Christ, Paul and Joseph Smith. He is at work in every life. He is at work in yours.

It is just as untrue and error-prone to view your life in exclusively secular terms as it is for a faithless critic to recast Joseph's life into a

---

[285]To paraphrase the Lord's statement: "He that hath eyes to see, let him see." (Matt. 11: 15.)

context other than the one Joseph came to understand through faith. Critics of Joseph miss the wonder of God's returning public involvement in mankind's lives. Do not make the same mistake in your own. Do not define your own life in terms which miss the sacred narrative disclosing what is going on. See it through the "eyes of faith." If you will permit yourself to do so, you will see that your own life is sacred too. Your own history is yet another history of God at work.

Chapter Eighteen

THE TEMPLE AS A TOOL

I was in the Jordan River Temple with four of the full-time missionaries. The full-time missionaries were allowed into the Temple once a week. We were in the Celestial Room after a session and I was talking with them about the symbols covering the clothing worn in the rites.

An elderly Temple worker was glaring at me from across the room. His stern look seemed calculated to alter our discussion. But we continued on.

Eventually, the Temple worker came over and 'whispered' to me: "If you are discussing the meaning of the Temple clothing, YOU'RE WRONG! We don't know what the symbols mean." It wasn't much of a whisper, really. It was calculated to let the missionaries overhear it. Particularly the "YOU'RE WRONG!" part of the whisper, which could be heard across the entire room it seemed.

It amused me. Probably shouldn't have, but it did. He seemed somehow fearful. I asked him to join us, and we continued the discussion.

I explained that the Temple has layers of symbolism and is intended to communicate great amounts of information through ceremony and symbolism. There was not a specific, individual meaning to any of the separate parts. All of the Gospel, in its fullness, was symbolized throughout the rites. It was an orchestra of meaning and was intended to elevate our thoughts. Each of us responds to it in varying degrees of comprehension, but it has depths and heights which allow for more than a lifetime of reflection and improvement. Our newly acquired Temple worker seemed to soften a bit as we spoke further.

I told them the story of my first eleven baptisms and of my ancestor's requests for more of the work to be completed that day. By the time we finished, our Temple worker was as friendly as the missionaries, and we departed as friends.

The Temple is where heaven, earth, life and afterlife all meet. It is the center place. Gathered in that center are all the phases of mankind's experiences, from before the creation into the eternities. The best way to view it is, I believe, as a tool.

I spent 25 years attending the Temple with little gain in understanding. But then it began to unfold. The unfolding came as I did work for my own ancestors. Name extraction cards hadn't produced the same results of insight. I believe those are connected, as well.

It is a tool intended to bind generations together. Used for that purpose it can free up great amounts of spiritual insight and power. Ancestors are freed to advocate your cause from the other side. Blessings flow as a result. The chief blessing in all of this is the added light and understanding which comes to you through obedience to the ordinances of the House of God.

The Temple is given to you as a tool in approaching God and godliness. It stands as a great signpost on the path to God. The Temple rites are intended to be both instruction and an example for you. Months before the rites had been revealed to the Saints, Joseph Smith wrote an outline of the coming rites in a letter to the Saints. He wrote in January, 1841: "Therefore, verily I say unto you, that your anointings, and your washings, and your baptisms for the dead, and your solemn assemblies, and your memorials for your sacrifices by the sons of Levi, and for your oracles in your most holy places wherein you receive conversations, and your statutes and judgments, for the beginning of the revelations and foundation of Zion, and for the glory, honor, and endowment of all her municipals, are ordained by the ordinance of my holy house, which my people are always commanded to build unto my holy name." (D&C 124: 39.) These are interesting phrases. They clearly suggest in concept form the coming Temple rites which would, on May 4, 1842, result in the presentation of the Temple endowment for the first time.[286]

Washings and Anointings are rites to cleanse and sanctify the recipient. The Lord wants us to be clean and pure. Some people view the rites as instilling holiness and cleanliness, itself. Others view them only as a symbolic call to attain such things. This difference in point of view is an important indicator of where the person's heart is.

The rites are intended to bring these things into the life of the recipient. Holiness comes from the Atonement. Forgiveness of sins and cleanliness comes from the Atonement. It is the Atonement that puts power into the Gospel and which delivers the promised forgiveness and reconciliation between God and man. However, the Atonement does not get applied in an indiscriminate or disorganized way to any person who promiscuously 'confesses Jesus,' but refuses to abide by His conditions. Christ has elected to bestow these gifts of grace to the Saints of God through the rites of His Gospel which He has ordained. Paul

---

[286]See *DHC* 5: 1-2.

reminded the Saints at Ephesus, there is only "one faith, one baptism," (Eph. 4: 5) and not many. Only one road leads back to Him. All others lead elsewhere.

Baptism is the first ordinance of the Gospel. Baptism is a whole-body experience. The entire person is immersed in water, nothing left above the surface. The symbol points powerfully to Christ's own burial and resurrection as the person baptized is "buried" under water and then brought again back to the air through a symbolic "resurrection." Left too long in a state of immersion, you would die. The ordinance is a graphic symbol of death and burial, because it literally places you in a position where you cannot breathe.[287]

The presence of water and total immersion also hearkens back to the time in the womb in which the infant is suspended in water before birth. This symbol, therefore, points to newness of life or rebirth. But it is more than just symbol. For the candidate who has prepared for baptism, the rite is the actual means whereby they are indeed forgiven of past sins and transgressions and given a new life in Christ by the rite.

Similarly the rites of the Temple are intended to convey to the recipient the actual promises, in their own name, which assure for them cleanliness and holiness before God. Washing you was to remove sins. If you were prepared for the rites when you received them, then through the washing you had the sins of this generation taken from you. Since earlier you had been fully washed in baptism, the rite of washing you anew was intended to remove those specific additional stains which have accumulated in your life since baptism. The washing away of the defects and errors of life take place within this ordinance, with a promise to you in your own name from God, if you are prepared.

Anointing confers holiness and sanctity. The olive oil used is a symbol of the Holy Spirit, as St. Cyril explained in his 21st Lecture. Cleansing you is not all the Lord intended for you through His

---

[287]The ordinance reminds us of the Egyptian *Book of Breathings*, where the various incantations and sacred formula are designed to restore breath, or life. The Egyptian approach was based upon an imitation of the truth, but not the truth itself. (See, e.g., Abraham 1: 26.)

Atonement. He intended also to make you sanctified.[288] The rites of washing and anointing are to sanctify you and tie you directly into the power of the Atonement. After receiving these rites, the promises made to others in an old book[289] are no longer the basis for your expectations from God. Rather you have promises made to you, in a covenant between you and God, through which you are personally entitled to receive promised blessings. Remember it makes no difference if the promises are made to you by God or by His authorized servants. From either source the promises are secure.[290] We are not supposed to let our hearts be troubled over the efficacy of these things. Instead we are supposed to rest secure in the knowledge we are entitled to the

---

[288]The power of sanctity comes through Christ's blood. As the Lord taught Adam: "Therefore I give unto you a commandment, to teach these things freely unto your children, saying: That by reason of transgression cometh the fall, which fall bringeth death, and inasmuch as ye were born into the world by water, and blood, and the spirit, which I have made, and so became of dust a living soul, even so ye must be born again into the kingdom of heaven, of water, and of the Spirit, and be cleansed by blood, even the blood of mine Only Begotten; that ye might be sanctified from all sin, and enjoy the words of eternal life in this world, and eternal life in the world to come, even immortal glory; For by the water ye keep the commandment; by the Spirit ye are justified, and by the blood ye are sanctified." (Moses 6: 58-60.)

[289]See, e,g., *DHC* 1: 282 – 283: "Then again we say: Search the Scriptures, search the Prophets, and learn what portion of them belongs to you and the people of the nineteenth century. You, no doubt, will agree with us, and say, that you have no right to claim the promises of the inhabitants before the flood; that you cannot found your hopes of salvation upon the obedience of the children of Israel when journeying in the wilderness; nor can you expect that the blessings which the Apostles pronounced upon the churches of Christ, eighteen hundred years ago, were intended for you. Again, if others' blessings are not your blessings, others' curses are not your curses; you stand then in these last days, as all have stood before you, agents unto yourselves, to be judged according to your works."

[290]D&C 1: 38: "What I the Lord have spoken, I have spoken, and I excuse not myself; and though the heavens and the earth pass away, my word shall not pass away, but shall all be fulfilled, whether by mine own voice or by the voice of my servants, it is the same."

promises given, and to let our minds meditate upon them as our own property. They are among the only things we will take with us into eternity.

After you have been washed and anointed in the Temple you are then clothed. The account of clothing Adam and Eve by God occurs in Genesis 3: 21[291] where they are given coats of skin. Remember the context in which Adam and Eve were clothed by God. Adam had previously named all the animals,[292] and these animals were his initial earthly friends and companions. There was an intimacy between these animals and Adam.

Through his and Eve's transgression, the two had become aware of their nakedness before God.[293] To remove this guilt and shame from being naked, Adam and Eve initially put on aprons made of fig leaves.[294] This initial unsuitable covering was a symbol of the newly acquired knowledge of good and evil, which gave to them their sense of guilt and awareness of their nakedness.[295] It was a sign they had become as God knowing the difference between good and evil.[296]

No doubt the shame remained, for Adam brings it up again with God, while wearing his fabricated fig leaf apron, saying: "I heard thy voice in the garden, and I was afraid, because I was naked; and I hid myself." (Gen. 3: 10.) To cure the guilt and remove the shame, God provides a covering for Adam and Eve. He provides this through the "coats of skins" with which He clothed them.

---

[291]"Unto Adam also and to his wife did the Lord God make coats of skins, and clothed them."

[292]Gen. 2: 19-20.

[293]Gen. 3: 10.

[294]Gen. 3: 7.

[295]Gen. 3: 22.

[296]Gen. 3: 22 "And the Lord God said, Behold, **the man is become as one of us**, to know good and evil:" (Emphasis added.)

Think for a moment what would have been involved in providing such animal skin clothing. It would have required that an animal, or animals, first be killed. God was the one who slew the animal, not Adam. God would not just kill an animal in these circumstances. The Fall necessitates the Atonement. Providing coats of skin to cover shame, like the Atonement itself, would involve ceremonial implications and rites. It is certain, therefore, the animals which were used for clothing Adam and Eve were slain by the Lord as He introduced the primeval worship rites of mankind,[297] through ceremonial killing and sacrifice. This primeval rite was to point forward to the real sacrifice which would be offered by the Son of God in the Meridian of Time.

The connection between removing shame and guilt, and clothing with garments is apparent in the Biblical record. The presentation of clothing, particularly in a ceremonial context with animal sacrifice, points toward Christ's future Atonement. Similarly, the Temple rite in which clothing is presented is also intended to cover one's guilt and shame, and cover you through the Atonement of Christ.

Having been washed and clothed, you are then presented with the endowment ceremony. Ritual teaching and covenant making are intended to bring you into harmony with God. It is through these means you acquire the "power of godliness" that was lacking in Christianity before the Restoration. D&C 84: 19-22: "And this greater priesthood administereth the gospel and holdeth the key of the mysteries of the kingdom, even the key of the knowledge of God. Therefore, in the ordinances thereof, the power of godliness is manifest. And without the ordinances thereof, and the authority of the priesthood, the power of godliness is not manifest unto men in the flesh; For without this no man can see the face of God, even the Father, and live." These higher ordinances of the Temple are performed by the Melchizedek Priesthood. These verses **do not say** the key to this

---

[297]It is no doubt from this event the diverse cultures following afterward would continue the system of animal sacrifice in various methods found throughout the ancient world. This is a subject beyond this work, however, and is acknowledged with only this passing comment.

knowledge requires a person hold this priesthood. Rather, they say this priesthood is required in order to obtain **the ordinances**, and it is **the ordinances** which prepare people for the power of godliness, receiving mysteries, and seeing the face of God. Anyone who has received these ordinances has the foundation for these things in their lives. It is a false notion that these things are confined to priesthood holders, even though thoughtless people do sometimes assert this notion. Men and women both receive Temple rites, and are equally entitled to the benefits the rites confer.

Compare this broad assurance given in revelation about the ordinances of the Temple with the Lord's indictment of Christianity in the First Vision. Speaking of the churches of our day the Lord said, "they draw near to me with their lips, but their hearts are far from me, they teach for doctrines the commandments of men, having a form of godliness, but they deny the power thereof." (JSH 1: 19.) Godliness in **form** only is powerless. It cannot call down revelations or visitations from angels, or teach truths which save. It matters little if that form of godliness is held by a person claiming to be a Methodist, or Presbyterian, or Lutheran, or Latter-day Saint. Powerlessness in one's faith is evidence of faithlessness. Faithlessness has, as its fruit, the absence of power.

The Lord opened this dispensation in order to return to the earth a faith which held the power of godliness within it. And in Section 84, above, He tells us how it is accomplished through the ordinances of the higher priesthood. Those higher ordinances include laying on of hands for the Gift of the Holy Ghost and Temple rites.[298] How then is the Temple an endowment of power?

There is a relationship between holding sacred knowledge *sacred* and profaning it by disclosing it to the unprepared or unworthy. This improper disclosure was called "casting pearls before swine" and has

---

[298]It includes also patriarchal blessings, grave dedications and other miscellaneous ordinances. But we are not concerned with those in this work and so pass over them without comment.

been discussed previously. You gain the Lord's confidence when you show the Lord you are willing to keep the things which are sacred as holy things before Him. The Temple allows you to do this. Without the Temple there is no institutionalized method of dispensing sacred knowledge. The Temple allows the Saints an opportunity to be proven in this necessary requirement. The Temple gives you teachings and experiences which you must covenant never to reveal. No other Church holds such rites and dispenses them to every member who is willing to abide the conditions for receiving them. The Church of Jesus Christ will allow all, male and female, access to these rites and therefore access to this qualifying requirement.

The Temple rites include symbols and instruction which orient the mind of man toward God and godliness. The whole of their teachings can be captured with this thought: We are to be prepared in all things to receive further light and knowledge by conversing with the Lord through the veil. The Temple prepares you to do that. The Temple includes, within its rites, the symbolic act of conversing with God in a symbolic version of "oracles in your most holy places wherein you receive conversations." (D&C 124: 39.)

In the Salt Lake Temple, the endowment rooms are oriented to the various directions of the compass. As you progress from room to room during the presentation of the endowment, you circumambulate the four compass directions. You are required to climb a staircase as you move from the Garden to the World rooms.[299] Each room is elevated in height from the floor of the one to the floor of the other. The architecture testifies of the process of growth and progress through the second estate.[300] The ordinance of the endowment is intended to bring

[299]Pictures of the various rooms are available for viewing in Talmage, James E. *The House of the Lord.* Salt Lake City: Signature Books, 1998.

[300]For further reading on Temple architectural symbolism, *Symbols in Stone* is one source. Brown, Matthew B. and Smith, Paul Thomas. *Symbols in Stone.* American Fork: Covenant Communications, Inc., 1997. Talmage's book, *supra*, treats the subject only in passing.

powerful symbols to the mind of the participant in a ceremonial setting. That setting and those symbols are intended to work on the mind and allow you to think deeply on the things of God. It is a vast display of material to allow for reflection and meditation over a lifetime.

When the Lord spoke about preparing the Saints to enter Zion, He taught: "And this cannot be brought to pass until mine elders are endowed with power from on high. For behold, I have prepared a great endowment and blessing to be poured out upon them, inasmuch as they are faithful and continue in humility before me. Therefore it is expedient in me that mine elders should wait for a little season, for the redemption of Zion." (D&C 105: 11-13.) We need still to receive that endowment of power. The Temple is the way that happens. It confers power when it is understood in the proper light.

Gaining a correct orientation into ceremonial learning is a great advantage and a great endowment for any person seeking the Second Comforter. Exposure to the culture of ceremony and symbols is a priceless advantage to anyone coming from a secularized and demythologized society. Unfortunately, many of the participants in Temple rites confuse the value of these things and come to the wrong conclusion.[301] The power of these rites lies in the reorientation of the

---

[301]David John Buerger, for example, completely misses the value to this exposure to the culture of ceremony and symbolism in his *Mysteries of Godliness* when he suggests: "From a strictly functional perspective, the amount of time required to complete a vicarious endowment seems excessive. If patrons do not need to hear baptismal and confirmation speeches prior to performing these proxy ordinances or talks on how to have a good marriage before vicarious sealings (as all living people traditionally receive before their own ceremony), it seems inconsistent that they must hear about events in the Garden of Eden or the lone and dreary world before vicariously receiving the signs, tokens, and key words which form the apparent essence of the endowment ceremony. If increasing the number of endowments were the primary objective, these elements could be performed in a few minutes instead of two hours." (Buerger, David John. *The Mysteries of Godliness*. San Francisco: Smith Research Associates, 1994, p. 180.) He would have the Temple turned into "McTemple" as a result of his regrettable Western orientation and focus on production.

individual and their minds from what is in society today to a different setting and different world-view. That different setting is one in which you are prepared for companionship with those who, behind the veil, live in a culture of symbols and ceremony where deep meanings and eternal patterns are seen endlessly and portrayed throughout the culture.

Just one example can be found in an article of Temple clothing. In the Temple a robe shoulder fringe has numeric and symbolic meaning. Three pleats divided into four rows remind us, in one simple symbol, of the entire Gospel of Christ. Three pleats remind us through symbol of God the Father, God the Son, and the Holy Ghost. The pleats also suggest, Abraham, Isaac and Jacob, the ancestors of the tribes of Israel. These suggest, too, the First Presidency -- or of presidencies generally -- where there is a President and two counselors. Such suggestions of presidency remind us of the Church as an institution and the restoration of things which existed once and exist again today. They will suggest even more to the reflective mind.

Divide the three pleats into the four rows, and you see the seven divisions suggesting the seven days of creation. The creation, in turn, reminds us of the power of God and that all of creation is His handiwork. This world is no accident. He planned it, and it reflects His power and majesty by its existence and order. The seven divisions also remind us of the Menorah, which suggests a chiasm as we have previously discussed. The balance and harmony of the number -- with three on one side, divided by the center arm, and three on the other side -- shows through their repetition that the first shall be last, and the last shall be first. This return of pattern around the center arm reminds us of the Atonement, which promises to return again to life all that went before. The Menorah also suggests the tree of life, in the Garden of Eden, which, again, reminds us of the Fall of mankind, and the need for the Atonement.

Take the pleat and multiply the three rows of the pleat by the four folds of the rows, and we have the number twelve. The months of the year, with the returning cycles of nature and the eternal round of God's creative drama are symbolized here. The Twelve Tribes of Israel, God's chosen people whose latter-day destiny is to be restored to full covenant status is also symbolized. The need for a people to be chosen in a world of apostasy and forsaking Him is symbolized here. The Twelve Apostles of the Lamb are also suggested with the return to Christ's ministry and the need for Christ's Atonement again echoing in the symbol. And the return of the Twelve Apostles to the earth through the Restoration of the Gospel is also symbolized. Christ's delegation to man of the authority of the Gospel, symbolized by the Twelve Apostles, is also found here.

These are only a few of the meanings. They are covered cryptically, and not exhaustively. But they are enough to see the symbolic nature of the Temple content. It is filled with symbolic meanings which offer endless opportunity for pondering and meditation.

In a mere fringe of a Temple robe, the entire Gospel of Christ, along with His Church, along with the history of mankind from Adam to Abraham, from Abraham to Christ to the present, are brought to mind. The endowment is a cascade of images, symbols and instruction. It is intended to convey in ceremony, to the mind of the participant, the kinds of thoughts which prepare you to receive the Second Comforter. Impatience with this form of communication is the hallmark of the unprepared. Patience and gratitude for this powerful form of preparation is the hallmark of those who are receiving the power of godliness and the mysteries of God into their lives. Reflection and pondering leads to the "stillness" required to hear the "still, small voice." That voice is, of course, our first and most enduring link to God.

In the Temple rites, every word and gesture is prescribed. The company of patrons who participate in the endowment are called upon to go through the progression from one degree to the next as a group. All words, phrases, acts and gestures are prescribed for them throughout the ceremony, until the last step qualifying them to receive further light and knowledge from the Lord through the veil. Before they are brought to that point, however, they must depart, for the first time, from prescribed ritual. They, as a company, must create their unique contribution to the ceremony. The prayer circle is the company's creative contribution to their endowment and the final step in preparation for conversing with the Lord.

The prayer circle is a powerful symbol, one of the most powerful in the rites, for here, the participants must redefine themselves from the role as recipient to the role of creator. They must change from their passive role as recipients to an active role as contributors. They must create within the ceremony, just as God has created this ceremony for them. They must reach out before they receive. They must petition God in actual prayer before God will symbolically return to speak directly with them. It is a powerful ceremonial teaching device which confers the power of godliness upon them through its message. It forms another chiasm as one reaches up, and One reaches down.

Anyone who suggests the endowment is not a useful tool in preparing the participant for passing through the actual veil which covers God's presence here in mortality is not likely to pass through that veil. They miss the point. And in our society, that sentiment is held much too often. This book attempts to disabuse you of that notion.

The Temple provides tools directly to you to help in your search for God's presence. It is perhaps the single most powerful tool for that purpose in the entire Gospel of Christ. Section 84 does not overstate the case. Within the rites the power of godliness is manifest, and without them no person can be prepared to see the face of God.

The Temple is also intended to educate you about the mysteries of God. The fact that God dispenses to man sacred knowledge with restrictions on its use is communicated in the Temple more powerfully than in any other place, including the scriptures. Nowhere is this message about God holding you accountable for sacred knowledge more clearly set out. He requires you to covenant not to reveal aspects of the rites.[302] As a consequence, you learn in the Temple as from no other source, that God expects you to be His confidant. And if you are unwilling to accept that burden, then you cut yourself off from receiving further sacred knowledge.

The Temple's rich symbolic ceremonial setting answers far more questions than you have asked. The Temple is a place where, just like the visions of heaven, more is given than was expected when you entered.

The Brother of Jared came to the Lord asking for help with an interior lighting problem in his boats. His petition to the Lord revolved about this limited issue. The answer to the inquiry provided much more than merely the solution to the lighting problem.[303] What resulted was

---

[232]The information contained in this work does not reveal any of the material which is required to be kept sacred and not revealed. General authorities, including Elder John A. Widtsoe of the Twelve, have spoken about the Temple's rites while avoiding matters which are not appropriate for public discussion. Elder Widtsoe's talk to the Genealogical Society on October 12, 1920, is reproduced in the Appendix to Signature Book's reproduction of Talmage's book *The House of the Lord*, beginning on page 185. (Talmage, James E. *The House of the Lord*. Salt Lake City: Signature Books, 1998.)

[303]The problem of light caused him to seek, but the answer led him to the fullness of light. He stated his problem to the Lord this way: "And I know, O Lord, that thou hast all power, and can do whatsoever thou wilt for the benefit of man; therefore touch these stones, O Lord, with thy finger, and prepare them that they may shine forth in darkness; and they shall shine forth unto us in the vessels which we have prepared, that we may have light while we shall cross the sea." (Ether 3:4.) In response we read: "behold, the Lord stretched forth his hand and touched the stones one by one with his finger. And the veil was taken from off the eyes of the brother of Jared, and he saw the finger of the Lord; and it was as the finger of a man, like unto flesh and blood; and the brother of Jared fell down before the Lord, for he was struck with fear. … behold, the Lord showed himself unto him, and said: Because thou knowest these things ye are redeemed from the fall; therefore ye are brought back into my presence; therefore I show myself unto you. … Seest thou that ye are created after mine own image? Yea, even all men were created in the beginning after mine own image. … Jesus showed himself unto this man in the spirit, even after the manner and in the likeness of the same body even as he showed himself unto the Nephites. And he ministered unto him

redemption from the Fall, knowledge of God, and Christ as Second Comforter ministering to him in the same way that He ministered to the Nephites (which is to say that He taught him ceremonial truths and the mysteries of godliness).

Similarly, when Joseph Smith went to pray about which Church to join, he received an answer which not only answered that inquiry, but went well beyond that single subject. Among other things, he received a visitation from God the Father and His Son Jesus Christ;[304] he received a remission of his sins;[305] he saw many angels;[306] he learned that all religious denominations were wrong,[307] the doctrines of Christian churches of his day were incorrect,[308] and the fullness of the Gospel would at a future time be made known to him,[309] and that when God visits you, it leaves you with a sense of calm and peace which is indescribable.[310]

---

even as he ministered unto the Nephites; and all this, that this man might know that he was God, because of the many great works which the Lord had showed unto him. And because of the knowledge of this man he could not be kept from beholding within the veil; and he saw the finger of Jesus, which, when he saw, he fell with fear; for he knew that it was the finger of the Lord; and he had faith no longer, for he knew, nothing doubting. Wherefore, having this perfect knowledge of God, he could not be kept from within the veil; therefore he saw Jesus; and he did minister unto him." (*Id.* v. 6, 13, 16, 17-20.)

[304]JSH 1: 17.

[305]See 1832 Recital of the First Vision, Appendix A in *Joseph Smith's First Vision*. (Backman, Milton V. *Joseph Smith's First Vision*, Second Edition. Salt Lake City: Bookcraft, 1971, p. 157.)

[306]*Id.*, 1835 Recital of the First Vision, Appendix B, p. 159.

[307]*Id.*, Wentworth Letter, Appendix D, p. 169.

[308]*Id.*

[309]*Id.*

[310]*Id.*, Orson Pratt's Account of the First Vision., Appendix E, p. 172.

When Nephi prayed to know the meaning of his father's dream, he too received far more than an answer to this single inquiry.[311] He received an audience with the Second Comforter and learned the fullness of God's revelations.

The Temple is a type of these things. You come to receive an endowment, but receive through it a ceremonial instruction into the mysteries of God. You receive a wealth of information about the culture of the heavens and a symbolic treasury of principles to meditate upon drawing you nearer to God than any other ordinance of the Gospel. The suggestions of David John Buerger in his *Mysteries of Godliness, supra*, illustrate just how little these things are recognized. The Temple is a tool. But it is apparently a sadly underused and widely misunderstood tool.

The Lord attempted to point the Saints toward understanding what He was providing to them in D&C 88: 119: "Organize yourselves; prepare every needful thing; and establish a house, even a house of prayer, a house of fasting, a house of faith, a house of learning, a house of glory, a house of order, a house of God." The house was to be a seven-fold blessing to the Saints: 1) prayer; 2) fasting; 3) faith; 4) learning; 5) glory; 6) order; and 7) God. This list of seven, ties the mind back to the original list of seven in the creation. The number seven is a symbol of completion, perfection or the entirety of the matter. The Temple is, therefore, a complete, perfect and entire presentation of the Lord's Gospel. This list, too, is a progression from one degree to another in grace, light and truth.

-**Prayer** prepares you to enter into the right frame of mind to receive these things.

-**Fasting** prepares your spirit and subdues the flesh.

-**Faith** grows from the prayer and fasting which precedes it and prepares you to learn.

---

[311]This has previously been discussed at some length and will not be repeated here.

-**Learning** in the highest sense comes from faith, fasting and prayer.

-This brings to you the "**glory** of God" or in other words "intelligence" or "light and truth." As you receive further light and truth, you gain an appreciation for the order of heaven and earth.

-This **order** requires a ceremonial orientation and understanding.

-All of which prepare you for the presence of **God**, or the Second Comforter.

This seven-fold list is, therefore, a perfect whole and complete description of the Temple's purpose.

The Temple rites are intended themselves to be a revelation. They reveal much about God if you are willing to receive it. You first see things through the eyes of faith before seeing the things themselves.[312] In the Temple you are permitted the opportunity of seeing, if you have the eyes of faith, the deepest things of God. They are presented before your mind as if seeing the visions of heaven themselves. Receive them as you would receive a visitation from God Himself. Then, when you have the eyes to see these things through faith, you are finally ready to receive the Second Comforter and the comfort coming from that experience; which will leave you with calmness and indescribable peacefulness "Therefore, sanctify yourselves that your minds become single to God, and the days will come that you shall see him; for he will unveil his face unto you, and it shall be in his own time, and in his own way, and according to his own will." (D&C 88: 68.)

Through the process of the Temple rites, you become holy, or potentially become so. Whether you are willing actually to accept the holiness offered or not is up to you. But if you choose to accept the holiness offered in the spirit with which it is offered, and to obey the covenants, charges and obligations found there, you then have a tool for recovering your lost association with God. The Temple can make *you* a

---

[312]Ether 12: 19: "And there were many whose faith was so exceedingly strong, even before Christ came, who could not be kept from within the veil, but truly saw with their eyes the things which they had beheld with an eye of faith, and they were glad."

Temple. You become the "House of God" with His Spirit dwelling within you. The Apostle Paul was not just using a useful analogy, he was rather describing a profound truth when he wrote: "Know ye not that ye are the temple of God, and that the Spirit of God dwelleth in you? If any man defile the temple of God, him shall God destroy; for the temple of God is holy, which temple ye are." (1 Cor. 3: 16-17.)[313]

You become a holy place He can and will visit from time to time. He will take up His abode with you.

Use the Temple to cleanse yourself. Use the Temple's rites to separate yourself from the world. Make yourself "sacred space" which is set apart from the world, behind a veil, where the Spirit of the Lord is unrestrained. These rites apply the power of the Atonement of Jesus Christ to cleanse, purify, wash, anoint, clothe and endow you with power. Accept them in faith, nothing doubting, and realize the "power of godliness" can and will be manifested to you through them.

---

[313]See also 1 Cor 6:19: "What? know ye not that your body is the temple of the Holy Ghost which is in you, which ye have of God, and ye are not your own?" 2 Cor 6:16: "And what agreement hath the temple of God with idols? for ye are the temple of the living God; as God hath said, I will dwell in them, and walk in them; and I will be their God, and they shall be my people."

Chapter Nineteen

WHAT IT MEANS AND WHAT
IT DOES NOT MEAN

My neighbor and friend, Antonio Antonelli, was talking with me about his testimony. He was preparing to teach an Elder's Quorum lesson on that subject at the time and was bouncing some of his thoughts off of me. He made the distinction between "believing" and "knowing." He said he believed the Church to be true, but he hadn't seen God, so could not know it to be true.

As we pondered the distinction, I asked him, "Suppose there was a voice that spoke to you, not an audible voice, but one you heard in your mind. Suppose it said to you: 'Prove me herewith; on the morrow, at sunrise, I will cause that the clouds will part, the rays shine down upon you and a flock of doves lands upon your roof-top. And by this you may know that I am.' Then suppose you got up and saw all that happen at dawn, exactly as the voice had said. Would you then 'know'?"

Tony thought about it for a few moments and responded: "I suppose that I would."

"Even if you hadn't seen anything other than perfectly natural events?" I asked.

"Yes, I think it wouldn't matter, because it says that is the proof, and if the proof comes, I think I would know."

"I think you're right. I think I'd agree. The problem for most of us is not that we don't have a basis to 'know.' It is that we haven't been willing to accept the proof we've already received. You should think about challenging the class with that thought."

Tony used that thought in his lesson the following Sunday. The discussions, both before and from Tony's class, have remained with me. Tony's lesson that day led to some of the later successes in my own spiritual journey.

Anyone who wants to receive a full witness to God's existence must be willing to accept the preliminary proofs He has already given us, but they will lead to knowledge. Knowledge will in turn lead to the Second Comforter. But by the time it happens, you will already have known for some time.

Receiving the Second Comforter means you will meet Christ. You will know, without a doubt, He exists. You will know through Him the Atonement has been provided, and the scriptures which testify of Him are true. You will have faith no longer in the existence of God nor in your standing before Him, but will have knowledge.[314] We are going to consider in this Chapter what it means and does not mean to have such knowledge.

As we have already seen, Nephi had the extraordinary experience of receiving the Second Comforter and being tutored in all the mysteries of God. His vision was so comprehensive he was not permitted, even in writing scriptures and prophecy for his descendants and for latter-day

---

[314]See, e.g., Ether 3: 19: "And because of the knowledge of this man he could not be kept from beholding within the veil; and he saw the finger of Jesus, which, when he saw, he fell with fear; for he knew it was the finger of the Lord; and he had faith no longer, for he knew, nothing doubting."

restored Israel, to record the full contents of the visions. Among other things, he was shown in vision the future life of Christ, His ministry in mortality and His Atonement, the mission of His Apostles and the subsequent apostasy and restoration of Christ's Church, as well as the unfolding history of all mankind until the end of the earth. Nephi's witness of the truth[315] was complete and he had the fullness. So he is a good source of telling us what receiving the Second Comforter means and does not mean.

Despite all that he received, Nephi made this observation about his mortal experience **after** having received these great things:

For my soul delighteth in the scriptures, and my heart pondereth them, and writeth them for the learning and the profit of my children. Behold, my soul delighteth in the things of the Lord; and my heart pondereth continually upon the things which I have seen and heard. Nevertheless, notwithstanding the great goodness of the Lord, in showing me his great and marvelous works, **my heart exclaimeth: O wretched man that I am! Yea, my heart sorroweth because of my flesh; my soul grieveth because of mine iniquities. I am encompassed about, because of the temptations and the sins which do so easily beset me. And when I desire to rejoice, my heart groaneth because of my sins**; nevertheless, I know in whom I have trusted. My God hath been my support; he hath led me through mine afflictions in the wilderness; and he hath preserved me upon the waters of the great deep. He hath filled me with his love, even unto the consuming of my flesh. He hath confounded mine enemies, unto the causing of them to quake before me. Behold, he hath heard my cry by day, and he hath given me knowledge by visions in the night-time. And by day have I waxed bold in mighty prayer before him; yea, my voice have I sent up on high; and angels came down and ministered unto me. And upon the wings of his Spirit hath my body been carried away upon exceedingly high mountains. And mine eyes have beheld great things, yea, even too great for man; therefore

---

[315]Used here as defined in D&C 92: 24: "And truth is knowledge of things as they are, and as they were, and as they are to come."

I was bidden that I should not write them. O then, if I have
seen so great things, if the Lord in his condescension unto the
children of men hath visited men in so much mercy, **why
should my heart weep and my soul linger in the valley of
sorrow, and my flesh waste away, and my strength slacken,
because of mine afflictions?** And why should I yield to sin,
because of my flesh? Yea, why should I give way to
temptations, that the evil one have place in my heart to destroy
my peace and afflict my soul? **Why am I angry** because of
mine enemy? Awake, my soul! **No longer droop in sin.**
Rejoice, O my heart, and give place no more for the enemy of
my soul. Do not anger again because of mine enemies. Do not
slacken my strength because of mine afflictions. Rejoice, O my
heart, and cry unto the Lord, and say: O Lord, I will praise thee
forever; yea, my soul will rejoice in thee, my God, and the rock
of my salvation. (2 Ne. 4: 15-30, emphasis added.)

From this we see Nephi acknowledged he had the following list of
personal troubles after his great theophany with the Second Comforter:

1. His heart sorrowed because of his "flesh."
2. He grieved because of his iniquities.
3. He was compassed about by temptations and sins which he said
    easily beset him.
4. He groaned because of sin, and could not rejoice.
5. His soul wept, and he lingered in the valley of sorrow.
6. He had afflictions and slackened his strength as a result.
7. He fought not to yield to sin and temptations.
8. He became angry because of his enemies.

This list of difficulties may seem to be inconsistent with the great
blessings and witnesses he had received, but problems like these are
neither odd nor inconsistent with what others with similar spiritual
experiences have suffered. Joseph Smith's great difficulties began with
a theophany. All of his life's difficulties stemmed, in one way or
another, from the visions and revelations he received. If it were not for

his visions, he would not have been hated and persecuted. While lingering in Liberty Jail, the Lord spoke to Joseph these words: "know thou, my son, that all these things shall give thee experience, and shall be for thy good. The Son of Man hath descended below them all. Art thou greater than he?" (D&C 122: 7-8.) Joseph's difficulties were for his good, no matter how terrible the experiences proved to be. This is true of anyone who receives such things.

In the case of Nephi's lament, his temptations and difficulties grew largely out of a family dynamic in which he was the younger brother who was called to lead older brothers. The cultural and familial positions of these older brothers presumed that Nephi would be the subordinate one. Yet Nephi was called by the Lord to lead, precisely because his older brothers were unworthy for the assignment. So Nephi was put into the position of being called to lead the unwilling and unworthy. If you take a moment to reflect on that, you will see a good deal about mortality encapsulated by this dilemma. What Nephi was asked by the Lord to do was *not* going to succeed. He was called in this instance on a doomed mission, yet told to do it anyway.

Life's experiences are intended to be for our benefit and development. It is supposed to contain a generous share of failure and setbacks. Without the experience of fighting a losing battle for some noble cause, we are not able to prove the depth of our commitment nor show faith in the face of opposition. Why should you receive any different challenge than one similar to the others who received the Second Comforter before you?

The Second Comforter never has and never will remove life's difficulties. Life will continue much the same as it did before, although the challenges may become greater. You are here to develop into the greatest form of "you" that it is possible to refine in mortality. None of us are here to coast along awaiting death. The Lord uses the words "anxiously engaged"[316] to describe a life of following Him.

---

[316] D&C 58: 27 "Verily I say, men should be anxiously engaged in a good cause, and do many things of their own free will, and bring to pass much

Having the Second Comforter will remove doubts about His existence. Though, as we have already explained, you must first develop such faith through obedience that doubts are far removed **before** you receive the Second Comforter. It would be more correct to say that after you have lost all doubts, you then receive the Second Comforter and have that faith confirmed as knowledge.

The Second Comforter will also remove any doubts about your standing with God. You will "rest" from all anxiety over your relationship with God. That was what Joseph sought when he prayed in September 21, 1823, "for a manifestation to me, that I might know of my state and standing before him; for I had full confidence in obtaining a divine manifestation, as I previously had one." (JSH 1: 29.) He wanted to remove doubts about his worthiness, but not to remove doubts about God, for about God, Joseph had no doubts.

The notion that one is "always saved," or cannot fall from grace, is a false Calvinist notion.[317] Most Christian denominations believe it possible to fall from grace and be damned despite conversion. The truth is you must not only convert, but must also "endure to the end" to obtain salvation.[318] But one of life's great anxieties gets solved for you when the Second Comforter ministers to you.

Remember Christ taught this whole possibility in the context of promising to His disciples "comfort." This "comfort" comes from knowing your standing before God is such that He will give you an audience with Him. That event alone will give you calmness and peace

---

righteousness."

[317]John Calvin taught the doctrine of "irresistible grace" which meant God could impose salvation upon you once He decided to elect to do so. If he did, you could not fail or fall from grace.

[318]See, e.g., D&C 20: 29: "And we know that all men must repent and believe on the name of Jesus Christ, and worship the Father in his name, and endure in faith on his name to the end, or they cannot be saved in the kingdom of God." See also, 1 Ne 13:37, 1 Ne 22:31, 2 Ne 9:24, 2 Ne 31:16, 2 Ne 31:20, 2 Ne 33:4, Omni 1:26, 3 Ne 15:9, Morm 9:29, D&C 14:7, D&C 18:22 and D&C 20:25.

which words fail to convey. Joseph said it "le[ft] his mind in a state of calmness and peace, indescribable."[319] But the feeling does not endure, for life returns and challenges remain to be confronted. Joseph's peace of mind did not last long. He was buffeted and persecuted throughout his life, beginning shortly after the First Vision. What remained with Joseph, however, was a satisfying reflection on the profound experience. Nephi summed it up succinctly in his observation about his experiences: "Behold, my soul delighteth in the things of the Lord; and my heart pondereth continually upon the things which I have seen and heard." (2 Ne. 4: 16.) You will have that in common with Nephi, Joseph, and others who have had similar experiences. The scriptures will take on a deeper meaning as you consider the sacred accounts of others' encounters with God and reflect upon your own.

Receiving a witness does not guarantee you will endure to the end; for that is left to you. The example of Aaron's sons, Nadab and Abihu, is instructive. They are among those who have seen God, as described in this passage, "Then went up Moses, and Aaron, Nadab, and Abihu, and seventy of the elders of Israel: And they saw the God of Israel: and there was under his feet as it were a paved work of a sapphire stone, and as it were the body of heaven in his clearness. And upon the nobles of the children of Israel he laid not his hand: also they saw God, and did eat and drink."[320] (Exodus 24: 9-11.) Yet, some time thereafter, these sons of Aaron departed from God's ways. While serving in the Tabernacle in a false and unacceptable way, they were destroyed by God: "And Nadab and Abihu, the sons of Aaron, took either of them his censer, and put fire therein, and put incense thereon, and offered strange fire before the Lord, which he commanded them not. And there went out fire from the Lord, and devoured them, and they died before the Lord." (Lev. 10: 1-2.) Clearly, receiving an audience from God does not mean you can then deviate from His commandments. Instead it will

---

[319]Orson Pratt's account of the First Vision, previously cited.

[320]Note the covenant/sacramental setting of this visit.

elevate the level of accountability and expectation for you. You get there by keeping the commandments. Thereafter you cannot willfully disobey (as these sons of Aaron) without incurring the Lord's displeasure.

The Second Comforter will also correct many false or incomplete impressions which exist about heaven. Joseph said, "Could you gaze into heaven five minutes, you would know more than you would by reading all that ever was written on the subject." (*DHC* 6: 50.) You will gain an understanding of some of the difficulties which inspired men have had in conveying the truths of Christ's existence and of his glory, peace and love. Spoken or written language simply fails in some respects when dealing with God and the infinite. In the closing verses of Section 76 this truth appears: "Neither is man capable to make them known, for they are **only to be seen and understood by the power of the Holy Spirit**, which God bestows on those who love him, and purify themselves before him;" (v. 116, emphasis added.) Even if you wanted to convey some things, it isn't possible to do so because the language of mortality fails to permit it.

How can you capture in words the feelings which Christ shares by His presence? You can say you felt "love," but the intensity of that is not captured by the word. John tried by using these words: "Beloved, let us love one another: for love is of God; and every one that loveth is born of God, and knoweth God. He that loveth not knoweth not God; for God is love." (1 Jn. 4: 7-8.) He goes from "love is of God" to "God is love" in an attempt to put into words the notion. Other attempts to put into words the notion include these:

Rom 5:5: "And hope maketh not ashamed; because the love of God is shed abroad in our hearts by the Holy Ghost which is given unto us." This is Paul's attempt, which gets followed later in the same letter with this improvement: "Nor height, nor depth, nor any other creature, shall be able to separate us from the love of God, which is in Christ Jesus our Lord." (Rom. 8: 39.) That is better than his first, but this still fails to put into words the reality and overwhelming nature of Christ's radiance of love.

Paul tries in another letter, 1 Cor 2:9: "But as it is written, Eye hath not seen, nor ear heard, neither have entered into the heart of man, the things which God hath prepared for them that love him." That language is coming from a man who was "caught up to the third heaven." (2 Cor. 12: 2.) He returns saying essentially that he can't put it into words.[321]

John uses these words in 1 Jn 4:16: "And we have known and believed the love that God hath to us. God is love; and he that dwelleth in love dwelleth in God, and God in him." That puts the equation on equal footing, making those who know Him to be loving, just as God is Himself love or loving. But it still does not capture the greatness of the love found in the Savior.

Here is yet another (my) attempt: His love will crush you. It will overwhelm and intimidate you. It will bring you involuntarily to your knees in adoration and humility. It is not possible to feel love of this kind from Him and remain aloof or unaffected. It brings you to awe, reverence and to the point of confessing, as Moses did: "Now, for this cause I know that man is nothing, which thing I never had supposed." (Moses 1: 10.)

And so if you receive the Second Comforter, you will join a sorority and fraternity of those who have both knelt with humility and leapt with joy at His presence; all of whom have returned and searched the lexicon of their languages and concluded that man is not capable of

---

[321]The words of Section 76 were given by revelation, and put the three heavenly degrees into language. We quoted some of the closing words above, but the section ends with a larger explanation: "But great and marvelous are the works of the Lord, and the mysteries of his kingdom which he showed unto us, which surpass all understanding in glory, and in might, and in dominion; Which he commanded us we should not write while we were yet in the Spirit, and are not lawful for man to utter; **Neither is man capable to make them known, for they are only to be seen and understood by the power of the Holy Spirit**, which God bestows on those who love him, and purify themselves before him; To whom he grants this privilege of seeing and knowing for themselves." (vs. 114-117, emphasis added.)

making them known. In our current state, the Lord reserves some instruction to dispense Himself. This is one of those things which can be learned but cannot be taught. From it, however, you will gain an appreciation of the meaning of the scriptures. And though the words fail, you will retain an understanding of what the words are attempting to convey.

You will generally not be able to tell anyone, except for close family members, about these things; although if commanded to do so, you must. These mysteries are given to you only if you have the willingness and ability to honor the requirement that "you shall not impart" of them to others. Only the Prophet is authorized to declare doctrine in this dispensation for the Church. And so you are not permitted to take upon you the right to teach anything the Church does not teach. Among you and your friends, associates or neighbors, there will appear to be nothing particularly noteworthy about you. Your opinions will be disregarded, just as they were before. People having less understanding will be your boss at work, your partner in businesses, your presiding authority in your ward, or your superior in civic organizations. They will not, and should not, defer to you because of your experiences. They should continue to treat you just as they did before. The things of the Spirit have little value in the affairs of men. The world does not and will not value them. Therefore having them does nothing here. This is between you and God. It must remain so.

You may find, however, on occasion a spiritually sensitive soul detects something about you and begins to inquire of you. There won't be many of these, if any. But some people whose own spirits are attuned to the infinite may gravitate to you and seek from you answers to their inquiries. For them, when moved upon by the Spirit to do so, answering their limited inquiries is appropriate, but only if you are not trying to "set yourself up as a light" and thereby practice priestcraft. In 2 Ne 26: 29 we read: "He commandeth that there shall be no priestcrafts; for, behold, priestcrafts are that men preach and set themselves up for a light unto the world, that they may get gain and praise of the world; but they seek not the welfare of Zion." If you love God, and obey His commandments, then you have no need to seek recognition from the world. Gain, praise, recognition and ambition are contrary to the things of God. Therefore, trading in spiritual things as a matter of commerce is just plain wrong. Whatever you do with whatever you are given should be for Zion's welfare, and not your self interest.[322] The inquirer must come to you, not you to them. And you do not get to impose anything on anyone. Without a question and constraint from the Spirit to reply, there must be no answer offered.

Alma does not say you cannot impart at all, ever, under any circumstances. Rather, he conditions imparting to those who have the required diligence and heed to receive them.[323] That instruction has a rule: Do not impart. And an exception: Only do so when there is sufficient heed and diligence on the part of the one to whom you pass along information. Even then, however, it remains the exclusive prerogative of the Prophet, as President of the High Priesthood, alone to declare *new* doctrine in this dispensation. To the extent you declare any new doctrine when answering an inquiry, you are out of harmony with the instructions given by the Lord in scripture. Therefore, you should not impart matters of new doctrine at any time to any person under any circumstances. If that is not how you approach sacred things, then you are unworthy of them and they will not be given to you.

There is a great difference, however, between declaring new doctrine, and bearing testimony. Declaring new doctrine is not appropriate with the current state of scripture. During the Millennium

---

[322]This book is not written for praise or recognition. Rather, this has been written with considerable reluctance to discharge an obligation imposed upon the author.

[323]Alma 12: 9 instructs anyone receiving mysteries of God that "they shall not impart only according to the portion of his word which he doth grant unto the children of men, according to the heed and diligence which they give unto him." This would normally be a decision made by the Prophet and First Presidency, and not by you.

that will change, of course.[324] For now, however, there is an appropriate and necessary limitation on who can declare doctrine. Were it to be otherwise, we would return to the confusion in the days of Hiram Page with his peep stone, leading to a schism in the Church.

Within the process of receiving great truths there is also some degree of loneliness and isolation. The common lament of being a stranger and sojourner on the earth[325] will become your lament, too.

The Second Comforter will not pay your bills, prevent you from aging, or relieve you of trials and difficulties. But mortality will take on a different light. The difficulties here can be viewed against a more certain background of the coming eternities. This life is a time to be tested and tried and in which developing spiritual abilities is possible in ways not possible in the pre-existence. Living here, with all the insecurities and uncertainties of life, with all the frailties and pains of mortality, is a wonderful and brief opportunity. It is only here you can risk sacrifice for a cause or death for a cause worth dying for. An immortal spirit or a resurrected being with body and spirit inseparably connected[326] cannot risk death, pain or injury for a cause. As a result, the place where the greatest development can take place is this changeable, transient, and painful second estate.

---

[324]See, e.g., D&C 84: 98: "Until all shall know me, who remain, even from the least unto the greatest, and shall be filled with the knowledge of the Lord, and shall see eye to eye, and shall lift up their voice, and with the voice together sing this new song." See also Jer. 31: 34: "And they shall teach no more every man his neighbour, and every man his brother, saying, Know the Lord: for they shall all know me, from the least of them unto the greatest of them, saith the Lord: for I will forgive their iniquity, and I will remember their sin no more."

[325]See, e.g., Heb. 11: 13 "These all died in faith, not having received the promises, but having seen them afar off, and were persuaded of them, and embraced them, and confessed that they were strangers and pilgrims on the earth."

[326]See, e.g., D&C 93: 33: "For man is spirit. The elements are eternal, and spirit and element, inseparably connected, receive a fulness of joy."

It is because people have been aware of these things in times past that they have been willing to be "tortured, not accepting deliverance; that they might obtain a better resurrection:" (Heb. 11: 35.) It was as a result of seeing these things, that Alma told Amulek they should not stop the killing of the innocent women and children who were believers. Alma said the Spirit told him: "I must not stretch forth mine hand; for behold the Lord receiveth them up unto himself, in glory; and he doth suffer that they may do this thing, or that the people may do this thing unto them, according to the hardness of their hearts, that the judgments which he shall exercise upon them in his wrath may be just; and the blood of the innocent shall stand as a witness against them, yea, and cry mightily against them at the last day." (Alma 14: 11.)

As perspectives change, the challenges of life are seen differently and in a broader context. What was before an unthinkable difficulty now becomes endurable. And the attitudes and reactions of prophets in scripture become something understandable in practice rather than just statements of philosophical truisms, interesting morality tales or noble theories. You can imagine yourself, for the first time, making those same difficult life choices. You can endure the things of this life with greater tolerance.

Receiving the Second Comforter does not make you a scholar. It may confer knowledge upon you of some things, but they are entirely otherworldly and have no scholarly value. Since they are forbidden to be revealed, they cannot be published. Since they pertain to eternity, they have no market value here. Since they are not able to please the carnal mind, they are not useful to others even if you were willing to share them.

You will not pick up any skills as a result. No second language is conferred, and no understanding can be shared beyond certainty of God's existence and Christ's status as Redeemer of Mankind.

People in Fast and Testimony meetings say that they "know" Christ lives. When, therefore, you make a similar statement, the full import of what that means when you speak it is lost in the din of others using the same words. Yet your meaning will be markedly different than others when using the same words, and you and the Lord will know that.

Having a witness of Christ as resurrected Lord gives you an apostolic witness. However, it *does not* make you an Apostle. There have been many who received the Second Comforter who have never held the office of Apostle. Recall that Paul recounts a list which includes "above five hundred" who saw Christ between His resurrection and ascension.[327] And in Paul's list he omits mention of Mary, who saw Him first in the Garden outside His tomb. From the lengthy list of these witnesses, only twelve were Apostles at any given time, and only fourteen of them were ever Apostles. Similarly, in the visit among the Nephites discussed in this work, over two-thousand five-hundred saw Him the first day. Many more, perhaps thousands, saw Him the next day. Yet from among all these witnesses there were only twelve chosen as Apostles. The witness is one thing, and the priesthood office is another. For ordination to the Apostleship, the requirement has always been the same: "And no man taketh this honour unto himself, but he that is called of God, as was Aaron." (Heb. 5: 4.) So it remains today. No one can assume any right, office, or entitlement no matter what their testimony or experiences. Unless they are called, an apostolic witness is simply a matter of individual testimony and not a point of public privilege. It remains a private matter.[328] Although you may be asked by the Spirit to bear testimony from time to time in selective settings and before selective audiences, you are not suddenly called to do more.

---

[327] 1 Cor. 15: 4-8: "And that he was buried, and that he rose again the third day according to the scriptures: And that he was seen of Cephas, then of the twelve: After that, he was seen of above five hundred brethren at once; of whom the greater part remain unto this present, but some are fallen asleep. After that, he was seen of James; then of all the apostles. And last of all he was seen of me also, as of one born out of due time."

[328] If the author had not been asked to write this work, the author's own experience would have remained a private matter, as it was for years before the writing of this book.

Nor does possession of such a testimony make you greater than the Lord's Apostles. Christ's instruction on the status of His called, ordained and sustained Apostles is clear: "Blessed are ye if ye shall give heed unto the words of these twelve whom I have chosen from among you to minister unto you, and to be your servants;" (3 Ne. 12: 1.) And in our own day the instruction has been repeated: "And the arm of the Lord shall be revealed; and the day cometh that they who will not hear the voice of the Lord, neither the voice of his servants, neither give heed to the words of the prophets and apostles, shall be cut off from among the people;" (D&C 1: 14.) It is a perilous thing to attempt to put yourself between the Lord's Apostles and the Lord. He called them and He expects our sustaining faith and confidence in them. None of us will ever progress to the point that we do not need Apostles and Prophets to guide us. So, if you assume you can acquire independence and superiority from obtaining such a witness you should disabuse yourself of that notion. Our salvation is related to the heed and diligence we give to the Lord's anointed ministers. And evil speaking of them, assuming superiority to them, and trying to bring others away from them will inevitably lead to your condemnation.

After the Brother of Jared received his audience with Christ, his life's challenges did not change. They continued along in the same dramatic-at-times and mundane-at-times way as before. The lighted stones were used to make the interiors of the ships serviceable.[329] But the boats had to be boarded and outfitted for a lengthy journey.[330] Then

---

[329]Ether 6: 2 "For it came to pass after the Lord had prepared the stones which the brother of Jared had carried up into the mount, the brother of Jared came down out of the mount, and he did put forth the stones into the vessels which were prepared, one in each end thereof; and behold, they did give light unto the vessels."

[330]Ether 6:4: "And it came to pass that when they had prepared all manner of food, that thereby they might subsist upon the water, and also food for their flocks and herds, and whatsoever beast or animal or fowl that they should carry with them — and it came to pass that when they had done all these things they got aboard of their vessels or barges, and set forth into the

they had to be taken on a 344-day[331] journey in a tempest-tossed[332] voyage to another continent. Certainly during this time normal human hygiene would be challenging, and the confinement of people to such narrow quarters, along with the disturbances of this kind of motion for 11 months would be unpleasant and alternatively threatening and boring. The participants, including the Brother of Jared, would no doubt wonder at their ultimate survival in this kind of on-going peril.

To cope with the stresses of the voyage, the occupants of the vessels resorted to daily worship and singing. In this, the Brother of Jared led by example.[333] After some 11 months of this circumstance, the party landed on the shores of a new land.

Though the account becomes quite cryptic about the events unfolding thereafter in the Brother of Jared's life, he seems to have lived thereafter with more limited spiritual experiences. None are mentioned. Perhaps none occurred. If they did occur, however, their significance paled in comparison to what had gone on before, since they held insufficient relevance to the record as abridged by Moroni. What does get mentioned is the landing, and the overwhelming gratitude

---

sea, commending themselves unto the Lord their God."

[331]Ether 6:11: "And thus they were driven forth, three hundred and forty and four days upon the water."

[332]Ether 6:5-6: "And it came to pass that the Lord God caused that there should be a furious wind blow upon the face of the waters, towards the promised land; and thus they were tossed upon the waves of the sea before the wind. And it came to pass that they were many times buried in the depths of the sea, because of the mountain waves which broke upon them, and also the great and terrible tempests which were caused by the fierceness of the wind."

[333]Ether 6:9: "And they did sing praises unto the Lord; yea, the brother of Jared did sing praises unto the Lord, and he did thank and praise the Lord all the day long; and when the night came, they did not cease to praise the Lord."

accompanying the landing,[334] and the labor involved in developing a new civilization.[335] The Brother of Jared's family life gets only spare mention, but Jared's sons not only get numbered but named as well. The Brother of Jared's own children are, initially, neither named nor numbered.[336] Later, as his life is about to end, this is corrected and brief mention is made.[337] This was in keeping with cultural norms for the Jaredite culture.

From this record it appears the Brother of Jared, whose visions were perhaps the greatest of any prophet's in history, led a mundane existence after his theophany without great deference by his peers. His audience with Christ did not qualify him to gain any great advantages in the struggles of daily life. He continued his life consistent with the cultural norms of his time and setting.

In Ether 6:17, we read this passing comment: "And they were taught to walk humbly before the Lord; and they were also taught from on high." This statement does not clarify if the teaching from "on high" consisted of the Spirit giving inspiration, or from further heavenly visitations. Whether it was the one or the other, the events were apparently not significant enough to justify preserving them in the record. The development of the culture and population is mentioned in

---

[334]Ether 6:12: "And they did land upon the shore of the promised land. And when they had set their feet upon the shores of the promised land they bowed themselves down upon the face of the land, and did humble themselves before the Lord, and did shed tears of joy before the Lord, because of the multitude of his tender mercies over them."

[225]Ether 6:13: "And it came to pass that they went forth upon the face of the land, and began to till the earth."

[336]Ether 6:14-15: "And Jared had four sons; and they were called Jacom, and Gilgah, and Mahah, and Orihah. And the brother of Jared also begat sons and daughters."

[337]Ether 6:20: "And accordingly the people were gathered together. Now the number of the sons and the daughters of the brother of Jared were twenty and two souls; and the number of sons and daughters of Jared were twelve, he having four sons."

passing,[338] followed by the final report of the Brother of Jared's life in Ether 6: 19: "And the brother of Jared began to be old, and saw that he must soon go down to the grave; wherefore he said unto Jared: Let us gather together our people that we may number them, that we may know of them what they will desire of us before we go down to our graves." What follows is a discussion about having a king, which the Brother of Jared opposes. But his opposition fails to persuade the majority and the king is appointed anyway.[339] It is in connection with the attempts to name a king, that the Brother of Jared's sons finally get named in the text.

The life of the man who received one of the greatest theophanies of all time ends with this account: "And it came to pass that Jared died, and his brother also." (Ether 6:29.)

From this account, we can learn much of what receiving the Second Comforter does and does not mean. There are still oceans to cross, towns to build, families to raise, difficulties to overcome and lessons to teach. These will be done while occupying your position in society, and without any great fanfare or notice. So you mustn't think of this process as an answer to life's difficulties or struggles. It is not. Your advice will be ignored, or not sought. And that is as it should be.

Even father Abraham, who had numerous revelations, was left to himself to decide some of his life's great struggles. One of them is commented upon by E. Douglas Clark in his article: *Cedars and Stars: Enduring Symbols of Cosmic Kingship in Abraham's Encounter with Pharaoh*, found in *Astronomy, Papyrus, and Covenant*. Edited by John Gee and Brian

---

[338]Ether 6: 18: "And it came to pass that they began to spread upon the face of the land, and to multiply and to till the earth; and they did wax strong in the land."

[339]Ether 6: 22-24: "And it came to pass that the people desired of them that they should anoint one of their sons to be a king over them. And now behold, this was grievous unto them. And the brother of Jared said unto them: Surely this thing leadeth into captivity. But Jared said unto his brother: Suffer them that they may have a king. And therefore he said unto them: Choose ye out from among our sons a king, even whom ye will."

M. Hauglid. Provo: FARMS. He writes about Abraham's trip to Egypt, on p. 38:

> Ironically, Abraham's steps were now leading him away from the land that God had promised. What a trial of faith it must have been to finally arrive at the land of promise only to find a grievous famine. Had it been only Abraham, it is easy to imagine him staying put and toughing it out there in the promised land, for one of the constants of his exemplary life was obedience at all costs. But he also had to consider the welfare of his wife and the saints whom he led. And so, he says in his autobiography in the Book of Abraham, "I ... concluded to go down to Egypt" (Abraham 2: 21). "Concluded," he says, implying that this was a deliberate decision he alone had arrived at, and probably not without some difficulty. For despite the many prior revelations he had received, no divine direction was now forthcoming. Abraham seemed forced to take matters into his own hands and head for Egypt, where crops depended not on rainfall but on the annual flooding of the Nile. Only when Abraham arrived at the border of Egypt did the Lord finally speak.

As with Abraham, so with all who receive an audience with God. There will be times of struggle and times when no direction from God will answer the difficult questions you will have to face. And so, nothing will change.

And yet, you will know for certain God lives. You will have certainty of that knowledge for yourself and not be dependent upon any creature under heaven for it. Much more importantly, you will also be certain the course of your life is acceptable to God. As a result, you will enter into "rest" in the sense of the term used in scripture. Reading about the Brother of Jared's "rest," or Nephi's "rest," gives you a good idea of how that term is used in scripture. It does not mean retirement, nor does it excuse you from this life's labors, difficulties, challenges or struggles. But you will know that God lives and your life is acceptable to Him. As a result of that knowledge, everything will change.

The definition of eternal life was given by the Savior and recorded by John, who wrote: "These words spake Jesus, and lifted up his eyes to heaven, and said, Father, the hour is come; glorify thy Son, that thy Son also may glorify thee: As thou hast given him power over all flesh, that he should give eternal life to as many as thou hast given him. And **this is life eternal, that they might know thee the only true God, and Jesus Christ, whom thou hast sent.**" (John 17: 1-3, emphasis added.) To know God is eternal life. To know God in the fullest of the sense[340] in this life is to receive the Second Comforter. Therefore this, yet again, is an invitation to receive this added witness and knowledge. From it you gain eternal life. As a result, all eternity will change.

Christ is the keeper of the gate to opening the heavens. He is the steward over the revelations of God. As He declared in revelation:

And he that will contend against the word of the Lord, let him be accursed; and he that shall deny these things, let him be accursed; for unto them will I show no greater things,[341] saith Jesus Christ; for I am he who speaketh. And at my command

---

[340]Of course, it is possible to have knowledge of Him through faith, and without the Second Comforter, as well. As King Benjamin asked: "For how knoweth a man the master whom he has not served, and who is a stranger unto him, and is far from the thoughts and intents of his heart?" (Mosiah 5: 13.) Implicit in this rhetorical question is the possibility of knowing Him by serving Him, i.e. keeping His commandments. Without keeping His commandments first, and thereby gaining a knowledge of Him in that manner, you cannot receive the Second Comforter. Through keeping His commandments, you incline your thoughts to Him and you thereby incline your heart toward Him. All of which King Benjamin is teaching in his questions here, and which we have discussed earlier in this book.

[341]Why should anyone who will not believe what has been given in scripture be entitled to receive more of the Word of God? Until people have accepted all that God has revealed, it is unreasonable to expect that He would now reveal more to you, and even less reasonable to expect that He would yet reveal many great and important things pertaining to the Kingdom of God to the unbeliever. (*Cf.* Article 9, Articles of Faith.)

the heavens are opened and are shut;[342] and at my word the earth shall shake; and at my command the inhabitants thereof shall pass away, even so as by fire. And he that believeth not my words believeth not my disciples;[343] and if it so be that I do not speak, judge ye; for ye shall know that it is I that speaketh, at the last day. But he that believeth these things which I have spoken, him will I visit with the manifestations of my Spirit,[344] and he shall know and bear record. For because of my Spirit he shall know that these things are true; for it persuadeth men to do good. And whatsoever thing persuadeth men to do good is of me; for good cometh of none save it be of me. I am the same that leadeth men to all good; he that will not believe my words will not believe me — that I am; and he that will not believe me will not believe the Father who sent me. For behold, I am the Father, I am the light, and the life, and the truth of the world. (Ether 4: 8-12.)

This progression in reasoning is also found in the oath and covenant of the priesthood, where receiving the Lord's ministers is equated with receiving the Lord.[345] Receiving the Lord is equated with receiving the Father. When you receive a prophet in the name of a prophet, you

---

[342]That is, He is the one who determines when the conditions have been met to qualify one to have the heavens opened to them.

[343]Whether we will accept it or not, there is a connection between accepting Christ's chosen ministers as His ministers and then qualifying to receive more. Those who reject, judge, condemn, belittle or disregard the ministers cannot please the Master who called and ordained them. Evil speaking of the Lord's anointed is as reprehensible an offense as evil speaking of their Master.

[344]This calls to mind Christ's parable which taught the lesson: "For unto every one that hath shall be given, and he shall have abundance: but from him that hath not shall be taken away even that which he hath." (Matt. 25: 29.) That is, to those who believe in and accept the witness of others found in scripture, they qualify to receive yet a further witness. But those who reject the scriptures will not qualify to receive anything further, and will lose what they might have received, had they believed the scriptures.

[345]D&C 84: 35-40.

receive a prophet's reward.[346] You will never receive an audience with the prophet's Master if you are unwilling to receive the prophet as a prophet.

There is no magic in any of these things. And your life will not suddenly become magical because you have seen the Lord. Life will continue as it was before. You still have meetings to attend and callings to fill and bills to pay. So you might ask yourself *why* you are seeking this witness. If you are doing so in the hope of getting something for this life, then you will be disappointed. It has no material value here. If you are doing so because you love God and want to know Him, you will not be disappointed. He is more glorious and loving than words can tell. He will teach you feelings of such tenderness toward Him, as words cannot express. You will learn He is love. As a result, your understanding will change and you will change.

---

[346]Matt. 10: 41: "He that receiveth a prophet in the name of a prophet shall receive a prophet's reward; and he that receiveth a righteous man in the name of a righteous man shall receive a righteous man's reward."

Chapter Twenty

TESTIMONY, SAYINGS AND CONCLUSION

C*hrist lives and comforts His followers today, just as He promised and did anciently. He is the Second Comforter. I know He lives, for I have seen Him. He has ministered to me.*[347]

There is nothing special about me. Many of my personal failures have been set out in this book. There are many other personal failures not mentioned here, but which I freely admit occurred. Despite all my personal failings, I have followed Him and have faith in Him. He has accepted my poor sacrifices. This book is not just

---

[347]The full content of these things are of course personal, never intended for public display, and not needed as a part of this text. This is about bearing testimony of the process itself and the already declared doctrines. I am adding my weak voice to those of others who proclaim this to be true. This is not about personal matters, the revelation of which would amount to improperly profaning the sacred, nor is it about preaching any new doctrines, which is altogether inappropriate.

about His Gospel. It is a personal account of what it has taken to get from being a stranger to God, to being a fellow-citizen with the Saints of God. I love being among the Latter-day Saints.

I have not written this book to call attention to myself but to call attention to these teachings and this part of the restored doctrines of Christ's Gospel and to bear testimony of the truth of these things. I am irrelevant except insofar as I can testify to what He does for us. It is the Lord and His promises which are relevant. I have been asked by Him to write this and have done so because of that request. The request has been a trial and fearsome to undertake. But who am I to withstand Him? If it pleases Him to have this written, then my personal discomfort in writing about it is unimportant.

The most significant thing about this account is I am nothing and nobody. It is unlikely you have ever heard of me. It is my obscurity above all else that is evidence God is no respecter of persons, and will allow anyone, in any circumstance, to approach Him on equal footing. You can do so.

It must be made clear I hold no keys, have no salvation to offer anyone, and must point you to others who have been chosen by Christ to hold keys and the power of salvation. The ordinances of the Gospel, and in particular the authority to minister in the Temples, are contained in the Church of Jesus Christ of Latter-day Saints and nowhere else. The President of the High Priesthood, who is the Prophet of the Church, alone has the right to exercise the keys in a fullness. If you would be saved, you must accept the Gospel and its ordinances. This means you must accept Christ's authorized ministers. They will lead you in the path of salvation and exaltation. I am a lay member of that Church and nothing more.

What I have done is to follow that path to the extent I have been able. I clearly have not been perfect in this effort. But the Lord, who judges the heart, has accepted my efforts. As a result I am able to testify it is true. If this book has distracted you from this path, then I have failed in my intent and in this effort. If, however, you realize just how vital the connection is between you and Christ through His Restored Church, then you know where you must look for saving truths and saving ordinances. In these can be found the power of godliness that can empower anyone to see the face of God and live.

1 Ne 14:10 tells us, in words from an angel, quoted by Nephi: "And he said unto me: Behold there are save two churches only; the one is the church of the Lamb of God, and the other is the church of the devil; wherefore, whoso belongeth not to the church of the Lamb of God belongeth to that great church, which is the mother of abominations; and she is the whore of all the earth." There are false theories, false religions, false teachers in the world, and even false beliefs within the body of Saints. The world offers you an almost endless selection of alternative ways of thinking about God and the meaning and purpose of life. As the angel has declared, there really are only two alternatives: One is correct and will lead to God. All the others are a distraction and will not do so.

This book attempts to put into words why this is so. The Lord is reaching down to mankind and offering all of us, equally, an opportunity to know Him. He is remarkably liberal and democratic in His offering. Anyone, regardless of age, position, sex, nation, or race is invited to come to Him, so He can come to them. But it is through a single, strait, narrow path we come to Him. If there is any other way, I know nothing of it. The path I am following teaches there is only one way.

To the extent any ideology or system of beliefs distracts you from this single, strait, narrow path, it is part of the "church of the devil" the angel warns us against. Such things are an invitation from the "great whore" to come and compromise yourself away from love and fidelity to God. Single-mindedness will get you back to God's presence. And that single-mindedness must be in the path which He has offered to you.

This is not to say other faiths, philosophies and thought systems have no value. They have great value. Some of them offer insights which are of extraordinary use in moving you closer to God. If other faiths did not have any truths, they would never appeal to the minds of men. All faiths contain some truths. All religions have something of value to offer. But as this work has attempted to convey, those other offerings must be measured and accepted inside the context of the Restored Gospel of Jesus Christ. The Gospel is not measured against them. They are measured against it.

All truth belongs to Christ's Gospel, as we have seen. But truths from any source must all be weighed against what Christ taught us. He was and is the living embodiment of a fullness of truth. He lived as an example of the fullness of truth. He taught us how to acquire the fullness for ourselves. The revealed lesson on His life in D&C 93:19 announces the purpose of His deliberate life and example: "I give unto you these sayings that you may understand and know how to worship, and know what you worship, that you may come unto the Father in my name, and in due time receive of his fullness."

We are benefitted from accepting all the truth we can find. There should be humility about this, too. Perfunctory rejection or condescending treatment of things others hold as sacred can result in overlooking many great truths which God has placed here for us. Some belief systems have great truths to offer us, and they understand some principles better than we generally do. We shouldn't be hasty in rejecting these things. But when any truth from any corner presents itself to you for your consideration, the truth must meet the test that it fits into the established framework of truths already contained in the Gospel. If it contradicts the Gospel's principles, then you can know it is false. All proposed new truths must be weighed against the revealed and Restored Gospel of Christ as taught in the scriptures of the Restoration. Truths must fit comfortably within the rites and ordinances of the Gospel, for these rites are also scripture and revelation.

The path to receiving the Second Comforter comes only to those who follow Christ's teachings contained in the Restored Gospel. He did not restore the rites, ordinances, rituals, and teachings of His Gospel to then have you look to other sources for foundational material. He restored it as the means for returning to Him and being redeemed from the Fall. If you attempt to build a path back to Him while abandoning the foundation He established, you build on the sand He warned you about. Build, therefore, on the Rock of Heaven.[348]

You already have the truth since you are a member of the Church of Jesus Christ of Latter-day Saints. But you must look at Christ's Gospel much more carefully if you want to realize all of what it offers to you. This book attempts to help you to see this. If it has done so, it has succeeded in its purpose.

Do not think having insight into these things means you will receive results in an instant. The gifts available from God are of such deep import, time and experience are required to find them. Careful, solemn and ponderous thought is necessary to accompany your walk in this path. Hopefully this book will help you with the journey. The path takes specific growth and development which does not happen overnight, and none of the steps or experiences are superfluous. They are all given to everyone who seeks, because there are laws which are irrevocably ordained upon obedience to which these blessings are predicated. Many of them require internal changes before you move to the next step. How quickly you are willing or able to change is left to you. But you should not think you can reasonably make those internal changes in a single year. It took me over thirty years, and I sought them diligently.

---

[348]That is one of Christ's names. See, e.g., Moses 7: 53: "And the Lord said: Blessed is he through whose seed Messiah shall come; for he saith — I am Messiah, the King of Zion, the Rock of Heaven,"

In words well worn in testimony meetings of every ward in the Church, I proclaim: I, too, know Christ lives! I have seen Him. I know He is the universal Savior of all mankind, whether they know Him or not. Whether they accept Him or not, He died for them. He suffered for them. He atoned for your sins, if you will receive Him. He paid a price for mankind which was infinite in scope and has the ability to heal every wound, repair every failure, forgive every wrong, and overcome every shortcoming. Much of that He will do without regard to whether we accept or reject Him. But the fullness of the blessings available through the price He paid is provided only to those who accept and follow Him.

Before the final end comes, His love will overwhelm every heart and bring every person to their grateful knees where they will all universally submit to His rule and acknowledge their debt to Him. Every knee will bow and every tongue will confess He is our Savior. The "compulsion" of that confession will come as we are clearly shown what He did for us. No one will be able to withhold gratitude to Him.

He is the Light and the Life. No one comes forth from the grave at the time of the resurrection, except by Him. His universal acclaim will come because of His radiant love, and we will finally and clearly see the great debt we owe to Him. The tongue of man fails when attempting to describe the Lord's love for mankind. This is why prophets speak of Him with the eloquence of few words. His accomplishments are best proclaimed in few words: He is Love. He is Charity. He is Kindness. He is Mercy.

The Second Comforter is the heritage of the Saints. He is as available to the least of the Saints as He is to the greatest. Joseph tried to have the Saints understand this and taught this principle throughout his ministry. These promises are to be taken literally. They are not cunningly devised fables. Nor are these blessings confined to the few who are called to preside in the Church. Often presiding authorities are

no better than the rank and file members in obtaining these things.[349]
The laws upon which these blessings are predicated are universal,
without short-cut, and must be obtained through obedience. No one
gets relief from the principles. Rank, station, family, or Church position
does not change anything. Similarly, lack of rank, lack of station, lack of
family or lack of Church position does not limit either. They are the
common right of every man, woman and child who receives the
ordinances of the Gospel of Christ. If you are willing to accept Christ's
Gospel on its own terms and exercise faith to receive these things, then
you too are called to the throne of grace to receive Him, and He to
receive you.

You may not realize just how high His regard is for us. He died for
us. He wants to redeem all of us. He suffered for us and thereby
perfected His capacity to love us. Infinite suffering by Him has
produced infinite love in Him for us. That price binds Him to you in a
way and at a depth which you will only realize when you are confronted
by Him. You will find there love which crushes you, because you
cannot love on that order in return. His devotion to us is beyond
comprehension. Words fail when we humans try to explain. It is best
put in Philip's words to Nathanael: "Come and see." (John 1: 46.) Don't
trust me. Come and see for yourself. Don't be dependent upon others
for your knowledge of Him. Come and get your own. I wish all
mankind knew Him and had no need to say to each other: "know the
Lord." From the least to the greatest, I wish all of us knew Him. Like

---

[349]There is an interesting account of President David O. McKay's
struggles in *David O. McKay and the Rise of Modern Mormonism* discussing his
spiritual growth. "[David O. McKay] had misgivings that stemmed from
unresolved doubts about the work he was being called to perform." (p. 6), and
this while functioning as an apostle. Quoting Hugh Nibley, they write: "[David
O. McKay's] whole talk was about how skeptical he had always been about the
gospel. He said he had never believed it for most of his life and was very
skeptical." (p. 7). Despite this, President McKay grew into a towering leader,
inspired Prophet, and Church President. That readable book tracks President
McKay's growth and makes it clear he was granted no favors allowing him to
receive progress without effort.

the gathering at the Temple in Bountiful, I wish He were commonly visiting us. He can and has promised He will. When we are prepared, He will come to us.

Shed your sins and doubts and come to Him. You will only gain the confidence to do so by repenting and obeying. He is real, He lives, and He is willing to receive you. All of you are welcome, whatever circumstances you find yourself in here in mortality. Your circumstances are His gift to you, because they are uniquely fitted to refine you so you can return to Him. Don't reject them as distractions, but use them to propel yourself upward. Gravity is at first the enemy of the infant, but soon becomes the play-thing by which all children learn to run. The faster they recover from the forward fall, the faster they run. Learn from your life's specific gravity to run back to Him. Be grateful for your lot in life. It was carefully given to you for your blessing and development.

I believe many of you already have received a personal invitation from Him through the Spirit to receive these things. Many of you have heard that still, small, and sometimes distant voice, beckoning you to come fully to Him. Few people respond to it because they lack the specific direction needed to allow them to respond meaningfully. This book has been an attempt to provide the direction I wished I had received years earlier and which conforms to my experience.

Perhaps had this book existed thirty-two years ago, it would have helped me. Perhaps it would not. Perhaps, instead, these things are best pursued without mentor, without guidance and as a solitary undertaking. I do not know the answer. Perhaps this book will prove to be a great help to some few who receive it in the way it is intended. Only time (and you) will answer that. This book provides nothing not already available in published works. It does not try to advance new material, but to gather existing material into a convenient place and to confirm, by personal testimony, the truthfulness of the material. The most important material of all comes from the Book of Mormon. It holds more truth and light than any other single volume of scripture.

In my quest for these things, there has been no mentor to call upon apart from the scriptures and the Spirit. This work is an attempt to provide for others what was lacking in the available curriculum and Church manuals for me. Given the criteria for receiving the Second Comforter, however, I cannot be certain any instruction from any person can help another. We all must put the oil in our own lamps. Someone can tell you how to do so, but everyone, individually, must actually gather the oil solely for themselves. These things cannot be rushed.

I am certain you can learn anything you are willing to learn. It is up to you to determine how much you are willing to receive, and whether you are willing to abide the conditions to receive it. The successes or failures of others around you cannot prevent you from having a fullness of knowledge in your life. The Lord has so organized things that when any person is ready to receive, the Lord is willing to teach.

It should be clear by now that the Church of Jesus Christ of Latter-day Saints is the sole custodian of the authority from Christ to minister in the ordinances of salvation. The mysteries of God are received by covenant and by ordinance. If you are not willing to receive the ordinances and to obey the commandments, then you are not going to qualify to receive the Second Comforter. Anyone can receive them but must do so through the gate which Christ has erected for entry into His presence.

Christ organized the Church anew through the Prophet Joseph Smith to provide the way for mankind to receive these things, again. Without the ordinances of the Gospel you cannot qualify for the kind of light and truth that comes from an audience with Christ. Those qualifying ordinances are exclusively available through the priesthood and keys held solely by the Church of Jesus Christ of Latter-day Saints. It is not necessary for you to hold those keys. Someone needs to hold them and to administer the ordinances to you. But once you have received the ordinances, it is up to you to continue in the path until the fullness is obtained. The rites themselves are preliminary, qualifying steps which must first be obtained in faith. But the rites are pointing you to the real thing. The rites are not the real thing. They are the promise to obtain the real thing. The real thing is received by obedience to the laws and ordinances.

There is opposition to the Restored Gospel as relentless and opposed to faith on the one hand as Christ is persistent in offering faith on the other. They hang in equal balance. You must choose between belief and unbelief. There will always be another explanation for everything in the Gospel. There are alternative explanations for Joseph's mission and accomplishments. There are rationalizations for why Joseph was not called of God, or if called, why he failed in his task. Or, if Joseph didn't fail in his task, then the Church officers following in his footsteps have failed in *their* tasks. Or, if past Church officers did not fail, then the current ones are in the process of failing. See, it doesn't really matter when and where the argument convinces you to go away from faith. The opposition only cares that at some point, somewhere along the path before you receive the Second Comforter, you accept some rationalization taking your feet off the path. One step to the side will keep your view on this side of the veil. Thin as a razor, but straight and true, the path lies before you. The opposition is trying to take you to the side, so you cannot see through the narrow opening. If you are willing to ignore the opposition, you can get along the path much quicker.

Christian Churches, irrespective of denomination, all hold some truths. Non-Christian faiths also have truths. Some of these have great truths, which can transform lives and make people better and more godlike. But they will not bring you the Second Comforter because that is not their aim.

The Christian world, however, lacked "the power of godliness" when Joseph Smith was called to be the Prophet of the Restoration. Christ set in motion the Restoration to allow for the return of the "power of godliness" in a faith recognized and authorized by Him. That power resides in the priesthood ordinances administered exclusively by the Church of Jesus Christ of Latter-day Saints. It is not necessary to hold priesthood authority to receive the ordinances, for they are ministered to all, male and female, alike. Any convert can receive them, just as I, as a convert, have received them. Faithfulness alone decides if you will receive the offered ordinances. It is up to you to determine if you will receive them, and then whether you will keep them afterward. You must receive these ordinances and be obedient to them, or the promised Second Comforter is not available.

The rites of the priesthood, celebrated from baptism to the endowment and sealing, are all intended to bring you closer to God. All of them instruct you, line upon line, precept upon precept, in the way to converse with God through the veil. They prepare you in all things to receive further light and knowledge by conversing with the Lord through the veil.

The path back is lonely and cannot be shared. Each person must elect to choose whether they will return or not. Throughout the scriptures the Lord affirms and reaffirms "few there be that find it." Section 76's promise that these great mysteries are to be received "while in the flesh, that they may abide His presence in the world of glory" suggests these things *should* be received here. It suggests receiving them here may be needed in order to be able then to receive them in the world of glory.

We qualified in the pre-earth life for the things obtained here. What we receive in this life is an extension of and fulfillment of the promises we obtained before birth. The bounds of our habitation are set for us now, based upon what we did then. It appears clear this life will set bounds for us in the next life, as well. Given the risk we may be limiting our eternity by what we fail to receive here, it makes the most sense to receive as much as is possible while in mortality. It makes sense we should seek the face of God here, so it becomes our inheritance to receive that presence in the next life.[350]

---

[350]In making this statement I do not exclude the possibility that such blessings may still be obtained hereafter. There is some evidence to the

SAYINGS

The following thoughts are a reminder of the things we have covered and things subsequently implied:

-The things of God really are of deep import. Only time, experience, and careful, ponderous and solemn thoughts can find them out, provided, of course, there is a real desire to know the things of God accompanied by obedience to His commandments. If you don't desire them, you won't ask and won't receive. And if you do desire them, you will ask and you will obey. It is self-regulated, in that sense. Everyone decides for themselves just how much of an advantage in the world to come they are willing to acquire here.

-Freedom or agency really means accountability. That is its chief, if not only, meaning. Unfortunately, because of political debate, it has assumed a much less rigorous meaning. We are free, therefore we are accountable before God for all our acts. The Atonement alone affords

---

contrary in Christ's parable about the laborers and their pay, where He suggests that those who begin here, even though they labor only on hour, will receive full pay. (See Mat. 20: 1-16.) Christ also taught: "He that receiveth a prophet in the name of a prophet shall receive a prophet's reward; and he that receiveth a righteous man in the name of a righteous man shall receive a righteous man's reward." (Matt. 10: 41.) Revelation in our day also affirms the principle that the varying gifts given the Saints include knowledge on the one hand, and faith because of the testimony of those with knowledge on the other hand: "For all have not every gift given unto them; for there are many gifts, and to every man is given a gift by the Spirit of God. To some is given one, and to some is given another, that all may be profited thereby. To some it is given by the Holy Ghost to know that Jesus Christ is the Son of God, and that he was crucified for the sins of the world. To others it is given to believe on their words, that they also might have eternal life if they continue faithful." (D&C 46: 11-14.) Therefore, "eternal life" may not be entirely dependent upon receiving this witness in mortality. Nevertheless, it seems foolhardy not to pursue the greatest principle of intelligence we can attain to here through our heed and diligence, as we are cautioned in Section 130: 18-19.

us relief from that accountability. Taking advantage of the Atonement for that purpose, however, does require us to obey Christ's conditions.

-It is not true that "seeing is believing." Rather, believing is to see. Belief will open your eyes. The Voice, three levels removed from us, is regained by your election to remove the veil which bars your hearing and your sight.

-It is a veil and not a wall you must pass through. You elect whether or not you will pass through.

-There is no one, other than you, who can make the decision to go forward. It is far more frightening to persist through the veil than to remain without a view of heaven.

-Revelation from heaven is also a revelation of yourself. For as you see Him, you see most clearly how very limited and dependent you are upon Him. You cannot be prideful after seeing yourself alongside Him.

-Heaven is steeped in ceremonial rites intended to preserve and declare the Glory of God and the wisdom of His acts. The depth, heights and majesty of His undertakings are beyond man's comprehension. Words fail in the attempt. It is best understood by seeing and not to be otherwise understood.

-God wants most for us to understand Him. He is as eager to meet with and touch us, as we should be to know and touch Him.

-God loves His children equally, but we love Him unequally in return. If we would love Him as He loves us, we would leap into His open arms and rejoice in the touch of our Lord.

-He bears seven wounds on His person: Two in His wrists, two in His palms, two in His feet, and one in His side. Seven is the symbolic number of completion or perfection. Seven wounds reflect the completion of His sacrifice and of that sacrifice's complete perfection.

-Christ's sacrifice has completely healed all that the Fall of Adam brought to pass. As Adam went before, so Christ came after, the one the antithesis of the other, and both making this creation a chiasm of Fall and Redemption. We stand in the center, where it is all in balance about us.

-The balance between Adam's Fall and Christ's sacrifice provides a neutral balance of opposites. We choose what we are willing to do with this balanced universe.

-We tip the scales by our choices, and by so doing, we change all eternity. We change eternity by the choices we make here.

-There is an eternal balance, with infinite results, hanging on our every choice. We stand in peril or stand in glory depending upon our every thought and deed.

-Five minutes of mortality are more precious than all the prior eternities of pre-earth life. Only here can you demonstrate the faith from which creation itself was born.

-Our failures are mourned in the corridors of heaven with groans for our shortcomings. We have angels and gods wishing our choices were always tipping the scale of balance in this life in favor of obedience to God.

-Our noble acts and righteous deeds are celebrated in joy and song in the corridors of heaven. As we choose God and His ways, the Hosanna Shout rings out in heaven for such choices.

-We are the place where eternity's conflicts are now being played out. We are the battleground between infinite good and infinite failure.

-Life is an open book test. We only need to realize the test is underway to be able to pass it.

-Joy cannot be found by subordinating the spirit to the flesh. Joy, peace and freedom come only by subordinating the flesh to the spirit.

-The meekness of the Lord as He supplicates us to follow Him is because of the great worth of souls. That great worth has been poured into us by the bitter cup from which He drank. Every person who has ever lived is an infinite creation.

-Within the coupling of the man and woman in the Lord there is found all eternity. They, together, are infinite. The Temple rites are intended to establish this infinite and eternal union.

-Adam and Eve were given by God to each other before death entered into creation. Had there been no Fall, the man and woman would have remained together forever.

-The eternal union of man and woman is a return to Eden before the Fall. The Temple and the ordinances found there are, for us, the return to Eden before the Fall and the completion of creation through the union of man and woman in an infinite covenant.

-Heaven does not need to await the afterlife, but you can be redeemed from the Fall here and now. Receiving the presence of God is to be redeemed from the Fall.

-The Millennium will happen as people prepare themselves for it. When the wheat is fully ripe, the Lord will return. You can receive Millennial blessings now, through the Second Comforter.

-It would do little good to have the Lord return if there were not people prepared for His presence awaiting Him. If that were to occur before people are prepared, the whole earth would be wasted at His coming.

-If you would have Him return, then you must prepare individually to abide His coming. When you are ready, He will return.

-There is nothing hidden but what will be made known, but it is up to you to be willing to see and receive what is hidden.

-God hides most things in plain sight. It is up to you, therefore, to be willing to draw back the veil and see them.

-The religiously blind refuse to see. Blindness born from religious error is the most recalcitrant form of the disease.

-Knowledge of the mysteries of godliness is obtained only through obedience to God. He ordained this method to make His greatest truths universally available to all His humble followers. If it were otherwise, we would all have to go to college to receive training for the ministry.

-Education is no real advantage in receiving light and truth from God. Humility is the only real, great advantage which any soul ever possesses.

-Since God is no respecter of persons, He has ordained truth to come to us without respect to persons. Whatever truths may exist, His true followers seek after these things and find they are freely given.

-In order to go forward, you must go back. Without a return to the humility and faith of childhood, you will not be able to see Him.

-When we elect to receive Him, He elects at that moment to receive us. We determine whether we are "elect" by our own election to receive Him.

-The proud will fail. Their failure will come as a natural consequence of their unfitness to be in God's presence. Their pride will keep them from doing what is required to be in His presence. Had Naaman not returned to wash himself seven times in the Jordan River, he would have died a leper. Many of us die lepers because we find such things as dipping in rivers childish. Too often we join Naaman in asking: "Are not Abana and Pharpar, rivers of Damascus, better than all the waters of Israel? May I not wash in them, and be clean?" And join him too in reacting: "So he turned and went away in a rage." (2 Kings 5: 12). Be humble enough to do as the prophets ask you and submit to the laws and ordinances of the Gospel. You will be healed if you do. For the Apostles and Prophets are Christ's chosen ministers.

-You must choose your world: this one or the next. You cannot choose both.

-Your past controls your now. You can only control the future by what you do now. But what you do 'now' controls all of eternity.

-The most important lessons in life, shedding the greatest light, are almost invariably the most painful as well. That is as it must be. Christ learned the most because He suffered the most.

-Things which seem perfectly normal here in mortality are completely mad when viewed from eternity. Had the rich man a broader view of things, he would have treated his beggar Lazarus more kindly. By the time his omission became clear to him, it was too late to repair.

-While mortal we are all rich because it lies within each of us to help others.

-We are better off taking advice and instruction from God than giving it to Him. Most of mankind is so unwilling to accept advice and instruction from Him, however, that they never hear Him.

-The Church of Jesus Christ of Latter-day Saints contains His tools for approaching Him.

-We are told to study out of "the best books." In this dispensation, apart from the scriptures themselves, very few have been written.

Choose your teachers carefully. Not every person who wants to lead you is worthy of your trust. It is far better to be led by the Spirit and the scriptures than to be led by an inadequate and self-vaunting teacher. You should reject anything you find in this book which is an error. I am no authority and hold no position or rank in any organization. This book is not endorsed by or approved by any person who does hold rank or position. It stands on its own, and it either holds a claim on your heart as a statement of truth and light, or it should be rejected and forgotten.

Even many Latter-day Saint writers and teachers cannot, and will not, lead you to Christ. That, too, is as it should be. You are given an opportunity to choose in all things. Therefore you must be given a choice. Don't choose to drink downstream from uninspired and uninspiring teachers. It is better to read the scriptures than fill your mind with drivel from authors more anxious about their own acclaim than teaching truths and helping others. We are commanded that "if ye receive not the Spirit ye shall not teach." (D&C 42: 14.) This should deter the uninspired from teaching and writing, but it does not seem to deter enough of them. Therefore it is left to you to choose.

As said in the introduction, if these are only the words of the author, the required two witnesses to truth do not exist and you should feel free to dismiss this work. But if the Holy Spirit has borne witness to the truth of this work as you read it, then you have two witnesses to the truth of these things, and you should feel obligated to accept it and act upon it. It is left entirely to you to decide if the required two witnesses exist.

In closing I adopt Moses' words: "I will not cease to call upon God, I have other things to inquire of him: for his glory has been upon me." And I commend it to you to do the same.

Having now discharged a responsibility imposed upon me to write this, I close this as an offering to God the Father and His Christ, and do so in the name of Jesus Christ; Amen.

CONCLUSION:

Hopefully this work will only be an opening statement in a renewed dialogue among the Latter-day Saints. This is *our* Dispensation. We are in control of what we do with it. All of us (not just the leadership) are accountable for how we act in relation to the powerful tools given to us in the ordinances of the Gospel. I have attempted to set out a rudimentary basis for grasping the awesome power of these tools.

Collectively, we have all of the gifts intended for the Saints. Section 46 of the Doctrine and Covenants tells us of a host of gifts intended to be the common property of His Saints. Among them are: those who *know* that Jesus Christ is the Son of God, and that He was crucified for the sins of the world (v. 13) and others who have the gift to believe on their words (v. 14). To some it is given to have faith to be healed (v. 19) or faith to heal (v. 20); to some is given the working of miracles (v. 21); to others it is given to prophesy (v. 22). It is given to some to speak with tongues (v. 24); to another is given the interpretation of tongues (v. 25). "And all these gifts come from God, for the benefit of the children of God." (v. 26.) It is not the obligation of an increasingly distant hierarchy to shoulder the burden devolving upon the Saints themselves.[351] *We* need to display these gifts. *We* need to seek and obtain them.

Again, Section 46 teaches us these gifts are to keep us from being deceived. For it is through the certifying presence of the gifts of the Holy Ghost, displayed in rich abundance among us, that both we and the world are given the assurance that the Latter-day Saints are His chosen, covenant people. Verses 8-9: "[T]hat ye may not be deceived seek ye earnestly the best gifts, always remembering for what they are given; For verily I say unto you, they are given for the benefit of those who love me and keep all my commandments, and him that seeketh so to do; that all may be benefitted that seek or that ask of me, that ask and not for a sign that they may consume it upon their lusts." Have them to avoid deception. But hold them aright, not as "signs" of a failed attempt to produce faith, but as fruit of those who already have faith.

We should be enjoying, displaying and rejoicing in these gifts. Young and old, black and white, male and female should all be the glad recipients of these things. We have no excuse for returning in our day to the conditions at the time of Eli: "And the word of the Lord was precious in those days; there was no open vision." (1 Sam. 3: 1.) We are living in the Dispensation of the Fullness of Times, in which God is bringing together all things in heaven and earth. We should not be quenching the Spirit and limiting the gifts we enjoy.

Our day is the time in which our "prophets shall hear his voice, and shall no longer stay themselves" (D&C 132: 26). Your voices should be among them, for the testimony of Jesus is the spirit of prophecy.

We are too inhibited, too busy attempting to conserve what has been given to us rather than spreading it and making more. Where are the daughters of Eliza R. Snow, the prophetess, whose hymns proclaim truths found nowhere else in our sacred works? We should be

---

[351]The Saints no longer occupy a single city, or single region, or single language or culture. As we spread further and further apart in geography and culture, we cannot reasonably expect the limited offices and numbers of General Authorities will fully service the individual spiritual needs of the Saints.

producing psalms, hymns and testimonies which make the hearers all confess that God is with us. Where are our great poets and writers, our works of art, our creative works that celebrate the great outpouring of the Spirit? We are too controlled and too disciplined in the wrong ways and not sufficiently controlled and disciplined in the right ways. We produce great numbers of "middle-management" whose defining virtue is the ability to follow direction, but we do not produce poets whose words resonate with the power of the Spirit as they communicate the greatest truths in prose which touches even the hardest of hearts.

We need more of those who say, "I know," and testify, "I have seen," and proclaim, "He lives!" Though authoritative declarations of doctrine may be limited to a single presiding office, the great confirming testimonies of witnesses of our Lord should be spread far and wide among us, as should the great abundance of the gifts of the Spirit.

You need to join the chorus of witnesses and seek for and obtain the gifts of the Spirit. You need to become the greatest, most inspired, and Spirit-filled version of yourself. You were sent here to do that, and you rob your fellow Saints when you fail so to do.

The overwhelming majority of us will, ten minutes after death, regret we did not do more with this second estate. Our regrets will be because we did not seek more earnestly, pray more devoutly, fast more frequently, and gain a greater measure of truth and light than we gained here. Change that for yourself. As President Benson reiterated, we remain under the same condemnation today as in 1832. Section 84: 54-57: "And your minds in times past have been darkened because of unbelief, and because you have treated lightly the things you have received — Which vanity and unbelief have brought the whole church under condemnation. And this condemnation resteth upon the children of Zion, even all. And they shall remain under this condemnation until they repent and remember the new covenant, even the Book of Mormon and the former commandments which I have given them, not only to say, but to do according to that which I have written." Only we can change that. No leader can do so, nor any presiding authority. It is the Saints alone who control when this condemnation will be lifted.

This text attempts to renew the dialogue on this subject. In the Dispensation of Meridian of Time, great spiritual gifts dissipated, faded from view, and were replaced by the work of the councils and scholars. Men of good faith and sincere desire doing their best to follow after God, lost the light of the Spirit, then lost sound doctrine, and ultimately lost their covenant status and drifted into darkness. We should war against the fading of the great spiritual light given to us. It is your individual responsibility to do so. And then take up the fight yourself in bringing to this life, in the life you live, the light of the Spirit to shine forth among us. We need you to develop your gifts and share them with the rest of us. Do not leave this life without having first sought for and shown your gifts for the edification and benefit of the rest of us, not through sentimentality or emotional storytelling, of which we seem to have an overabundance, but in the power of the Spirit, which opens to the mind a flood of light and truth.

The Spirit brings a calm, peaceful understanding and broadens the mind and views of the recipient. Angels do not come to those of an unstable and emotional constitution. Rather, they "minister according to the word of his command, showing themselves unto them of strong faith and a firm mind in every form of godliness." (Moroni 7: 30.) These things come from careful, solemn and ponderous thought, not such as you would obtain through the "arm of flesh," but which comes from the "power of the Holy Ghost." 2 Ne. 28: 31: "Cursed is he that putteth his trust in man, or maketh flesh his arm, or shall hearken unto the precepts of men, save their precepts shall be given by the power of the Holy Ghost." You cannot obtain a PhD and be the better off in this arena, but must go from grace to grace, through obedience to the commandments, if you want light and truth.

The words of Moroni from the Book of Mormon seem particularly apt as a closing statement: He bids his readers farewell "until we shall meet before the judgment-seat of Christ, where all men shall know that my garments are not spotted with your blood. And then shall ye know that I have seen Jesus, and that he hath talked with me face to face, and that he told me in plain humility, even as a man telleth another in mine own language, concerning these things; And only a few have I written, because of my weakness in writing. And now, I would commend you to seek this Jesus of whom the prophets and apostles have written, that the grace of God the Father, and also the Lord Jesus Christ, and the Holy Ghost, which beareth record of them, may be and abide in you forever. Amen." (Ether 12: 38-41.)

The heavens opened anew on the morning of a clear Spring day, early in 1820. They remain open to all who will seek it and who obey the conditions upon which receiving such an audience is predicated. I do not know if I have yet said enough, or already too much, but will end with this final assurance: They are open to you.

THE END

SELECTED BIBLIOGRAPHY

Astronomy, Papyrus, and Covenant. Edited by John Gee and Brian M. Hauglid. Provo: FARMS, 2005.

Backman, Milton V., Jr. *Eyewitness Accounts of the Restoration.* Salt Lake City: Deseret Book Company, 1986.

————. *Joseph Smith's First Vision,* Second Edition. Salt Lake City: Bookcraft, 1971.

Barker, Margaret. *The Great Angel: A Study of Israel's Second God.* Louisville: Westminser/John Knox Press, 1992.

————. *The Great High Priest, The Temple Roots of Christian Liturgy.* New York: T&T Clark Ltd, 2003.

————. *THE LOST PROPHET: The Book of Enoch and its Influence on Christianity.* Sheffield: England, 2005.

————. *The Older Testament: The Survival of Themes from the Ancient Royal Cult in Sectarian Judaism and Early Christianity.* London: SPK, 1987.

Barzun, Jacques. *FROM DAWN TO DECADENCE: 500 Years of Western Cultural Life.* New York: Harper Collins, 2000.

Benson, Ezra Taft. *A Witness and a Warning: A Modern-Day Prophet Testifies of the Book of Mormon.* Salt Lake City: Deseret Book Company, 1988.

Bickmore, Barry Robert. *Restoring the Ancient Church, Joseph Smith and Early Christianity.* Ben Lomand: Foundation for Apologetic Information and Research, 1999.

Brown, Hugh B. *An Abundant Life: The Memoirs of Hugh B. Brown,* edited by Edwin B. Firmage, Salt Lake City: Signature Books, 1988.

Brown, Matthew B. and Smith, Paul Thomas. *Symbols in Stone.* American Fork: Covenant Communications, Inc., 1997.

_____. *Receiving the Gifts of the Spirit,* American Fork: Covenant Communications, Inc., 2005

Buerger, David John. *The Mysteries of Godliness.* San Francisco: Smith Research Associates, 1994.

Burtt, Edwin Arthur. *The Metaphysical Foundations of Modern Physical Science,* Revised edition. New York: Humanity Books, 1999.

Cannon George, Q. *Gospel Truth: Discourses and Writings of President George Q. Cannon.* Selected, arranged and edited by Jerreld L. Newquist. Salt Lake City: Zion's Book Store, 1957.

Cases on the Law of Torts, Second Edition. Green, Leon; Hawkins, Carl; Pedrick, Willard; Rahl, James; Smith, Allen; Thode, Wayne and Treece, James. St. Paul: West Publishing Company, 1977.

Chiasmus in Antiquity. Edited by John W. Welch. Provo: The Foundation for Ancient Research and Mormon Studies, 1981.

Doorly, William J. *Obsession with Justice: The Story of the Deuteronomists.* Mahwah: Paulist, 1994.

Early Christians in Disarray: Contemporary LDS Perspectives on the Christian Apostasy Edited by Noel B. Reynolds. Provo: FARMS, 2005.

Ehrman, Bart D. *The Orthodox Corruption of Scripture: The Effects of Early Christological Controversies on the Text of the New Testament.* Oxford: Oxford University Press, 1993.

Featherstone, Vaughn J. *The Incomparable Christ: Our Master and Model.* Salt Lake City: Deseret Book Company, 1996.

Friedman, Richard Elliott. *Who Wrote the Bible?* New York: Summit Books, 1987.

Glimpses of Lehi's Jerusalem. Edited by John W. Welch. Provo: FARMS, 2004.

Hofstadter, Douglas R. *Godel, Escher, Bach: An Eternal Golden Braid.* New York: Basic Books, Inc, 1979.

Hope. Compiled by Deseret Book Company, 1988

Journal of Discourses, 26 vols. London: Latter-day Saints' Book Depot, 1854-1886.

Kimball, Spencer W. *Faith Precedes the Miracle.* Salt Lake City: Deseret Book Company, 1972.

Levi-Strauss, Claude. *Myth and Meaning: Cracking the Code of Culture.* New York: Schocken Books, University of Toronto Press, 1978.

_____. *The Raw and the Cooked, Mythologiques, vol. 1.* Chicago: The University of Chicago Press, 1983.

Lord, Increase Our Faith, Ezra Taft Benson, Provo Utah Tabernacle Rededication, 21 September 1986.

McConkie, Bruce R. *A New Witness for the Articles of Faith.* Salt Lake City: Deseret Book Company, 1985.

_____. *Doctrinal New Testament Commentary.* Salt Lake City: Bookcraft, 1965.

_____. *Millennial Messiah.* Salt Lake City: Deseret Book Company, 1982.

_____. *Sermons and Writings of Bruce R. McConkie.* Salt Lake City: Bookcraft, 1989.

McConkie, Joseph Fielding. *Here We Stand.* Salt Lake City: Deseret Book Company, 1995.

McConkie, Mark L. *Remembering Joseph; Personal Recollections of Those Who Knew the Prophet Joseph Smith.* Salt Lake City: Deseret Book Company, 2003.

Maxwell, Neal A. *If Thou Endure It Well.* Salt Lake City: Bookcraft, 2002.

Messages of the First Presidency of The Church of Jesus Christ of Latter-day Saints, 6 vols. Compiled by James R. Clark. Salt Lake City: Bookcraft, 1965-75.

Nibley, Hugh. *Approaching Zion.* Salt Lake City: Deseret Book Company, 1989.

_____. *Brother Brigham Challenges the Saints.* Salt Lake City: Deseret Book Company, 1994.

_____. *Mormonism and Early Christianity.* Salt Lake City: Deseret Book Company, 1987.

Oaks, Dallin. *Alternative Voices, Ensign,* May 1989 beginning at p. 27

Packer, Boyd K. *Things of the Soul.* Salt Lake City: Bookcraft, 1996.

Palmer, Grant H. *An Insider's View of Mormon Origins.* Salt Lake City: Signature Books, 2002.

Quinn, Michael D. *Early Mormonism and the Magic World View.* Salt Lake City: Signature Books, 1987.

Roberts, B. H. *Studies of the Book of Mormon,* Second Edition. Edited by Brigham D. Madsen. Salt Lake City: Signature Books, 1992.

Robinson, Stephen E. *Are Mormons Christians.* Bridgend: Seren Books, 1998.

Shakespeare, William. *A Midsummer Night's Dream; The Complete works of William Shakespeare.* New York: Barnes & Noble Press, 1994.

Smith, Joseph. *History of the Church of Jesus Christ of Latter-day Saints,* 7 vols. Salt Lake City: Church of Jesus Christ of Latter Day Saints, 1932-1951.

Sperry, Sidney B. *The Voice of Israel's Prophets.* Salt Lake City: Deseret Book Company, 1952.

Talmage, James E. *The House of the Lord.* Salt Lake City: Signature Books, 1998.

Teachings of the Prophet Joseph Smith. Arranged by Joseph Fielding Smith. Salt Lake City: Deseret Book Company, 1972.

Teachings of Spencer W. Kimball, The. Edited by Edward L. Kimball. Salt Lake City: Deseret Book Company, 1982.

The Worlds of Joseph Smith: A Bicentennial Conference at the Library of Congress. Edited by John Welch. Provo: Brigham Young University Press, 2006.

Thompson, William Irwin. *The Time Falling Bodies Take to Light: Mythology, Sexuality & The Origins of Culture.* New York: St. Martin's Griffin Edition, 1996.

Toscano, Paul. *The Sanctity of Dissent.* Salt Lake City: Signature Books, 1994.

_____.*Kings and Priest v. Secular Priests.* Student Convocation Speaker, J. Reuben Clark Law School Graduation 1978.

Twain, Mark. *Extract from Captain Stormfield's Visit to Heaven; The Complete Short Stories of Mark Twain.* New York: Bantam Book, 1958.

Warner, Terry C. *Bonds that Make us Free: Healing Our Relationships, Coming to Ourselves*. The Arbinger Institute, Incorporated, Salt Lake City: Shadow Mountain Press, 2001.

Words of Joseph Smith, The. Compiled by Andrew F. Ehat and Lyndon W. Cook. Provo: Religious Studies Center Brigham Young University, 1981.

Young, Brigham. *Discourses of Brigham Young*. Selected and arranged by John A. Widtsoe. Salt Lake City: Deseret Book Company, 1973.

Millennial Harbinger, 7 February 1831, *Delusion,* by Alexander Campbell.

Prosser, Law of Torts (3d Edition); Prosser

Saints Herald 26, no. 19 (1 October 1879) 289-290, Joseph Smith III, "Last Testimony of Sister Emma."

Temple Worship, John A. Widtsoe; address given in Salt Lake City, 12 October 1920.

They of the Last Wagon, President J. Reuben Clark, Jr., Conference Report, October 1947, Afternoon Meeting, p.160.

Women of Covenant: The Story of Relief Society, p.44, by Jill Mulvay Derr, Janath Russell Cannon, and Maureen Ursenbach Beecher.

The following websites were also consulted:

www.fairlds.com and www.byu.edu.org.

www.dialoguejournal.com

INDEX

D

opposite, 233, 241, 286

opposition, 9, 8, 80, 300, 321, 345, 347-349, 359-361, 364, 388, 401, 415

ordinances, 8, 6, 12, 26, 27, 35, 111, 121, 132, 134, 146, 164, 175, 202, 216, 223, 250-254, 259, 260, 264-267, 292, 293, 320, 358, 367, 372, 373, 375, 407-410, 412, 414-416, 420, 421, 423

ordination, 118, 152, 245, 284, 397

other sheep, 93, 94, 97

overwhelming, 90, 112, 392, 399, 425

P

Packer, Boyd K., 7, 70, 346

Page, Hirum, 11, 13, 16, 96, 98, 115, 213, 238, 239, 363, 379, 395

Palmer, Grant, 350

papyrus, 401, 429

patriarchal blessing, 129, 226

pattern, 11, 21, 45, 66, 67, 89, 90, 93, 239-242, 376

Paul, i, iv, 12, 16, 27, 32, 38-40, 43, 79, 144, 145, 147-150, 156, 232, 234, 264, 293, 294, 298, 315, 345-347, 358, 364, 368, 374, 383, 392, 397

perceive, 74, 96, 97, 138, 221

perception, 78, 192, 226

perfect, 5, 9, 15, 20, 25, 29, 37, 52, 57, 58, 84, 99, 107, 149, 154, 176, 220, 256, 259, 276, 293, 297, 299, 300, 302, 319, 320, 323, 339, 351, 380-382, 407

perfection,, 16, 20, 78

perpendicular, 287

Peter, 89, 127, 138, 147, 149, 232, 234, 235, 242, 271, 292, 301, 347

phaenomena, 39

Pharaoh, 72, 203, 401

Pharisee(s), 35, 98, 230, 236, 246, 263

philosophers, 39, 41

physical, 4, 74, 76, 80, 81, 84, 85, 92, 192, 258, 279, 316, 356, 358

poet, 39

ponder, 24, 89, 96, 97, 108, 151

ponderous, 80, 410, 417, 426

pornography, 51

position, vi, 9, 21, 22, 77, 85, 119, 128, 133, 138, 144, 153, 154, 164, 171, 197, 208, 209, 229, 230, 236, 279, 351, 353, 360, 363,

369, 388, 401, 408, 412, 422

power, 19, 20, 22, 26, 30, 31, 56, 69, 78, 85, 89-92, 102, 103, 106-108, 122, 124, 126, 130, 135, 137, 139-142, 144, 145, 147, 149, 150, 152, 156, 165, 168, 183, 185, 190, 197, 202, 205, 208, 209, 213, 214, 216-220, 223, 230-234, 243, 245, 251-255, 258, 259, 263, 265-268, 276, 292, 301, 310, 340, 342, 343, 350, 353, 356, 359, 361-363, 367, 368, 370, 372, 373, 375-379, 383, 391, 392, 403, 407, 408, 415, 423, 425, 426

power of godliness, 137, 139, 140, 142, 223, 251, 252, 259, 263, 266, 268, 359, 361, 372, 373, 377, 378, 408

powerlessness, 373

Pratt, Orson, 84, 103

pray, 3, 49, 66, 68, 70, 96, 100, 102, 135, 138, 151, 176, 193, 194, 222, 274, 281, 287, 380, 425

prayer, 63, 65, 68, 70, 71, 87, 90, 92, 100, 101, 104, 105, 107, 111, 125, 169, 176, 181, 182, 193, 217, 220, 222, 225, 245, 263, 290, 314, 331, 345, 378, 381, 382, 386

Prayer Circle, 100, 176, 217, 220, 378

precious, 43, 64, 123, 246, 334, 419, 424

prefer, 90, 188, 354

preferable, 58, 90

preparation, 7, v, 12-14, 19, 26, 85, 87, 88, 108, 110, 143, 176, 177, 224, 226, 252, 264, 267, 323, 377, 378

prepare, 14, 73, 75, 79, 89, 90, 96, 97, 104, 113, 155, 173, 177, 179, 201, 207, 223, 246, 254, 262, 264, 275, 291, 344, 362, 373, 377, 379, 381, 382, 416, 420

Presbyterian, 137, 373

president. of the U.S., 202, 283, 284, 312, 412

pre-exile Judaism, 338

pre-existence, 122, 296, 344, 395

price, 45, 129, 171, 272, 297, 411, 412

pride, iv, 16, 18, 40, 43, 44, 108, 139, 189, 227, 236, 246, 247, 253, 275, 311, 312, 336, 421

priesthood, 17, 22, 35, 50, 116, 127, 132-134, 147, 168, 223, 224, 230, 231, 247, 251, 252, 259, 260, 265, 268, 293, 311, 355, 372, 373, 394, 397, 404, 407, 414-416

process, iii-vi, 2, 9-12, 15, 17-20, 22, 23, 31, 33, 36-40, 43, 48-50, 54, 57-60,

A Note About the Author

Denver C. Snuffer, Jr. is an attorney living in Sandy, Utah. He has an Associates of Arts degree from Daniel Webster Jr. College, Bachelors of Business Administration from McMurry University, and Juris Doctor from the J. Reuben Clark Law School at Brigham Young University. He was admitted to practice law in 1980 in Utah, and has been a practicing attorney since then. He was a convert to the LDS faith in 1973 when 19 years old, and has now been a member of the LDS Church for over thirty-two years. Currently he serves as a member of the Stake High Council in the Sandy Crescent Stake. Previously he has taught Gospel Doctrine and Priesthood classes for twenty-one years in Wards in Pleasant Grove, Alpine and Sandy, Utah. He has instructed Graduate Institute classes at the University of Utah College of Law for two years, and instructed at the BYU Education Week for three years. He also currently teaches a weekly class on the Book of Mormon. After writing *The Second Comforter: Conversing With the Lord Through the Veil*, he has written two follow up books: *Nephi's Isaiah*, 2006, and *Eighteen Verses*, 2007.

A Note on the Type

This book was set in Garamond. The fonts are based on the fonts first cut by Claude Garamond (c. 1480-1561). Garamond was a pupil of Geoffroy Tory and is believed to have followed the Venetian models, although he introduced a number of important differences, and it is to him that we owe the letter we now know as "old style." He gave to his letters a certain elegance and feeling of movement that won their creator an immediate reputation and the patronage of Francis I of France.

Designed by Mill Creek Press
Cover by George Foster
Fairfield, Iowa
Printed and bound by BookSurge, LLC,
Charleston, South Carolina

Made in the USA
Lexington, KY
22 December 2009